Spoilt Children of Empire

NICHOLAS R. CLIFFORD

Spoilt Children of Empire
Westerners in Shanghai and the Chinese
Revolution of the 1920s

MIDDLEBURY COLLEGE PRESS

Published by University Press of New England

Hanover and London

Middlebury College Press
Published by University Press of New England, Hanover,
New Hampshire 03755

Printed in the United States of America   5   4   3   2

CIP data appear at the end of the book

FOR DEBORAH

The British residents in Shanghai are the spoilt children of the Empire. They pay no taxes to China, except that landowners pay a very small land tax, and no taxes to England. Judges and consuls are provided for them; they are protected by the British fleet, and for several years they have had in addition a British army to defend them; and for all this expenditure the British taxpayer pays.

L. A. Lyall, *China*

Contents

Eight pages of illustrations follow page 164.

Preface

Seventy years ago, Shanghai occupied a position very much like that of Hongkong today. Though not formally a colony, it was largely under foreign control. Everyone agreed that it was a Chinese city and must revert some day to Chinese rule, but no one was sure what its fate would be under Chinese authority. Would it flourish, as Chinese patriots maintained, once set free from the yoke of foreign imperialism? or would it decay, as old China hands feared, once the foreign barriers to Chinese chaos and Chinese corruption disappeared? To many, Shanghai in the twenties seemed a vision of what China might someday become. It was China's largest, richest, and most advanced city, the center of trade and industry and banking, an example of what modern ways might mean to China. So too, today, Hongkong—its economic success built on an openness to the greater world beyond China—may provide the model for the kind of modernized nation that Deng Xiaoping and his colleagues profess they wish to build.

The theory of "one country, two systems" that Deng's government promises Hongkong—that she can go her own way for fifty years after 1997—is not new. Shanghai's prosperity in the early decades of the twentieth century—and it was a prosperity by no means enjoyed by all its inhabitants—came in large part from its relative independence from China itself. In the first place, the enclaves of foreign control formed by the International Settlement and the French Concession provided a security and a stability denied China as a whole during her long years of decline in the nineteenth and early twentieth centuries. Secondly, the weakness of the Chinese government, particularly after the downfall of the Manchu dynasty in 1911, left the city's Chinese entrepreneurs largely their own masters, free to pursue their interests away from the stifling controls of the government. So too, Hongkong has profited from a political stability since the end of the war, a stability denied China as she has passed through the decades of continuous revolution imposed by the Maoists after 1949.

Finally, Shanghai and Hongkong were both in many ways the products of foreign imperialism, largely Western imperialism. Seventy years ago, many foreigners believed that it was precisely foreign enterprise that had made Shanghai a great city and one of the largest ports in the world. "However admirable they may be in other respects, the Chinese arc not yet good managers in the Western sense," an American reporter could write as late as 1946, after Shanghai had reverted to Chinese control. "Left on their own, they would almost certainly make a botch of the fabulous trading mechanisms that western enterprises, beginning with the British, founded on a malarial swamp nearly a century ago."[1] While the public expression of such views is no longer fashionable, many no doubt believe the same of Hongkong today. Yet to emphasize the foreign role too much in the building of these cities is to ignore Chinese energy, Chinese organization, Chinese investment, and Chinese enterprise. Of course Shanghai and Hongkong profited from the foreign presence, particularly from the stability and security it brought. But it was not the foreign presence that built the cities; indeed that foreign presence, in the shape of Japanese invaders, almost destroyed them in the years between 1937 and 1945.

Shanghai never fulfilled its promise as the model for China's future. The Japanese invasion of the 1930s was only partly responsible. Even before that, Chiang Kai-shek's new Nationalist government, formed in 1927, sought to bring to an end the independence the city had earlier enjoyed. The privileges of the foreigners were cut back, though by no means ended. Chinese businessmen, who had prospered during the years of independence, were now brought under the new central government's control. Nor did the coming of communist rule in 1949 allow Shanghai to flourish. While Western Marxists might look to the city and the industrial proletariat that it spawned as the vanguard of a new social order, Chinese Marxists in the age of Mao were deeply suspicious of urban ways and urban outlooks and sought to bring to cities like Shanghai the austere virtues of the Chinese countryside wherein their movement had grown to power. More recently, Deng Xiaoping seemed for a while to promise a new China in which her cities could come into their own, and his regime has encouraged the rapid development of such urban centers as Shanghai, Tianjin, Canton, and Wuhan. Then, however, with a swift and sudden brutality in the early morning of 4 June 1989, the government showed the limits of its tolerance for the dangerous ideas the city could produce, and in so doing sent a sharp spasm of fear through Hongkong.

We know that 1997 will see Hongkong's reversion to Chinese control, even if it is not clear what that control will mean. Sixty or seventy years ago, Shanghai's future was equally uncertain. For years, Shanghai's foreigners had fought off the occasional attempts of an enfeebled dynasty to increase its voice in the city's affairs. Then, in the 1920s, a new kind of challenge arrived in the form of a revolution based upon the mobilization of a modern mass nationalism, a challenge that, because of its communist aspects and its links with the Soviet Union, raised the spectre of international revolution as well. The Chinese revolution of the 1920s in a sense represents one of the first great Third World movements against foreign colonialism, and although today the phenomenon has become a familiar one, then it was new and—to many foreigners in Shanghai—frightening. This book is a study of that experience, and of the way in which such a crisis illuminates the workings of a particular kind of colonial society.

Thus, although the book is set in China and will, I hope, be useful to Chinese specialists, it is primarily a study of a facet of Western colonialism rather than Chinese history. Or, to put it another way, it is about Chinese history in the same way a study of American expatriates in the Paris of Stein and Hemingway and Pound would be about French history. Yet the Chinese side cannot be seen only through Western eyes, so I have tried to give the general reader an understanding of the Chinese revolution of that time. Here I have profited from a number of works published recently in China that break with the relatively unsophisticated analyses of the Maoist era.

Though I have long been interested in the history of Shanghai, I am not an old China hand, nor do I have ties to that world. Hence I owe many people debts of gratitude for the help they have given me. Middlebury College has been generous in its support of my research. I owe thanks to the archivists and librarians of the institutions where much of the research for this book was done: the National Archives in Washington; the Public Record Office in Kew; the Quai d'Orsay in Paris; the Archives of the Episcopal Church, at the Episcopal Seminary of the Southwest in Austin, Texas; the Hoover Institution; the Union Theological Seminary; the French Jesuit archives at Chantilly; the British Library; the Shanghai Municipal Library; the Academia Sinica in Nangang, Taiwan; and the libraries at Harvard and Princeton universities, and the School of Oriental and African Studies of London University, have all been very helpful. Director Han Weizhi of the Shanghai Municipal Archives kindly made available some of the records of the Shanghai Municipal Council that remain closed. Fleur Laslocky of the Middlebury College library was both tireless and imaginative in tracking down obscure works both in English and Chinese and obtaining them on interlibrary loan. Other scholars have been kind enough to let me read their works in progress, particularly James Huskey and Jeffrey Wasserstrom. John Rawlinson helped me find graduates of the Shanghai American School willing to share their memories. I learned much from the papers and discussions that formed part of the Conference on the History of Modern Shanghai, sponsored by the Shanghai Academy of Social Sciences and the Committee on Scholarly Communication with the People's Republic of China, held in September 1988. David Bain and Upton Brady read earlier drafts of the manuscript, and their comments have done much to improve it. Careful readings by C. Martin Wilbur and Arthur Waldron have helped me catch some errors and to modify some of my interpretations. Sherman Cochran and Jeffrey Wasserstrom have both made helpful suggestions on parts of the manuscript. Finally, my wife Deborah has been extraordinarily patient about discussing my work, a patience I have tried to repay by raising intelligent questions about abolitionism and reform in nineteenth-century America, the subject of her own work.

Virginia Molesworth has kindly allowed me to quote from the very interesting letters her mother wrote from Shanghai during these years. Permissions to quote from unpublished works have also kindly been given by Professor Lee Feigon of Colby College, Brian Martin of the Australian National University, the Episcopal Seminary of the Southwest, the Hoover Institution, and the Missionary Research Library of Union Theological Seminary; and Kelly and Walsh, Ltd., have allowed me to reproduce photographs from *Shanghai of Today*. Parts of chapters 6–9 appeared in somewhat different form in my *Shanghai, 1925: Urban Nationalism and the Defense of Foreign Privilege*, Michigan Papers in Chinese Studies, no. 37, Center for Chinese Studies, University of Michigan, 1979.

I am indebted to Amanda Tate for the preparation of the maps, to Erik Borg and Greg Staley for their help in reproducing several of the photographs, and to the Bettmann Archive for providing photographs of Shanghai in early 1927.

Note on Romanization of Chinese Names

A nyone writing about China today must face the problem of Romanizing Chinese names, and it is almost impossible to be entirely consistent and escape pedantry at the same time. Thus I have kept to standard Western spellings of well-known people and places, such as Peking, Nanking, Canton, Sun Yat-sen, or Chiang Kai-shek. I have used pinyin where spellings are easily recognizable (Ningbo, Hankou). I have also used the spellings for most places in and around Shanghai that were used by the people I am writing about: Siccawei rather than the French Zikawei or the Chinese Xujiahui, Jessfield rather than Fawangdu, and the Soochow Creek rather than the Wusong Jiang, though again where recognition is easy (Pudong, Zhabei), I use pinyin. Nonetheless, the following table of equivalents may be useful.

PINYIN	CONVENTIONAL
Bai Chongxi	Pai Ch'ung-hsi
Baoshan	Pao-shan
Beijing	Peking
Chongqing	Chungking
Chen Yuren	Chen, Eugene
Feng Yuxiang	Feng Yü-hsiang
Fujian	Fukien
Guangdong	Kwangtung
Guangzhou	Canton
Guling	Kuling
Guomindang	Kuomintang

Hankou	Hankow
Hebei	Hopei
Hongkou	Hongkew
Hongqiao	Hungjao
Huangpu	Whangpoo
Hubei	Hupeh
Jiang Jieshi	Chiang Kai-shek
Jiangsu	Kiangsu
Jiangwan	Kiangwan
Jiangxi	Kiangsi
Jiujiang	Kiukiang
Kunshan	Quinsan
Laozha	Louza
Pudong	Pootung
Qing	Ch'ing
Qingdao	Tsingtao
Shandong	Shantung
Shantou	Swatow
Sichuan	Szechwan
Song Ziwen	Soong, T.V.
Songjiang	Sungkiang
Sun Zhongshan	Sun Yat-sen
Suzhou	Soochow
Tianjin	Tientsin
Wang Jingwei	Wang Ching-wei
Wang Zhengting	Wang, C. T.
Xiamen	Amoy
Xujiahui	Siccawei, Zikawei
Yangshupu	Yangtszepoo
Yu Rizhang	Yui, David
Zhabei	Chapei
Zhang Zongchang	Chang Tsung-ch'ang
Zhang Zuolin	Chang Tso-lin
Zhejiang	Chekiang
Zhenjiang	Chinkiang

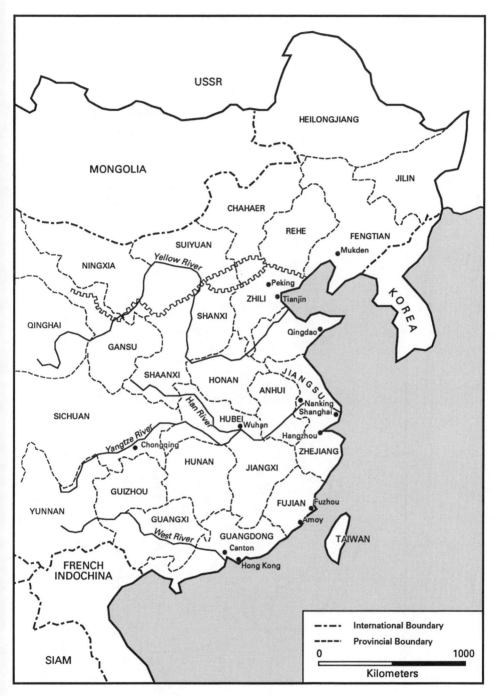

China in 1925.

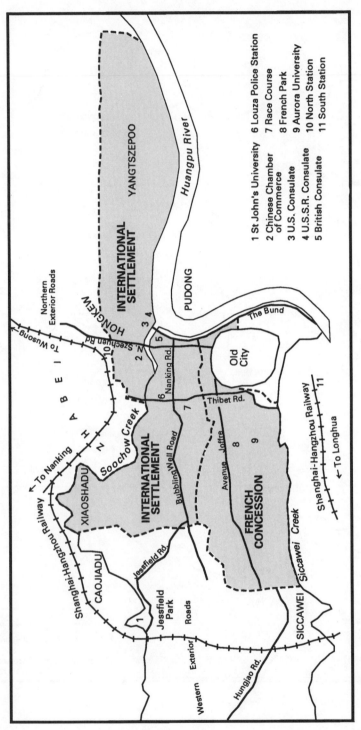

City map of Shanghai.

Legend:
1 St John's University
2 Chinese Chamber of Commerce
3 U.S. Consulate
4 U.S.S.R. Consulate
5 British Consulate
6 Louza Police Station
7 Race Course
8 French Park
9 Aurora University
10 North Station
11 South Station

Spoilt Children of Empire

Introduction

At noon the factory whistles sound, their voices echoed by the sirens of the rusting Chinese ships lying in the Huangpu River, under the solid gray buildings of the banks and trading houses that line the Bund. From the cotton mills and silk filatures of Xiaoshadu and Zhabei, from the docks and godowns of Pudong and Yangtszepoo, from stores and offices, from hundreds and hundreds of little workshops crowded into the mean streets that cut the slums, the workers spill out into the roads where trams and buses now stand still, abandoned by their crews. Suddenly Shanghai is on strike, and within an hour will come the rattle of gunfire as the insurrection begins. The twenty-first of March has been one of the first warm days to break the raw winter of 1927. Last night, the vanguard of Chiang Kai-shek's National Revolutionary Army reached the city's gates, and within Shanghai, the communists who are his uneasy allies have called a general strike as the prelude to an armed uprising that will deliver China's greatest city into the hands of the revolution. Yet the Chinese will not be allowed to decide Shanghai's fate for themselves. Everywhere in the city's foreign settlements, barbed wire barricades and machine gun emplacements have hastily been thrown up as protection against the expected invasion of the revolutionary forces. Almost ten thousand British soldiers already patrol the streets of the International Settlement, and before night falls on an embattled city, American marines will join them and the other foreign troops that have come to protect the city's forty thousand foreigners from the real and imagined dangers of China's first revolutionary war.

The Shanghai crisis of 1927 captured the world's headlines, and that spring brought the specter of conflict between China and the West. Its challenge was ideological as well as military, for the armies closing in on the city, the strikers and insurrectionists within it, were part of the great wave of revolution breaking across the country that year, and they saw the foreigners who dominated Shanghai as antagonists who must be overcome if China were to regain the independence and self-respect she had lost during the disastrous years of the nineteenth century.

Therein lay the real danger to Shanghai's foreigners, for the fighting itself was nothing new. Almost three years earlier, in the late summer of 1924, a very different sort of war had come to the city. Then it had been an old-fashioned war, a war that summed up, at least in the minds of the old China hands, all the serio-comic aspects of a typical battle between contending warlords, fought for purely personal gains. Throughout the month of August in that year, the generals had prepared by requisitioning supplies, seizing food, clothing, and blankets, commandeering railway trains, junks, sampans, trucks, carriages, to marshal their troops and move them into position against one another. From their headquarters came a stream of statements, to fellow generals, to politicians in Peking and the provincial capitals, to guilds and chambers of commerce, to newspapers, and to the people at large, each side condemning in tones of high Confucian righteousness the disloyalty and selfishness of the other, each promising a new age of unparalleled peace and order after victory.

In 1927, revolutionary war brought both hope and fear to millions of people. In 1924, however, far from rallying to the support of the generals, the people in the war zones took the only action that made sense. Under the hot yellow haze of August, an unbroken line of refugees began to pour into Shanghai, as men and women abandoned their villages, their homes, and their goods, hoping to find safety in the city from the marching armies. They came on foot, by oxcart, by truck, over roads made almost impassable by the summer rains; they came by boat, following the thousands of creeks and canals that criss-crossed the Yangtze delta; and they came by rail. "At every station," wrote an Englishman coming down from Nanking in late August, "crowds of refugees—mostly well to do people—forced their way into the train determined to seek shelter in the foreign concessions of Shanghai."[1] The lucky ones were the rich or those who could turn to relatives in the city for shelter. Most were poor, however, and they came into a Shanghai already crowded, its grossly inadequate public services taxed to the limit, and now threatened with a shortage of food because of the military's disruption of transportation. On 2 September, the fighting began.

None of this was new. For eighty years, ever since the Taiping rebels had driven north into the Yangtze Valley to fight the Qing dynasty's armies, destroying the lives and livelihood of millions in China's richest provinces, the disintegration of China's political and social order had brought violence and insecurity to the country. The fall of the Manchu dynasty in 1912 and the founding of the Chinese Republic only weakened further China's social and political fabric, and when the would-be unifier Yuan Shikai died in 1916, the last hope of a central government was lost. The country fell into chaos that nurtured the warlords, generals who commanded provinces or groups of provinces, who fought for no principles higher than greed, and whose gray uniformed armies marched over the face of the country, from the mountains of Yunnan to the forests of Manchuria, from the rice paddies of Guangdong to the deserts of Gansu.

The war of 1924, or the Jiangsu-Zhejiang war, to give it the name that distinguished it from other conflicts of the period, was essentially a battle between two of these opposing warlords. To some extent it reflected a similar conflict being fought out in north China that autumn for control of Peking, but it was primarily a local campaign fought for local ends. The war is important to our story for two reasons. The first is that Shanghai was the prize for which the two sides took up arms. Shanghai was the most important city in Jiangsu province, in many ways the most important city in China, and control of Shanghai could be an important source of strength. "Shanghai is the richest prize of the whole country for whatever Chinese military and political faction may be able to seize and control it," wrote the American consul-general in 1927.[2] Not only would its rulers profit from its general wealth and revenues, with their opportunities for forced levies, but there was also a substantial profit to be made from its illicit opium trade. It also had strategic importance, with its arsenal, ammunition factory, and naval base, and a harbor convenient for the import of munitions. The control of Shanghai was thus not one to be surrendered easily.

Though Shanghai lay in Jiangsu province, because of the pattern of warlord intrigues, it had come to be controlled not from Nanking, the provincial capital of Jiangsu, but rather by the neighboring province of Zhejiang. Yuan Shikai, coming to power after the downfall of the Manchus in 1912, had put his own troops in Shanghai to keep the governor of Jiangsu from becoming too powerful. Within a few years of Yuan's death in 1916, however, the city had drifted into the sphere of influence, if not the outright control, of the militarists in Hangzhou, the capital city of Zhejiang. Few in Chinese Shanghai objected to this, for a good deal of the wealth, banking, and commerce of the city was in the hands of businessmen from Ningbo in Zhejiang province.

By the summer of 1924, the provincial government in Nanking, worried by the growing strength of the Zhejiang armies, prepared a campaign to reclaim Shanghai and its wealth for Jiangsu's benefit. Since Jiangsu was at least nominally allied with the Peking government, the Nanking generals could denounce their rivals in Hangzhou as rebels against the established order, invoking what little moral authority remained to the weak and grasping politicians of Peking who comprised the official government of the Chinese Republic. No one was likely to be swayed for an instant by such claims; everyone knew that the real issue was control of Shanghai, with its arsenal and its wealth.[3]

The second reason for the war's importance to us is that it had no importance. It was short, violent, and destructive. It was a war that no one wanted, save for the commanders on each side. It was a war that would solve no problems, would bring no change either to the provinces it affected or to China as a whole. Except that it was fought with rifles, modern artillery, and even an occasional aircraft, there was little to distinguish it from one of the regional brawls of the late ninth century, when after three centuries of glory under the Tang dynasty, China broke up into a group of quarreling provinces. There were no real political or social issues, there were no ideological issues, and the classic moralism of the official pronouncements did little to disguise the ambitious greed of the leaders who issued them.

Foreign Shanghai treated the hostilities with all the contempt they seemed to deserve. War was an interruption, no more and no less, in the business of the day. British trade associations in Shanghai called on London to take steps to end the fighting, blaming the war on the unwillingness of the foreign governments to hold China to her international obligations.[4] Ultimately, it made little difference to the foreign colony which side won. The complications of warlord politics, the factionalism, the infighting, were beside the point. Good warlords were those who allowed trade to continue; bad warlords were those who interfered with it or who were too weak to guarantee the peace and order it needed. The generals could fight, villages could be pillaged and burned, men, women, and children could die—that was the business of the Chinese, and the foreigners had no wish to interfere (openly, at any rate). But when the war approached Shanghai, then the soldiers trespassed on what was the business of the foreigners, for Shanghai was a foreign enclave that must be kept immune from the political and military games of Chinese generals. The refugees swarming into the crowded city seemed to testify to this view, and so did the powerful and well-established Chinese groups like the chambers of commerce, who now asked for foreign protection against the depredations of their own countrymen.

Within a year, however, this foreign attitude of weary contempt and Chinese anxiety for foreign protection would be possible only for those who could not, would not, see the changes that were taking place. The Jiangsu-Zhejiang war, and the simultaneous fighting in the north, is at best a footnote in China's modern history and had little to do directly with the real upheaval of those years. Today, Chinese historians see the period from 1925 to 1927 as China's first revolutionary civil war, and the foreign position of privilege that Shanghai exemplified was one of its chief targets. It was a revolution of a kind familiar to us now, but at the time it faced Shanghai's foreigners with an entirely new kind of challenge. The crisis of those years thus becomes a backdrop against which to examine a Western enclave in an Asian land, and the size, wealth, and importance of this particular society can help us understand how Westerners dealt with one of the first great revolutions against imperialism.

Western imperialism has been much written about, but rarely have Western colonial communities been carefully examined. Shanghai, of course, was a colonial community of a very particular kind, and the sources for its story are limited, thanks in part to the destruction brought by later invasion and war. We know, for instance, little about the backgrounds of the thousands of its foreign inhabitants, or about what brought them to China. Business and professional men, of course, came to work for houses engaged in the China trade or to cater to the needs of a growing foreign community. Some, like the demobilized British soldiers who made up much of the International Settlement's police force, came because after the First World War Shanghai seemed to offer greater scope than did life in Europe. Americans came to be part of their country's expanding role in the Pacific. Missionaries came to save souls and, some have suggested, to work in a climate that seemed more promising than the increasingly secular world of the West. And many must have been lured by the excitement of life in a foreign country, a life conveniently lived among people of their own kind in a place where they did not need to learn a new language.

But these are no more than generalizations. Foreign Shanghai left surprisingly few chronicles of itself. Most of the records of the foreign settlements themselves remain closed in the Shanghai Municipal Archives. There are the diplomatic and official records, the best of them American, a few newspapers and journals, and a handful of memoirs by missionaries, journalists, and others. There is almost no literature worth the name. Somerset Maugham's *On a Chinese Screen* gives some sketches of treaty port life, but no one did for foreigners in China what Rudyard Kipling or Paul Scott or E. M. Forster did for the British in India. For many, their image of Shanghai comes from the one great novel of the period: André Malraux's *Man's Fate*, set in the climactic spring of 1927 when revolution and counter-revolution battled for possession of the city's streets. After that, Grace Zaring Stone's *The Bitter Tea of General Yen*, about the same episode, is a comedown, and Henry Misselwitz's *Shanghai Romance*, best forgotten. Or the images come from the movies: Marlene Dietrich as Shanghai Lilly, Gary Cooper uttering vaguely leftist sentiments (by Clifford Odets) as he faces down the warlord Akim Tamiroff in *The General Died at Dawn*, or the young Gene Tierney and Victor Mature in a very loose screen adaptation of John Colton's very scandalous play of 1926, *The Shanghai Gesture.*

Malraux's book, of course, is not really about particular historical events in a particular Chinese city. It is about the human condition in the twentieth century, and its setting in Shanghai is no accident; this city between worlds, unconstrained by the rules and conventions of more ordered societies and hence bound only by the laws of human nature and human mortality, becomes an image of that condition. History, of course, also seeks to illuminate the human condition. But, as Aristotle reminds us, the historian's purpose is more modest than the poet's, for we deal precisely with particularities. Yet a study of the particularities of foreign Shanghai can tell us something about the more general phenomenon of imperialism, of the meetings of cultures. Here was a large, international expatriate colony, living a highly privileged existence in the country that was its unwilling host. Because of its privileges, it was an enclave of a very particular sort. Except for the white Russians, its foreign inhabitants were there by choice; they were not refugees forced to flee their own countries. They were not, like Americans in Paris or Rome, living in a culture and among a people whom they regarded as their equals; racism and a sense of cultural superiority were always present in Shanghai. Nor were they, like the British in Bombay or Nairobi, part of the world of formal colonialism, and they lacked both the direct political control of a mother country and the moral sense of mission that was so important at least in the rhetoric of imperialism.

In the 1920s, Shanghai's foreigners faced an immense revolution that made that privilege one of its targets. To control that threat, it had to deal with the different Chinese authorities, political and military, who emerged from the turmoil. It had to deal with its own home governments, from whom it sought support and protection. For though foreign Shanghai assumed that its own well-being was important to its mother countries, Washington and London and Paris were more interested in keeping the problem of Shanghai from complicating their larger foreign policies. How important to Britain and America, for example, was the maintenance of foreign Shanghai's privileged position? For whose good should it be maintained? For the good of its foreign inhabitants? For the good of traders and manufacturers at home? For the good of the British or French or American empires? For the good of China itself? How far was foreign Shanghai responsible for looking after itself? And how far could it call on the support of the home governments?

There have been, of course, other cities with foreign colonies in them, cities like Cairo or Bombay or Calcutta, where large groups of Westerners have lived for years or even decades. Shanghai was different, however.

Egypt and India were parts of the British empire, but China was independent. Yet her independence was severely bounded by the treaties that the West and Japan had forced on her in the nineteenth century. The effect of both China's independence and the limitations on that independence was to give foreigners in China a kind of freedom they were unlikely to enjoy in a colonial possession. Furthermore, China's foreign population was much more genuinely international than that of British India or French Indochina. Though the British dominated Shanghai, after the First World War they were outnumbered by the Japanese, the Americans were growing more important, and the French had retained a significant stake. Finally, the Shanghai community was old and established; the first foreigners, traders, and their diplomats had settled there in 1843, and although many of its inhabitants were birds of passage, seeking adventure or quick fortune, by the end of the First World War an increasing number of men and women had put down roots, invested both their energies and their money in the city, and saw it as their home.

Even among China's foreign settlements, Shanghai was unique. It was far larger and far richer, and ultimately far more important to the home countries of its inhabitants, than were the British, French, Italian, or Japanese concessions in cities like Canton, Tianjin, Hankou, or Amoy. In 1920, there were perhaps 2,500 foreigners in Hankou and some 8,700 in Tianjin (in both cases, somewhat more than half were Japanese). Even British Hongkong had only about 13,000. But for the International Settlement and the French Concession, which comprised foreign Shanghai, the census of 1925 listed 37,638 foreigners, more than a third of whom were Japanese. In other ports, foreign settlements perched on the edge of great Chinese cities; they did not dominate their cities. Though foreign Shanghai had started out this way too, by the twentieth century it had overpowered the city of which it was a part; the International Settlement and the French Concession accounted for over a million of its inhabitants and included by far the greater part of its wealth, its commerce, and its industry.

Since China was independent, the treaty port settlements were not subject (as were British Hongkong or French Hanoi or Japanese Taiwan, for instance) to a colonial office responsible to a mother country. Of course, the home government played a large role, and in most of the settlements and concessions, the diplomats could veto any actions by foreign municipal administrations that might embarrass the mother country's relations with China. In Shanghai, the French consul-general had this kind of check over his own *Conseil municipal*. In the International Settlement, however, whatever official sanction existed was very weak, and the Shanghai Municipal Council was largely mistress of its own house—or thought it was, at any rate, a point that will become an important part of our story.

Shanghai also differed from other foreign settlements in China because of its reputation. When the outside world thought of foreigners in China—if it thought about them at all—it pictured small groups of businessmen living in weary exile to bring the benefits of foreign trade and foreign goods to the Chinese. Or it pictured small groups of missionaries sacrificing themselves to save China by proclaiming the word of God. Oil for the lamps of China (preferably from the Asiatic Petroleum Company or Standard Oil) would illuminate ten thousand dark peasant villages, while the Gospel would bring the white radiance of eternity to four hundred million Chinese souls (never mind that in the increasingly secular world of the twenties, the missionary schools, run largely by Americans, were now more apt to teach salvation through subjects such as law, medicine, and business).

Shanghai conjured up a different vision altogether. In the popular imagination, the man of God and the man of business faded into the background. Everyone knew that Shanghai was a city of sin. Everyone knew that the Chinese, if not actually sinful, at least had different morals, and everyone knew that before he got to Shanghai, the white man left his own morals behind in Suez or San Francisco. It was not only missionaries who were horrified to discover that in the early years of the century, the term "American girl" meant a prostitute who worked the treaty ports of the China coast. Some blamed the moral climate on the seductive ability of the Orient to overcome Western standards; some blamed it more directly on the lovely Russian girls who streamed into the city after the October Revolution of 1917 drove them from their homeland. As an English journalist wrote in 1927, despite the clean-up a few years earlier of the "Trenches" (a notorious red-light district on Kiangse Road), "Shanghai, in parts, is still no Sunday School. . . . Nowhere in the world, I should think are there so many cabarets in proportion to the total white population. They range from the cheap and respectable *palais de danse* to more select resorts with exotic names like 'Paradise,' where beautifully dressed professional dancers, mostly Russian, obligingly dance with all comers on the sole condition that they order champagne."[5] The American missionaries and community leaders who in 1924 tried to bring the blessings of Prohibition to their fellow countrymen in China were clearly deceiving themselves.[6] Opium, prostitution, gambling, extortion, violence—every form of depravity was said to flourish in a way that had no match even east of Suez. "If God lets Shanghai endure, He owes an apology to Sodom and Gomorrah," said a Christian evangelist in the early twenties, and he expressed a common enough view.[7]

Perhaps Shanghai's reputation for wickedness was overdrawn, for there were always a few who found in the city on the Huangpu all the excitement of rural New Jersey on a Sunday morning. "Dancing (and to a lesser extent the cinema) provides generally the only alternative to boredom," complained a local newspaper.[8] The world, however, knew differently, and the phrase (common in English and Chinese) "paradise of adventurers" testified to the common image of the Paris of the Orient. By the twenties, too, wickedness had come to mean more than simply the fleshly pleasures denied the inhabitants of small towns on the midwestern prairie. To lib- erals and radicals of all sorts, the sins of Shanghai included the social con- ditions that allowed beggars to starve in the streets while rich men dined in their clubs, that allowed children not yet ten years old to work twelve- or fourteen-hour shifts in cotton mills for pennies a day while rich women played mah-jong and bridge to pass the time. Shanghai was a city of sin because of the disease that stalked the filthy slums of Pudong and Zhabei, because of the corruption, the kidnapping, the extortion, the killing that took place as warlord gave way to warlord in the unending civil strife that followed the collapse of the Manchu empire in 1912. Even to missionaries, or at least to those of a modernist view, the sins of Shanghai seemed to owe less to the Fall than to the rapacity of foreign imperialism and to the warlords who were, in the popular mind, imperialism's Chinese agents.

Finally, Shanghai was unique because of its role in China, a foreign city even in its own country. It was the largest city in China, one that had grown rapidly after its opening as a port from an estimated 544,000 in 1852 to over two million by 1915 and to over two and a half million by 1927.[9] It was the most industrialized city in China, a sign of hope both to those who thought the country's salvation lay in developing modern capitalism and to those who thought it lay in a revolutionary urban pro- letariat that would lead China into the red dawn of socialism. It was the intellectual center of China as well (though Peking's inhabitants might dispute the claim). The new Chinese nationalism of the teens and twen- ties was by no means restricted to Shanghai, but Shanghai was its center. Shanghai's burgeoning Chinese middle class, its industrialists, its heads of shipping lines and insurance agencies, its modern bankers and brokers, responded enthusiastically to the new nationalism of modern China; the city also teemed with students from its schools and universities, and it swarmed with journalists writing for the scores of newspapers and week- lies and monthlies, radical, conservative, some long-lived, some publishing only a few issues, that catered to a growing readership. Just as Western visitors to Shanghai discerned a "treaty port mentality" or a "Shanghai mind" among its foreign residents, so, too, its Chinese residents were said to reflect a "Yangjingbang culture," which drew its name from the creek separating the two foreign settlements.

Thanks to the protection of foreign laws, students, writers, and journalists in the International Settlement and the French Concession enjoyed an editorial liberty that, while far from absolute, surpassed anything found in Chinese cities. Chinese businessmen in the Settlement could run their enterprises relatively free both from the restrictions of the Confucian tradition and from some of the more extreme forms of modern corruption and rapacity. Politicians and military men down on their luck, revolutionaries who detested the foreign presence in China, found a haven in Shanghai's foreign settlements when the outside world was unsafe. Sun Yat-sen, ousted from Canton by the warlord Chen Jiongming in 1923, negotiated his alliance with the Russians from his house on the rue Molière in the French Concession. The Soong family, Chinese by birth, American by education, and active in the Nationalist movement, kept a base in Shanghai. It was no accident that the first congress of the Communist party met in July 1921 in a school on the rue Wantz, and that in 1927 Zhou Enlai, from his in-laws' house in the Concession, helped plan the great rising that almost delivered Shanghai into communist hands.[10]

Such characteristics gave Shanghai an extraordinary complexity, reflected in the difficulties of governing a city under three administrations—more, in fact, since the various districts of Chinese Shanghai were not brought under a single municipal government until 1927. The International Settlement and the French Concession lay right astride the Chinese city, physically dividing Nanshi to the south from the industrial district of Zhabei to the north, while the Huangpu river—which even today remains unbridged—cut the main city off from Pudong to the east. The uncertain relationship between the Shanghai Municipal Council and the consular and diplomatic authorities was mirrored on the Chinese side by an uncertain relationship between civil and military officials, between changing military authorities as warlord succeeded warlord in the struggles of the early twentieth century.

But Shanghai's complexity came not from the foreign presence alone. Its rapid growth meant that even its Chinese population made it a city of immigrants. Most people came from the nearby provinces of Jiangsu, Anhui, and Zhejiang, but many were drawn from further afield. Historians argue, just as they argue over the growth of British cities in the nineteenth century, whether most were attracted to Shanghai by the promise of jobs in its growing industry or were forced into the city by the appalling poverty and social dislocation of much of the countryside (Shanghai was built on the back of "widespread economic ruin," a Chinese historian tells us, echoing one view, while other evidence suggests that industrial wages in the city were well above the national average).[11] But they brought with them their own customs and their own dialects. They brought their own loyalties, their own ties, their own organizations, such as the native place associations (*huiguan* and *tongxianghui*), groups that gathered people from the same provinces or districts and offered support and shelter in an alien world. In this sort of unsettled and unstable environment, with its lack of tradition, its lack of customary local control mechanisms, and its divisions of authority, vice and crime flourished. By the 1930s, Shanghai reportedly had a hundred thousand prostitutes, graded in different ranks for different clienteles. A burgeoning underworld, much of it growing out of old secret societies, took advantage of the city's divided jurisdictions and played an increasingly important role as the city became a center for the smuggling of arms and drugs in a way that could corrupt policemen, customs agents, and other officials, both Chinese and foreign.[12]

Shanghai thus stood alone in the tortured China of the 1920s. There was no other city in the country, no other city in the world perhaps, where foreigners wielded so independent a power in a land that was not theirs, where their doings had such an influence not only on their host country but also on the policies of their home countries and caused so much concern in the ministries and parliaments of the world. There was no other city where so many foreigners lived so close to the men and women who were trying to bring a new nation into the modern world.

In the years after 1925, a great revolutionary movement would sweep through large parts of China. It was a movement that, on the one hand, represented the fruit of much of what Shanghai stood for as the pioneer of China's modernization, the leader of China's commerce, manufacturing, and banking. Yet it was also a movement that had as one of its chief aims the destruction of the old order that had brought modern Shanghai into being and had allowed such a foreign anomaly to continue to exist.

Modern Shanghai was very much the product of the Western invasion of China in the nineteenth century. Ever since her defeat at the hands of Britain in the first opium war, China had been forced into a position of diplomatic subjection that had denied her many of the rights of a sovereign nation. The treaty of Nanking, which had ended the war in 1842, was the first of what the Chinese called unequal treaties, imposed upon her by force of arms. These agreements allowed foreigners to live and do business in the dozens of "treaty ports," as the cities opened to foreign commerce were called. The treaties, or at least the foreign interpretation of them, allowed foreign settlements to grow up in several of these ports, and to become enclaves virtually free from Chinese jurisdiction. The treaties gave foreigners immunity from most Chinese taxation and established the limits within which China could set her tariffs. The treaties allowed foreign merchantmen and foreign men-of-war to ply the coastal and inland waters of China. They allowed foreign troops to be stationed in China, after 1901 even in the imperial capital of Peking itself.

The treaties allowed missionaries to propagate Christianity freely, to live and work in the interior, to buy and lease land for their churches, their hospitals, their orphanages, and their schools. Above all, the treaties gave these foreigners the right of extraterritoriality, remaining subject to the laws of their own country rather than the laws of China, and it was this right that lay at the center of foreign privilege in China.

The system thus established by the unequal treaties seriously limited China's sovereign rights and was a continuing affront to Chinese nationalism. Yet sovereignty and nationalism were modern terms. For most of the nineteenth century, resentment of the foreigner, hatred of the foreigner, and even violent resistance to the foreigner arose primarily from a sense that the outsiders were violating China's cultural integrity rather than her geographical territory. The strange alliance of 1900 between Boxer peasant rebels and the Qing court in Peking, which led to a Chinese war against foreign imperialism, is seen by some as representing the birth of modern nationalism. That stretches the meaning of the word, but there is no doubt that by the first decade of the twentieth century a growing sense of national pride, a modern nationalism, was spreading throughout many levels of Chinese society.[13]

As Joseph Levenson and others have suggested, China's traditional view of herself as the center of civilized humanity began, by the late nineteenth century, to give way to a view of China as a modern nation-state in a world of competing nation-states, a view in which China's civilization was to be valued because it was something uniquely Chinese, not because it was ecumenically human. Such a view was bound to erode the faltering legitimacy of the Qing dynasty, for not only were the Manchus foreigners themselves, but it was their weakness and their ineptitude that had, in the eyes of the nationalists, allowed imperialist privilege to establish itself so thoroughly on Chinese soil. Hence the first task was to overthrow the alien dynasty so that political power might be restored to Chinese hands. The revolt that broke out in October 1911 accomplished that; one by one, the provinces seceded from their dynastic allegiance, and in February 1912, the infant emperor abdicated, bringing to an end the two thousand-year-old Chinese empire.

Yet the revolution of 1911 fell short of overturning the old order. Sun Yat-sen's principle of People's Livelihood might suggest radical social and economic change, but the military, gentry, and merchant leaders who led their provinces away from allegiance to the dynasty wanted to safeguard the growing financial and political independence of the provinces from Peking, wanted to ensure that the overthrow of the Manchus would not also overturn the customary social institutions of the country. They also hoped that the new Chinese nation would work through modern constitutional forms to strengthen and legitimize a new republican government, and here the revolution faltered. Sun Yat-sen, elected leader by the revolutionaries in 1911, gave way to Yuan Shikai in 1912, and Yuan Shikai, the republican president, gave way to Yuan Shikai, the unsuccessful dictator and would-be emperor of 1915. Republican China proved too weak to stem the flow of power from the center to the provinces, and the merchant-gentry localism of the late Qing turned into the warlordism that spread after Yuan died in 1916, broken by the resistance to his monarchical restoration.

Meanwhile, the growing sense of nationalism was stimulated by the First World War, by the Russian revolution, and by China's humiliation at the hands of the peacemakers of Versailles. The May Fourth Movement of 1919 marked a new stage in China's consciousness. On that day, thousands of students took to the streets of Peking to protest against the Allied statesmen who had given Japan title to the old German imperial holdings in Shandong province. From the capital, the demonstrations spread to the other great cities like Shanghai, where the protest was taken up in a great burst of self-confidence by journalists, publicists, student unions, chambers of commerce, labor associations. The narrow grievances against China's treatment at Versailles swelled into a far broader movement that sought to birth a new Chinese consciousness and a new Chinese culture that would be informed by the spirit of democracy, whether in its American or Russian form.

The May Fourth Movement was largely spontaneous and diffuse, lacking clear leadership. Nonetheless, out of this turmoil was born the Chinese Communist Party. (The building where it held its first congress in July 1921 is reverently preserved as a museum on Xingye Road in what was the old French Concession.) Out of this turmoil, too, Sun Yat-sen's movement pulled itself back together in Canton, and the Nationalist Party, or Guomindang, gathered its strength, drawing a new sense of discipline and organization from the Soviet advisers who came to Canton in 1923. Such organizations, with their ability to use modern journalism, modern means of education, and propaganda, did much to help build a new sense of Chinese nationalism that was different from the older nationalism of the first two decades of the twentieth century.

It was new because it was radical as the old nationalism was not. China's old nationalists saw the expulsion of the Manchus as the key to China's salvation; the new nationalists found a domestic Chinese enemy in the selfish ambitions of the provincial warlords. The old nationalists thought that the passing of the Manchus would restore China to the Chinese and would enable them to deal with the foreigners as equals; the new nationalists held that warlordism and imperialism went hand in hand, that one could not be destroyed without the other. The old nationalists drew back in the face of social revolution and sought to maintain the old structures of power; the new nationalists saw their cause as cutting across class lines, wanted to bring all Chinese, high and low, into their camp, and were ready to undertake the far-reaching social changes this inclusion would demand. The old nationalists wanted to protect provincial autonomy in a kind of federation under Peking; the new nationalists knew that provincialism meant warlordism, and both the Guomindang and the Communists tried to build new institutions that would transcend provincial and regional lines, providing China with the kind of disciplined and organized leadership that had been so lacking in the May Fourth Movement of 1919.

If Chinese nationalism had changed since 1911, so had foreign imperialism, and with it, the foreign position in China. The Great War and the Bolshevik revolution destroyed the earlier imperial order. Four years of slaughter on the western front, four years of destruction and economic drain, had weakened both victor and vanquished in the old world, destroying the myths of Western military and moral superiority. When the Pacific powers met at the Washington Conference in late 1921, the British and French empires were larger than ever before. But imperial problems were not Britain's chief concern; rather, she was harried by unemployment and labor unrest, by the collapse of the prewar economic order, and by socialism and the demands for a greater equality in the distribution of economic wealth.

America and Japan, not the old empires of Europe, were the new powers of the Pacific world. The Washington Conference tried to come to terms with the new world that was emerging after the fall of the Manchu dynasty, the Russian revolution, and the Great War. Foreigners, however, wanted no sudden threat to their privileges; China was not yet ready for full independence and must be kept in a position of tutelage. No one, except the Chinese delegates, talked in Washington about abolishing the unequal treaties outright. The statesmen promised to examine China's right, lost eighty years earlier, to set her own tariffs on foreign trade; they promised to help China build a modern legal system so she could look forward to the day when extraterritoriality would disappear and foreigners become subject to Chinese law. Outside diplomatic circles, other voices called for even broader changes. Many missionaries wanted the old treaties done away with entirely, and liberals and radicals in Britain and America wanted foreign privilege ended so that a new democratic China could be born.

If Chinese nationalism was stronger and foreign imperialism weaker in the postwar world, Washington and London perceived the change more clearly than did the inhabitants of foreign Shanghai. They still expected the support of their home countries in maintaining the privileged position they enjoyed, and thus played the part (in the eyes of one of their critics) of "the spoilt children of empire." They scorned the hopeful prospects held out by the protagonists of New China. As Arthur Ransome wrote in 1927, what Britons in Shanghai remembered was not the revolution of 1911 nor the First World War, but rather the Boxer uprising of 1900, the fire and sword that had laid waste to so much of north China that year, taking the lives of so many foreign missionaries and their Chinese converts.[14]

Statesmen in their capitals might realize how weak and incompetent the old imperial structures were for coping with the new challenges of the twenties, and they might thus be willing to pursue gradualist and reformist policies in China, willing to modify the treaties to protect their greater national interests. Liberals and internationalists might see in China's upheaval the birthpangs of a healthy nationalism. The foreign establishments of the treaty ports like Shanghai, however, could only see in the political and military chaos of China in the 1920s a Boxer-like threat, proof not only that they need not change their ways but that their concessions and settlements were a boon to China herself, the only islands of security in a country torn apart by civil war. "The doctrine that China must work out her own salvation has been tried and found wanting," declared A. O. Lang, chairman of the Court of Directors of the Hongkong and Shanghai Bank at the ceremonies opening its new building in Shanghai in June 1923. "It is not only derided by most intelligent Chinese, but has been abandoned by all thinking foreigners."[15] Foreigners were in China for China's own good, and responsible Chinese knew it.

Today there is much in the Chinese revolution that seems familiar to us. Since the end of the Second World War, country after country has seen its people and their leaders rise up to overthrow the imperialism that had held them down. The Chinese revolution of the twenties, however, was one of the first great Third World revolutions of our century. Precisely because it was a spectacle so unfamiliar to those who saw it, precisely because it faced them with a crisis, it gives us a useful background against which to realize the purpose of this book: to examine the workings of a particular kind of colonial society, to understand its culture, particularly its political culture, and thus to piece together a bit more clearly the long decline of the Western empires.

Omnia Juncta in Uno
The Government of Foreign Shanghai

Eighty years before the events of the 1920s, Shanghai had been one of the first five ports opened to foreign trade by the treaty of Nanking, which marked Britain's victory over China in 1842. Hongkong island, ceded in perpetuity to Britain, became an outright colony. The treaty ports did not, and nothing in the original agreement suggested that China in any way surrendered its control or its sovereignty over them. British subjects and their families were allowed to live in the ports "for the purpose of carrying on their mercantile pursuits without molestation or restraints," and a supplementary agreement of October 1843 allowed them to buy or rent land and houses. Fifteen years later, after another war, the treaty of Tientsin confirmed these privileges, adding that foreigners might also build churches, hospitals, and cemeteries.

That was all the treaties said about foreign settlement in China—that British citizens, and those of countries like France and America who signed similar agreements with Peking, could live and work in the treaty ports, could own property, and could provide themselves with certain physical and spiritual amenities. The treaties did not say that they could carve out particular pieces of Chinese territory and establish their own virtually independent municipal governments with powers to regulate and tax the foreigners who lived within their boundaries. They did not state foreigners could build roads, provide their own water, light, or power, or establish their own police or defense forces or call on outside military forces for protection. Still less did they imply that such governments could impose their powers upon the *Chinese* who lived within their borders, effectively excluding them from the purview of Chinese authority.

Yet, in several treaty ports, and most particularly in Shanghai, there grew up a system that had all the marks of this kind of *imperium in imperio*. Although it may have been unplanned, the system was hardly developed in a fit of absence of mind. Rather, it was the cumulative result of years and years of particular decisions made to meet particular problems, years and years of foreigners guarding and expanding their own interests against a weak China, stretching the treaties as far as they possibly could. Finally, the treaty port system grew from a need to provide an institutional authority for the polity that had thus evolved, and in the end only the diplomats and the lawyers could distinguish what the foreigners held by treaty and what they held by custom.

Treaty ports might contain two kinds of foreign jurisdictions: concessions [*zujie*] and settlements [*juliudi*]. The words were used with no great precision and are often interchangeable (the Chinese term *zujie*, for instance, served for both foreign districts in Shanghai). For the more legally minded, however, a "concession" was a piece of land granted or leased directly by China to a foreign government in return for the payment of a nominal ground rent; a "settlement" was simply a place set aside where foreigners might live and deal directly with individual Chinese owners in buying or leasing land.[1] Concessions existed in several cities such as Hankou, Tianjin, and Canton. But in Shanghai, what was called the French Concession was in fact, like its neighbor, technically a settlement.

By whatever name, both settlements and concessions infringed upon China's authority. The most important infringement from a legal standpoint was the provision of extraterritoriality.[2] The treaty of 1843 stipulated that British subjects involved in criminal cases in China be subject to British, not Chinese, law. When the American treaty of 1844 enlarged the provision to include civil cases as well, it became a model for future agreements. The treaty powers thus built upon the original British foundation a system of privilege far greater than originally intended. Over the years, the scope of extraterritoriality grew (it came to include freedom from most Chinese taxation, for example), undergirding the whole structure of foreign privilege.

The American treaty of 1844 also enlarged the reach of foreign prerogative by including a most favored nation clause, guaranteeing that American citizens would benefit from whatever rights or privileges China might grant to others. Though Americans were later prone to boast that their country had never used force to extort concessions from China, they were always quick to take advantage of the gains made by others. They profited from British and French victories in mid-century, and when in 1895 the treaty of Shimonoseki allowed Japan to build factories (as opposed simply to commercial establishments) on Chinese soil, Americans, like the other treaty powers, profited from the defeat of China by Japanese arms.

The right to establish industries on Chinese soil, the rights of trade and residence in the open ports, of extraterritoriality, of most favored nation status, all formed the basis by treaty of foreign privilege in China. To this list, one more item must be added: the right of Christian missionaries not only to propagate their religion, but to live and build churches, schools, and hospitals in the interior as well as in the treaty ports. Yet the reach of foreign privilege extended well beyond the strict provisions of the treaties. Westerners drew on their own international law to interpret the treaties in ways favorable to themselves. If China could not provide adequate protection for Shanghai's foreign residents, for instance, an internationally recognized right of self-protection justified the establishment of a police force or a militia.[3] Nor did nineteenth-century Chinese negotiators at first consider unusual the kinds of concessions that twentieth-century nationalists would see as shameful derogations of sovereignty. To them, the treaty system was simply a way of fitting the Westerners into a long tradition of barbarian management, allowing foreign traders to handle their own affairs, troubling the imperial government as little as possible.[4] By the time China developed an understanding of sovereignty and a core of experts in the new diplomacy, she was powerless to resist foreign encroachments. The erection of the foreign system of privilege did not cause the decline and fall of the Chinese empire, but it did take place against the background of that decline and fall, leaving China hard put to reclaim what she had lost.

Not long after Shanghai's opening as a treaty port in 1843, more concrete arrangements, almost always in favor of the foreigners, were added to the general and imprecise provisions of the treaties. In November 1845, the first British consul and the local *daotai* [circuit intendant] agreed to set aside a piece of land bounded by the Soochow Creek and the Huangpu River within which British subjects could buy or rent land. Under these arrangements, called the Land Regulations, foreigners assumed certain municipal duties, including the formation of a Committee of Roads and Jetties to undertake the building of roads, the development of the waterfront, the hiring of watchmen, and so forth. Nothing was said about the establishment of a municipal government.

Perhaps if Shanghai had remained purely British, this simple system would have lasted. But the first, rather uncomplicated, set of Land Regulations broke down for several reasons. One was the increasingly international character of Shanghai. By 1849, the French had established their own settlement, and in 1854 the American consul put forward a claim to an American settlement north of Soochow Creek in Hongkew. More important was the influx of thousands of Chinese into the settlements when the city was threatened by the civil wars of mid-century. The land set aside for foreigners suddenly found itself with a large Chinese population as well.[5]

To deal with these problems, in 1854 Sir Rutherford Alcock, the British consul, drafted a new set of Land Regulations with his French and American colleagues. They went well beyond the earlier ones, for they now allowed the foreigners not only to establish a police force but also to set up a committee to raise money through taxes, rates, and dues to pay for a widening range of public services. The new Regulations also sought to give the Settlement a legal status (at least in the eyes of foreigners) that would allow it to call for foreign military help in emergencies. It was according to these principles, for example, established by custom rather than by treaty, that allowed the Municipal Council to ask for the landing of foreign sailors in the autumn of 1924, when once again a Chinese war threatened to spill into the foreign settlements.

On 11 July 1854, the foreign renters of land adopted the new Regulations. Though the *daotai* gave his approval, no reference was made to the imperial government in Peking; yet, out of this code was born the Shanghai Municipal Council, a foreign political authority on Chinese soil. In 1863, the Americans amalgamated their own tract of land with the British holding, thus formally bringing the International Settlement into being. The French, however, went their own way. In 1862 they formed a *Conseil municipal* for their settlement south of the Yangjingbang Creek (this stream, paved over in 1914–1916, would become the avenue Edward VII, dividing the two settlements). In 1869, the ministers of the treaty powers in Peking approved a new set of Land Regulations for the International Settlement and a corresponding *Règlement d'organisation* for the French Settlement. This time the Chinese government played no role, and it is not clear that the *daotai* was even notified.

Further revisions followed, and in 1898 the modern Land Regulations came into force without formal Chinese approval (neither the viceroy in Nanking nor the Zongli Yamen—a kind of proto–foreign ministry in Peking—wanted to interfere in a matter of purely foreign concern). A year later, the *daotai*, in agreeing to an extension of the Settlement's borders, recognized the authority of the Land Regulations throughout the Settlement, save for "temples founded by Imperial sanction and sites employed officially by the Chinese government." [6]

Under the Land Regulations, a foreigner buying land from a Chinese seller would receive a title deed from his consul after Chinese authorities had surveyed the land and verified the sale. The lot would be assigned a number and recorded in the consular register, and if it were resold to a foreigner of a different nationality, it would be registered in the new owner's consulate. The purchaser was not getting outright ownership, for all land was supposed to be held by the Chinese emperor, but rather a deed of perpetual lease, for which he paid the Chinese government a land rent of one tael a year per *mou* (the tael was a monetary unit originally equivalent to an ounce of silver, and the *mou* was about a sixth of an acre). Though the settlements included land still held by the original Chinese owners, once a lot passed to a foreigner, it was not supposed to revert to Chinese ownership. Yet well before the turn of the century, Chinese were buying back land and registering it with the appropriate consulate in the name of a foreigner, usually a lawyer or a real estate agent or architect. Later, as the benefits of foreign security became more evident, many Chinese owners simply converted their own titles into foreign deeds registered in foreign names, thus gaining a measure of extraterritorial protection for their holdings. By the end of 1927, of the 10,065 lots in the International Settlement surveyed and taxed, about 3,700 were held for Chinese interests, and in the Central District, the wealthiest and most crowded region of the city, 522 of the 700 lots were Chinese.[7] No one denied that the system was an abuse of the Land Regulations; but the Chinese owners benefited from consular protection, and the foreigners, particularly lawyers and land agents, benefited from the fees that they drew.

Even this brief description should show that the history of foreign Shanghai raised all kinds of unanswered questions and, more than that, gave rise to all sorts of grievances that the new nationalism of twentieth-century China would find intolerable. Elsewhere in China, the municipal administrations of individual foreign concessions were clearly responsible to the foreign consuls on the spot and to the ministers in Peking above them. The same was true of the French *Conseil municipal* in Shanghai. But precisely to whom was the Shanghai Municipal Council responsible? From what superior body did it draw its authority? What limits, if any, were there on its jurisdiction, on its powers of taxation and coercion over the Chinese residents of the International Settlement, men and women who in no sense renounced any part of their Chinese citizenship by living there? How valid was the largely implicit assent given by the Chinese to the Land Regulations? Should there have been a more explicit approval?

These were the sorts of questions over which councilmen, lawyers, politicians, and diplomats—Chinese and foreign—would wrangle in the years to come. Usually they had the texts of treaties, agreements, and memoranda to back up their positions, but sometimes the archives were empty and the historical record silent. More important than the legal and diplomatic concerns, however, were the new questions that arose with increasing urgency in the twentieth century, questions that grew out of China's growing national consciousness and that posed a new challenge to the foreigners. By what right were these enclaves of foreign privilege such as the International Settlement maintained in a sovereign nation?

Foreigners answered that the treaties had granted that right; but then, the question really being asked was, On what *moral* basis did the foreign position stand? By what *moral* right was it maintained? Had not the treaties been dictated to the Chinese at gunpoint? And had not the birth of the Chinese Republic in 1912 radically changed the state of affairs? How far, in short, could the new China tolerate the arrangements of an earlier day? How far could it tolerate arrangements that went beyond the letter of the treaties? Foreigners answered that the Chinese would do better to put their own house in order before raising such questions. They should study the orderly and efficient government of the International Settlement as a model for the corrupt and chaotic administration of their own cities. Of course, the foreigners were right, and, of course, they were entirely missing the point.

The highest authority within the Settlement was the Shanghai Municipal Council (or, to give it the official name that no one used, the Council for the Foreign Settlement North of the Yang-king-pang). It was elected annually by the roughly twenty-seven hundred ratepayers who could meet the qualifications for the franchise: foreigners who owned land worth at least 500 taels (Tls.; about US $365), paying an annual assessment of at least Tls. 10 (roughly $8); or householders paying an assessed rental of at least Tls. 500 annually. A single individual might have more than one vote by virtue of owning several different units of qualifying property (a house and a business, for instance) or by holding the proxies of non-resident ratepayers. In 1926, for example, a lawyer named G. H. Wright held no fewer than twenty-five separate votes; his nearest competitor, A. W. Burkill, the head of one of Shanghai's leading real estate firms, held eleven. Father Noury, the head of the French Missions Étrangères, who lived in Siccawei, had nine votes, thanks to properties owned by his order in the Settlement. The principle, in short, was not one man one vote, but one interest one vote. (The American Methodist Bishop Birney found this out when he tried to increase his mission's voting strength by splitting its properties.)[8] It was no accident that the property qualification severely limited the number of voters; as a British memorandum put it, the Regulations were designed to keep control of the Settlement in the hands of hard-headed foreign businessmen, for only they would protect the city's commercial prosperity. Other interest claims—residence, education, social service, or even non-propertied wealth—had no voice.[9] Moreover, the control would be British; of the Settlement's 2,742 votes in March 1925, the British held 1,157, the Japanese came next with 552, and the Americans ran a poor third with 328.

The Municipal Council's nine members, all foreigners, were elected annually. Though there were no official stipulations about nationality, a gentlemen's agreement provided for six Britons, two Americans, and a

Japanese, the last occupying what had been a German seat before the war. In theory, any qualified person could stand for office; in practice, American and Japanese councillors were usually chosen by informal agreement before the election to avoid splitting the vote of those communities. Hence, usually the only real contest was among the British. Since each enfranchised ratepayer had nine votes to cast, the American and Japanese votes remaining after their own nominees had been chosen might well determine which British candidates (assuming there were more than six) would be seated.[10] By the 1920s, however, the problem was not in deciding between well-qualified candidates but in inducing such men to stand for election. Councillors were not paid, the amount of work had grown considerably, and businessmen with large responsibilities were less and less willing to take on the burdens of office.[11]

The Council elected its own chairman. Today, in the Shanghai Historical Museum, one can see the ornate oak chair from which he presided, its back inscribed with the Council's motto, *Omnia juncta in uno*. In 1923 they chose the American Stirling Fessenden, a native of Maine, a plump and affable bachelor, gregarious, well liked, and much in demand as an after dinner speaker. A graduate of Bowdoin College, he had come to Shanghai in 1906, built up a law practice on Kiukiang Road, and was one of a handful of Americans (like his partner, Major C. P. Holcomb, and V. G. Lyman of Standard Oil) who had reached the highest levels of what was otherwise a very British Shanghai establishment. Yet, he obviously owed his position to the support of that establishment (which referred to him as the "Lord Mayor of Shanghai"). Though few would agree with the American diplomat who saw him as a man gone to pieces in the East and unfit for his position,[12] some disgruntled Americans found Fessenden more British than the British themselves, a pawn occupying a position of eminence to give a veneer of internationalism to what was otherwise an almost entirely British show.

The Shanghai Municipal Council normally met every fortnight, less often in the heat of summer, and more often in emergencies. Aided by twelve advisory committees, it oversaw the Settlement's affairs, but the real work of governance was done by a large municipal administration in the new Town Hall at the corner of Foochow and Kiangse roads. In large part, the Council simply approved their actions.[13] Twelve departments—Police, Public Health, Legal, Secretarial, and so forth—handled the Settlement's business, and to coordinate them the Council created the post of commissioner-general in February 1925, appointing to the position Major A. H. Hilton-Johnson, the former acting commissioner of police. No Americans held any high posts in this international administration, nor did any Japanese, Italians, Swiss, or Scandinavians. The Council's own figures showed that in 1925, of the 1,031 foreign members of the municipal staff, 857 were British, only 47 were American, and 7 were Japanese, and British citizens held virtually all the responsible positions. There was one exception: The conductor of the Municipal Orchestra, Mario Paci, was an Italian.[14] All in all, concluded the American consul-general, the Council's employees were chosen more for nationality than for competence, and vacancies were filled by advertising in the London papers rather than locally.[15]

To pay for the regular costs of administration, the Council imposed upon its citizens—foreign and Chinese—a variety of rates, taxes, and license fees. Though there was a land tax, the largest single item was the municipal rate, assessed as a percentage of rent paid. The heaviest burden was thus on the tenant rather than the owner of the land, and, as some complained, those of middle income were taxed proportionally higher than the rich.[16] Ordinary Council income and expenditures, projected at somewhat over Tls. 9,400,000 (roughly £1,500,000 or $6,800,000) in 1925, would rise to over Tls. 12,000,000 (£1,875,000 or $8,700,000) by 1928 and covered the routine costs of administration, most important of which were those for the police, public works, health, and education. Extraordinary expenses, on the other hand—primarily capital improvements such as the purchase of land, the construction of buildings, roads, and bridges, the laying of sewer lines, and so forth—were met by floating loans through the issuance of municipal debentures and could add several million more taels to the budget. Though the Council prided itself on its fiscal management, there was some grumbling about the salaries drawn by its servants. "Modern business principles have not been introduced into the Municipal Council," complained the American consul-general in 1929, pointing out that the police commissioner was paid half again as much as his equivalent in New York and that the Council's prosecuting attorney earned more than twice as much as the American district attorney for China. Fringe benefits, he added, increased the total compensation "to a figure that would be regarded as unconscionable in the United States." A special commission on economy in 1929 agreed that as new appointments were made, salaries should be lowered.[17]

The Municipal Council's Annual Reports provide a good deal of information about the Settlement's machinery and its finances but say little about the activities of the Council itself. The French *Comptes-rendus* and *Bulletin Municipal*, on the other hand, while publishing far fuller accounts of the meetings of the *Conseil municipal*, unfortunately reveal much less about the operations of their government. It is a sign of the insularity of the foreign communities in Shanghai that, despite the large numbers of Britons and Americans living and working in the French Concession, despite the presence there of companies like Butterfield and Swire and institutions like the American School and American Community Church, there is so little news about Frenchtown in the Settlement's newspapers or in British and American consular reports. Even a paper like the *China Weekly Review*, with its offices on the very road that divided the two settlements, says virtually nothing about the affairs of the Concession—except occasionally to use the real or supposed liberality of the French authorities as a stick with which to beat the British. The parochialism extends to current scholarship as well; even the French ignore the subject of their Concession.

What the Land Regulations were for the Settlement, the *Règlement d'organisation* of 1868 was to the Concession. It set up a *Conseil municipal* consisting of the French consul-general or his deputy and eight elected members, four French and four foreign (again there was a property qualification for the vote). It differed from the Shanghai Municipal Council in several ways. It met more often (four or five times a month was not unusual) in the imposing, late nineteenth-century building on the rue de l'Administration, which served as *hôtel municipal*. While the Land Regulations made no provision for a Chinese voice, the *Règlement* allowed the consul-general, with the assent of the *Conseil*, to appoint several *notables Chinoises* to participate without vote in discussions affecting Chinese interests. Not until 1914 did the French implement the provision, and then it was as part of the price paid for Chinese agreement to an extension of the Concession's boundaries. Most important, the *Conseil municipal* was purely advisory to the French consul-general. He or his deputy usually acted as president; it met at his call, by and large discussed the matters he put on the agenda, and only the decisions he approved took effect, although the *Conseil* could appeal his veto to the French minister in Peking.[18]

The Concession's budget was a good deal smaller than that of the Settlement, and it had a much smaller administration. In 1927, for example, there were only about 248 Europeans on the payroll, of whom 105 were in the police force. Since it was responsible for less than a third of the Settlement's population, how much this smaller budget affected the provision of public services is less clear. Certainly it rewarded its servants considerably less well. The secretary, who was the most highly paid member, drew only Tls. 12,000 in 1927, compared with the Tls. 30,000 paid to Commissioner-General Hilton-Johnson or the chief engineer of the Shanghai Municipal Power Company. The chief of the *Garde municipale* received Tls. 11,100, while the commissioner of the Shanghai Municipal Police drew Tls. 18,000, and there was a corresponding difference in the salaries of other officials, from public works engineers to schoolteachers.[19]

Nonetheless, the French Concession grew rapidly in the early twentieth century; the number of foreigners rose from 622 in 1905 to 7,811 in 1925, and the Chinese population, from 91,646 to 289,281.[20] In January 1924, Consul-General Auguste Wilden gave a brief but optimistic report on the Concession's development since his arrival in 1917, looking not only at its business interests but at the growth in social and public services as well: at the Compagnie Française des Eaux, des Tramways et de l'Éclairage Électriques, which was recovering from earlier troubles under a newly appointed chief engineer; at the two schools, one for Westerners and one for Chinese; at hospitals and sanitation, the fire company ("Le Torrent"), the volunteer force, and so forth. It was by no means a perfect picture though. Wilden mentioned opium smuggling and the corruption of an underpaid police force, though fortunately Captain Étienne Fiori, the Corsican commander of the *Garde municipale*, was above suspicion. Above all, he returned to the question of Chinese representation, warning that to keep the sympathy of its Chinese population, the French Concession must deal with the question in a liberal spirit whatever the neighboring Settlement might or might not do.[21]

Both settlements were thus run by foreigners for foreigners, and therein lay their strength and their weakness. Historically, the arrangements might make perfect sense; politically, however, they made no sense by the early years of the twentieth century. In its size, wealth, and importance, foreign Shanghai dominated the Chinese city. In 1925, over a million Chinese lived in the settlements, and many more earned their living there, streaming out of the slums of Zhabei at dawn or dusk to work in the textile mills of the Northern and Eastern districts or crossing the river from Pudong to labor on the jetties of the Bund or the wharves of Yangtszepoo. Chinese shopkeepers catered to the daily needs of foreign and Chinese alike, Chinese merchants and bankers did business in the settlements, Chinese shippers used the settlements' river frontage as well as that of the Chinese city, and above all, Chinese paid the same taxes and rates as did the foreigners, contributing (in 1927) about 55 percent of the International Settlement's ordinary income.

Yet it was the 38,000 foreigners, not the million and more Chinese, who were the main beneficiaries of foreign Shanghai's social and municipal services. Chinese gained, of course, from modern roads and public transport, from clean water and dependable electricity; they gained from the public health measures that helped prevent the spread of disease; and they benefited above all, as Westerners were never tired of pointing out, from the physical and political security of the settlements. Nonetheless, the Chinese could and did argue that they did not get their fair share of the tax tael. Provisions for public education, particularly for Chinese, were skimpy, and the most modern and best equipped hospitals were reserved for foreigners. Of course, the missionaries—Catholic and Protestant—ran schools and hospitals both in and out of the Shanghai settlements, but these were private concerns, not supported from tax revenue. Finally, the Chinese were kept out of the public parks the foreigners had set aside for themselves in the Settlement. It was not true, as many of Shanghai's critics said, that beside the entrance to the Public Gardens, across from the British consulate, was a sign reading, "No dogs or Chinese allowed." But it is true that one regulation said that no dogs could enter, and another said that no Chinese could enter (except, of course, for amahs tending their small foreign charges). The exclusion of Chinese may seem a small point, but it was a constant irritant and would become an issue all out of proportion to its intrinsic importance. The French, for their part, allowed Chinese in Western dress into their park at Kouzaka, but excluded anyone not dressed respectably, and those in kimono, as well as dogs.

The two settlements were much more similar than they were different, and in an age of growing Chinese nationalism, both looked like parasites on the body of China—taking but not giving. They were channels through which the country's wealth passed on its way to enrich London and Tokyo, New York, and Paris. Both settlements were undemocratic, denying the vote to all Chinese and most foreigners. In the Settlement, there was no campaigning for office; municipal councillors were usually chosen by arrangements worked out by different nationalities and different parties rather than by open contest (though by 1925, the French Concession saw something of a campaign). Finally, neither administration could move swiftly enough to meet changing times. The ratepayers met once a year, in January in the French Concession and in April in the International Settlement, and there was little time or inclination to discuss important business. Though the Settlement's Land Regulations could be changed by vote of the ratepayers at a special public meeting, not for years had it been possible to turn out a quorum.

Nonetheless, the differences between the two settlements are interesting and important. The potentially autocratic powers of the French consul-general gave his Concession a flexibility missing in the Settlement, for the Council must refer any substantial change to the ratepayers. Moreover, for one reason or another, Chinese residents of foreign Shanghai had better relations with the French than with the authorities of the Settlement. The French thought the reasons obvious: They were free of the pervasive sin of racism that marked the British and Americans in their dealings with the Chinese. Americans and Englishmen considered the Chinese presence in the International Settlement as something to be tolerated, not as implying any obligations, wrote Consul-General Wilden, and he worried that their blindness would hurt all foreign Shanghai.[22] The inhabitants of the Settlement, for their part, admitted that the French dealt better with the Chinese, and were puzzled by it. They could only suggest that the French curried favor with the Chinese. A good deal of gossip suggested that the French authorities, unhampered by Anglo-Saxon ideas of recti- tude and legality, had made their peace with a variety of Chinese forces— radical and reactionary, overworld and underworld—using them to keep order in their domain and to deflect the ire of the Chinese against their neighbors north of the avenue Edward VII.[23] Yet, as Sidney Barton, the British consul-general, pointed out rather testily, the Chinese residents of the Settlement never held up the governance of the French Concession as a model to the Shanghai Municipal Council.[24]

In neither settlement did the Chinese have much of a voice in Shang- hai's governance. The *notables Chinoises* were rarely called to meetings of the *Conseil municipal* and had attended none since 1922.[25] After the protests of the May Fourth Movement of 1919, Chinese demands for a voice in the Settlement led to the formation of a Chinese Advisory Board, but the body had little influence with the Council.[26] The settlements were run, after all was said and done, primarily for the benefit of the foreign businessmen who had built modern Shanghai. To them, the Chinese were at best guests who had no right to demand a voice in the governance of those areas set aside specifically for foreigners. The business of Shanghai was business; except among the missionaries, there was little concern for the *mission civilisatrice*, none of the passion for tutelage and improvement that was common to colonial officials in, say, Africa or India. China was not a colony; the talk was not of the mother country's responsibilities toward her subject people but rather of treaty rights, safeguards, and secu- rity for foreign lives and foreign property, all of which militated against Chinese participation in government.

Besides the grievance arising from the lack of a Chinese voice in the settlements, two other sore points are important. The first had to do with the growth of the International Settlement. By 1899, it had reached its modern size of 5,584 acres or 8.66 square miles (an attempt to extend the borders in 1915 came to naught). Yet it grew more and more crowded, par- ticularly after the revolution of 1911. Beyond the Settlement, the Municipal Council was allowed to buy land and build roads, and as commerce and industry developed downtown, foreigners fled to the more open spaces of the west where building lots on Council-owned roads could still be had at a reasonable price. Though the extension of 1899 brought many of these roads and their populations within the Settlement's borders, by 1925 there were 7,100 foreigners living on these roads outside the Settlement compared to the 22,850 who lived within its borders.[27] The French solved a similar problem by extending their Concession west to Siccawei in 1914.

There were two main concentrations of these Extra-Settlement Roads, as they were also called. To the north was a small area along Dixwell Road and North Szechuen Road, which included Hongkew Park and which was inhabited mostly by Japanese. To the west, a far larger area of 7,640 acres stretched from the Settlement border beyond Jessfield Park, beyond Rubicon Road, all the way to Monument Road near the present airport. All in all, by 1925, there were just over five miles of outside roads in the north and forty-three in the west, the most important of which lay within Keswick Road and the railway loop that curved west of the city and that joined the Shanghai-Nanking railway with the line to Hangzhou.[28]

The Municipal Council did not claim control of all this land, which remained indisputably Chinese territory, but it did claim ownership of the roads and parks it had bought. Because of that ownership, it also claimed the right to police them and to tax the residents, both foreign and Chinese, who drew on the Council's municipal services. Foreigners living here did not have the vote, and they paid a municipal rate generally set 2 percent lower than that for the Settlement proper. For fifty years, the Chinese challenged the Council's administrative claims over the roads, and Chinese and foreign police clashed from time to time over the right to patrol them. Nothing in the treaties or the Land Regulations justified the Settlement's continual encroachment on Chinese territory. Its usurpation of authority represents perhaps the clearest example of the way in which foreign Shanghai managed to stretch its original privileges over the years, making it more and more difficult to challenge a system that was becoming sanctified by custom.

The other major irritant came from a question of legal jurisdiction. The movement of Chinese into the settlements raised the whole troublesome question of foreign authority over them, a question on which both the treaties and the Land Regulations were silent. At first, the authorities took the common sense view that the Chinese government retained jurisdiction over its own subjects. Easy enough in theory, the system was difficult in practice, and over the years, more by custom than by formal agreement, the Municipal Council managed to establish the principle that no Chinese taxes were to be collected in the Settlement save the land tax and customs duties, and that no ordinances binding Chinese citizens were to be promulgated without Council approval.[29] After many battles both with the consuls and the Chinese, the Council also managed to exclude Chinese police from the Settlement. Furthermore, the Settlement's own Municipal Police would not hand any Chinese over to their own authorities until the

Settlement's own legal authorities were convinced that there was a *prima facie* case against them. That question was determined by an institution known as the Mixed Court, which was founded in 1864 to deal with cases between Chinese in the Settlement or, under certain circumstances, between Chinese and foreigners.

To understand the Mixed Court, we must start with the administration of justice in foreign Shanghai. Foreigners enjoying extraterritoriality were tried in their own courts: a British Supreme Court for China, established in 1905, an American Court for China, set up in 1906, or consular courts, presided over by the consul-general himself or (in the case of Japan, France, and Italy) by a judge assigned for that purpose. Rightly or wrongly, some of the consular courts (the Italians and Portuguese in particular) had a reputation for dishonesty, for shielding their nationals and allowing Chinese opium smugglers or gun runners to claim extraterritorial protection by registering as foreigners. According to one British resident, every consulate except the British, Dutch, and Scandinavians used its power to shield criminals. According to an American, his countrymen had the worst reputation for dishonesty because Americans tried their criminals with full publicity rather than sending them discreetly home as others did.[30] In any case, there is no doubt that the consular administration of justice did little to enhance the reputation of foreign Shanghai among the Chinese.

Foreign legal cases were relatively easy to deal with. But how about Chinese charged with criminal offenses or engaged in civil suits with one another or with foreigners? The Mixed Court, housed in an unpretentious red brick building on Chekiang Road, handled questions of this sort. Under a Chinese magistrate appointed by the *daotai*, it tried Chinese accused of offenses in the Settlement, it tried foreigners who did not enjoy extraterritoriality (after the war, that included Germans, Austrians, and Russians), and it heard civil cases brought by foreign plaintiffs against Chinese defendants. In the latter actions, the treaty power concerned had the right to be represented by a foreign assessor (the consul or his deputy), who would sit with the Chinese magistrate and help reach a decision. Again, this was a customary practice rather than a treaty right and further diminished Chinese authority, since over the years the assessor often acted as the real judge in questions brought before the court. To make matters worse, when the revolution broke out in the fall of 1911, the Chinese magistrate and his colleagues fled after resigning control of the Court to the consular body. Thenceforth, the Mixed Court became for all practical purposes the creature of the Municipal Council, which now took over the responsibility of appointing and paying the Chinese magistrates. After 1911, foreign assessors sat on all cases, and foreign lawyers could plead all cases, even when no foreign interests were at stake. These new arrangements were sanctioned neither by treaty, by local agreement, nor even by tradition.

Some argued that, with its new practices, the Court could provide swifter and more impartial justice in a system whose burden grew year by year (in 1923, the Court heard 84,999 criminal cases and 2,629 civil cases).[31] Yet, although the old system had been vulnerable to Chinese corruption and Chinese political influence, the new court only became open to different kinds of corruption and politics. If a consul claimed that the interests of one of his nationals was concerned in a particular case, his deputy could try the case as assessor with the Chinese magistrate. It was, in the words of a later British consul-general, a completely unjustified system as far as purely Chinese cases were concerned, and it "kept in affluence a legal fraternity far in excess of the genuine requirements of the foreign community."[32]

A notorious case in early 1925 illustrates some of the problems. In January, two foreigners, N. E. B. Ezra and G. Dadunashvili, brought to the Mixed Court a case against the Chinese proprietors of an opium shop on Canton Road in the Settlement (where the drug traffic had been illegal since 1917). Ezra and Dadunashvili claimed to be the owners of a shipment of opium worth $1,250,000, which they had legally bought in Constantinople and legally consigned to Vladivostok. The Japanese steamer carrying the drug had, they claimed, been waylaid enroute, and the opium was offloaded near Shanghai for illicit sale. Now they sought to recover its value. The Municipal Police raided the shop, where they not only found some opium but also a great many interesting documents about drug smuggling. They thereupon brought their own charges against the proprietor, a Mr. Yi, who was convicted and sentenced to eighteen months in jail for selling opium.

The Court then turned its attention to the case brought by Ezra and Dadunashvili. Dadunashvili was a Georgian, and since Russians no longer had extraterritorial rights, the Mixed Court clearly had jurisdiction over him. Ezra was more complicated. He had been born either in Baghdad or India (accounts varied) and had been a British subject until either 1911, when he registered as an Ottoman subject at the French consulate, or 1923 (accounts varied again), when he had registered at the Spanish consulate, claiming that, since he was a Sephardic Jew, Spain was the land of his ancestors. Hence, he could ask the Spanish consul to claim an interest in the case and could ask that it be heard before a Spanish assessor. "It is really carrying matters rather far," wrote the *Peking and Tientsin Times*, "when a Spanish Consul in Shanghai claims that he can actually confer Spanish protection and jurisdiction upon a British born Jew, who, to the best of our belief, has never resided in or even visited Spain."[33] The British assessor contested Ezra's claim, finding no proof that Ezra had ever renounced his British citizenship. By now, Ezra admitted that he was not the owner of the opium; he was simply helping Dadunashvili in his claim, for his years of work (he said) with the International Anti-Opium Association had given him knowledge of Shanghai's narcotics underworld! In return for his help, Dadunashvili was to pay him 5 percent of whatever sum was recovered.

As time went on, it became clear to the Court and its British assessor that Ezra's only association with this case was to try to extend to Dadunashvili the benefits of extraterritoriality, to arrange for a Spanish assessor, less familiar with such shenanigans than were the British, to hear the case. By now, Ezra had also considered claiming Chilean citizenship, but to his dismay, the Court decided that if he had indeed renounced his British citizenship, he was neither Spanish nor Chilean but (because of his birth) Turkish! Since Turks did not enjoy extraterritoriality, the case would be heard before the regular assessor who was British. As the testimony dragged on through 1925, the Court also became convinced that the unfortunate Yi had not stolen the opium from Dadunashvili but had bought it from the Georgian, who—wisely—had skipped town by now. Apparently, Ezra and Dadunashvili had never meant the case to come to trial but had used the threat of legal action only to blackmail Yi into paying them off. In January 1926, Ezra lost his case; Yi was found innocent of larceny, though he continued to serve his term for selling opium.[34]

Such confusion obviously made Shanghai a lawyer's paradise. Imagine the enormous and lucrative complications that could arise from a large, foreign, polyglot population, most of which enjoyed extraterritorial rights, subject to the different laws of their different countries, living in the midst of an even larger population made up of Chinese subjects. With the complicated system of courts in foreign Shanghai, an attorney who knew some Chinese, some French, and some English and who knew something of Chinese law, English law, and the Code Napoléon, could do quite well.[35] Admitted after 1911 to a practice from which they had hitherto been excluded, Shanghai's foreign lawyers made the most of it, and their behavior was often a scandal even to the Municipal Council.[36]

Even before the revolution of 1911, the Mixed Court, and particularly the assessors's powers, had become an issue between foreign and Chinese Shanghai. In 1905, the question of the Court's right to extradite a prisoner to the Chinese authorities had led to the outbreak of a serious riot in which several people were killed and the Louza [Laozha] Police Station on Nanking Road was destroyed. Though there was no logical connection between the Court's status and the problem of the outside roads, they became linked when, under British initiative, negotiations began in 1913 to try to solve both problems. When an agreement was drafted in 1915 for a further extension of the Settlement to include many of the outside roads, the Chinese refused to move until the Court was returned to their jurisdiction. Foreign Shanghai was not ready for the step; the Americans insisted that the Chinese appoint only magistrates with certain qualifications, and the China Association, cheered on by foreign lawyers terrified by the specter of lost income, managed to block any agreement transferring the Court to Chinese jurisdiction.[37]

In October 1922, the Foreign Ministry in Peking (the *Waijiaobu*) asked once again for the Court's return. That request brought forth the most ambitious, the most interesting, and the most far-sighted attempt to solve the problem yet seen, in a grand package presented by the Diplomatic Body to the Chinese government in March 1923. The Court would be "returned" to Chinese control, and three Chinese would join the Municipal Council. In return, the foreigners would get an extension of the Settlement's boundaries four miles west to Rubicon Road, well beyond the railway loop, and north above Hongkew. Two foreigners would be seated on the Zhabei Municipal Council, and a Sino-Foreign Municipal Council would be set up to administer Pudong and the land beyond the Settlement on both sides of the Huangpu down to its mouth at Wusong. Finally, a grand consultative body, formed by representatives from all these councils (and including the French) would be established to discuss problems of common concern.

This plan for a Greater Shanghai, as it was called, came largely from the pen of Sidney Barton, the British consul-general. Built on a clear vision of Shanghai's future, understanding the need for the city's rational and unified development, it was a highly intelligent plan in all ways save one: It completely ignored political reality. Such a plan might have worked in 1890; thirty years later it could not. One did not have to be a communist to agree with the local Party journal that the effect would be to detach Shanghai from any Chinese control.[38] Why should China bargain for the return of what she already owned? Why should she surrender yet more control over yet more territory to get back what had been illegally taken in the first place? Did not the corruption of so many foreign lawyers and the self-serving nature of so many consular courts support her claim that she could not put her own house in order until foreign jurisdiction on Chinese soil was ended? These were difficult questions, but the outbreak of the autumn war of 1924 postponed any real discussion about them.[39]

Questions about Chinese representation in the Settlement's governance, about the external roads, and about the Court all fed the nationalism of Chinese Shanghai. To them, the Settlement was rightfully Chinese; to foreigners, it was rightfully international. Perhaps both views were wrong: The Settlement was British. It was physically British—anyone could see that. From the Shanghai Club at the southern end of the Bund, past the great dome of the Hongkong and Shanghai Bank and the twin towers of the *North China Daily News*, past the Glen Line building, Jardine's, the Chartered Bank, and up to the British consulate-general at the northern end—the famous skyline that greeted the arriving traveler was virtually all British (though the new Yokohama Specie Bank building that opened on the Bund in 1924 was a harbinger of things to come). A block behind the Bund, among the shops and counting houses of the Central district, the Gothic tower of Holy Trinity remained a symbol of the link between the Anglican establishment and the British overlords of foreign Shanghai. "A stranger arriving at Shanghai by the P. & O.," wrote a British diplomat, "would scarcely realize that he was not in British territory. The Shanghai Foreign Settlement was mainly 'made in England' and a creation of which there was every reason to be proud."[40]

Hence, as a former British consul wrote, it was very much in his country's interests to leave Shanghai's polity as it was.

Any revision at all [of the Land Regulations] would almost certainly damage British authority in Shanghai, which under the existing regulations enjoys an entrenched position of privilege, e.g., the restricted municipal franchise leaves the control in British hands; municipal posts (some of them highly salaried) are reserved for British subjects who in the P.W.D. [Public Works Department] and the Electricity Department . . . favor the purchase of British machinery; the Police are recruited in England; the Volunteers are controlled by British officers; the schools are staffed by British, &c.&c. Jealousy of these prerogatives explains much of the effort in the past on the part of Latins and Scandinavians, and in a lesser degree of the Americans and Japanese, to revise the constitution of the Shanghai Municipal Council, ostensibly in favor of the Chinese.[41]

"It's about as international as the Tower of London or Westminster Abbey," sniffed an American about the Settlement.[42] Yet, if the benefits of rule accrued to the British, so did the disadvantages. Their very prominence in the affairs of foreign Shanghai made them vulnerable when things went wrong, and in the mid-1920s, they went wrong, so to speak, more often than they went right. British Shanghailanders and the British government argued that the Shanghai Settlement was not British, but international (look at its American chairman!), and that Britain could not make unilateral changes. Yet it was obvious that without British initiative or at least assent, no changes could take place. To the Chinese, at any rate, it was clear where the power lay, and although the International Settlement was officially known as the *gongong zujie*, or "common concession," they popularly called it the *Ying zujie* or "English concession."

British predominance among the voting ratepayers, their control of the Municipal Council and administration, the influence of the major British business houses, organized through the British Chamber of Commerce and the China Association, and the *North China Daily News*'s role as spokesman for so much foreign opinion made a combination difficult to overcome. This group was particularly formidable when it had the support of the British consul-general, himself the most powerful member of the consular body. The man who occupied that position is worth a moment's attention. Sidney Barton has been called the most powerful man in Shanghai,[43] and his influence over China policy sometimes eclipsed even that of the British minister in Peking. Though he was on home leave in 1924, he returned in the spring of 1925 just in time to see the first wave of revolution break over foreign Shanghai. Forty-nine-years old that year, he had first come to China at the age of nineteen. Decorated for his part in the allied expedition that relieved the Boxer siege of the legations in 1900, he had become Chinese secretary to the British Legation in 1911. At that time, G. E. Morrison, the Peking correspondent of the *Times* of London, dismissed him as "a narrow-minded man who has had no experience outside of the consular service in China, and who is much dominated by his wife" (whose father had been head of Jardine, Matheson in Shanghai). Yet, after being named consul-general in Shanghai in 1922, he became, in the words of one of his colleagues, "practically the autocrat of Shanghai, a position which he has usurped by sheer ability, brains, a very forceful personality and an unusually comprehensive knowledge of the Chinese language, customs, and Chinese personalities. He has the whole of the British community solidly behind him—and the British are the lords of Shanghai."[44] Although never the dean of the Shanghai consular corps, he was unquestionably its unofficial leader, and, to the distress of some in the American community, he often found in the American consul-general, Edwin S. Cunningham, a willing follower.

Barton was a man of extraordinary abilities, with a passion for hard work and a mind untroubled by doubts. John Van Antwerp MacMurray, the new American minister to Peking in 1925, found him "reactionary, failing to take account of anything but purely local necessities, as viewed by one who emulates the colonial administrators of the Victorian era."[45] There was something of the proconsul, or at least of the district officer, about him, with his strong belief that the man on the spot knew best how to decide what course to follow in difficult and dangerous times. He was jealous of his autonomy, and the sketchiness of his reports to his superiors, which could exasperate both his minister in Peking and the Foreign Office in London (to say nothing of the historian), may well have been intended to leave him as much freedom of action as possible. "Barton is such a busy man that he rarely tells us what is happening—but only sometimes that something has happened or is about to happen," complained a member of the Foreign Office in early 1928, deploring the paucity of news from Shanghai.[46] This reserve became even more pronounced when, during the revolution of the twenties, he found himself increasingly out of sympathy with the main lines of British policy, torn between his loyalties to the government that he served and to the British community in Shanghai of which he was so important a part.

And, as the revolution of the 1920s developed, it grew more and more evident that London's policy was not Shanghai's policy, Britain's opinion was not Shanghai's opinion, and British Shanghai was more often a hindrance than a help in shaping Britain's response to the rapid changes taking place in the Far East. The same might be said of Shanghai's position vis-à-vis Washington, Tokyo, and even Paris, although the peculiar powers the French consul-general held over his municipal administration helped keep those divergences in check. The differences between the International Settlement and its home bases in London, Washington, and Tokyo were the products of foreign Shanghai's peculiar polity. Whatever may have been the intentions of its founders, by the second decade of the twentieth century, the International Settlement had become an entity unto itself, and it was by no means clear to what higher authority its governors were responsible.

The Shanghai view—that of the Council, the *North China Daily News*, and many other influential leaders—was that the Council and the Settlement's administration were ultimately responsible only to the ratepayers, just as the government of the United States was responsible only to its voters. Its international nature set it apart from, say, British Hongkong or British and French concessions in other treaty ports. Here is the American lawyer and Council chairman Stirling Fessenden arguing the point in 1927:

Shanghai as a municipality was not created by and does not derive its powers of government from the legislative assembly of any single state or country, nor from the mandate of any single sovereign power. It was created by and derives its powers from an agreement made between the so-called "Foreign Powers" on the one part and the Chinese Government on the other part.

This agreement, which for want of a better name is known as the "Land Regulations," has all the sanctity of a treaty, being as it is a solemn and inviolable compact between sovereign nations.

In substance and effect, although not in form, it is a treaty of the highest class, being as it is not merely a bi-lateral agreement, between two sovereign powers, but an agreement to which many sovereign powers are parties.[47]

Defending the Council in court, he would also argue that since the Settlement was not bound by Chinese law and since the laws of the foreign countries represented were so dissimilar and inappropriate to local needs, the foreign residents had had to come together to form what was not so much a municipality (for municipalities derive their powers from the superior authority of the state) as a voluntary association. The members of that association bound themselves by laws and regulations that they themselves devised. It was pure social contract theory, sounding rather as if the original builders of foreign Shanghai found themselves in a state of nature (presumably because extraterritoriality removed them from any part of the Chinese polity), but Fessenden made no appeal to Hobbes, Locke, or Rousseau in his argument. Instead, perhaps recognizing the analogy most familiar to his audience, he took as his model for such a voluntary association none other than the Shanghai Club![48] (The Club was another polity in which Chinese played only the part of servant; whether it kept life in Shanghai from being nasty, brutish, and short is another matter.)

Legally, Fessenden had much on his side. The Diplomatic Body had delegated many of its powers to the Municipal Council and the ratepayers under the Land Regulations, and there was little it could do to assert a superior authority as long as the Council acted within the scope of those Regulations and as long as the Regulations went unchanged. In London, the Foreign Office's legal adviser conceded such points but was also realist enough to point out that, in the last resort, Shanghai depended on the protection of the treaty powers.[49] And how much protection did the powers *owe* foreign Shanghai? Protection of strict treaty rights, perhaps; but what of the privileges that went beyond the treaties?

As long as Shanghai remained peaceful—another way of saying as long as China could not resist the imposition of foreign privilege in the country—such questions might have only an academic interest. By 1925, however, although the Chinese government itself was still as powerless as ever, the increasingly organized force of Chinese nationalism was challenging a foreign imperialism that to a large extent had lost both the confidence and the strength it had enjoyed earlier. Then, both legally and morally, foreign Shanghai's claim to its own independence proved to be a severe embarrassment to the governments of the very powers that had protected it.

THREE

Businessmen, Missionaries, and Educators

Seeing Shanghai today shocks you back into a world long gone. If you stand on Zhongshan Road, the old Bund, and look at the buildings that line the Huangpu waterfront, immediately you drop back a half century and more to a time when Shanghai was one of the great international cities of the world. The massive architecture of the Bund—the word is an Anglo-Indian one, meaning quay—speaks of a confident foreign ascendancy, yet here, among students and journalists, new politics and new intellectual currents were being born while old Europe, the Europe of empires, was destroying itself on the battlefields of Flanders and Tannenberg, Ypres and Gallipoli. Here a new generation of Chinese businessmen, bankers, and industrialists, profiting from the wartime retreat of the West and the needs of postwar reconstruction, were making their own economic miracle.[1] Here too the first labor organizations among the stevedores of Pudong, the factory and mill workers in the slums of Zhabei and Yangtszepoo, were giving birth to a new kind of radicalism. Out of this ferment, fed by the new nationalism of the May Fourth Movement of 1919, came the revolution of the twenties, and here in Shanghai, communists and Guomindang alternately fought one another or joined with one another to reclaim their country from the foreigner.

For all its importance to modern China, Shanghai, with its foreign past, had always been something of an exotic growth on the country's periphery. By the 1920s, Chinese were at once captivated by the power and possibilities that modern cities like Shanghai promised and humiliated by the knowledge that the treaty ports owed so much to foreign enterprise.[2] Shanghai's urban ways and cosmopolitan outlooks seemed to threaten the peasant ethos that triumphed in 1949, and communism's attempts to integrate the city, to make it truly part of the People's Republic, did not tame its qualities. Meanwhile, the old radical tradition, born in the revolution of the twenties, lived on. Forty years later, Shanghai would become more Maoist than Mao, a center of the Cultural Revolution with its utopianism and its destruction, its idealism and its cruelty. The Gang of Four had its base in Shanghai, but when Mao died and they fell in 1976, the radical phase ended. Today, under Deng Xiaoping's reforms, the city is once again trying to draw foreigners and their enterprise, once again dreaming of becoming one of the great international centers of the world.

On a hot summer evening, as the light falls in the hazy orange sky to the west and the day's sharpness fades, the shadows of the past are evoked by the very mass of the buildings on the Bund, looking east across the Huangpu to the wharves and factories of Pudong on the other shore. Most of them were put up during a great construction boom that lasted from about 1910 to the mid-thirties, and, seen from the river, the city's skyline has hardly changed in the last half century.[3] Look more closely, and you will see that the details are different. Sir Robert Hart, the Ulsterman who built the Chinese Maritime Customs, no longer looks down from his pedestal (its inscription by President Eliot of Harvard) above the river, no longer do the statues of Sir Harry Parkes and Augustus Raymond Margary[4] remind the passer-by of Britain's role in opening China; no longer does Li Hongzhang's monument to the Ever Victorious Army recall Shanghai's battles against the Taipings in the 1850s. The Cenotaph, unveiled in 1924 to honor those who fell in the Great War, has disappeared, remembered only by the truncated, gray stone base on which it once rested. The harbor semaphore, which since 1906 warned ships and seamen of approaching typhoons, no longer responds to the Jesuit meteorologists of the Siccawei observatory.

Today, trees line the Bund where none stood before. Though the sailing junks have largely gone, the river is still alive with barges, ferries, steamers, and the ugly but utilitarian container ships that berth under the great unloading cranes of Pudong. But gone are the passenger ships that once carried foreigners and their goods to the city: *Ajax, Idomeneus, Patroclus,* the Blue Funnel liners with their classical names; the Peninsular and Orient's *Khyber* and *Kashmir,* evocative of empire; and the white-hulled *Empress of Japan* and *Empress of Canada* of the Canadian Pacific. The *President Jefferson* and *President Lincoln* of the Robert Dollar Line brought the American flag to Shanghai, while farther south, in Frenchtown, the ships of the Messageries Maritimes—*Porthos, Amazone, Chenonceaux*—arrived from Marseilles, from Alexandria, from Saigon. Slim gray warships lie moored in the river as they did sixty years ago; but today they are Chinese. The American destroyers, the Japanese and

British cruisers that once reminded China that Shanghai was not hers to control have vanished.

At the corner of the Bund and Nanking Road stands the Peace Hotel, capped by a tower that echoes Venice's campanile, secure in a past that today's new Hiltons and Sheratons cannot rival. Built by Sir Victor Sassoon, it opened in 1928 as the Cathay Hotel, the most luxurious in the Far East. Though it is a bit dingy today, the art deco friezes still grace its entrance, and the restaurant on the top floor still looks down over the old banks and business houses, out across the harbor to Pudong or north where the river curves right to flow down to Wusong and the great Yangtze. In its bathrooms, you still see the ponderous British fixtures of old London hotels: washbasins and toilets built to last as long as the Empire itself, but which have outlived the Empire, a triumph of plumbing over politics.

Nearby is the Customs Building, opened in 1927, seven stories high and a monument to the foreign oversight of the China trade. When Chairman Mao was alive, the English bells in its tower (larger than any in Big Ben)[5] marked the hours by playing "The East Is Red," but today in Deng's China, they again sound the Westminster chimes. Down the street is the Hongkong and Shanghai Bank; when it opened in 1923, it was the second largest bank building in the world. Built in a massive English adaptation of the Beaux Arts style, a pair of bronze lions guarding its entrance, the inside of its great dome was decorated by a mosaic that combined figures of Greek gods with inscriptions from the Chinese classics.[6] Today the lions are gone, and it houses the municipal Party and government offices. The bank itself has long since moved to the upper floors of a dingy, red brick building in a back street. Here on the Bund, too, are the buildings that once housed the other great financial concerns of the China coast, done in the neo-classical style designed to inspire confidence in their conservative security: the Chartered Bank and the Yokohama Specie Bank, whose English architects introduced into the Ionic capitals of the facade small, helmeted Japanese masks.[7] Near the south end of the Bund, next to what was once the headquarters of the Asiatic Petroleum Company, stands the old Shanghai Club, its Italianate cupolas capping a colonnaded facade built of Ningpo granite. Inside, from the black and white marble floor of the grand hall, a staircase of white Sicilian marble once rose to the dining room, itself over a hundred feet long, while above it were a library, a reading room, and billiard rooms. Opened in 1910, it was the center of British social and financial privilege, a place where the taipans and their juniors met for lunch or gathered in the oak-paneled Jacobean room at what was said to be the longest bar in the world; lay your cheek on it, said Noel Coward, and you will see the earth's curvature (he was in Shanghai, staying at the Cathay and writing *Private Lives*). Since 1949, it has become the Dongfeng [East Wind] Hotel, its gloomy entrance hall filled with counters under pale blue fluorescent lights showing off Chinese kitsch for the tourists. In 1990 came a new transmutation: the downstairs, a bright oasis of glass and chromium, is filled with young women in uniform, almost looking like girl cadres out of "The Red Detachment of Women," that classic of the Cultural Revolution. But the uniforms are brown and bear the logo of Colonel Sanders' Kentucky Fried Chicken. It is hard to know which of the ghosts of the past—the taipans or the Maoists—are most upset by what has happened.

Away from the Bund, although there have been more changes, much still recalls Shanghai's foreign past. The brick and granite American Club on Foochow Road might have come from Philadelphia's Rittenhouse Square. A few blocks away, although Holy Trinity Cathedral has lost its spire and plywood covers its rose window, Sir Gilbert Scott's design still echoes the Gothic revival of the nineteenth century. The Shanghai Race Club's building on Nanking Road is now the municipal library; behind it, what looks like a small replica of McKim, Meade, and White's New York Municipal Building used to house the China United Assurance Society. The old British consulate, set amidst its immaculate lawn and gardens near the Bund, is now a research institute; several blocks away on Foochow Road, miniature skyscrapers in gray concrete suggest America of the thirties. Everywhere in the city there remain the thousands upon thousands of smaller houses in which foreign Shanghai—and many of its wealthy Chinese—lived. Some houses continue the colonial bungalow style that came up the China coast from Hongkong and southeast Asia; some veer toward Chinese domestic architecture in an attempt to marry the styles of East and West; but many are purely Western, making no compromise with local geography. Some are half-timbered, in the Tudor style dear to suburban architects between the wars; some are red brick or faced with a stucco now grimy from the smoky air. Today, these dark houses still stand behind the high walls that protect them from the noise of the streets, their steep-peaked roofs of red tile surmounted by great chimneys. Looking as if they had been transplanted from the outskirts of Manchester or Chicago, they concede nothing to the Chinese landscape, and the larger ones, like those on Hongqiao Road out near the airport, face their gardens in the back, a suburbia of sixty years ago juxtaposed with what is still Chinese farmland. They are ugly, complained an observer in the mid-twenties. "Most cities have an individuality expressed in some way by their houses. Shanghai expresses an irritableness, a restlessness, and a total lack of beauty."[8]

In 1925 a census taken by the foreign authorities showed 29,848 foreigners and 810,378 Chinese in the International Settlement and 7,790 foreigners and 289,210 Chinese in the French Concession. Since all Shanghai in those days had just over 2.5 million inhabitants, the figures show that over 40 percent of the city—some 1.1 million—lived under foreign administration and that, within those foreign settlements, only some 3.3 percent were actual foreigners.[9] The largest single group was the fourteen thousand Japanese, most of whom had come since 1914 and who lived largely in the Settlement's northern district along Dixwell and North Szechuen roads. But it was the 8,200 British who were the most influential; they had come first, saw themselves as the founders of foreign Shanghai, and largely set the tone of the foreign community. There were about 3,100 Americans, growing in importance since the end of the war. But there were only some 1,100 French, by now a decided minority even in their own Concession, a point that worried the authorities. Some twenty other nationalities were represented: the Germans were coming back, and there were Italians, Portuguese, Indians, and handfuls of Norwegians, Swedes, Swiss, and others.

The census lists only about four thousand Russians living in the two Settlements, but there may have been as many as ten or fifteen thousand of them in the city as a whole. Almost all were refugees from the Bolshevik revolution, the largest group arriving from Vladivostok in 1923. These exiles were put ashore to do the best they could in a city whose ways they did not know, whose languages they could not speak, yet within a few years they had changed the character of much of foreign Shanghai. A few were drawn into the business and administrative life of the city; many continued to depend on charity; others found employment as chauffeurs, watchmen, or bodyguards, or drifted into the world of cabarets, cafés, and dance halls that sprang up as Shanghai enthusiastically entered the jazz age. Some simply did what they must to keep body and soul together, and for the first time, Shanghai saw penniless white men competing with Chinese coolies for the most menial jobs of the streets.[10]

The British dominated foreign Shanghai economically, just as they dominated it politically. An estimate from early 1927 put a total of £200 million of foreign investment in the city, with almost a third—some £63,250,000—in British hands, including capital in land, buildings, factories, manufacturing stocks, and debt instruments.[11] The figure may well have been low, for a careful study a few years later suggested that by 1929 British business investments in Shanghai had reached £151,527,500, comprising 76.6 percent of British investments in all of China and Hongkong.[12] There are no good figures for American and Japanese holdings in the city, but clearly they were far less. G. B. Rea of the *Far Eastern Review* estimated in 1927 that there were $30 million in American properties in Shanghai registered with the consulate, and a survey in early 1928 found $58,549,593 invested in the consular district, most of which, of course, was within the city itself.[13] The British lead in landholding was even more pronounced. Within the International Settlement, £44 million of the £52.6 million worth of foreign registered land was held in British names. (America accounted for only just over £3 million and Japan for almost £4 million.) Even in the French Settlement, more than half the land by value was held by the British (£4.6 million of a total of £9 million), while the French themselves only held £2.6 million.[14]

There were, roughly speaking, four kinds of foreigners who lived in Shanghai. First came the businessmen, merchants, and bankers who traded with the Chinese, financed the trade, or ran the city's foreign factories and mills. Second were those drawn to the city by its growth and the opportunity to cater to the needs and wants of the foreign settlements: lawyers, doctors, real estate agents and developers, engineers, insurance agents, ship chandlers, shopkeepers, the teachers of foreign children, the journalists, musicians, and entertainers. Third came the officials, those who ran the International Settlement and the French Concession or who staffed the consulates and other foreign governmental offices in town. Finally there were the missionaries, the evangelizers, and the educators of the Chinese— the "uplift element" as they were sometimes derisively called by those who disliked their politics and policies.

At the top of foreign Shanghai's hierarchy stood the China traders, particularly the taipans of the great commercial houses. It was for them that the port had first been opened, and virtually all others save the missionaries were there for their benefit. Some, particularly among the British, represented houses long established in the China trade. Jardine, Matheson, the largest trading firm in China, went back to 1832, getting its start in the so-called country trade by carrying legal Indian cotton and illegal Indian opium up to the China coast. From its headquarters in Hongkong, Jardine's oversaw branches in all the larger treaty ports of China, and its Shanghai offices in the Ewo Building at 27 The Bund (Ewo, *Yihe*, "mutual harmony," was the firm's Chinese name) overlooked the harbor the company's pioneers had helped build. Butterfield and Swire, founded in 1867 and a subsidiary of John Swire and Sons of London, was its chief rival, its offices down on the French Bund. Firms like these had grown with the China trade, and Jardine's subsidiaries came to include, among other things, a major shipping line, the Shanghai and Hongkew Wharf Company, three cotton mills and a silk filature, an insurance company, and a brewery.[15] Any list of important British firms must also include the Asiatic Petroleum Company, a subsidiary of Royal Dutch Shell, and C. H. Arnhold and Company, which acted as agent for Metropolitan Vickers and many English and American machinery manufacturers and which owned a textile mill in the city. British-American Tobacco (B.A.T.), based in London but until the early twenties largely under American managers, had three factories in Shanghai.[16] A. R. Burkill and Sons owned the Kiangsu

Chemical Works, and there were a handful of other large firms, such as Ilbert and Company and Mackenzie and Company, acting as agencies for British goods.

American trading firms were smaller and less important. Most of the early American enterprises, such as Russell and Company—which in the nineteenth century had been powerful enough to rival British shipping for primacy on the China coast—had disappeared, in several cases swallowed by their British competitors.[17] Newer and usually smaller firms took their place. Andersen Meyer on Yuen Ming Yuen Road was an exception, a large engineering and contracting firm that also acted as agent for such giants as Baldwin Locomotive and U.S. Steel. So was Standard Oil on Canton Road, whose aggressive sales techniques had carved out a substantial market in the Yangtze Valley by the late nineteenth century. Several other firms handled exports, but while there were two or three small American factories, the Americans had only a small stake in the textile industry, one of the bases of Shanghai's modern economic development.

When the First World War drove so many Europeans back to their homelands, American and Japanese companies flourished. Peace brought the British back, however, and the Americans had to hustle to maintain the position they had captured. They suffered from certain disabilities in their competitive position. British firms in China were usually organized under the Hongkong Companies Ordinance, which freed them from taxes levied at home. American companies in China had no such shelter. Some took advantage of the Hongkong Ordinance, until the British decreed in 1919 that all such firms must have a majority of British directors. Others incorporated themselves under state laws that were not designed for foreign enterprise. They still had to pay the 12.5 percent federal corporate income tax, even on profits earned outside the United States, as Americans living overseas had to pay taxes on incomes earned outside the United States. "No other nationals operating in China have been so taxed by their home governments as Americans," complained an official of the Bureau of Trade and Commerce in Shanghai, and she maintained that the differences in corporate taxation allowed the British to undersell comparable American goods by 1.5 percent.[18] The passage of the China Trade Act of 1922, and more particularly its revision in 1925, designed to rectify these inequities, was one of the early triumphs of the lobbying efforts of the Shanghai American Chamber of Commerce.[19] No firms enjoying extraterritorial status, of course, paid any taxes to the Chinese government.

In 1895, after her defeat of China, Japan extracted the right to build and own factories on Chinese soil. Thanks to the most favored nation clause of the treaties, other countries now profited from the Japanese victory and put up their own factories and workshops staffed with cheap Chinese labor. The Japanese had thirty-two textile mills in the city, giving them a major role in that important industry. But apart from the cotton mills, the silk filatures, and the B.A.T. factories, manufacturing was a good deal less important to the economic life of foreign Shanghai than was trade, and there were only a handful of other Western-owned plants in the city.

Textiles, machinery, and metals—these made up the bulk of British exports to China in these years. According to what was admittedly a somewhat expansive estimate by the British Chamber of Commerce in Shanghai, some 160,000 Britons—roughly 30,000 of them Lancashire cotton workers—depended for their livelihood on the British export trade (as did some 200,000 Shanghai Chinese).[20] In the earlier days of the China trade, Western import-export firms had largely restricted their business to the treaty ports. Under what Sherman Cochran has called the "Shanghai system," such companies established their headquarters in Shanghai, and although Westerners retained managerial control, they depended largely upon a network of Chinese traders and bankers—starting with the Chinese compradors in their own firms—to handle the financing and marketing of goods in the interior.[21] Thus, the goods they imported were sold to Chinese merchants in the ports, who then handled their distribution in the interior. So too, exporters depended upon Chinese merchants to bring their goods to the waterfront, where the foreign houses bought them and shipped them abroad.

By the early twentieth century, however, some companies had moved beyond the ports. Thanks to the pioneering efforts of such firms as Standard Oil, Asiatic Petroleum, and British-American Tobacco, some of the larger companies began to build up their own transportation and distribution networks in the interior (or more accurately, they moved into the existing Chinese commercial system with their own agents, foreign and Chinese). There they built their own storage and transshipment facilities and sold, if not directly to the Chinese consumer, at least to merchants closer to the consumer. This meant a lower risk (foreign-owned goods were less likely to be tampered with in the interior than were Chinese goods), the elimination of many middlemen and their fees, and hence lower prices and a larger market. On the other hand, since the Western firm now owned large stocks of goods in the hinterland and depended so much on its own distribution network, its business became more than ever dependent upon the maintenance of peace and an orderly framework for trade.[22] These distributing firms, as they were sometimes called, dealt largely with such goods as oil, tobacco, chemicals, and certain foodstuffs. They did not include trade in machine goods or textiles, the woollens, and the cotton piece goods that remained the most important item of British trade during these years and that were handled by the import-export firms of Shanghai and Hankou. Despite the vulnerability of the Western distributing firms, giants like B.A.T. or A.P.C. or Brunner Mond were worldwide multinational companies whose Chinese enterprises represented only part of the picture seen from the head office. The trading firms, however, more often than not had no business outside China and thus depended for their very existence on political stability and an unimpeded access from Shanghai to the interior and to the other ports of the China coast and the Yangtze Valley. The large distributing firms could ride out several years of trouble in China; the Shanghai trading firms—like C. H. Arnhold—could not, or at least thought they could not. Finally, there were any number of small firms catering largely to the needs of Shanghai's foreigners and its rich Chinese with few, if any, interests beyond the city's limits. Their position was an anomalous one. On the one hand, they profited from the safe haven offered by the foreign settlements during the troubles of the twenties (a substantial rise in real estate prices was one of the consequences of civil war); on the other hand, precisely because they had no interests beyond Shanghai, they tended to confuse the general problems of China with the particular problems of Shanghai and to assume that what served their interests would serve the interests of all connected with China.[23]

Most trade with the outside world was carried by foreign ships, financed by foreign banks, and insured by foreign companies. Roughly as far from the harbors of western Europe as from eastern North America, Shanghai could draw goods competing on equal terms from the two great industrial centers of the world and was a major port of call for a score of freight and passenger lines. From London, the traveler could reach Shanghai in five weeks by the Blue Funnel Line (first class only) or the Glen Line or the Ellerman Line, among others; those with more pressing business could hurry to Marseilles or Brindisi by train, to board the ships of the Messageries Maritimes or the Lloyd-Triestino (the fastest way out, however, was by the Trans-Siberian Railway, which in 1927 restored the prewar service from Moscow to Harbin). A mere two weeks would bring the passenger from the west coast of North America by the Dollar Line or the American Mail Line, or (for those who preferred an earlier release from the rigors of the eighteenth amendment) by the Nippon Yusen Kaisha, or aboard the White Empresses of the Canadian Pacific, the largest and most luxurious ships to call at Shanghai.

An incoming ship, having entered the Yangtze through Steep Island Pass, Bonham Strait, and the Saddle Islands, would drop her anchor near the Fairway Buoy and take aboard a European pilot. There she would wait for the tide to flow so that she could ride across the Fairy Flats, a great bar of silt that even at times of high water limited entrance to ships drawing thirty-two feet or less. Leaving the brown waters of the Great River astern, she would turn into the Huangpu at Wusong, steaming through the Astrea Channel, eighteen miles upstream to Shanghai. Moored off the Bund, she would be surrounded almost immediately by the small river craft, the lighters, sampans, and the tender that would carry her passengers to the Customs Jetty for their entrance into China.[24] Shanghai, however, is a delta city, and only continuous dredging by the Huangpu Conservancy Board (a Chinese government agency established in 1905 and largely under foreign administration) to clear two to three million cubic yards of silt every year kept open the channel from Wusong to the Shanghai docks. Not until 1924 could ships like the Empresses tie up in Shanghai proper; before that they had to anchor at Wusong, sending their passengers and cargo on by tender up the Huangpu to the city, and many continued to do so.

Ships coming from foreign lands made up only part of Shanghai's maritime traffic. Well before the Westerners arrived, the city had been a leading entrepot for domestic trade, dividing the coastal routes of north and south China. Descriptions of the Shanghai's maritime activity in the early nineteenth century contradict the foreign myth that nothing more than a sleepy village on a mudflat existed before the treaty of Nanking. The lower Yangtze delta is criss-crossed by an extraordinary network of canals that are the most important, and sometimes the only, access routes to the thousands of villages and towns that sprawl across the flat countryside west and south of the city. Through them cuts the greatest of all waterways, the Grand Canal, begun twelve hundred years earlier by the Sui dynasty, running up from Hangzhou to carry food from the rich granaries of the delta to the capital in the north.

Over these watercourses that fed the Huangpu River and into the Siccawei and Soochow creeks, in sampans, on rafts, in small junks, flowed —and still flows—much of the produce of the delta and most of the food on which the city depended. But it was, of course, the Yangtze, the Great River, that made the fortune of modern Shanghai and the river ports upstream. The Yangtze watershed covers roughly half of China and included almost half of China's population. Because north China's topography allows no single deep-water port to serve it, Shanghai and the Yangtze have acted as the route for much of the trade from that part of the country too. Into the Yangtze flow several tributaries that are navigable for as much as two hundred miles, and at the mouth of each stood a treaty port, like Hankou or Yichang or Jiujiang, that served as a subsidiary center for the concentration of cargo to and from Shanghai. Ocean-going ships, up to five thousand tons during winter's low water and ten thousand tons in the summer, could reach Hankou in four days, six hundred miles upstream from Shanghai. By the early twentieth century, smaller steamers piloted by Chinese watermen had begun to climb the narrow channels of the majestic Three Gorges above Yichang, cliffs rising a thousand feet and more above them, where in times of flood the water could rise a hundred feet a day, around the hundreds of whirlpools, rapids, and shoals, all the way up to Chongqing, fourteen hundred miles from the ocean.[25]

By the First World War, four firms dominated shipping on the river. Three were foreign: Jardine's Indo-China Steam Navigation Company (which accounted for roughly a third of the 303,000 tons of British-owned shipping in the coastal and river trade), Butterfield's China Navigation Company, and the Japanese Nisshin Kisen Kaisha. The fourth was the China Merchants Steam Navigation Company, founded in 1872 under Peking's sponsorship to try to wrest a share of the market away from the foreign shipowners. These lines had almost daily sailings from Shanghai to Hankou and the river ports and frequent service to Hongkong and ports of the China coast. Their shipping notices boasted of the comfort of their accommodations ("staterooms, saloon, and smoking rooms fitted with steam heating; excellent cuisine and service," ran an advertisement for Jardine's *Luenho*). A few small ships maintained a direct service from the river ports to Japan, but most transoceanic business passed through Shanghai; an estimate in 1926 put 40 percent of Shanghai's gross trade in the reexport business.[26]

It was the foreign banks, whose offices lined the Bund and the roads of the central district, that financed foreign trade and much of the internal trade as well. The Hongkong and Shanghai Bank, founded in 1864, was the largest foreign bank in China, and next came the Chartered Bank of India, Australia, and China. Most important of the American institutions was the International Banking Corporation (it took the name National City Bank of New York in 1927), which came to the city in 1902, joined later by several smaller American banks. The Yokohama Specie Bank and Bank of Taiwan were the most prominent of the Japanese institutions, and there were branches of French, Belgian, Dutch, and other banks.[27] Britain's long experience in financial management gave the firms of that country a commanding position in insurance. Both Jardine's and Butterfield had their own companies and acted as agents for others, and British firms dominated both the Shanghai Fire Insurance Association and Shanghai Marine Underwriters Association.[28] American Asiatic Underwriters, the parent of today's American International Group, was started on a shoestring by C. V. Starr in 1919 and by the mid-twenties was the most important American enterprise in the field, spreading out through China, Manchuria, Southeast Asia, and the United States.[29] Starr's firm was unique in another respect; it was, as one of its members remembered, probably the only foreign business in Shanghai where white-collar Westerners might find themselves working under Chinese supervisors.[30]

Besides large firms like these, there were hundreds of smaller foreign houses, some of which acted as agencies for foreign firms or simply met the needs of the other residents. In 1923 the Chinese Maritime Customs counted 228 British, 165 American, 70 German, 63 French, 56 Russian, and 1,047 Japanese firms in Shanghai—a slight decrease in number from the postwar boom year of 1920.[31] About forty of the larger local firms traded their shares on Shanghai's foreign stock exchange at 12 The Bund, an annual *China Stock and Share Handbook* recording their fortunes as well as those of firms elsewhere in China.[32] National chambers of commerce were organized to advance the interests of their members. Most important, of course, was the British Chamber, its offices in the Asiatic Petroleum building at 1 The Bund, and allied with it was the local branch of the China Association of London, which for years had lobbied for the interests of the China traders.

To China's foreign traders, it had long been an article of faith that trade and progress went together, that China's opening to the outside world would not only bring profits to the merchants but a better life to her people. These men, looking at the figures published by the Chinese Maritime Customs showing the rising value of trade, saw there evidence of China's resiliency. The total value of China's net imports and exports had risen 72 percent between 1913 and 1923, from Haikwan (Hk.; Customs) Tls. 973,468,000 (US $710,631,640) on the eve to the First World War to Hk. Tls. 1,676,320,000 (US $1,341,056,000). Of that amount, Shanghai accounted for roughly 40 percent, rising from Hk. Tls. 421,311,000 (US $307,557,030) in 1913 to 694,709,000 (US $555,767,200) in 1923.[33] If she could do this well in the face of political turmoil and civil war, there was hardly any limit to future possibilities when peace and order returned.

The revenues drawn from the Maritime Customs benefited the Chinese treasury as well as the bankers in London, Paris, and New York, who were the holders of China's external loans secured on those revenues. They did not directly benefit the warlord masters of Chinese Shanghai in the 1920s, since they were held by foreign banks in trust for Peking. There were, however, other economic advantages that came from the control of Shanghai, from the collection of a variety of internal trade duties, local taxes, licenses, and the like. On another aspect, however, the official figures were silent: the traffic in narcotics and, above all, in opium.

Here some background is necessary, for by the 1920s the role of opium in the China trade and in the life of Shanghai had changed radically from earlier decades.[34] Ever since the eighteenth century, the drug, smuggled in from India by the British and from Turkey by the Americans, had been one of the great lubricants of Western commerce with China. Under pressure, the Chinese had legalized the trade in 1858, and although a treaty of 1880 forbade American participation, the British and others continued. Yet one of the most startlingly successful of the reforms launched by the Qing dynasty in its waning years was a campaign against opium. A great drive against drug use and against cultivation of the poppy led Britain in 1907 to consent to a gradual reduction in the exports of Indian opium to China, stopping it completely when the Chinese could prove they had wiped out domestic production. An international conference at The Hague in 1912 agreed on measures to suppress opium smuggling into China, and in 1913 London announced that, in view of China's extraordinary progress against the drug, she would no longer allow sales of Indian opium for export to China.

The decision faced Shanghai's opium traders and opium speculators with the prospect of ruin. In 1913, a group of foreign merchants formed an Opium Combine—including some of the great names of foreign Shanghai such as the Sassoons, the Ezras, and the Abrahams—to work with Chinese opium guilds and to take advantage of rising prices as the supply of legal opium grew shorter. By 1917, as China's ten-year program for opium suppression was ending, they made a corrupt bargain with the local Opium Prohibition Commissioner to sell their remaining stocks to the Chinese government at Tls. 8,200, a chest for "medicinal purposes" (in 1908, a chest had fetched Tls. 1,000). The public outcry forced the Chinese government to back down, and Peking ordered the destruction of the remaining chests, which had now risen to a value of Tls. 16,000 each. In 1919 they were burned in Pudong in special kilns, and the ashes were thrown into the river. Meanwhile, both the Settlement and Concession authorities had agreed to a gradual prohibition of the sale and use of the drug, and thus, by the time of the burning in Pudong, the legal traffic in opium, both Chinese and foreign, had come to an end.

China's triumph was short lived. In the chaos that followed the fall of the dynasty and the death of Yuan Shikai, the poppy bloomed again in the hinterland. By the early 1920s, China was—according to the International Anti-Opium Association—producing more than eight times as much opium as all the rest of the world and twelve times as much as India.[35] Once again Shanghai became the center of China's drug trade, but it was a trade that was now illegal and underground. From the inland provinces, above all from distant Sichuan, the opium came down the Great River in steamers under foreign and Chinese flags, brought in by a vast smuggling ring that stretched throughout the Yangtze Valley and that dealt in foreign opium—particularly Persian—as well. The drug was sometimes dropped over the side of the steamers for pick up by junks, sometimes sunk in watertight containers for later retrieval, and occasionally even put in small containers and forced down the gullets of ducks, who would then carry it ashore. Increasingly, however, it would be offloaded near Wusong and then carried by Chinese gunboats upriver to Shanghai, to be stored near the arsenal under military guard while it awaited distribution.[36]

The foreign settlements were thus left trying to fight a battle against opium in a city where Chinese official connivance allowed the trade to flourish almost unchecked. Both the French Police and the Shanghai Municipal Police wanted to legalize the trade, arguing that only through a licensing system could they solve what had become an impossible problem.[37] Many foreigners agreed; in 1923, Sir Francis Aglen, the inspector-general of the Chinese Maritime Customs, proposed the reestablishment of an opium monopoly, but public sentiment (and the strong opposition of Sir John Jordan, the former British minister) ensured that nothing came of the idea.[38] Aglen worried, among other things, about the way in which opium smuggling was disrupting and corrupting the Customs service through bribes and intimidations, and the same fears motivated the foreign police in Shanghai. "One of the chief problems with the present situation is the fact that members of the foreign police forces are exposed to temptations that are too great for them. Sometimes they give way," wrote French consul-general Auguste Wilden in 1924. He pointed out that two years earlier he had had to dismiss a whole police post who were getting $500 to $1000 a month simply for looking the other way. The sergeant in charge had taken his accumulated capital of Frs. 600,000 and gone home to become a *gros industriel* in the Midi.[39] Corruption reached higher levels as well. In 1924, Wilden had to fire Chief Traissac of his Sûreté for taking bribes. (There was not enough evidence to prosecute him, however; the case would have been dismissed, and Traissac could have sued for his reinstatement.)[40] Such episodes led to suspicions, anonymous denunciations, and demoralized police.[41] Worse yet, Traissac's successor, Sidaine, had to be sacked in early 1926 on charges of corruption.[42] Nor was the problem only a French one. When the unfortunate N. E. B. Ezra brought his charges against Mr. Yi in 1925 (see chapter 2), the police raid on the latter's premises at No. 51 Canton Road revealed the existence of a smuggling ring that depended upon Swiss, Japanese, American, and Persian participation.[43] Indeed, in the spring of 1927 a former American district attorney for Shanghai was convicted of taking a bribe to drop the investigation of an opium smuggling case, and some charged that the Settlement's police were also in the pay of the gangsters.[44]

In 1922 and 1923, the Municipal Police carried out a series of sweeping opium raids in the Settlement, driving the bulk of the trade out into Chinese territory and, more particularly, into the French Concession. There the drug traffic was taken in hand by Huang Jinrong, the chief of Chinese detectives in the *Garde municipale* and a leading member of the underworld Green Gang (*Qingbang*), and by his enterprising protegé Du Yuesheng.[45] Du, born into poverty in Pudong, quickly became one of the leaders of Shanghai's underworld and a commanding force in the Green Gang, which was then making a transition from a nineteenth-century secret society to a modern manipulator of rackets in drugs, prostitution, gambling, and labor recruitment. "Ten years ago," wrote John Pratt, the acting British consul-general in 1924, Du "was a fruit hawker, but by sheer brains, villainy and force of character, he has raised himself to a position of untold wealth."[46] He had also had the foresight to register with the Portuguese consulate-general, thus enjoying the privileges of extraterritorial status and virtual immunity from prosecution in either the Chinese or foreign courts.

Missionaries and social reformers railed against such scandalous practices, while self-styled realists like Aglen and the foreign police chiefs sought to come to terms with them. The arguments for and against legalization bear an uncanny resemblance to the contemporary American debate on drugs. "The British communities and the British administrations in the Far East," wrote Pratt (no partisan of legalization), "quite sincerely do not believe that opium smoking by Chinese is a serious evil, and . . . believing that opium is to the Chinese what alcohol is to the European, see no harm whatever in drawing a revenue from opium." Unlike whites, who became addicts, wrote the French consul-general, Chinese could use the drug in moderation; "le tempérament spécial des jaunes le leur permet."[47]

Opium was, after all, legal in British Malaya, British Hongkong, and French Indochina, and government opium monopolies contributed handsomely to the revenues of those and other colonies. It is impossible to say how large the illegal opium revenues of Shanghai were, and contemporary estimates ran from $48 million to over $100 million a year (roughly $25 to $50 million American dollars). Nor can we say how big were the slices taken by warlords, naval commanders, officials, gangsters, or their foreign collaborators. But the amount was huge, and it kept growing. As the *North China* wrote of the fighting in 1924 and 1925, "The keynote of all the recent turmoil in Kiangsu and Chekiang was simply possession of the wealthy district of Shanghai. And in that it is no exaggeration to say that the richest jewel of all is the 'squeeze' on illicit opium. This is and has been so notorious for years past that it can hardly now be said to occasion any scandal among the Chinese."[48] Like Aglen and the foreign police, the *North China* also wanted some kind of legalization to bring the trade under control in the interests of Shanghai's future. "It is impossible for a municipal government to develop independently of the militarists in China, as things are here, unless this attractive offering disappears. . . . There is a fortune to be made here by a military man in command of troops in the enterprise of assisting in and protecting the smuggling of opium, and there can be no free and scientific development of a municipality as long as that fortune remains here to lure on the voracious."[49] In May 1925, the Municipal Police reported an agreement between the Chinese police, the navy, and General Zhang Zongchang with an opium syndicate that promised to pay the authorities $1500 for each chest smuggled into Shanghai.[50] Opium, in short, remained very much a part of big business in Shanghai and, as we will see, became thoroughly intertwined with the politics of revolution and counter-revolution in these years.

From a discussion of trade, whether licit or illicit, to one about the Christian missions may seem a sudden jump, and it would be an exaggeration to say that, just as Britain was in Shanghai for business, America was there for evangelism. Yet there is some truth in the statement. Informal estimates of American interests in China during the twenties suggest that, both in numbers of people and in economic investment, the Protestant missionaries were as important as the merchants and perhaps even outweighed them. Some four or five thousand of the ninety-eight hundred Americans in China were missionaries and their families. Their land and property holdings were valued at anywhere from $43 to $80 million (of a total of $150 million in American investments in China), and they spent roughly $10 to $15 million a year in the country.[51] Many of them were outspoken, not only about their own roles but about the policies of their own country and the politics of China as well, and there is no doubt that they had a substantial influence in America. Unlike American businessmen, who had no lobbying group comparable to Britain's China Association, American missionaries, through their home boards and their church networks, held the ear of a significant part of Protestant America. They made the most of it, and Washington listened.

"Next to London and New York," wrote the Presbyterian E. C. Lobenstine in the *China Mission Yearbook* of 1925, "Shanghai is the most important center of missions in the world" (it is revealing, of course, that he made no mention of Rome). It was certainly the largest center in China. A quick check of the annual *Directory of Protestant Missions in China* shows the luxurious flowering of the reformed churches in the rich soil of that pagan city. China as a whole was home to no fewer than two hundred Protestant mission societies, mission publishers, mission associations, and mission schools and colleges. In the mid-twenties, representatives of fifty-nine of them could be found in Shanghai. Most were American; a few were British. Although German, Scandinavian, and Swiss Protestants were active in China at the time, they had no Shanghai representatives. One can only presume that the sheer weight of the Anglo-American presence, its numbers, its organization, and its wealth, discouraged non-English-speaking toilers in this particular vineyard of the Lord. In postwar Protestant Shanghai, even the British came off second best, well outnumbered by the Americans. The American presence and its financial support irritated some. An Anglican missionary saw the Red Cross's famine relief work as a business proposition with the Ford Company, and a French writer suggested caustically that the Americans were "less intent on conversions than commerce, . . . commercial travelers preparing the way for the financiers and promoters of their country."[52] Or, as the French minister in Peking put it, "The American schools and colleges are engaged not in religious propaganda, but in an Anglo-Saxon propaganda, a propaganda of language, of society, of politics. . . . The Americans, with their universities, their schools, their Protestant works such as the Y.M.C.A., play a political role in China."[53]

Largest of the mission headquarters in Shanghai was the American Church Mission of the Protestant Episcopal Church, outside the Settlement's borders at Jessfield and near the campus of its own St. John's University. It was one of the oddities of clerical Shanghai that the Anglican bishop was not English but American, for in 1908 the archbishop of Canterbury and the presiding bishop of the Protestant Episcopal Church had signed a concordat at Lambeth formally delimiting the geographical and parochial spheres of their churches. For missionary purposes, Shanghai and much of the Yangtze Valley fell into the American zone. Thus, though Holy Trinity Cathedral was thoroughly English, thoroughly Anglican, and under the English bishop of central China, the episcopal authority in the missionary diocese of Shanghai was held by the American Frederick R. Graves, bishop since 1893, from his pro-cathedral in Jessfield.[54] Graves, together with Roots of Hankou and Mowll of west China, made up the trio known irreverently as the "underground bishops" of China.

Shanghai also served as headquarters for many other mission groups: Northern and Southern Methodists, Northern Presbyterians, the China Inland Mission, the Y.M.C.A. and Y.W.C.A., the W.C.T.U., the Bible Societies of Britain, America, and Scotland, down to such exotic or local groups as the Bethel Mission, the Christian Endeavour Union, and the Shanghai Mission to Rickshawmen and the Coolie Class. Although interdenominational cooperation was not one of the strong features of the period, the first fruits of ecumenical endeavor were beginning to take form in the early decades of the century. Their visible symbol was the new Missions Building, which opened in June 1924 at 23 Yuen Ming Yuen Road in the heart of Shanghai's business district. Six stories high, built of gray brick and reinforced concrete—its aspect calling to mind a midwestern department store—it looked down over the lawns and gardens of the British consulate to the ships rounding the bend in the river, a continuing physical reminder of the self-identification of American Protestantism with universal Christianity.

From the Missions Building was published the *Chinese Recorder*, the most important Protestant periodical of the day, its heavy American slant reflecting the predominance of the United States in the field. Its editor, the Reverend Frank Rawlinson, printed articles dealing with the prospects and policies of Protestantism (and sometimes Catholicism) in China and tended to look with a hopeful, if somewhat wary, eye on the rise of the nationalist movement of the mid-twenties ("lenient in dealing with Chinese shortcomings," complained a confidential report of the Shanghai Municipal Police).[55]

Most important of the ecumenical groups was the National Christian Council (N.C.C.), born in 1922, a body that spoke with considerable voice about the affairs of Protestant evangelism. Though its director, the Reverend E. C. Lobenstine, was an American Presbyterian, Chinese Christians already held most of its important positions, and it sought to build a Chinese church as independent as possible of Western control (if not of Western financial support). During the troubled years of the mid-twenties, the N.C.C. showed little hesitation in jumping into complicated political questions, and a good deal of friction arose between its leaders and those who either generally disliked the church's engagement in the world of politics or particularly disliked what they saw as the council's radical views.

Despite the numbers and the money, by the 1920s the malaise that had overtaken Christianity at home was beginning to affect the foreign missions. Though the first few years after the war saw the high point of the American Protestant effort in China, by 1926 both volunteers and contributions from home were falling off. The growth of secularism and the new liberal theology divided missionaries abroad just as they divided churchmen at home, contributing to the problems of the Church in China. It has been argued that the continued presence of American missionaries in China had almost as much to do with the health of the church back home as it did with the prospects for evangelization among the Chinese. If native America's Protestant heritage was being threatened by Jewish and Catholic immigration, to say nothing of secularism, China at least remained malleable, and the prospect of a Christian Orient would refute the arguments of those who held that religion's day was past.[56] Yet, despite the efforts of groups like the National Christian Council, despite the hopeful emergence later on of the Protestant Chiang Kai-shek as putative leader of a united China, the missions would never regain the position they enjoyed before the troubles of the twenties.

To most Shanghai missionaries, to most Americans, and indeed to most American historians of the missions (apart from Kenneth Scott

Latourette), Christianity meant Protestantism, more particularly, Anglo-American Protestantism. From their writings, one would hardly realize that the Catholics (or, for that matter, continental Protestants) even existed. There were many fewer Catholic missionaries in China than Protestants; a count from 1927 listed only 1,854 foreign and 1,234 Chinese priests.[57] Given American ignorance of foreign countries and foreign languages, given the small role played by American Catholics in China at this point (they did not appear until after the First World War), and given the lingering enmities of the Reformation, this ignorance is scarcely surprising; but in fact there were some considerable similarities as well as differences between the two groups.

Catholic Shanghai in the early 1920s was a firm French Jesuit preserve. The province of Jiangsu was entrusted to the vicar apostolic (in effect the bishop) of Nanking, the French Jesuit Monsignor Prosper Paris. His seat, however, was in Shanghai, not only because of the well-developed Catholic establishment in the city but because of the convenience of communications with other parts of his district. From Siccawei, located just outside the southwestern corner of the French Concession, he oversaw the various facets of life in Catholic Shanghai: Aurora University, a Jesuit seminary, and various schools, hospitals, orphanages, and convents.[58]

Though neither side would have been flattered by the comparison, France's relationship to the Catholic missions in China was not so different from America's relationship with the Protestants. Neither country had the kind of economic stake in China enjoyed by Britain or Japan, and the missions thus tended to play a larger role in their policies. A series of treaties and conventions in the nineteenth century had recognized the right of the French to act as protectors of the Catholic missions, thus putting relations between France and the Catholic church on a more formal, if not ultimately very different, basis than that which existed between Britain and America and the major Protestant denominations. Though the French might not use their missionaries as travelling salesmen, successive French governments, whether clerical, neutral, or downright anticlerical, all made the most of this provision to push French interests. Even the victory of the leftist parties, bound together in the *cartel des gauches* in May 1924, seemingly made no difference in the government's view of the Church essentially as a cultural arm of the state.

Thus, like the American missions, the French missions to some extent were instruments of national propaganda in China. American Protestants, for their part, tended to combine the preaching of Christianity with preaching about the American way and were by no means reluctant to use their voices to influence Washington's policy for their own benefit. In France's case, however, the situation was reversed; rather than the Vatican lobbying the diplomats for its own interests, it was the Quai d'Orsay that lobbied Rome to maintain as much French influence over Catholic missions as it could.[59] All the while, of course, both American missionaries and French diplomats maintained that the spiritual and temporal spheres should remain separate.

What particularly upset Paris were the signs that Rome was trying to extricate itself from French protection and therefore from French influence. In 1919, the French minister in Peking blocked a Vatican initiative to open direct relations with China. But in 1922, the Italian Celso Constantini arrived in Peking as the first apostolic delegate to that country. He understood the need to come to terms with Chinese nationalism, to depend less on foreign protection, and to forego the reparations and indemnities demanded earlier for the mistreatment or murder of missionaries. He also understood the need to establish a Chinese hierarchy so that the Church could put down firm roots and depend less on foreign help and foreign administration. Such ideas, not very different from those of the National Christian Council, were bound to upset the more conservative missionaries and particularly to upset the French diplomats, Gallicanists to a man, who resented these signs of ecclesiastical independence and knew that they could not extend the protectorate to Chinese clergy.[60] But Constantini had Rome's backing, and his calling of the first Church council in Shanghai in June 1924 opened the gate to fulfillment of his program.[61]

These Christian efforts to come to terms with a new China after the May Fourth Movement came up against the new nationalism's view of Christianity as a foreign doctrine in the service of imperialism. The Protestant triumphalism evident in a book tactlessly called *The Christian Occupation of China* (issued by the forerunner of the National Christian Council) contributed to this view and helped stimulate a new anti-Christian movement in the twenties.[62] Many of the older missionaries saw this movement as a throwback to Boxerism and the rebellion in which tens of thousands of Chinese Christians and their missionaries had perished. Yet the new movement was far from a blind defense of China's tradition (the missionaries could deal with *that*); rather, it was a movement often led by intellectuals who were at the same time leading an attack on China's own tradition. The list of those who participated in, or publicly sympathized with, the anti-Christian movement reads like an honor roll of the new culture movement, including among others Hu Shi (John Dewey's student at Columbia and later ambassador to Washington), Chen Duxiu and Li Dazhao, two of China's first communists, the Guomindang anarchist Wu Zhihui, and Cai Yuanpei, former chancellor of Peking University and a man thoroughly trained both in the Confucian tradition and in modern

German scholarship. Such men opposed Christianity not only because they considered it foreign cultural imperialism but also because, like many Western intellectuals of the time, they firmly believed that religion was little better than superstition. In the age of the new scientific humanism, religious claims could no longer be taken seriously. Not surprisingly, they had a substantial impact on students in Chinese colleges and universities, an impact particularly felt in the great cities like Shanghai.

Well before the twenties, many missionaries in China and their societies, dispirited by the slow work of conversion and influenced by the social gospel, began to turn from pure evangelism to social and educational work. The most impressive achievement of this new orientation was the emergence of no fewer than twenty Christian colleges and universities, run by a variety of denominations. These, while requiring courses in Christianity and attendance at church, also introduced their students to modern secular knowledge. They thus attracted many who had no particular religious interest but were anxious for a modern education in a Western language. Three of the leading Christian institutions of higher education in China sat in Shanghai: St. John's, belonging to the Protestant Episcopal Church, Shanghai Baptist College (also American), and Aurora University [Chendan], run by the French Jesuits.

St. John's University, lying out near Jessfield Park on a pleasant forty-five-acre campus, hard by the gritty industrial slum of Caojiadu, was one of the oldest and most eminent of these schools. Founded by the American Bishop Schereschewsky in 1879, it began as a secondary school, but its real growth began when the Reverend F. L. Hawks Pott was named president in 1888. Pott put up buildings, strengthened the faculty, and expanded the curriculum into new fields. Though it perhaps never quite reached the intellectual eminence of Peking's Yanjing University—probably the pre-eminent missionary university in China—St. John's attracted many students seeking preparation for graduate and professional studies in the United States. By the twenties, it had already established a reputation as a training ground for the sons of the rich and influential, and enough St. John's graduates (like W. W. Yen, Wellington Koo, and T. V. Soong) had gone into politics that the press occasionally spoke of a "St. John's clique" or a "Christian party."[63]

The other Protestant institution of higher education in the city began in 1905 as Shanghai Baptist College and Theological Seminary, changing its name in 1918 to Shanghai College (in 1931 it became the University of Shanghai). Under the presidency of Dr. Francis J. White, it grew larger than St. John's, with over four hundred students in the college and three hundred more in the middle school. It stands out, among other reasons, for its social work; in 1913, the college opened the Yangtszepoo Social Center in the center of the textile mill district, which came to include schools, a reading room, and in 1919 an industrial hospital.[64]

Among the most interesting of the foreign educational experiments in Shanghai was the Comparative Law School, founded under the aegis of the Methodists's Soochow University in 1915. Its purpose, according to the school's catalogue, was "to turn out students who can contribute to the making of a new and better jurisprudence for China."[65] What better place for this than Shanghai with its extraordinary mix of legal systems— old and modern, Chinese and Western, Anglo-American and Continental? To attract working students and to allow Shanghai's practicing lawyers to teach its classes, the school offered its courses in the late afternoon and early evening. Students also attended a practice court, which met on Saturdays in three sections and reflected the complexities of legal Shanghai: a Chinese court, with proceedings in Chinese; a Mixed Court, with proceedings in both Chinese and English, the students interpreting for one another; and an Anglo-American court, whose proceedings were in English only.[66]

Catholic higher education in China was nowhere near as developed as Protestant. But Aurora University, at Loukawei [Lujiawan] on the avenue Dubail in the French Concession was one of the great Chinese universities of its day. Like Peking University, it was in part an offspring of the reform movement of 1898, started by a collaboration between the Christian scholar Ma Liang (Ma Xiangbo) and the Siccawei Jesuits.[67] Soon coming under the control of the Jesuits, it offered courses in law, the sciences, medicine, and liberal arts, all of which (save for those in Chinese studies) were taught in French, just as those of the Protestant colleges were taught in English. Good Sinologists as many of the Jesuits were, they insisted on speaking French rather than Chinese with their pupils and—to the amusement of the Americans who came in 1928—affected the wearing of long beards, presumably to appeal to a Chinese sense of venerability.[68] Jesuit scholarship was not confined to Aurora, and the order also maintained observatories at Siccawei and Zosè [Sheshan] outside Shanghai, ran the Musée Heude for natural history and Chinese antiquities, and published several journals such as the Variétés Sinologiques.

Although the Christians brought modern higher education to China, the Chinese were not long in following their lead. A Chinese guidebook of 1926 lists thirty universities in the city and many specialist schools. The more prominent ones like Nanyang, founded in 1896 by the statesman Sheng Xuanhuai, and Fudan ("New Aurora," also founded by Ma Liang) helped make Shanghai a center of student culture in the twentieth century. They, and a handful of others, made up the more or less orthodox side of Chinese higher education in the city, attracting students who sought a modern education without the foreign, and particularly Christian, veneer of the missionary institutions. But there were others as well, some of them more recently founded, such as Shanghai University in the Settlement and the Shanghai College of Law [Fazheng Daxue] in the Concession that seemed—to foreigners, at any rate—to be little more than training bases for radicals.[69] On them, the foreign police kept a wary eye. Students could be dangerous, whether they came from Christian or secular colleges. At home, the young might be caught up in the thoughtless pleasures of the jazz age, but in China, things were different. The concern was not just that their juvenile heads could be easily turned by denunciations of imperialism and talk of democracy. In China, students spoke with a moral authority that they lacked in the West, and they spoke to a respectful audience. Students had taken the lead in the demonstrations of the May Fourth Movement against China's treatment at Versailles, they formed the backbone of the anti-Christian movement, they wrote, published, and distributed polemical magazines and tracts. Students, in short, could make good revolutionaries.

FOUR

A Memory of Another Clime
Society and Culture in Foreign Shanghai

Shanghai's very geography emphasized the mastery of outsiders; streets were named for foreign men and for Chinese places. In the Central District, roads bearing the names of provinces—Chekiang, Honan, Shantung, Szechuen—ran north and south, while those with the names of cities ran east and west—Peking, Ningpo, Foochow, and, the greatest of them, Nanking Road. The foreigners thus paid homage to the Chinese landscape, but the millions who had built a historical tradition on that landscape remained anonymous. Other roads celebrated the glories of empire—Penang, Rangoon, Macao, Singapore—or occasionally suggested, as did Broadway, Edinburgh Road, and the Great Western Road, a longing for another geography. But when streets were named for people, it was foreigners, not Chinese, who were honored: emperors like Edward VII and the Roi Albert; warriors like Gordon, Pershing, Joffre, and Elgin; priests like Boone, Young Allen, and Mercier; or statesmen like Colbert, Lafayette, and Lincoln. In the French Concession, the name of an occasional thinker or artist would appear: Corneille, Molière, Massenet, and Wagner. The Settlement favored practical achievement: Hart Road recognized the great builder of the Chinese Maritime Customs; Medhurst Road, an early British consul; and Dent Road, an opium merchant whose illicit trade had helped open China. No street honored the emperor Han Gauzu or the poet Du Fu or the philosopher Zhu Xi or the patriot Yue Fei.

Along these roads arose the new offices, stores, houses, and factories that marked Shanghai's growth after the war. Chinese industry expanded rapidly during the war, and the demand for raw materials for postwar reconstruction stimulated trade and brought a brief boom to the city for both foreign and Chinese firms. British exports to China, which had stood at almost £15 million in 1913, jumped to almost £21 million in 1919 and to over £43.5 million in 1920 before dropping back rapidly to £23 million in 1924.[1] Even after the boom was over, Shanghai's growth and its political security meant good times for architects and contractors like Léonard and Veysseyre or Palmer and Turner, the British firm that designed the Hongkong and Shanghai Bank, the Customs House, and the Yokohama Specie Bank. The same factors drove up land prices during the revolutionary years. The huge Shanghai Land Investment Company saw its net profits rise 145 percent between 1924 and 1928, and, in the French Concession, the profits of the Foncière et Immobilière de Chine, after faltering during the troubles of the mid-twenties, were up substantially by 1928.[2]

For its foreign inhabitants, postwar Shanghai was becoming a more comfortable place to live, modern amenities adding to the charms of low costs and the virtual absence of taxes. As a journalist remembered it, even junior members in foreign firms could afford to keep a pony and belong to two or three clubs.[3] For those who could pay, virtually anything was available, and what Shanghai did not make or grow it brought in for foreign tastes. Refrigerator ships unloaded beef, lamb, and fruit from Australia, New Zealand, and North America, and local dairies produced safe milk, butter, and ice cream. There were over a hundred wine and spirits merchants in the Settlement alone, according to the Shanghai Municipal Council's 1925 report, including American firms who presumably found their supplies beyond the borders of a dry United States. (Safe, machine-made ice to cool one's drinks came locally from the improbably named Dombey and Son on Bubbling Well Road.)

Stores of all sorts, Western and Chinese, catered to foreign shoppers: bookstores and publishers, like Kelly and Walsh, music stores and sporting stores, drug stores and silk stores, like the famous Laou Kai Fook on Kiukiang Road with its bright bolts of material piled high on its shelves. There were curio stores, hardware stores, fur stores, and fashion stores, like the Yang Kwei Fei Atelier, named for the concubine whose fatal beauty had almost brought down the Tang dynasty. Nanking Road was Shanghai's Oxford Street, its Fifth Avenue, running from the dowdy Palace Hotel on the Bund out to the Public Recreation Ground beyond Thibet Road. There it became Bubbling Well Road and led west from the congestion of the inner city to the airy houses of the rich in the Western District. Crowded with cars and cyclists, with rickshaws and human-drawn carts dodging the trams that ran down the middle of the street, Nanking Road was thronged with shoppers, with sailors on shore leave, with tourists from cruise ships. Here, under the bright scarlet and gold advertising banners that hung down from the upper floors of the storefronts, they strolled among the rickshawmen and the countrymen with their baskets of ducks or cabbages on bamboo carrying poles, indifferent to the blasting horns of the cars and trucks or the commands shouted by the red-turbanned Sikhs of the Municipal Police.

Along Nanking Road near the Bund could be found the Shanghai branches of Hall and Holtz, Weeks and Company, Whiteaway Laidlaw, and Lane Crawford, the old English retail houses that had come to the China coast in the nineteenth century. Most striking were the three great Chinese department stores: Sincere's, Wing On, and Sun Sun. Here, within the huge new buildings whose extravagant spires still surprise the city's skyline, one could find clothes from Paris, buy Chinese or Western furniture, perfume, and cooking appliances, or choose from a display of food and wine that rivaled London's Fortnum and Mason. Their upper stories housed hotels, restaurants, theaters, amusement centers, skating rinks, and roof gardens (from which, during the troubles of 1927, radicals threw down fiery pamphlets denouncing imperialism into the streets seven stories below). Built by overseas Chinese money, Sincere and Wing On got their start in Hongkong at the turn of the century. Stores like these seemed to symbolize the new China, a China discovering the spirit of Western entrepreneurship, albeit protected by the codes of the foreign settlements. Protected by legal codes, at any rate; the codes of gentility were something else. Barbara Walker, growing up in the nearby cathedral compound at Holy Trinity, remembers the exuberance with which the Chinese discovered outdoor electrical advertising, as signs flashed above Nanking Road in the twilight sky. One evening, a shocking new one appeared. "High overhead a giant Chinese baby was shown at its mother's breasts, refusing to suck. It turned away with a grimace of disgust, then complacently accepted a long drink of patent milk, which glugged visibly in the bottle. Finally the giantess' milk was squirted out of her nipples in a fireworks display of stars."[4]

After the war, a growing number of hotels and restaurants were built, catering both to residents and to the increasing number of travellers. At the corner of Nanking Road and the Bund, the old Palace Hotel, opened in 1906, still stands. The Astor House on Whangpoo Road, with its palm garden and its French chef, was the largest and best place to stay, until the new Majestic opened in 1924 on Bubbling Well Road—only to close a few years later, a victim of the Depression. Restaurants of all sorts abounded, from the most expensive to the Chinese Y.M.C.A. on Szechuen Road, which advertised "first class meals" in the Western style for as little as sixty-eight cents. By the mid-twenties, there was scarcely a street in Frenchtown without a Russian restaurant, opened by one of the thousands of refugees who had fled from the troubles up north. Hongkew was crowded with Japanese restaurants, and on Foochow Road, Westerners could be introduced gently to the joys of Chinese cooking. "The average American or Briton finds an occasional selected Chinese meal delightful," wrote a British journalist, "but would find a continuous Chinese diet unpalatable and unnourishing."[5]

By the end of the war, foreign Shanghai had come to expect the essential services of a modern city. The Municipal Electricity Department, whose huge Yangtszepoo station was the largest in China, provided light and power for the Settlement, the British-owned Shanghai Electric Construction Company ran the Settlement's trams, and in 1924 C. H. Arnhold introduced the first motorbuses. Similar companies served the French Concession and the Chinese city. More than fifty-five miles of meter gauge tram line linked the city's districts, yet passengers still had to change cars as they crossed from one administration to another. The Settlement's streets, until recently paved with broken stones and clay, now began to be properly surfaced, often to the distress of horseback riders. Cars and trucks became common, and over 130 firms, Chinese and foreign, brought in automobiles and auto parts, largely from America. By 1927, Shanghai's 8,800 motor vehicles accounted for fully half of China's total, and the Shanghai Horse Bazaar and Motor Car Company on Bubbling Well Road found the second part of its business (it sold Studebakers, among others) rapidly overshadowing the first. The contentious free-for-all of downtown Shanghai's streets, where cars and trucks competed with pedestrians, rickshawmen, carters, and carriages, led the Municipal Council to set up a Traffic Commission in 1926 in a vain attempt to bring some order to the Settlement.[6]

By the 1920s, new engineering techniques had begun to make possible the construction of large new banks and office buildings that transformed the Bund and the Central District. Shanghai rests on alluvial mud and silt, and big buildings, like the Hongkong and Shanghai Bank or the Customs House, were planted on concrete rafts, giant horizontal slabs locking together the fifty-foot piles driven vertically into the soil. Though the engineers warned that no buildings could rise higher than fifteen stories, the increasing price of land drove buildings upwards, and Shanghai, with both pride and trepidation, began to think of itself as a city of skyscrapers.[7] Yet it became more difficult than ever for the average person to find a place to live. In the mid-twenties, downtown land already cost well over £140,000 an acre (higher, it was often said, than comparable land in the heart of London), and sites on the Bund or along parts of Nanking and Szechuen roads went for twice that much.[8] Only the very rich could still afford houses in the Central District or on the Bund, where, as George Spunt remembered, they had to put up with the endless noise from the river, "the shrill piping of tenders and the blast of funnels over the persistent chant of the wharf coolies."[9] Some of the larger British firms provided bachelor quarters for young men, but others had to make do with a variety of dingy boarding houses, though by the mid-twenties, a new foreign Y.M.C.A. was rising on Bubbling Well Road to provide some housing. Blocks of flats opened, like the Park and Blackstone apartments on the avenue Lafayette ("the finest living accommodations in China," boasted an advertisement for the latter in 1924), and a few years later came the sumptuous Cathay Mansions on the route Cardinal Mercier, at fourteen stories the highest building in the city at the time. Today the Cathay Mansions is a hotel, and in one of its buildings, Zhou Enlai and Richard Nixon signed the Shanghai communiqué in 1972.

South of the avenue Edward VII, the pace of life in Frenchtown remained less frenetic. In the early 1920s, the Concession did not yet have the reputation for vice and corruption that would later plague it, and its western reaches became a favorite place to live, particularly for Americans. Here, along the avenue Joffre or the smaller streets sheltered from the summer sun by dusty, thick-leaved plane trees, they built their houses, furnished them in a Western style, cultivated their gardens, and (particularly if they were British or American) tried to plant a patch of scrubby lawn. Near the avenue Pétain, the Americans built their Community Church in a style best described as generic Presbyterian and the new buildings that would house the Shanghai American School.

Not only rich Westerners lived here. So many White Russians settled here that parts of the avenue Joffre were known as the "Russian concession." Frenchtown was also a favorite spot for rich Chinese merchants, for politicians, for intellectuals, even for warlords to maintain their pieds-à-terre, insurance against a downturn in political fortunes. Leftist authors like Mao Dun lived here; so did the gangster philanthropist Du Yue-sheng, and Sun Yat-sen's house at 29 rue Molière remains a revolutionary shrine.[10]

In the Western District of the Settlement, behind the poplars lining Bubbling Well Road, stood the large houses of the rich, their verandahs and porticoes recalling the style of the first taipans.[11] Beyond the Settlement, despite Chinese challenges to the Municipal Council's authority on the external roads, hundreds of new houses each year went up along Yu Yuen and Jessfield roads, which led west to the botanical gardens at Jessfield Park opposite St. John's University. Even farther out, the shaded reaches of Hungjao Road were popular with those who could afford them; here there was a view of real country, yet the Bund's office buildings were only thirty minutes away.

Shanghai's reputation for luxury could be overdone, as Americans found out when they moved into a city reflecting British ideas of building and creature comforts. In the mid-twenties, it was still possible to build a house with no sanitary installations or even a connection to the nearest sewer, so that wastes still flowed in open drains. Western houses had high ceilings, and rooms had large double doors to allow air circulation in the summer. Yet, as the French journalist Jean Fontenoy put it with some exaggeration, Shanghai's climate brings not only Saigonese summers but Russian winters.[12] "How about heating these infant dance halls?" wrote an exasperated American. "Here is a wonderful sample of a certain race's idea of heating—if you look carefully about it is probable that you will find, tucked inconspicuously under a mantel shelf, a fireplace!" which, however, would be far too small to do any good. Bathrooms also reflected British shortcomings. "Some houses have real bathtubs. Some have Soochow water tubs into which a long individual can pour himself. Some have Japanese tubs into which long people cannot pour themselves under any circumstances. And some haven't any bathtubs at all." Kitchens were tiny and inadequate, with no proper provision for waste, and, like as not, the servants and their families would do their laundry there. "An appetizing place, a Shanghai kitchen," he continued. "No wonder women like to eat at clubs and hotels." Compare the comforts of a real Chinese house in Peking, and you will see, he concluded, how much Shanghai had to learn about designing for Chinese conditions.[13] But for most of Chinese Shanghai, of course, a real Chinese house meant not the luxury of a gentry villa in Peking style but a tiny, airless, overcrowded flat on a filthy back alley with no sanitation. "A prison without guards where the sun never shone," the writer Yu Dafu described his quarters on Bubbling Well Road, but even they were better than the loft he later occupied on Dent Road. "Here, edging one's way through heaps of rags, old tins and bottles and other junk, one came to a rickety ladder," which was the only way up the dark opening that led to a low, small room. "If, standing upright, I had wished to stretch my arms and yawn, my hands would have gone through the dusty gray roof."[14]

Men (and to a lesser extent women) came to Shanghai to make money, and though the city was one of the world's leading seaports, not even its most ardent admirers would pretend that it was a center of high culture. The Settlement alone, however, supported no fewer than twenty-nine foreign newspapers and other journals, according to a police listing of 1924. At what was once No. 17 The Bund still stands the seven-story, twin-towered building that opened in 1924 to house the *North China Daily News*. With its daily circulation of some five to eight thousand, this newspaper had indisputably become the most famous and most influential foreign paper on the China coast since its founding in 1854. Many assumed that the Old Lady of the Bund spoke for the British government, which it did not; many more assumed that it spoke for the Shanghai

Municipal Council. Although the latter was closer to the truth, the *North China* could still be critical when it found weakness and vacillation in the Settlement's governing body. "Independent but Impartial," it called itself, and its voice reflected a good deal of unofficial British treaty port opinion. O. M. Green, who edited it from 1910 to 1930, saw his paper as one that dared tell the unflattering truth about China to a world hypnotized by the flummery of diplomats and politicians in Peking, Whitehall, and Washington and by the deceptive dreams of missionaries and uplifters who saw a bright future amidst the chaos of China's unending civil wars. Precisely because so many people thought of it as an official organ (it published the Council's *Municipal Gazette*), its reactionary voice was a perpetual embarrassment to British officials and policymakers, and sometimes even to the Municipal Council itself. The Municipal Police suspected that the paper's one Chinese editorial writer used his columns to plead the cause of the warlord who subsidized him.[15] A visiting Labour member of Parliament complained that, while the American press in China helped Washington's policy, the British press hindered London's, and a Foreign Office observer called the *North China* the sort of paper that would "confirm to the Chinese that the British are really what the Russians make them out to be."[16] "Many of us feel," wrote an English social worker, "that Mr. Green is quite frankly a serious menace to British interest in this country," and Viscount Gort, serving as chief of staff to the Shanghai Defence Force in 1927, also warned of the great harm the paper did by stirring up anti-British feeling.[17] (On the other hand, the revolutionary hero of one of Ding Ling's stories found that, despite the paper's imperialistic line, its reports were more accurate than those of the Chinese press.)[18] Like it or not, no one could escape the *North China*; it was one of the foreign community's commanding features, and when outsiders spoke of the "Shanghai Mind," it was often O. M. Green and his paper they thought of. The *North China* also issued several useful annual publications, such as currency conversion tables and the *North China Desk Hong List*, a business and residential directory of foreigners and their firms.

No other daily could match the *North China*, and all were short staffed and in financial trouble. "Journalism in Shanghai was not a career," one veteran of those days put it. "Only one newspaper job in the city was worth having, that of O. M. Green. . . . The rest of us just battled with the wolf." Informal arrangements helped cope with such problems, and every morning the writers for the lesser dailies would gather at the Broadway Club, a bar near the Astor Hotel, to divide the day's work between them. Some would cover the law courts, one the Central Police Station, others would handle incoming shipping, and the rest would cover the main sporting events. Each wrote his story and dropped off a carbon at the club so that his colleagues and rivals could share the news.[19]

Yet, some individual reporters did well. George Sokolsky was one; he had come to Shanghai in 1919 where he wrote for a variety of different papers, including the *North China*, and espoused a confusing variety of political opinions. He went on to become one of the best-known interpreters of the Chinese revolution for foreigners, particularly for Americans.[20] Some individual papers also pulled through. The *China Press* on Kiukiang Road, founded by Thomas Millard in 1911, brought an American style to Shanghai, and its rapid circulation (by the mid-twenties it was selling four to five thousand copies a day) badly worried the editors at No. 17 The Bund. Shaky finances, however, by then had forced its sale to Edward Ezra, a British citizen and former head of the Shanghai Opium Combine, and the paper was controlled by his estate after his death, though Stirling Fessenden headed the American-incorporated company that published it. It continued to be thought of as the American paper, even after its American editor, John B. Powell, left or was fired (it is not clear which) in 1925. A journalist joining the staff remembered two instructions from the city editor: first, that American prestige must be upheld at all costs, and second, that foreigners should not study Chinese—it made them queer.[21] In the Concession, *L'Écho de Chine*, owned by the Missions Étrangères in Paris, trumpeted a forceful French patriotism and a contempt for Chinese nationalism as outspoken as the *North China's*, thus seriously embarrassing both its clerical patrons and the authorities. There were two Russian papers, one White and one Red, while the Japanese had two papers of their own.

Other weeklies and monthlies spoke for trading interests, like *Finance and Commerce* or the British *Chamber of Commerce Journal*. So did the American *Far Eastern Review*, whose editor, G. B. Rea, propagated an increasingly anti-Nationalist and pro-Japanese line; it was finally banned in December 1932, after Rea became a publicity agent for Tokyo's Manchkuoan puppet. Most interesting of all was the American weekly that was founded as *Millard's Review* in 1917 but was edited by John B. Powell, a recent graduate of the University of Missouri School of Journalism. In 1922, Powell assumed full control of the magazine, changing its name to *The China Weekly Review*. A man of enormous energy, he also edited the *China Press* from 1923 to 1925, represented several English and American papers, lobbied for the China Trade Act in 1922, and spent several weeks as the captive of Chinese bandits in 1923. Years later, after almost dying in Japanese internment, he received a commendation from Chiang Kai-shek for his wartime heroism. From the *Review's* editorial offices on the avenue Edward VII, he opened his pages to the writings of Chinese political observers, playing particularly for young, English-speaking Chinese subscribers.[22] Though in 1924 and 1925 the *Review's* politics mirrored treaty port opinion, by the revolutionary year of 1927 its outspoken criticisms of the Municipal Council and its liberal stance towards the Chinese revolution would win Powell the enmity of much of the American and British communities of the Settlement.

Few foreigners, of course, could read the Chinese papers. But the protection of the foreign settlements was as attractive to Chinese journalists as it was to Chinese businessmen, and more daily papers were said to be printed in the International Settlement than in all the rest of China together.[23] Some enjoyed foreign protection: the *Sin Wan Pao* [Xinwen Bao] on Hankow Road was registered in Delaware and its principle shareholder was the American missionary J. C. Ferguson, while the *Shun Pao* [Shen Bao], China's oldest daily (it began in 1872), was Chinese owned but registered in the French consulate.[24] Nonetheless, in 1924 the Mixed Court ruled that such registration would not enable Chinese papers to escape the Court's jurisdiction, a decision welcomed by the Settlement authorities who had railed against what they saw as the irresponsibility, ignorance, and falsehoods of the Chinese press.[25]

Despite the luxurious growth of the press, some found foreign Shanghai's cultural life sparse. The Public Library's twenty thousand volumes—all in Western languages—were fewer than those to be found on the shelves of the Shanghai Club.[26] Apart from the Musée Heude at Siccawei, there was no museum worth the name, and an annual art exhibit in the old Post Office Building seems to have shown primarily the work of local amateur painters. The stage did better, with the Shanghai Amateur Dramatic Society and the Shanghai American Players putting on several productions, often of drawing room comedies, at the Lyceum and the Carlton. Occasional touring companies came through, like the Wilbur Players from California who staged the "raging American play sensation," *Her Unborn Child* (from which children under fourteen were excluded). Movies were increasingly popular, and by the mid-twenties there were six foreign theaters in Shanghai. Under Mario Paci, the Municipal Orchestra gave weekly concerts from October to May in the Town Hall and in the summer played outdoors in the Public Gardens and in Jessfield and Hongkew parks. Its performances were well attended, but the orchestra suffered from various disabilities, as when it had to settle for a mezzo (Mme L. Spunt) to perform Walther's *Preislied* from *Meistersinger*. Visiting artists complemented Shanghai's musical life, and during the war of October 1924, the Italian Opera Company "direct from Milan" brought ten days of Donizetti, Verdi, and Puccini to the Olympia. Concert soloists on world tours played in Shanghai: Mischa Elman, Fritz Kreisler, Emilia Galli-Curci, Feodor Chaliapin; and in September 1924, Master Emil C. Danenberg, "the Hongkong Prodigy," gave a piano recital at the Lyceum. The *North China* praised "the little fellow's dexterity and his no less wonderful powers of memorization. . . . He has an undoubted future before him. . . . One wishes the youngster all the success he deserves."[27] The little fellow went on to become a concert pianist and president of Oberlin College.

Though most foreigners may have been concerned with China only as it affected business,[28] there were some who showed a considerable interest in the history, language, culture, and problems of the land in which they lived. The missionaries produced some notable scholars: Jesuits like Leonard Wieger and Pascal d'Elia at Aurora, George Cressey at Shanghai Baptist College, Harley MacNair and C. F. Remer at St. John's, to name some of the more important. Some groups, like the American Women's Club, studied aspects of Chinese culture and published their findings. The British consul-general, Sidney Barton, presided over the North China Branch of the Royal Asiatic Society, which met to read papers and issued a journal from its headquarters on Museum Road. The *China Journal*, edited by Arthur de C. Sowerby (no friend of modern Chinese culture or politics), investigated Chinese history, art, and science. But a common attitude towards high culture (to say nothing of Chinese culture) was perhaps best expressed by the bemused reviewer at the *North China Daily News* into whose hands there fell a copy of *To the Lighthouse*. "Doubtless there are many in the British Isles," he wrote of Virginia Woolf's audience, "who have both the leisure and the inclination to fathom what the author was trying to get at in this story. Here in China, alas, the times are altogether too trying to justify the attempt." And when Lu Xun's searing indictment of his countrymen, "The True Story of Ah Q," appeared in English, the *China Weekly Review* could find only a series of "piquant, animated scenes of people in villages who delight us with their quaint whims and utterances."[29]

Neither the Settlement nor the French authorities felt themselves bound to provide for the schooling of their children, either Chinese or foreign, arguing that they lacked the resources to assume the responsibilities common in Western cities. But though education depended generally on private associations or charitable institutions, the Shanghai Municipal Council did begin making small grants-in-aid to several schools and eventually took over some smaller foreign schools altogether. An English education for foreign children came from the Public Schools for Boys and for Girls, and the Thomas Hanbury Schools, which were originally founded for Eurasian children, were now open to all. The École Municipale Française provided a French curriculum for foreign children. Other nationalities and religions ran their own schools—the Cathedral Schools for Anglicans, a Shanghai Jewish School, St. Francis Xavier College and St. Joseph's Institute for the Catholics—all depending primarily on their own resources, though sometimes supplemented by small grants from the Municipal Council. The Shanghai American School (founded by missionaries in 1912) grew rapidly after the war, and its move to large new quarters on the avenue Pétain in 1924 was a sign of the American community's coming of age.[30] Boarders, particularly "mish kids" from the hinterland church stations, made up much of its constituency, and in the twenties its strongly Protestant mind still found Catholics and Jews more outlandish than Buddhists; even Episcopalians were on the borderline.[31] Still, it sent its graduates off to the best colleges in America and built up a fiercely loyal alumni body that meets for reunions to this day. Its education was thoroughly Western, although the mid-twenties saw the beginnings of the study of China and things Chinese. On the whole, wrote one observer, foreign Shanghai provided an education that was "for a boy going into business good enough, as the careers of many Shanghai-educated children prove. It is for other reasons that people send their children home, as for instance, to teach boys subordination" by denying them the spoiling effects of having adult servants at their beck and call.[32] Another observer in the nineteenth century had made the same point, commenting on the rudeness with which those brought up in the East treated the natives: "The real cause of this I believe to be a partial arrestment of moral development at the boisterous schoolboy stage, owing to a too early acquirement of power among people of a different moral code from that of their own countrymen."[33]

If public education for foreign children was sparse, such schooling for most Chinese children was out of the question because of the expense. The École Municipale Franco-Chinoise had about eight hundred pupils, and the Municipal Council helped support a few Chinese schools in the Settlement, though not until 1931 did it begin to plan for primary education. So too, missionary and benevolent societies filled some of the gap left by the Council's failure or inability to provide for adequate social and medical services. Groups like the British Women's Association and the American Women's Club played an important role, and much of the income of the Shanghai Race Club went to charitable undertakings. The Door of Hope offered refuge to women and children who had been sold into, or drifted into, prostitution. The Institution for the Chinese Blind gave courses in industrial work, and the Jesuits ran an impressive vocational training center for men and women at Siccawei. Nowhere in China, wrote the missionary W. E. Soothill, was there such philanthropy and generosity as in Shanghai.[34] Despite the efforts of such groups, however, no voluntarism, however well meaning, could make up for the almost complete absence of proper laws and proper social services in both the foreign and Chinese districts. "Shanghai, which is a city of luxury, ought to think much more about the misery which is so common there," wrote the French consul-general in 1924. "But the municipal councils are usually made up of businessmen of practical outlook, who have little altruism and no sympathy for anything Chinese."[35]

Such charitable organizations represented simply a few of the enormous number of clubs and associations that were such a mark of foreign Shanghai. At the top of the social pyramid stood the Shanghai Club, founded in 1863, whose immense building was one of the dominant features of the Bund. For those proposed for membership (no women or Chinese, of course), the opposition of a fifth of the membership meant a blackball. Election was a sign of arrival in Shanghai society, which is not to say that all the members were equals. Junior members of the leading British firms who were fortunate enough to gain admission remember the strict hierarchical lineup at the Long Bar, its polished mahogany shining under dark Jacobean panelling—the taipans at one end and the griffins, or newcomers, at the other.[36]

In 1917 an American Club started up in a building at 33 Nanking Road. It quickly outgrew its quarters, and in March 1925, a splendid new building was opened on Foochow Road, a sign, as J. Harold Dollar said in his welcoming speech, that the American community was in Shanghai to stay. It was notable, among other things, for the fresh apple pie available at any hour of the day or night and for a mah-jong room in the style of a Peking temple (such were the concessions to Chinese culture). On special occasions like Washington's Birthday and Independence Day, it held an open house for the American community. On such days, women were admitted as guests. Despite the efforts of some of the more liberal members, it was not until May 1929 that Chinese were allowed to join (the Shanghai Club held out until 1941). Nonetheless, there were several organizations that were founded to serve as meeting grounds between foreigners and Chinese, the latter often those who had studied abroad or in China's Christian universities. The International Institute (1897) and the Shanghai Y.M.C.A. were among the earliest. The American University Club (1905) was open to all graduates of American colleges, Chinese and foreign, and in 1919 a group of British, Americans, and Chinese founded the Union Club of China whose purpose was to improve relations between Chinese and foreigners (meaning, of course, Anglo-Saxons). The Shanghai Rotary Club (1919), many of whose members were American educated, was another example of a successful Sino-foreign social organization.[37]

The Union Club played an important role in the troubles of the forthcoming years, but its membership declined soon after its opening perhaps because, as an American commented, the Chinese looked on the club "as a sort of no man's land where foreigners condescend to meet Chinese."[38]

Downtown clubs like these (there was a Japanese one as well) were used for midday tiffin or for special events such as dinners, lectures, or evening meetings. Farther out and closer to the houses of the rich, other institutions served for afternoon and evening entertainment. British and American country clubs offered swimming, tennis, and other sports. Everyone agreed, however, that by far the liveliest spot in town—at least the liveliest respectable spot—was the Cercle Sportif Français, whose new building opened on the route Cardinal Mercier in January 1926. Not only was it the largest club of its kind, not only did it have the best sprung dance floor in Asia and, by common consent, the best table in town, but there one could also find a broader international circle than the Anglo-Saxon retreats allowed; it admitted not only Chinese members but even women! At its inauguration, Consul-General Meyrier spoke of his pride in seeing the tricolor raised over the magnificent structure, "Où l'art le plus délicat de la décoration s'allie à une originalité puissante et neuve." (The opening program, however, testified to the small size of the Concession's French population; a gipsy chorus was followed by Russian songs and dances, and the entertainment finished with an Italian baritone singing Neapolitan songs.)[39] Designed by Léonard and Veysseyre with an outside that looked like a pavilion for an international exposition and an interior as daringly modernist as Shanghai would allow, it was also one of foreign Shanghai's architectural gems, done with a light touch missing from the conservative solidity of the Bund. Today, though a skyscraper hotel stands in its place, much of the old facade has been incorporated into the new building, a rare example of careful historic preservation in the city.

There were dozens of special interest groups: Freemasons, Daughters of the American Revolution, the Shanghai Horticultural Association, Oxford and Cambridge clubs, a Harvard Club. British veterans met at the United Service Club, and Americans, at the American Legion's Frederick Townsend Ward post, named after the scapegrace from Salem whose command of the Ever Victorious Army ended when a Taiping bullet felled him in 1862. National societies flourished (the foreign equivalent, perhaps, of the Chinese *tongxianghui*, or native-place associations). For the British Isles alone there was a St. George's Society, a St. Andrew's Association, a St. David's Club, and a St. Patrick's Club (the last presumably for Ulstermen; the appearance of an Irish Association after the war suggests that citizens of the Free State went their own way). There was even, for a mercifully brief period in 1924, a Chinese branch of the Ku Klux Klan (the "*San K*"), started with the help of Captain L. D. ("Pegleg") Kearney, an American adventurer, arms smuggler, and sometime propagandist for the Chinese revolution.[40]

Other groups were devoted to sport, a passion unhampered by the climate. British firms in the Far East liked young men who were good at games and tended to distrust any too obvious intellectual accomplishments. There were clubs for such pastimes as tennis, swimming, sculling, sailing, shooting, golf, football, and baseball, among others. The pink-coated huntsmen of the Shanghai Paper Chase Club followed trails laid by riders in red cowls who took the place of nonexistent foxes. Although the club maintained a fund to repay farmers whose fields its riders damaged, not surprisingly the horsemen were often unwelcome beyond the limits of the foreign settlement. Above all, there was horse racing, popular since the coming of the Westerner to Shanghai. The major meets of the Shanghai Race Club, held at its course on Bubbling Well Road in May and November, had almost the character of public holidays, and there were lesser meets at other times. Out at Jiangwan [Kiangwan] to the northeast, the International Recreation Club was the center for Chinese racing, but Westerners were full participants. The horses were really Mongolian ponies, short and shaggy but with enormous stamina, though rumor had it that the occasional small Arab was smuggled onto the race course. Their riders were gentleman jockeys, but it was generally known that some of the most successful riders owed their employment in downtown offices more to their horsemanship than to their business talents.[41]

It was for its general social life, and particularly for its fast-paced night life, that foreign Shanghai became famous or infamous. People who disliked it were apt to blame the burgeoning of night clubs and the proliferation of cafés and cabarets on the unhealthy influence of the White Russian refugees who ran so many of them. But Shanghai, which prided itself on being as modern as any city in the world, would have been hard put to resist the currents coming in from New York, London, and Paris. By the mid-twenties, spots such as the Del Monte, the Little Club, the Eddie Café ("the only real night club in China," it called itself), the Premier Café, and the Mumm Café had appeared. On Ningpo Road stood the Carlton Café, started by Al Israel, "the Ziegfeld of the East," whose bar on Powell Street in San Francisco had survived the earthquake of 1906 but not the Volstead Act of 1918.[42] The Carlton not only had its own movie house and its own ballroom and orchestra, but also had its own company of *artistes* for floor shows. On its Roof Garden, it staged boxing matches bloody enough on occasion to call down the wrath of the Municipal Council. These were all relatively respectable; other watering holes, like those near the French Bund on "Blood Alley"—so-called because of its frequent brawls—were less so.

This was the Shanghai visitors from the outside wanted to see, and it is the Shanghai they pictured in their writings. Take this sketch of evening in Shanghai, for instance, as it comes from *Vogue* in 1924. We begin with afternoon drinks in the old American Club, looking down on Nanking Road below. "One accepts all the Chinese, dun coloured and inert, without personality, as a background for the white 'foreigners' who are the high spots of colour in the parade dominating the street crowd just as the small foreign population dominates and colours the life of the city." Shanghai women are well turned out, but "everyone is just a shade, and just the same shade, behind the fashions of Paris, London, and New York."

Shanghai social life is a cluster of glittering, dashing bodies of foreigners with a nimbus of servants. The Chinese themselves, in daily touch with foreigners, are nonetheless continents away. To the Chinese, we are magnificent barbarians. They copy our luxuries and conveniences, but they scorn our philosophies and our habits. However both Europeans and Americans love China, because it is so completely flattering to the Anglo-Saxon sense of racial superiority. Democracy becomes a memory of another clime, while the present is a continuing experience of real supremacy. The poorest junior can afford at least one personal servant and moderate wealth commands an establishment. . . . The whole background of life in China is made up of these flawless Chinese servants.

At eight, as the streets darken, everyone leaves the club and goes home to dress: evening dresses for women, black trousers, a white mess jacket, and soft shirt for the men. A dinner party can be a spur of the moment affair, the adaptability of the flawless Chinese servants making it possible to provide for ten or a dozen guests at an hour's notice. But dinner itself is eminently forgettable. "A distinguishing mark of Shanghai's social life is that one almost never hears a phrase, much less a conversation, worth repeating" (and a bored Somerset Maugham made the same observation). So, it's off to the Carlton to dance to the latest American jazz orchestra. "Everyone in Shanghai, except the missionaries, is there sometime during the week." Then on to the Astor ballroom, which perhaps is too much like the Carlton, so the party winds up in some of the less reputable dives on Siccawei Road in Frenchtown—places like the Crest or the Delmonte that only begin to come alive after midnight. The night ends with a ham and egg breakfast at five, and so to bed. (Is this how Jake Barnes and Brett Ashley would have behaved in the Far East?)

How the businessman was supposed to work efficiently the next day is beside the point: "Out there it is a gay, hectic, carefree life. Ask any man who has been there if he would return. He would. If he would not, he was one of the lame, the halt, or the really conscientious. Such never really taste Chinese life, but those who have tasted are bound to it. They can not escape from its call if they would, and they would not if they could—and so that is the colour of Shanghai!"[43]

"I reflected one afternoon," recalled an American journalist, "as I tea-danced around with a swain at the Astor House, . . . that when, if ever, the sun did set for foreigners in Shanghai, it would go down to the popping of champagne corks." Recently divorced and job hunting in Shanghai in 1927, Milly Bennett was a radical of independent mind who discovered little good in her brief acquaintance with Shanghai society.

I was finding out that practically all of the British in Shanghai were die-hard re-actionaries, and that the only way to gain access to the business and social circles that they controlled, was to echo their hidebound dogma which came to something like that the Chinese were a dirty, low, mongrel race, that they should be everlast-ingly grateful for being booted around by the extremely superior British, and how what the Chinese really needed was the firm British government to guide them.

The backbone, so to speak, of these British arbiters were small fry, cashiers in banks, vice-consuls, traders, newspapermen, folk who would be lucky at home to have a charwoman in once a week, but here could staff their flats as a princely menage—every $300 a month employee had cook, helper, amah, table boy, six or eight full time, well trained servants. Surrounded by the appurtenances of wealth and grandeur, the humorless ego of these little British quite explainably became confused and they mistook their own pompous ways for power.

Her own countrywomen were even worse.

It is appalling what can happen to the average American housewife when she gets within hailing distance of what she thinks is high society, especially if it happens to have a British accent. . . . It made my flesh crawl to hear American women go around imitating the la-de-da manners of the British and "cheerioing" one another and imitating what was obviously a lower class British accent although they did not know it, and filling up their heads with imperialistic nonsense.

In such a climate, men, though in a majority, found themselves sought after by the "squads of well-established matrons in whom the fires of spring still glowed. . . . Easy wine, easy women and the gayeity [sic] never ending and the big boss off in New York or London and the local boss, if any, also posturing like a millionaire at the racetrack or the country club. Boozing went on excessively and ceaselessly, pickmeups in the morn-ing, heavy, boozy tiffins and cocktail parties, teas, receptions and the late dinners, and the whole, long night of drinking, dancing and carousing, stretching ahead of it. Few flesh and blood young men could resist it. Few did."[44]

"I've discovered how a lot of people live out here and at the pace they do," wrote the wife of a Texas Oil representative in 1922.

They work on as large an overdraft as the bank will allow them. The bank, in order to get their Company business, finds it profitable to allow individuals considerable overdraft on their personal accounts, secured maybe by a guarantee of a third party as brake on the original borrower, or a lot of flimsy furniture. Then, when going home time comes, they sell the lease to their house and the furniture and everything else they have, clean up enough to pay the bank and go home broke, but apparently they should worry. They've made a big splurge here and lived on top of the world for three years on the bank's money. Well, they can have that sort of business, but I prefer to pay my bills every month, even if I can't run a car and gamble and belong to every club in town."[45]

Was Shanghai social life really like this? The *North China* doubted it. "Shanghai is sometimes known as the 'Paris of the East,' though how far such an appelation is justified is a matter of opinion and of doubt," it wrote.[46] Yet Bishop Molony of Ningpo worried enough about the lures of Shanghai by night to urge the British Women's Association to do what they could "to produce the best British home life here in Shanghai. The young men who come out here from simple and refined British homes, and who will do so much good or ill in China don't want a whirligig of gaiety. They want manly sports and a quiet home life. They want those who will take the place of their mothers and sisters. Don't let your love of gaiety deprive them of the joys of quiet evenings in the home circle. . . . Books, art, music, needlework, and above all religion: these are the beautiful things, the things that go to make our British home"[47] (never mind what materialistic Americans might say about the shortcomings of British plumbing and central heating).

Such characterizations of Shanghai can easily be exaggerated, and they come largely from the pens of visiting journalists, celebrities, travellers, and—of course—critics of Western imperialism, all of whom pilloried or parodied foreign Shanghai in these years, forever repeating the truism that Shanghai was not China. And it is certainly easy enough to see the institutions of foreign Shanghai as an attempt to keep China at arms length, to build groups and associations that spared their members the need to come to terms with the country in which they lived. Of course this arrogant aspect of Shanghai existed—witness the contempt of the *North China* for so much that was Chinese and the judgments called down on foreign Shanghai by such long-term residents as J. B. Powell and L. A. Lyall. But to lay too much stress on such behavior means overlooking another, equally important side of Shanghai society as well, for there was a desire by an increasing number of men and women to consider Shanghai their home, to build the kind of ordered and settled community in which they could live peacefully, raise their children, and ensure a kind of security for themselves and their families.[48]

Regardless of Shanghai's glamor, after the postwar boom ended, civil war kept trade and business depressed. Shanghai was no longer a place to seek one's fortune, however plentiful the servants and low the taxes, to say nothing of the attractions of a society that made no pretense of democracy. "It cannot be too often repeated that Shanghai is no longer an Eldorado to the man seeking a billet," admonished the *Municipal Gazette* in 1925. "There are hundreds of men and women in this Settlement who are earning a hand to mouth existence, and the prospect of a change in these conditions is very remote."[49] In late 1924, the American consul-general warned that many of the young Americans who came looking for work would find their hopes dashed. Most of the positions that paid decent salaries were filled by appointments made at home, and there were many more applicants than positions at the lower level. Although a business executive might make US $5,000 or more a year, most had to do with far less, and many who earned about $2,000 found that they could just make ends meet (given the expense of maintaining face among the Chinese) and could save nothing. Credit was easy for those with steady incomes, "but for a man out of work there is probably no more inhospitable place anywhere on earth. . . . At the present time, there is no hope of a stranger's obtaining employment in Shanghai. For every job, no matter how small or poorly paid, there are several men in line."[50] A year later, the consul-general warned a would-be secretary that, even in the unlikely event she found a job, out of a monthly salary of $300 (about US $160) she could expect to pay $125 to $175 for a boarding house, $190 at a hotel, another $6 to $10 a month to tip servants, $20 for a private rickshaw (the most economical way to travel), and $15 a month for coal in the winter or an electric fan in the summer.[51]

Yet, not only for the taipan but for any white foreigner with extraterritoriality and reasonably secure employment, life in foreign Shanghai could be very pleasant in those years. The creature comforts—food, drink, servants, companionship of various sorts—could be got with relatively little money. For the curious, there was all China to explore; for the uncurious, Shanghai reproduced Western society in a city whose problems could be largely ignored since they were China's problems. Perhaps it was easier to turn a blind eye to the beggars, to the slums, to the children working twelve- or fourteen-hour shifts in the mills, to the indigent swarming in from the countryside, than it would have been to ignore impoverished southern sharecroppers or unemployed Welsh coal miners at home. With democracy only a memory of another clime, as *Vogue*'s writer put it, many in foreign Shanghai enjoyed the assumption of privilege that a white skin brought them in a brown-skinned country. If the tragic side of Shanghai's revolution in those years found its writer in André Malraux, there was also a side that needed Dickens—or perhaps Trollope. He would have had fun with Anglicans and Episcopalians dividing their spheres; with the competition of northern and southern Baptists, Methodists, and Presbyterians. But he would have also seen the relentless pursuit of the almighty dollar and its corrupting influence. There was material here for the gentle teasing of *Barchester Towers*, but there was also material for the astringent moral commentary of *The Way We Live Now*.

FIVE

A Tragedy of the Most Violent
and Bloody Sort
Shanghai and the War of 1924-1925

In the late summer of 1924, Shanghai faced its most serious armed threat in over a decade. Not since 1913, when the would-be dictator Yuan Shikai had sent his troops in to take control, had the city faced the prospect of becoming a battleground. Crime, violence, minor disorder—these were common enough; but the continuing movements of contending armies and the possibility that Chinese warfare would spill over into the foreign concessions represented a more serious danger. In February 1919, representatives of China's rival armies had met at the old German Club on the Bund in an unsuccessful attempt to resolve their differences. Their failure to end the civil wars coincided with the European armistice. Though the major foreign powers decided in 1919 to embargo arms sales to China, they could not prevent Europe's sudden surplus of weapons from surreptitiously entering China's inexhaustible arms market. And with the guns came the soldiers of fortune, the military advisers, and military adventurers—British, German, American, Italian, French, Russians, both Red and White—men left without a profession by the return of peace to Europe and ready to sell their skills abroad. Modern weapons and modern tactics would change the character of war in China and make it more dangerous than ever.[1]

Over the years, foreign Shanghai had devised ways of guarding itself against the disorders of the Chinese world. In the Settlement, the Shanghai Municipal Police consisted of some 2,700 men commanded by a British commissioner (the number would rise to 3,600 by 1928). About seventeen hundred were Chinese, and seven hundred were Sikhs recruited from India by the Municipal Council. There was a small Japanese branch, and the rest were mostly British, many of them (like the commissioner himself) veterans of service in the army or the Black and Tans of the Royal Irish Constabulary. Most dealt with routine matters like crime prevention and traffic control, but the plainclothes men of the Police Specials were there to ferret out political intelligence and to stay in touch with similar units of the French and the Chinese police. The French Concession's *Garde municipale* was much smaller. In 1924 it was comprised of 84 Europeans, 283 Tonkinese (the French, like the British, recruited their colonial subjects for work in China), and 580 Chinese. Over a hundred detectives, French, Chinese, Korean, and White Russian, made up a *Service de Sûreté* to keep an eye on any who might subvert the good order of the Concession.[2] Unlike the Shanghai Municipal Police, who were answerable through their commissioner to the Municipal Council, the *Garde* obeyed the orders of the French consul-general, and his *Conseil* had little voice in their activities.

Though foreigners prided themselves on the good order of the concessions, the press was often critical of the level of crime in those years (according to the Shanghai Municipal Council, cases of armed robbery in the Settlement rose from 47 in 1922 to 1,458 in 1927).[3] Foreign Shanghai blamed the rise in crime on the laxity of authorities in the Chinese city; Chinese Shanghai blamed it on the presence of foreign enclaves where criminals could seek asylum. Even with cooperation between the police of the different districts, the existence of three different administrations undoubtedly eased the burden of the criminal if it did not encourage outright lawlessness. Moreover, in keeping order among the complex and rootless Chinese populations of the settlements, the foreign authorities came to depend upon a variety of informal allies both above ground and underground. Huang Jinrong's positions both as chief of Chinese detectives in the *Garde municipale* and as Green Gang leader have already been noted. Nor was he alone in such dual allegiance; his opposite in the Municipal Police was leader of the Big Eight Mob, which had run the Settlement's drug traffic.[4] The gangs, with their control over large parts of the Shanghai underworld, could be useful in ensuring that foreign Shanghai was disturbed as little as possible both by ordinary crime and by China's social and political upheavals. Of course, the gangs demanded a price, and the price would rise as civil war and revolution came to the city.

Such arrangements, of course, were almost never revealed publicly, and even the foreign consular reports for the most part were silent about matters that the old Shanghai hands tell us were common knowledge. In a city where foreigners liked to contrast the stability of the settlements with the disorder of the Chinese city, no one at this point wanted to wash foreign linen in public. Nor had the picture in the early 1920s become as dark as it would be later, when the vice and corruption of the French administration became a scandal great enough to threaten the very continuation of foreign privilege.

The police were not the only force at the disposition of the foreign authorities. The loose interpretation of the treaties, which allowed the settlements virtual independence from China, also allowed them to build up their own amateur soldiery. Just as the political disintegration of late nineteenth-century China spawned gentry-led militia units [*tuanlian*] at the local level, so in Shanghai an unpaid local militia appeared. The Shanghai Volunteer Corps traced its origins back to 1853, when foreigners rallied to defend the Settlement against the rebels who had seized the Chinese city. In 1870 the Volunteer Corps became a formal institution of the Settlement and, by the twentieth century, had grown into a uniformed force of seventeen hundred men of various nationalities who would be called out to stand guard when emergencies arose. Service was considered a civic duty, although both the members and their employers could begrudge the days spent away from the office during periods of mobilization. To increase the sense of national pride (and no doubt also to decrease the possibility of clashes between disparate national ideas), the units of the Volunteer Corps were usually organized along national lines. The British had formed the first unit, and others followed: Germans, Americans, Japanese, and Austrians. Though the German and Austrian detachments vanished during the war, more units came later: an American cavalry troop in 1923, a White Russian company in 1927, and even two Jewish units in the 1930s.[5] In 1906, after serious riots in the Settlement, a Chinese company was formed. Though the Municipal Council had originally insisted on putting an English officer in charge by the 1920s the unit was under Chinese command.[6] The emergency of 1924 itself gave birth to a tenth company, made up of Swiss, Dutch, and Scandinavians, a combination of nationalities presumably reflecting the participants' Nordic affinities.

The Shanghai Volunteer Corps was commanded by a regular British officer seconded to Shanghai by the War Office. It was well equipped, including two cavalry troops, a field artillery battery, three machine gun companies, and nine companies of infantry. Together with the police, it gave the Municipal Council a force of roughly three thousand men to call upon in emergencies. In the French Concession, an earlier *Compagnie Française de Volontaires*—of about a hundred and twenty men—was reconstituted in 1923 and was joined by a small Chinese unit in April 1925; enough men, the French consul-general pointed out, to avoid being embarrassed by having to call on the Settlement for help.[7]

If police and volunteers were not enough, as a last resort the authorities could ask for landing parties from the warships in the harbor. Destroyers, cruisers, and gunboats from Britain, Japan, France, and America were moored off the Bund, and these countries, occasionally joined by Italy, considered themselves unofficially the naval powers of Shanghai with a special role in its defense. Their sailors and marines usually watched over strategic spots like the power station and waterworks, the major public transportation routes, and above all the boundaries between the settlements and the Chinese city where trouble might come. The French consul-general could go directly to the French naval commander when he wanted men put ashore. The Municipal Council had no such power, and the chairman had first to declare a state of emergency (martial law, in effect) and then put his request to the senior consul, who would discuss the matter with his colleagues and the naval commanders.[8]

Usually (not always) the men were landed. The question of withdrawal was more delicate, and the Council and the naval commanders did not always agree. Many in Shanghai seemed to think that the landing parties should come ashore in sufficient number to relieve the Volunteers and let them get back to their banks and businesses. But how much protection did the foreign countries owe foreign Shanghai? The International Settlement was not a colony, after all, and in choosing to live abroad, its inhabitants presumably accepted both the risks and the opportunities that were entailed. Though no one ever put the question quite so bluntly, at least some naval commanders (like Rear Admiral Charles B. McVay, commander of the American Yangtze Patrol in 1925) maintained that, except in real emergencies, foreign Shanghai should look after itself and not use their sailors as extra policemen.[9] Indeed, the Municipal Council itself, while always ready to call for military help, considered itself responsible for the Settlement's defense and saw no need always to tell the consuls what measures it was taking.[10]

The war of late 1924 and early 1925 shows how foreign Shanghai responded to an emergency that seemed to jeopardize its life and business. It also brings out some of the differences that were emerging between foreign Shanghai and its home governments. Unlike the revolutionary crises that were to come, this threat was purely military and had few ideological or political aspects. Although that summer the Peking government had recognized the Soviet Union and the old Russian consulate-general on Whangpoo Road was now in Soviet hands, and although foreign Shanghai worried about the Bolshevik proclivities of Chinese students and labor leaders, even the *North China Daily News* could see no signs of Russian meddling in the fighting. While the war took place against a background of deepening nationalist sentiment, there were no issues to stir patriotic feelings, no issues to pit foreign Shanghai against Chinese Shanghai. In fact, quite the opposite: During the fighting, Chinese Shanghai would look to foreign Shanghai for protection in ways that only a few months later would be inconceivable.

The war that broke out in the summer of 1924 was fought for no more than local issues and local gain. The control of Shanghai was its goal, and the rivals were the military leaders of Jiangsu and Zhejiang provinces.[11] Lu Yongxiang was defense commissioner of Shanghai and Wusong in 1917, and when he moved to Hangzhou to become the military governor of Zhejiang province, he left General He Fenglin to guard his interests in Shanghai. One of several minor warlords who had gotten his start in Yuan Shikai's armies, Lu had held on to Zhejiang and to Shanghai as different generals marched in and out of Peking. An uneasy alliance with Zhang Zuolin, the former bandit whom the foreigners called the Old Marshal and who was contending for power in the north, gave him some security in Peking. Not until early 1924 was Lu's position threatened. At that point, Wu Peifu, who had earlier defeated the Old Marshal, sent one of his subordinates, General Sun Chuanfang, to take control of Fujian province, bordering Zhejiang on the south. A graduate of a Japanese military academy, General Sun was a vigorous leader who would play an important role in Shanghai's future. His invasion of Fujian that summer drove thousands of soldiers north into Zhejiang, swelling the armies of Governor Lu Yongxiang. When Lu refused to disband them, the Jiangsu authorities had an excuse to move. By late summer, Qi Xieyuan, the military governor of Jiangsu, was rallying his forces for an attack, denouncing Lu as a rebel against the government and thus invoking the shadowy moral authority of the Peking government in his cause.

Foreign Shanghai had little interest or understanding of these complicated intrigues and distrusted the claims of the generals that they would bring unity and order to the country. In foreign eyes, all warlords, no matter what their allegiances and no matter what their public principles, were simply self-seeking men, to be judged only in terms of how far they hurt or helped foreign interests. The foreigners wanted only to lessen the damage that war would bring the city they regarded as their own, and even before the fighting broke out, they insisted on a neutral Shanghai as their prerogative. On 23 August, at the suggestion of the Japanese consul-general (who thought the move would help a trembling stock market), the senior consul warned the commanders on both sides to keep the war away from the river and the rail lines leading into the city.[12] When the movements of Chinese warships on the Huangpu conjured up visions of a naval battle that would leave the foreign settlements a smoldering ruin, the British, Japanese, French, and American ministers warned Peking on 30 August that, if the Chinese would not keep the river neutral, they would send in their own warships.[13] They did not tell the Chinese that they had to restrain the enthusiasm of the commanders, who wanted to seize the old forts at Wusong that guarded the mouth of the Huangpu and raise their flags above them to warn the Chinese away. Precisely how the foreigners could keep fighting away from the river is not clear. In a marvelously ambiguous series of messages that left the American chargé E. T. Bell scratching his head in perplexity, Washington reminded him that, although he must use his men of war only to protect American lives and property, they might also have to cooperate with other navies in using "all proper means" to keep the Huangpu open.[14] The equivocation is worth noting simply because it was typical of the American approach to such questions in later years. It is small wonder that the United States from time to time stood accused of privately benefiting from the risks run by others while publicly trying to keep its own hands clean.

The great naval battle never took place, partly because the two Chinese admirals backed down and partly because several Zhejiang ships went over to the other side. Meanwhile, the gray and black warships of the naval powers began steaming up the Huangpu to moor off the Bund: *Durban* and *Despatch* flying the White Ensign, a squadron of destroyers wearing the Stars and Stripes, *Libia* under the arms of the House of Savoy, and *Jules Ferry* and *Colmar* with the French tricolor at the masthead. When fighting erupted on 3 September, Contre-amiral Frochot landed his marines in the French Concession, and on 9 September when a state of emergency was declared in both settlements at dawn, the Shanghai Volunteer Corps was mobilized and sixteen hundred sailors came ashore. That afternoon, as black clouds piled up overhead and a violent thunderstorm drenched the city with five and a half inches of rain, the combined force took up stations along a sixteen-mile cordon that included not only the International Settlement itself, but also some of the roads where foreigners lived beyond the boundaries.[15]

It took several weeks for the fighting to reach Shanghai. From Fujian province, Sun Chuanfang drove north into Zhejiang, and Lu Yongxiang, betrayed by one of his commanders, abandoned Hangzhou and fled to Shanghai. Sun continued his advance, and when Lu's defensive lines cracked, the way to Shanghai lay open. On 13 October, Lu and his defense commissioner, He Fenglin, deserting their soldiers, crept aboard the *Shanghai Maru* under cover of darkness and sailed in secret for Nagasaki.[16] A day later, a detachment of Hubei troops commanded by Zhang Yunming in loose alliance with Sun Chuanfang reached Shanghai's North Station, just beyond the Settlement boundary, and that afternoon occupied the arsenal and the Longhua military headquarters south of the city.

The war was much more serious and more bitter than anyone had expected. Though there was never any real danger of an attack on the settlements, there was always the danger of fighting on their borders, of arson and looting in Zhabei to the north or Nanshi to the south, of trouble from the military press gangs that were rounding up coolies to serve as laborers for the armies. Nightfall would bring some fifteen thousand people over from Zhabei to sleep in the streets of the Settlement, returning to Chinese territory at daybreak. Only when Defense Commissioner He Fenglin cracked down on the press gangs did things get better.[17] Every day some five to seven thousand refugees poured into the settlements, so that by the end of September there were as many as half a million in the city, some seventy or eighty thousand in the International Settlement alone. Their numbers strained the capacity of the centers hastily thrown up to care for them, and though the disruption of the transportation lines slowed their flow into the city, it also threatened the supply of food.[18]

Above all, there was the problem of the defeated armies. The precipitous flight of Lu and He on 13 October left some thirty thousand troops without leaders in Shanghai and the surrounding countryside. In Zhabei, seven to eight thousand Zhejiang men, tired, dirty, and hungry, took over the North Station, camping out in the waiting rooms and in the railway cars that stood abandoned in the yards. Others spread out along nearby Markham Road, which divided Zhabei from the Settlement, digging trenches to protect themselves. There, a former warlord and politician who was living in the Settlement—Xu Shuzheng, or "Little Xu" as the foreigners called him—sought to mobilize them, to use them as his own military force and perhaps to extract protection from the Zhabei merchants.[19] That was too much for the Municipal Council and the consuls; they had already ordered Xu out of the Settlement back in 1921 as a troublemaker, and he remained *persona non grata*. At the urging of John Pratt, the acting British consul-general, the police nabbed him on the afternoon of the 15th, when he crossed over from Zhabei into the Settlement driving in a car with the ganglord Du Yuesheng. The consuls charged him with violating the neutrality of the Settlement and put him on a ship bound for Hongkong and ultimately to Europe to keep him out of trouble.[20] Under the circumstances, no one seriously questioned the legality of the extraordinary move, which saw a Chinese deported by foreigners from his own country.

Nonetheless, the city remained very tense for several days. Some of the consuls wanted to occupy the North Station, and 140 Chinese business groups, guilds, and civic associations in Zhabei asked the Municipal Council and the consuls to extend the foreign defense lines around Zhabei. The Chinese Chamber of Commerce dipped into its own pockets to feed the deserted troops and keep them from looting. It also negotiated an agreement on 18 October with Qi Xieyuan, the Jiangsu commander, allowing the abandoned soldiers to enlist under the generals who had defeated them, thus (as a local paper pointed out) providing Sun Chuanfang, "who has hitherto had no troops of his own worth mentioning, . . . with a brand new army of some one else's manufacture." The North Station was cleared out and cleaned up, and the trains started running again. For the time being, at least, the emergency was over, and Consul-General Pratt had high praise for the fundamental decency of both the Chinese soldiers and police who kept order among themselves after the sudden flight of their leaders.[21]

Shortly after the fighting began in September, the Peking government had stripped Lu Yongxiang and He Fenglin of their titles, denounced them as rebels, and ordered the Jiangsu authorities to suppress them. With that act, what had been a local campaign became part of a wider war embracing most of northern and eastern China. From Manchuria, the Old Marshal Zhang Zuolin and his Fengtian army (Fengtian was the old name of Liaoning, a Manchurian province) had begun an advance on Peking. Wu Peifu, appointed by Peking as commander in chief of its forces, sent his ally Feng Yuxiang (the so-called "Christian warlord" and a great favorite of Protestant missionaries) into action against Zhang Zuolin. Feng advanced rapidly at first. Then, in a stunning change of sides (perhaps encouraged by a massive Japanese bribe), the Christian warlord seized Peking on 24 October 1924, imprisoned the president, joined forces with Zhang Zuolin, and called for peace. Desperately trying to rally his forces, Wu was defeated, stripped of his titles, and ordered to a new position in Kokonor, a thousand miles off in the deserts of the northwest. He chose retirement instead, leaving his treacherous former subordinate dividing the control of the north in an uneasy alliance with Zhang Zuolin. Feng then summoned the old warlord Duan Qirui from retirement, and in November he put together a new administration in Peking.

For the moment the fighting was over, as winter settled over north China, and life in Shanghai began to return to normal. Yet the city's position remained more uncertain than ever. The victorious Qi Xieyuan had brought Shanghai into the Jiangsu camp. But because of Feng's coup, his party had lost its hold on Peking. His two local allies—Sun Chuanfang, now the military governor of Zhejiang, and Zhang Yunming, whom he had named defense commissioner of Shanghai—were out for themselves, simply waiting for a chance to enlarge their power. Thus, as the American consul-general in Nanking wrote in early December, Qi was weaker for his own victory.[22] He had won the autumn's campaigns; but the larger war was not yet over.

On 12 December, the new rulers in Peking dismissed Qi as military governor of Jiangsu, leaving Zhang Yunming in control of Shanghai from his headquarters at the Longhua Arsenal. Qi now moved into the safety of the Settlement (he had a house on Love Lane) and promptly began intriguing with Sun Chuanfang for a return to power.[23] On the night of 10 January 1925, he left his base in the Settlement, driving into Zhabei to an enthusiastic reception by his old troops. That night they marched south along the railway loop from the North Station to Longhua, and at four the next morning attacked Zhang Yunming's army near Siccawei, just southwest of the French Concession. Zhang's troops fell back toward the French lines, hurriedly manned by police and volunteers. At one point, the defenses gave, and several hundred armed men poured into the Concession, but the line was restored before there was any trouble. Within a few days, Qi and Sun had triumphed, although not before a good deal of destruction and looting had taken place in Nanshi and the western suburbs, not before the Siccawei cathedral had been damaged, and not before several shells had landed in the compound of the new Shanghai American School. Zhang Yunming fled to the French Concession, while ten thousand of his defeated troops streamed into the foreign settlements, allowing themselves to be disarmed and interned.

The destruction caused by this latest round of fighting was substantial, and one Western paper estimated that the entire country around Shanghai for twenty or thirty miles had been devastated and millions of people made homeless.[24] "Perhaps the suburbs of Shanghai have never seen such ruthless looting as has taken place since the 11th," wrote Edwin Cunningham, the American consul-general. "Shops were pillaged; residences were robbed of all their belongings; gangs of soldiers went from shop to shop, selecting articles of gold and silver after smashing in the doors, breaking the windows, and taking everything that they could lay their hands on. In the miles of stores in Nantao and the Chinese city to the west of the Settlement, not a shop was voluntarily open on the 11th or 12th." More refugees than ever poured into the settlements, and the missionaries at Siccawei alone took in seven thousand. "They certainly are a pitiful sight," wrote an American woman living in the French Concession. "There are usually three or four youngsters in each family, with a roll or two of bedding, and a few odds and ends of clothes and furniture. A few of them were wounded from stray bullets, and what is to become of them I can't see." [25] The *Écho de Chine* railed at the failure of the authorities to take adequate steps for the defense of the Concession ("A couple of well-placed shells would do more good for security than the barbed wire barricades . . ."), and on 13 January, the Volunteers were again called out. Two days later, the sailors and marines again came ashore.[26]

Meanwhile, Lu Yongxiang, the loser in the autumn war, had returned from Japan, having been appointed pacification commissioner of Jiangsu and Anhui by the new government in Peking. Thus, as the American minister pointed out, Shanghai's circumstances were now the exact reverse of the previous September. Then, Qi Xieyuan, in Nanking, had wanted to reclaim Shanghai from Lu Yongxiang, who was holding it for Zhejiang; now, Lu Yongxiang was in Nanking, wanting to expel Qi Xieyuan and his Zhejiang ally from Shanghai.[27]

Qi now pushed his luck too hard, however, by following his coup at Shanghai with a drive up the Yangtze. Though Suzhou fell peacefully on 16 January, his forces suffered two quick defeats at Wuxi and Zhenjiang and had to retreat in disorder to Shanghai. In pursuit came a new element in Shanghai's affairs. An army from Shandong province, loosely allied with Zhang Zuolin, had moved down from the north. This army was unusual for two reasons: first, because it included some White Russian detachments ("soldiers of misfortune," some called them), and second because of its commander, Zhang Zongchang, the "Dog Meat General" (the name came from his predilection for a gambling game called "throwing dog meat"). A huge man, six and a half-feet tall, the son of a witch and a trumpeter who had fought his way from banditry to military prominence on the Manchurian frontier, he exhibited a violence and brutality unusual even in that bloody age. (He had, one of his critics wrote, "the physique of an elephant, the brain of a pig, and the temperament of a tiger.")[28]

By early February, Zhang had set up his headquarters at the North Station. Sun Chuanfang, always a discreet man, agreed to pull his armies back to Hangzhou if Zhang would withdraw his own forces back beyond Kunshan [Quinsan], thirty-six miles northwest of the city.[29] The compromise seemed to promise at least the partial demilitarization of Shanghai. On 9 February, the Chinese Chamber of Commerce gave a dinner for both Chinese and foreign authorities, and there, in front of this large audience, military representatives on both sides pledged an end to the fighting and promised that Shanghai would now enjoy an unparalleled reign of peace and prosperity.[30]

The local war was thus brought to an end. Foreign Shanghai was saved, partly because of the defensive measures taken by the two municipal councils and the naval commanders, but mostly because there was no reason for the contending generals to look for trouble with the settlements. Nor were the foreigners alone in wanting to keep the peace in Shanghai. Organizations like the Chinese Chamber of Commerce had little stake in the war, and they too wanted to keep Shanghai neutral. Even before the campaigning began in September 1924, they had appealed to the foreign chambers to use their influence to avoid hostilities, a move that came to nothing. On 3 September, they proposed to both sides the creation of a neutral zone fifteen miles around Shanghai, a hopelessly unrealistic suggestion given the presence of the arsenal and the economic benefits that the ruler of Shanghai would enjoy.[31]

On 11 October, representatives of various civic and business groups in Zhabei had asked the Municipal Council to allow the Chinese company of the Shanghai Volunteer Corps to cooperate with their own volunteers. Two days later, the Zhabei municipal authorities asked the Municipal Council and the consuls to extend the foreign naval cordon around their district (a similar step had been taken in the fighting of 1913.)[32] Most startling was the proposal of 23 September made by an emissary from a number of Chinese business groups that the foreign defense lines take in not only Zhabei, but Nanshi and Jessfield as well, thus enclosing most of the city west of the Huangpu. In return, he continued, his committee would support the efforts of the Municipal Council to extend the boundaries of the Settlement to include those districts. The proposal was a tempting one. For years both the Council and several of the consuls, including Barton and Cunningham, had wanted to enlarge the Settlement, giving it room to grow and at last putting to rest the vexed questions that arose from the external roads. But the consuls agreed that they could do nothing unless they had a request in writing, and it proved impossible to get that.[33] Nor did anything come of another request by the Federation of Street Unions several months later asking that the foreign diplomats in Peking expel Qi Xieyuan from Shanghai.[34]

In 1924, foreign Shanghai relied on warnings to the Chinese and on its own police, volunteers, and landing parties to keep peace in the concessions. The China Association—a group representing the major British firms in the country—blamed the troubles on the hopelessly optimistic policies of the Washington Conference and the dithering of the Diplomatic Body in Peking. They wanted to use force to back up treaty rights.[35] When fighting broke out again in January 1925, their Shanghai branch proposed sending an international military force to guarantee Shanghai's neutrality. Though the consuls were unwilling to go that far, on 17 January they did ask the Diplomatic Body for a detachment to keep Chinese troops from coming within rifle shot of the settlements. The American minister in Peking smelled a rat; too many British and Americans in Shanghai had long wanted this sort of foreign intervention, and if troops did arrive, they would try to keep them there permanently. His military attaché, just back from Shanghai, thought the local foreign forces capable of keeping order, and Sir Ronald Macleay, the British minister, agreed that intervention would be justified only if there were a danger to foreign life.[36]

The episode is interesting not only because it raised the question of Shanghai's defense against outside troubles but also because it points up the increasingly important differences between foreign Shanghai, the

Peking legations, and their home governments toward that question. Calls from Shanghai for intervention of this sort were becoming increasingly frequent, and the appeals made by Chinese business groups for foreign protection seemed to prove that responsible Chinese—unlike greedy militarists and rabble-rousing leftist demagogues—were grateful for the foreign presence. The ministers in Peking and their home governments were unconvinced. "For my part," J. G. Schurman, the American minister, wrote home in early February, "I have a profound suspicion of any policy which involves intervention by an international military force in China. It is a survival of the imperialistic methods of the nineteenth century which is wholly out of harmony with the general spirit of this age, and also with the awakening nationalism of the Chinese people. While the British and some other foreign merchants in the treaty ports hark back to it on the slightest provocation, it is to be condemned both on grounds of principle and expediency."

Principle, because intervention would violate the spirit of the Washington accords; expediency, because the move would hurt America. If he had backed intervention, Schurman claimed, the other Western ministers would have gone along (a point, incidentally, contradicted by Macleay's report to Whitehall), leaving the field clear for Tokyo to step forward as China's champion. "This would have been another important step in the Japanese policy of undermining American-Chinese friendship, while at the same time it would have furnished an excellent opportunity of separating Japan from the 'imperialistic' nations of Europe and America." But he also warned that the problem of Shanghai's defense would not go away and that the powers must reach a policy on that question as soon as possible.[37] They did not; and in 1927, the city would face a far greater crisis.

"That the United States, a nation still in adolescence, with no past, no history, no tradition, falls for such *chinoiseries*, is natural," fumed the *Écho*, castigating the powers for their weakness, "but for old countries, like France or England, who have known China for centuries, who have considerable interests and a whole moral and financial heritage to preserve, for them to remain simple spectators of the work of destruction, content with one, two, twenty platonic protests, . . . that is simply incomprehensible."[38] In the end, nothing came of these proposals, foreign or Chinese, to neutralize Shanghai. The presence of the arsenal made Shanghai a military prize worth taking, and, even more, its enormous revenues made it an economic prize worth taking. "The Arsenal at Shanghai is a menace to the commercial port," wrote Cunningham on 20 October, and over and over again he called for its removal. "It has been the bone of contention for the present war and it will be for another if it is allowed to remain here. The revenues for the Chinese officials at this rich port are immense, and it will always be a coveted prize for politicians and militarists. Neither the troops, the Arsenal, nor the powder factory should be allowed to remain on the border of the Concession, where they can take refuge in future wars." [39] By early 1925, the consuls as well as the foreign and Chinese chambers of commerce all agreed that the arsenal should be moved. In February 1925, Sun Chuanfang and Zhang Zongchang agreed to allow the Chinese General Chamber of Commerce to take it over and use it for peaceful purposes. But it was not moved, and within the year it was at work again producing munitions. [40]

Though the arsenal might provide the instruments of war, access to the wealth to pay for them was no small consideration. As we have seen, not all Shanghai's revenues came from legitimate trade and taxes. Many Chinese referred to the struggle between Jiangsu and Zhejiang as a new opium war, fought for the enormous profits wrested from the drug trade. Just before He Fenglin fled to Japan in mid-October, reported Pratt, the price of opium dropped sharply, apparently because Ho dumped a thousand cases of the drug on the market. When Zhang Yunming took control of the Longhua military headquarters, Du Yuesheng immediately sought his protection for the traffic, and it was the prospect of huge bribes that made Zhang reluctant to give up Shanghai. "Even without opium," Pratt concluded of the smuggling network, "there would probably still be civil wars in China, but it seems certain that it is this vast criminal organization, controlling and even taking possession of the machinery of government, that constitutes the most serious menace today to the life of the Chinese people and to foreign trade and enterprise in China." [41]

The fighting, with its disruption of transportation networks, badly hurt foreign traders, leaving many trading firms insolvent and some near bankruptcy. Stocks of British textiles filled Shanghai's godowns, as dealers in the interior failed to take delivery, and importers of machinery suffered from the natural reluctance of Chinese capitalists to invest in new enterprises in a climate of political instability. [42] Yet, when the guns at last fell silent in January 1925, had anything really changed? After all the appalling suffering and bloodshed, after the autumn's heavy casualties, after the destruction and looting by the warlord armies, the old military governor of Zhejiang—Lu Yongxiang in 1924—lost control of Shanghai to a new pacification commissioner of Jiangsu—Lu Yongxiang in 1925. What clearer proof, foreigners asked themselves, of the comic opera nature of Chinese politics and Chinese war? They had no reason to expect the prosperous future promised by the generals and the speechmakers who celebrated the shaky peace of February 1925. The tentative suggestions made by various Chinese groups that foreign troops take parts of the Chinese city under their wing simply proved to foreign Shanghai that the Chinese were not yet fit to determine their own future, that the foreign presence in China remained a beneficial one. "With a view to establishing confidence," wrote a sarcastic British observer shortly after the fighting broke out, "General Lu Yung-hsiang on the 20th September issued invitations to all the leading Chinese merchants and gentry to come to attend a tea party at his Headquarters at Longhua on Sunday 21st. However, on receipt of the invitations all the recipients packed up their chairs, spittoons, concubines, and other valuables, and fled to the Settlement." He also noted, though, the ferocity of the battles and the high rate of casualties: "There is no doubt that this is a new era in Chinese fighting." [43] Or, as J. B. Powell put it in the *China Weekly Review*, "China is merely the trysting ground for the prowess of a handful of selfish militarists at the head of a rabble who find soldiering with its looting and lawlessness a pleasanter occupation than any other. It is not a war for freedom, nor a war to end wars in China, nor a war for anything but for the personal aggrandizement of whichever faction is victorious: and China itself at home and abroad, must emerge from the conflict in a more pitiful state of helplessness than heretofore." [44]

War was no comic opera for those who had to fight it, and even less so for those caught up as bystanders. "The most likely predictions have turned out to be wrong," wrote the French consul-general of the fighting early in October 1924. "The whole business should have lasted a week; but it has now gone on a month. It should have been a comedy whose actors would bring no passion to their roles; instead it has become a tragedy of the most violent and bloody sort, and both Lu's soldiers and those of Qi have fought tooth and nail." He cited the aircraft that nobody had expected to be used but that were making daily bombing runs against both sides. [45] Both armies suffered terribly in the fighting of early October, and one can only speculate about the damage done to peasant villages, about the innocent victims of the war. The lucky ones were the quarter of a million refugees who had crowded into the foreign settlements by early 1925.

In late 1924 it was still possible for foreign Shanghai to pretend that little had changed. But the revulsion against warlordism that grew out of campaigns such as these was an important element in the making of the Chinese revolution of the 1920s. Rightly or wrongly, many Chinese were becoming convinced that foreign imperialism was in league with warlordism and that the two were exploiting China's misery for their own profit. For such people, Sun Yat-sen's rebel government in Canton seemed to offer the brightest hope for China's future, and they welcomed his announcement on 10 November that he was going north to discuss with the Peking clique a grand unification of China. In foreign Shanghai, however, the opinion about Sun was quite different. When it was learned that the leader of Chinese radicalism would pass through Shanghai on his way, the *North China Daily News* saw red. "Shanghai does not want Dr. Sun Yat-sen," it wrote on 7 November. "It has no business to admit him, and . . . it is to be hoped that the authorities will prevent him landing here. . . . All his life, all his influence, all his energies are devoted to aims which keep China in turmoil, and it is utterly undesirable and improper that he should be allowed to prosecute those aims here. . . . If Dr. Sun must plot, let him go and do so elsewhere."[46]

The *China Weekly Review* was almost as vituperative, particularly after the Canton authorities arrested J. B. Powell's Chinese correspondent in that city.[47] Many treaty port foreigners thought that Sun, for all his Anglo-American education and for all his Westernism, was little better than a Bolshevik, and that his Protestant Christianity, which so endeared him to the missionaries, was nothing more than a false front to conceal his real inclinations. "I should not trust Sun a yard," wrote Sir William Tyrrell in the Foreign Office. "The worst day's work we did was to save him twenty-four years ago from the clutches of the Chinese minister who had him kidnapped" (a reference to the famous episode when Sun was impris-oned in the Chinese legation in London until public pressure forced his release).[48]

Sun's bombastic promises that he would lead a great northern expedi-tion to unify the country might have made him a figure of fun had his base in Canton not also by now become the center for a large group of Chinese radicals and Soviet Bolsheviks. In January 1923, after a passionate court-ship by Russia, Sun had agreed to seek Soviet help for his cause. Willingly and unwillingly, the members of the tiny Chinese Communist Party were brought into line, convinced that history demanded a union between the party of the proletariat and the "bourgeois nationalists," as Moscow re-ferred to Sun's party (Chen Duxiu, the Chinese Communist leader, was only one of several party members who did not trust the Guomindang). In the summer of 1923, the first united front was born, Nationalists and Communists joining one another in a common effort directed against im-perialism (the foreigners) and feudalism (the warlords and their landlord supporters).

To help the cause, a Soviet mission arrived in Canton in the autumn of 1923. At its head was Michael Borodin, a former student at Valparaiso University in Indiana and married to a Latvian emigrée. Borodin was a veteran of labor organizing in Russia, Mexico, Scotland, and Chicago. By all odds the most colorful and magnetic foreigner in China during these years, he brought with him a team of military and political advisers who were to help the Guomindang do what it appeared to be unable to do for itself (Western imperialists were not the only ones who believed that

Chinese needed foreign leaders). In January 1924, the Guomindang was reorganized along Leninist lines, giving the party a disciplined tightness it had earlier lacked, and Sun Yat-sen, the leader of the party, stood at its head. It took as its ideology, however, not the ideas of communism, but rather Sun's own Three Principles of the People—Nationalism, Democracy, and People's Livelihood—first developed before the revolution of 1911 but now given a much more leftist and anti-imperialist cast. The Guomindang's first congress in January 1924 ratified these changes and put Chiang Kai-shek, just returned from a visit to the Soviet Union, in charge of building a school to train the future leaders of the revolutionary army. The Whampoa Military Academy, which grew out of these plans, was intended to give the Party its own army so that it need no longer depend on the untrustworthy warlord allies with whom Sun had been forced to work earlier. It opened its doors to its first class of five hundred cadets in May 1924. Chiang Kai-shek was its commandant, and a few months later the communist Zhou Enlai, just back from Paris, became deputy head of the academy's Political Department.

Sun's new power within the Guomindang and the nascent military force under his control did much to increase his stature within China. Nonetheless, his announcement in September 1924 that he would join Zhang Zuolin and Duan Qirui against Wu Peifu was little more than a sideshow in the autumn war. More important in terms of the world's view of Sun was the contest that October between his forces and a conservative group called the Canton Merchant Volunteers. Although its immediate cause was a dispute over a shipment of arms to the Volunteers (secretly underwritten, it turned out, by the Hongkong and Shanghai Bank), the clash reflected a broader disillusionment and distrust by the propertied classes with the increasing radicalism of Sun's movement. His decision on 15 October to suppress the Volunteers led to a battle in which many were killed and much of Canton's commercial section burned. The outcry that followed damaged Sun politically, even as his victory strengthened his government militarily.[49]

Public outrage, however, did not keep him from going to Shanghai (a horrified Whitehall quickly vetoed the British commander-in-chief's offer to send a warship to intercept him, and the British minister vetoed a consular suggestion to keep him out of the Settlement).[50] He arrived on 17 November with an entourage of eighteen people, including his wife Song Qingling (who would die years later an honored leader of the People's Republic) and Wang Jingwei (who would die years later as a collaborator with Japan). Four hundred of his admirers greeted him, reported the French police, who also noted the radical leaflets calling for an open struggle against the foreign concessions—a tactic, they thought, designed to widen the breach between Sun and the West and drive him into Russian arms.[51] He met the Jiangsu and Fengtian leaders at his house in the rue Molière, but it was his interview with Japanese reporters that caught the attention of foreign Shanghai. "I want to tell the foreigners this," he cried, denouncing those who sought to bar him from the city. "Shanghai is China—foreigners are guests here, we are the hosts, and if this fact is not realized, we shall have to take drastic measures. The concessions must be returned; the Chinese are determined on this point."

"This," wrote the shocked American consul-general, "is probably the most defiant message that has ever been uttered by any Chinese entitled to be heard on any public occasion. . . . It is likely to ignite whatever smoldering embers there may be of anti-foreign feeling. Dr. Sun has maintained himself before the public in China since the Revolution more continuously than any other public man. He has done, so far as can be discovered, no constructive work but his activities have been destructive in every case."[52] Sun did not stay long and was gone on the twenty-third (his suppression of the Merchant Volunteers had turned many in the Cantonese community against him). To newspapermen at Kobe he praised Russia and bitterly criticized the West. He suggested the possibility of a Sino-Russian-Indian combination against Western oppression and called (as he had earlier) for Japan, China's younger brother, to help China in a great pan-Asian alliance against imperialism. (There was also a rumor that he had offered Japan an opium monopoly in China.)[53]

Perhaps foreign Shanghai, preparing for Christmas and concerned as it was with the more immediate threat from the warlords, could not worry long over Sun's words, which, as the press said, "reveal him simply as an agent of the Bolsheviks in China, whose business it is to stir up animus against other powers in China by fair means or foul."[54] Yet, though he had no more than a few months to live, Sun's statement at Kobe suggested the eventual constellation of forces that one day would drive Western imperialism from East Asia. Over the next three decades, as effectively as if they had been allies, first the Japanese and then the Communists would succeed in finally ending the position of Western privilege in China.

That lay in the future though. Meanwhile, on 16 December 1924, Yu Xiaqing, the president of the Chinese Chamber of Commerce, presented a cup to the Municipal Council as a gesture of gratitude for the protection afforded by the Volunteer Corps. His speech of thanks, however, reminded the foreigners—far more gently than Sun Yat-sen had—where they stood. "Since the Chinese residents here constitute the majority of the population, and since the foreign nationals in our midst are but guests on Chinese soil," he said, "the success of the emergency measures should mean and does mean more to us than to our foreign neighbors." Colonel W. F. L.

Gordon, the British commander of the Volunteers, was quick to answer: "You can rest assured that should circumstances arise where the safety of the Settlement and its neighborhood is again threatened that the Volunteer Corps will once more prove a very present help in time of trouble. What Shanghai has, Shanghai holds." "A passage of arms in the Council room," noted a local journalist, suggesting that though the gauntlet dropped by Yu had been very neatly picked up by Colonel Gordon, it might have been better to leave the challenge unanswered.[55] It was, as events would soon show, a prescient comment.

China's Bastille
May Thirtieth and Its Background

On the afternoon of Saturday, 30 May 1925, a unit of the Shanghai Municipal Police, under the command of a British officer, opened fire on a crowd of demonstrators on the Nanking Road. In a country torn apart by violence, where even local military campaigns left thousands dead, the eleven men slain in Shanghai that day hardly counted. But it was foreign gunfire in the International Settlement, not Chinese fire on Chinese soil, that shot down the victims on Nanking Road, and that made all the difference. The tragedy provoked a furious response that would affect virtually every facet of China's relations with the outside world, bringing an immediate focus to the still blurred sense of national feeling in the country. Suddenly, the nationalist movement had martyrs in the dead of Nanking Road, had a cause in the uprooting of a murderous imperialism, and had a visible enemy in the British and Japanese whom it held responsible. What at first seemed to many foreigners to be a mere incident—a schoolboy demonstration with an unfortunate (but necessary) bloody ending—that could be settled by the proper combination of diplomacy and force, became instead a movement that spread rapidly from Shanghai through much of the country. In the words of one historian, it was an emotional outburst that would only be matched by the Cultural Revolution forty years later.[1] Before it was over, it threatened to overturn the whole little world that encompassed the foreign position in China. Today the Communists look on the May Thirtieth Movement as the start of the first Chinese revolutionary civil war, a war that sought not only China's unification under a modern political system but also the recovery of her sovereign rights after eighty years of subordination under the weight of unequal treaties.

It is easy today to see and understand the events that led to May Thirtieth, and it is easy to criticize those who were blind to them at the time. We know that May Thirtieth marks a crucial juncture in China's modern consciousness, in the conflict between an emergent nationalism and the old structure of foreign power in China. Of course, we know how the story came out; at the time, most foreigners could see little more than the endless round of wars, like the one through which Shanghai had just passed. They congratulated themselves for keeping their city immune from the dangers of Chinese politics and Chinese militarism, observing that in times of crisis, tens of thousands of ordinary Chinese looked to the settlements for safety and support.

Not that foreigners were blind to the changes that were taking place. Sun Yat-sen's November visit was a reminder of the presence of radical Canton with its cadre of Russian advisers. That Christmas brought a new outburst of anti-Christian demonstrations and propaganda, and though most missionaries shrugged it off, others remembered 1900 and shuddered at the prospect of old Boxerism joined to new Bolshevism. Most foreigners agreed that the Chinese could never become Communist by themselves (they are "hopelessly individualist," with a long democratic tradition, wrote the American minister),[2] but they worried that Borodin and his colleagues might play on an ingrained xenophobia to bring China under Soviet control. "All young Chinese intellectuals dream only of a new Boxerism, *à la sauce bolsheviste*," wrote the *Écho*, "and in a few years we will have thousands of minds *malades à la Sun Yat-sen* to terrorize the Chinese and the peaceful foreigners who only want to go calmly about their work."[3]

Sun's northern trip did nothing to end China's civil strife. Already ill when he arrived in the capital, on 12 March 1925, he lay dead of cancer in the hospital of the Peking Union Medical College, leaving an uncertain mandate to be fought over by those claiming to succeed him. Meanwhile, in February Chiang Kai-shek had led his new Whampoa-trained army, accompanied by its Soviet advisers, on its first campaign against Chen Jiongming, the warlord who still controlled much of Guangdong province. Though Chiang's troops fought well, politics ended their drive when they had to turn back to save Canton from falling into the hands of a rival coalition of generals. In a climactic battle that lasted from 6 to 12 June, Chiang's army subdued the city, bringing it more firmly than ever under Guomindang control. On 1 July, a new National Government was proclaimed in Canton, challenging Peking's claim to national leadership. Yet even as they chanted their slogans of unity, even as they invoked the memory of their lost leader, the Nationalists wrangled among themselves and with their Communist allies for control of that memory and of the revolution that must shape China's future.

Sun's November visit and the welcome given him by Shanghai radicals may be one reason why, on the afternoon of 9 December 1924, a detachment of British and Indian policemen carried out a raid on the premises of Shanghai University on Seymour Road in the Settlement's Western District. The institution was a new one, founded in 1922 as one of the first fruits of Guomindang cooperation with the Communists. The acting head, Shao Lizi, now charged before the Mixed Court with violating the Settlement's publication regulations, was himself a veteran Guomindang revolutionary and former Communist organizer. By 1924, Shanghai University had become the most important training ground for young Communists in the city. Its faculty included several who were already becoming known as radical activists, thinkers, and writers. Qu Qiubai, back from the Soviet Union and combining a career in literary criticism with labor organization, Shen Yanbing, who under his pen name Mao Dun was one of the leaders in the postwar flowering of Chinese literature, and Deng Zhongxia, a labor organizer and labor historian, all at one time or another taught there.[4] Though the police failed to uncover the editorial offices of the Communist party's influential *Xiangdao Zhoubao* [Guide Weekly], they did seize a good many books and journals from the university library, including copies of the *Xiangdao* and the *Xin Qingnian* [New Youth], a magazine that had been one of the heralds of the new culture movement and was now under Communist control.[5]

The raid itself seemed to be of little importance, and the charges against Shao were dropped because—according to John Pratt—the Council badly bungled its case.[6] Shanghai University was one of a handful of institutions that the Municipal Police suspected (quite rightly) of being nurseries of radicalism. The Shanghai College of Law [*Fazheng Daxue*] on the rue Auguste Boppe in Frenchtown was another. Founded about 1922 by the Guomindang leftist and St. John's graduate Xu Qian [George Hsu], who had become an Episcopalian when his prayers for Yuan Shikai's death were answered, its faculty included several other Johanneans as well as a recent graduate of Columbia.[7] The existence of such institutions here and the availability of journals like the *Xiangdao* and the *Xin Qingnian* showed that the concessions could be havens not only for defeated warlords and discredited politicians but also for Chinese revolutionaries. Though the authorities had largely left them alone as long as they did not actively attack the structure of foreign power in Shanghai, perhaps the police now believed that the *Xiangdao* had overstepped the bounds. Certainly it had become vituperative in its assaults on imperialism, by which it meant virtually all foreign activity in China apart from that of the Soviet Union. It accused the powers of supporting the warlords to keep China weak and divided, denounced the foreign press for its opposition to Sun Yat-sen, and accused the Municipal Council of trying to use the autumn war to achieve its dream of a "Greater Shanghai" and ultimately to "concessionize" [*zujiehua*] all China.[8]

Just as alarming to the Settlement was the wave of strikes in Japanese textile mills that began on 9 February 1925. That day, workers walked out of the Naigai Wata Kaisha No. 5 mill in Xiaoshadu to protest the firing of forty of their number who had allegedly tampered with the mill's machinery. The strike broke a period of some two years of labor dormancy in the city. As it spread to other Japanese mills, the rhetoric of its leaders took on a more stridently radical and anti-imperialist tone. Within two weeks, over thirty thousand workers in twenty-two Japanese mills had gone out. Laborers mauled several Japanese supervisors at the Toyoda Mill on Jessfield Road on the fifteenth, and one of the victims died two weeks later. The Japanese demanded action, but since most of the mills affected were in Chinese territory, the Municipal Police could do little except complain that the Chinese police stood idly by while the strike organizers went about their business.[9] Only when disorder spilled over into the Settlement on the seventeenth did they arrest several demonstrators, including Deng Zhongxia. Then, on the twenty-first, the Municipal Police raided the headquarters of the Guomindang daily paper *Minguo Ribao* [National Daily News]. Its editor was Shao Lizi of Shanghai University.[10]

The strikes were fed both by specific grievances and by the generally appalling conditions under which Shanghai's laborers worked. Though the state of the foreign mills was no worse, and probably better, than that of the Chinese enterprises, stories of the brutality of Japanese foremen and managers made them an obvious target and gave the strikes a nationalist undercurrent. Both the foreign press at the time and historians in China since have given the Communists credit for starting and guiding the strikes.[11] The American consul-general may have been closer to the mark when he reported that they came in only after the movement had begun, though he also added that the Soviet embassy in Peking was sending Shanghai University $3,000 a month to help the movement.[12] The strikes reflected a new rise of activism by the Chinese labor movement, and Communist and Guomindang leftists, quick to see the possibilities here, founded the West Shanghai Worker's Club in late 1924 to organize and educate the workers. Moved from the Settlement to Zhabei to escape harassment by the Municipal Police, the club, under Communists like Liu Hua—a student at Shanghai University—Li Lisan, Deng Zhongxia, and others, became the headquarters of the strike movement and the center from which later union activity would grow. The strikers also won the sympathy of other sectors of Chinese society. Students, particularly those from Shanghai University, were active as fund raisers and organizers, and efforts at mediation (a mediation that began, said the Municipal Police, only after the strike had been broken!) by merchant organizations such as the General Chamber of Commerce, helped prevent the defeat of the strikers.[13] Though they had made few economic gains by the time they returned on 2 March, both the workers and their Communist organizers learned much from the episode. In particular, in a period of sometimes uneasy cooperation with the Guomindang, they had seen how it was possible to use the propaganda of the united front to win for labor a support that went considerably beyond working class circles. There were other strikes in other cities that spring, and in May the second National Labor Congress gathered in Canton where it established a new All-China Federation of Labor to build on the new activism.[14]

The Municipal Council had other matters on its mind. In February, the commissioner of public works prepared a grandiose plan to extend the Settlement, bringing within its boundaries not only most of the external roads but also much of the Pudong waterfront and parts of Zhabei, which were important as centers both of industry and of radical labor organization.[15] More immediately, it wanted to pass four new bylaws that spring. One called for an increase in wharfage dues; another, for the licensing of Shanghai's stock exchanges; a third was intended to crack down on the radical press, insisting that all printed matter carry the names and addresses of the editor and publisher. A fourth called for the gradual regulation of child labor in the Settlement, following the recommendations of a commission of inquiry the Council had appointed a year earlier.[16] A special meeting of ratepayers called on 15 April to consider the laws failed to turn out a quorum. It was a bitter disappointment to the men and women who had worked hard for adoption of the child labor laws, and at the insistence of a group of foreign Shanghai's leaders (and against Stirling Fessenden's better judgment), the Council scheduled a second special meeting for 2 June.[17] Much of Chinese Shanghai opposed the licensing and fee proposals, and groups like the General Chamber of Commerce denied the Council's right to impose such measures. Though they did give qualified endorsement to the principle of child labor regulation, they also argued that the proposed measures were unnecessary since the Chinese government itself had passed perfectly adequate laws governing the matter (they did not point out that the laws were hardly ever enforced.)[18]

Thus, as spring came to Shanghai, not only were the workers and their student allies showing a growing radicalism, but propertied Chinese were increasingly resentful of the proposed bylaws, of the Municipal Council's continued expansion along the extra-Settlement roads, and of its continued deafness to their appeals for representation. On 15 May, after strikes broke out again in the Japanese mills, Japanese foremen opened fire, wounding six workers. When one of them, Gu Zhenghong, died two days later in the hospital, the movement found its first martyr. Strike leaders wanted to expand the protests, and Li Lisan, one of the leaders of the new All-China Federation of Labor, hoped to swell them into a general movement against Japanese imperialism. Over the next few days, a flurry of organizational activity took place. Students rallied to the strikers' cause, flooding the Settlement with propaganda pamphlets and collecting money for their support. The Municipal Police arrested several of them on 23 and 24 May, and their hearing at the Mixed Court was set for the thirtieth. Meanwhile, laborers gathered in Zhabei to commemorate Gu Zhenghong's death and to hear speeches by delegates returning from the Labor Congress in Canton.[19]

Although different groups in Chinese Shanghai might have different grievances, they all resented the Municipal Council's high-handed ways. The death of Gu Zhenghong, the arrest of the students, and the offensive bylaws gave Shanghai's radical leaders a splendid basis on which to build a true united front movement that would transcend class lines and bring different levels of society together in a common effort against imperialism. The Communists were quick to see their chance. On 27 May, Yun Daiying, an instructor at Shanghai University, called a meeting of students from various institutions, who decided that the time had come to link proletarian protests against Japanese treatment of mill workers with bourgeois protests against the new laws. The next day, an emergency session of the Central Committee confirmed a decision to send students into the International Settlement on 30 May to demonstrate further against Japanese brutality, against the bylaws, and against the trial of their fellows.[20]

That, in any case, is the Communist version of the story. Guomindang writers, not surprisingly, claim that their own party deserves the credit for the inception of the movement, and that its purpose was not to spread communism but rather to uphold Sun Yat-sen's Three Principles of the People.[21] Politics defeats the historian here; it is almost impossible to tell, from secondary sources at any rate, how well Guomindang and Communist leaders cooperated during this high point of the united front. Nor is it clear whether Chen Duxiu, the Communist party's general secretary, really opposed the decision to launch the movement, as party historians later alleged. Chen fell from power in 1927 in disgrace, and until his partial rehabilitation several years after Mao Zedong's death, it was customary for Communist historians to see him as little more than a cowardly opportunist. Nor should we overestimate the level of Communist strength and Communist control at this point: according to a recent estimate, there were no more than 295 members of the party in Shanghai on the eve of May Thirtieth.[22]

On Saturday, 30 May, the Mixed Court met to try the students arrested a few days earlier for breaching the peace. Most of foreign Shanghai was on holiday, for that weekend saw one of the spring meetings at the Kiang-wan Race Club beyond the Settlement. Later in the afternoon there was to be a cricket match at the Recreation Ground just beyond Thibet Road, and in the meantime, many had made their way thirty miles upriver for the spring regatta of the Rowing Club at the place foreigners called Hen-li. Though summer's full heat had not yet come, the day was a fine one, and by mid-morning crowds of shoppers, foreign and Chinese, were making their way from store to store along Foochow Road, Nanking Road, and the other streets of the Central District.

That morning the news came that police had killed several strikers in a Japanese mill at Qingdao a day earlier. The report further inflamed the students who were meeting to plan the day's demonstrations, forming themselves into small groups of five to seven to speak from street corners and to hand out leaflets. Outside the Mixed Court's grimy brick building on Chekiang Road, representatives from Fudan and Shanghai universities gathered, waiting for the hearings to end and assailing the Settlement authorities for their actions: Foreigners who shot down Chinese workers on Chinese soil went unpunished, while those who supported them were arrested. As the sun rose higher, more demonstrators flowed into the Settlement, placarding walls, telephone poles, and tramcars with their slogans: "Down with imperialism!" "Boycott Japanese goods!" "Oppose the printing regulations!" "Oppose the extension of the Settlement Roads!" "We are bearing the unbearable," read one of the pamphlets. "We, the united students of Shanghai's universities, together with the patriotic workers, will go into the Settlement this afternoon to speak out and awaken the Chinese citizenry of the city, calling on them to rise against imperialism! We are ready to sacrifice ourselves, to run any risks, face any dangers, in order to mount a popular anti-imperialist revolution throughout the country."[23]

At 11:35, Municipal Police headquarters telephoned a warning to its posts that crowds were gathering around the student propaganda teams in the streets. Forty minutes later, at 12:15, an all-stations alert ordered special precautions. Just about that time, Police Commissioner Kenneth McEuen decided to call it a day and, without telling any of his subordinates, left for lunch. For the next several hours, he would be both in and out of the Settlement, at the Shanghai Club, the Kiangwan Race Course, and the Recreation Ground, and although he would pass near Nanking Road that afternoon, he missed the trouble.[24]

On the north side of Nanking Road, about a block east of its busy intersection with Xizang [Thibet] Road and near the old Public Recreation Ground and the race course, a plaque now marks the spot where the

Louza [Laozha] Police Station once stood. "A bold and well proportioned building," a guidebook of the day called it, within which "permission to see the prisoners in their iron exercise cages may usually be obtained."[25] In 1905, Louza had been the scene of rioting against the Mixed Court, and when a crowd besieged the station, the police had opened fire, killing several people. The building stood back some fifty feet from Nanking Road itself, and a narrow alley, guarded by iron gates, led to its entrance. On 30 May 1925, the officer in command at Louza was Inspector E. W. Everson, a veteran of nineteen years in the Municipal Police. Under him was a detachment of about a hundred Chinese and Sikh constables. Near Louza, crowds now began to collect to listen to the student speechmakers, and at 1:55, Everson arrested three students who were assailing the Japanese, taking them off to the station to be charged. Fifteen others followed, for they had decided earlier that if any were arrested, all would insist on going to jail. At 2:45, an assault on an English policeman nearby in Thibet Road led to more arrests. Meanwhile, the crowds outside the station continued to grow. Everson, who had been trying to reach the absent McEuen by phone, finally got through to him at about 3:15 to report that some forty students had been arrested, but he thought he could cope. Five minutes earlier, McEuen himself had passed the station on his way to the Recreation Ground, and later he testified that he saw nothing unusual.

Then things began to turn ugly. When demonstrators forced their way into the station's charge room, Everson ordered them evicted, and he and his fellow policemen pushed them back out into the street. All traffic had now halted on Nanking and Thibet roads. The Sikh police, their black beards set off by the bright turbans they wore, charged the crowd, carrying off a student who started haranguing the mass from an impromptu podium at the Thibet Road intersection. Some fifteen hundred or two thousand people had quickly gathered outside the station, demanding the release of those held inside. Seventy or so actually broke in but, after a scuffle, were driven back out to Nanking Road. By now, Everson was seriously worried about the safety of his station and particularly about the large store of arms and ammunition kept there. Some witnesses remembered that the crowd tried to charge the station; others, that the demonstrators who had been driven out into the street were unable to disperse because of the press of the crowd. Whatever may be the truth, at 3:37 Everson shouted a warning in both English and Chinese that he would shoot if the crowd did not fall back. Ten seconds later, he ordered his men to open fire. Forty-four shots were heard, and within a few minutes, four people lay dead, seven more were dying, and twenty were wounded. A sudden silence followed the gunfire. Then, the crowd, stunned by what had happened, fled for shelter. Police patrols ran out of the station into the streets, and a few minutes later the ambulances came for the dead and wounded; within an hour, fire trucks arrived to wash the blood from the street. "I had to do it, or they would have got my station," a horrified Everson told McEuen when he arrived a few minutes later.[26] Only two of the dead were students; one of them was He Bingyi, a young Sichuanese, who a few months before had written a fiery article describing the police raid on Shanghai University.

Thus occurred what some called the May Thirtieth incident [*shijian*], others the tragedy [*can'an*], and still others the butchery or slaughter [*tusha*]. The terms—the same that would be used years later to describe the massacre of 4 June 1989 in Peking—reflected the different outlooks of different observers. Most of foreign Shanghai held the students responsible for what had happened and thought the police justified in shooting to prevent the even greater disaster that would have followed had the mob got its hands on the weapons in Louza. "It is to be deplored that there was a loss of life on May 30th," wrote Cunningham, "but it is inconceivable that this could have been prevented if the police were to make any pretense of preserving order. The mob had unquestionably overpowered the police and were attempting to take the arms of at least one when the order was given to fire."[27] Only later were the awkward questions asked, and they were never asked very loudly: Why had the police not sent for reinforcements? Why had they not fired first into the air? Why had they not shut the heavy gates that would have cut Louza off from the crowd? And where, during all these troubles, was Commissioner McEuen?

To Chinese of all persuasions and classes, the May Thirtieth affair was a brutal and unprovoked attack on a group of unarmed students who had no thought of harm, who had been crowded into a very small space, and few of whom could possibly have heard Everson's warning ten seconds before the firing broke out. The comparison with the massacre at Amritsar in 1919 was inevitable. There, an Indian crowd, unable to obey orders to disperse, had been fired on by troops commanded by a British officer; here, Chinese blood had been spilled by foreigners on Chinese soil. The Settlement authorities saw the Nanking Road affair as a regrettable incident that could be settled by discussion. If there were some faults on the foreign side, they could be remedied by (for instance) changes in police regulations. But to the Chinese temper of 1925 (and this was by no means true only of the radicals), what had happened in front of Louza station was no accident. It was rather the inevitable result of the whole structure of foreign presence and foreign privilege in China, and until these larger issues were resolved, there could be no question of considering the affair settled. These different perceptions of precisely what had happened on the afternoon of 30 May were to color all the negotiations that grew out of it.

"The material has long been accumulating and is now ready: the long-drawn-out misery and malaise of civil wars, the increasing disintegration of all responsible political forces, the increasing self-assertion, half fanatical, half dishonest—of the noisy 'educated' minority," wrote S. P. Waterlow of the Foreign Office in London two weeks later. Quite rightly, he realized that what had happened on the afternoon of 30 May could not be forgotten after a settlement had been patched up, that the response to the shooting would be of a size and kind never seen before. "Thus there is now a combination of forces making for a big outburst with a progressive rate of acceleration. This is what makes the present occasion different from previous moments of tension when we thought things looked bad."[28] Six months later, another diplomat drew a longer parallel. "May 30th will be one of the great dates of Far Eastern history, like the fall of the Bastille in Europe!"[29]

In spite of all the problems caused by the fighting a few months earlier, nothing in the Jiangsu-Zhejiang war had forced foreign Shanghai to take stock of itself, nothing suggested that it would presently face a new sort of challenge. Whatever immediate dangers they might bring to the city, battles between competing generals did not threaten the legal and quasi-legal foundations on which foreign Shanghai was built. Nor did they threaten the state of mind that took the position of foreign privilege for granted. Inspector Everson's order to open fire suddenly changed all that, suddenly changed the easy assumptions that for so long had undergirded the foreign position in China. Above all, it challenged the foreigners' conviction that their position in Shanghai rested not only on a legal basis but on a moral basis as well: moral because in a chaotic China the settlements were havens of order and efficiency, moral because foreigners did for China what she could not do for herself, moral because the foreign presence ultimately served China's good. On that sunny Saturday afternoon in late spring, such self-righteous arguments were suddenly called into question.

Much of foreign Shanghai was slow to understand this change; the Chinese leaders of the May 30th movement were not. The special commissioner for foreign affairs immediately protested to the senior consul, asking for the release of the jailed students (Commissioner McEuen tried to let some of them go, only to discover that none would leave unless all were released). Within hours of the shooting, groups of activists—student associations, labor unions, business groups like the Federation of Street Unions—were meeting throughout the city to plan their response. Local Guomindang leaders hastily gathered to plan a general strike; Du Yue-sheng, a power in the Shanghai labor world, was among those present. That evening an emergency meeting of Communist leaders decided to bring the whole city of Shanghai into the movement through a triple strike of workers, students, and merchants. On Li Lisan's initiative, the Communists also decided to form a Shanghai General Labor Union to help them control the movement, and no doubt also to bring pressure to bear on any merchants who might be reluctant to join the protest.[30]

The next day, the students were back out in the streets. Overnight, the weather had changed, and a chilly spring rain now fell over the city, but Nanking Road was once again thronged with demonstrators making speeches, handing out leaflets, enjoining the city's citizens to support the triple strike. This time the police were ready, their armored cars and machine gun posts guarding the main intersections, waiting outside the garish New World Theater on Thibet Road and in front of the forbidding bulk of Louza station. More people were arrested, and by late afternoon the crowd had left, many of them drifting north up Honan Road across Soochow Creek to the Temple of the Queen of Heaven [*Tianhou gong*], where the crucial meeting of the day was taking place.

Because of a quirk in the Land Regulations, the temple compound was one of a few enclaves in the International Settlement over which the Council and its police exercised no jurisdiction (the Customs House was another). There was thus nothing they could do about the gathering taking place there. The original temple is long gone, but the four-story brick building that once housed the offices of the Chinese General Chamber of Commerce still stands. The chamber represented the larger Chinese business houses and banks in Shanghai, and its thirty-five man executive committee now found itself split into two factions over the strike question. Since the chairman, Yu Xiaqing, was in Peking at the time, it fell to vice-chairman Fang Jiaobo to try to mediate. That afternoon, its representatives gathered in its meeting room on the upper floor, while in the rooms next door the Chinese Ratepayers' Association and the Federation of Street Unions, which represented the smaller merchants, held separate gatherings. Downstairs, a larger impromptu assembly gathered, led by the Communist Lin Jun of the Shanghai Students Union, which passed resolution after resolution calling for a strike. Under a sky darkened by a heavy rain, the crowd in the courtyard grew, drenched to the skin but refusing to allow anyone to leave the building before the chamber had done its patriotic duty. Finally, around six o'clock and only after a good deal of browbeating, Fang appeared on the balcony to announce to the cheering throng below that the chamber would join the movement and agree to a general shutdown of shops in the Settlement and to a demand that the Municipal Council withdraw the proposed bylaws and return the Mixed Court.[31] Later that evening, he sent word privately to the Municipal Council that his chamber had acted under coercion, a statement greeted with some skepticism by the police, which suspected him of radical lean-ings.[32] Nonetheless, the chamber's decision brought most of Shanghai's merchants into line, since by then the Federation of Street Unions had agreed to join the movement.

Thus on 1 June, the city awoke to find some fifty thousand students out of classes and most stores in Zhabei and the Settlement closed, though many continued to do business surreptitiously. Only on Nanking Road did some of the big stores such as Sincere and Wing On stay open, until public pressure forced them to put up their shutters. Many workers in the foreign mills, both Japanese and British, walked out that day, and over the next few days others joined them. Tramcar and bus operators left their jobs, as did domestic servants in the city's hotels and clubs; Chinese employ-ees of the foreign press struck, and eventually the Seamen's Union joined the strike as dockers, longshoremen, and the Chinese crews of British and Japanese ships quit working. Chinese electrical and power workers in the Settlement went out, as did the telephone company's employees, threaten-ing the Settlement's public services. By mid-month, some 150,000 workers were on strike, primarily from British and Japanese concerns, although some American and Chinese firms were also hit. Stores in the French Con-cession shut down on 5 June in a one-day sympathy demonstration, but otherwise continued to work.[33]

Convinced that any sign of weakness would lead to disaster, the Munici-pal Council responded swiftly. On 1 June it declared a state of emergency and mobilized the Shanghai Volunteer Corps for the third time in less than a year. Fessenden asked the consuls to land enough sailors and marines to guard the public utilities and to protect workers who wanted to stay on the job. Admiral C. B. McVay, commanding the American Yangtze Patrol, arrived on the fifth,[34] and by 6 June, some twenty-two foreign warships, including three British cruisers, were in the harbor. Over thirteen hundred men came ashore, and another 850 waited aboard their ships. American and Italian bluejackets guarded the power station and the waterworks where White Russians kept emergency services going, the Japanese pro-tected their enclave in Hongkew, and the British watched over the Race Club and once again moved beyond the boundaries of the Settlement to Jessfield Park.[35] On the surface, Shanghai looked much as it had several months earlier, as foreign sailors and marines joined Volunteers and police in patrolling the roads of the Settlement. But this time, the situation was radically different. An ominous sign of the change could be seen in Zha-bei, where Chinese police and merchant volunteers sided openly with the demonstrators. On 5 June, fully 30 percent of the Settlement's Chinese police went out on strike, and two days later, ninety-one constables were dismissed. Though most of the others were back in a few days, their action raised a question: How far could they be trusted as guardians to foreign Shanghai?[36]

The Chinese press, watching crowds battle with police and foreign sailors, decried the events of the next few days as a reign of terror. Four people died in a clash on Nanking Road on 1 June, and Japanese police killed two more the next day. That afternoon, the police used a fire hose to control a crowd in Thibet Road and eventually opened fire, killing another man. On 3 June, several more workers were killed in Yangtszepoo. According to the Municipal Police's reports, between 30 May and early June twenty-two people were killed and thirty-six wounded. The figures published by the new General Labor Union, however, were far higher, alleging that by 2 June over a hundred Chinese had died in what the Communists now called "the slaughterhouse of modern imperialism." Meanwhile, police and Volunteers raided several schools and colleges in the Settlement, including Shanghai University. Once again they seized masses of Communist propaganda, and the institution now fled Seymour Road to reestablish itself in Chinese Zhabei.[37]

From every side during these days came a flood of manifestos, appeals, demands, condemnations, in Chinese and English, from students, professors, merchants, tradesmen, workers, Christian and anti-Christian groups—some of long standing, some hastily organized. They filled the pages of the Chinese daily press, were placarded in the Chinese city as wall posters, or were distributed surreptitiously in the Settlement when the police were not looking. Impassioned cries to strike, to boycott Japanese and British goods, joined cartoons of fat British capitalists, morning-coated and top-hatted, ordering policemen to fire on defenseless workers, while sinister Japanese statesmen manipulated their warlord puppets. The behavior of the British authorities was reprehensible, not just by Chinese standards but by any modern, enlightened standards, cried the Guomindang. It "ought to make all Christians and Anglo-Saxon lovers of freedom and independence ashamed." The police were not to blame, said the Communists; the real murderers were the great foreign banks and business houses, and all imperialists, not just the British, must be held to account for the butchery taking place in Shanghai.[38]

The explosion of feeling in Shanghai was largely spontaneous, and the participants in the movement knew they were riding a wave of popular sympathy. "We did not make May 30th," Borodin is supposed to have said later. "It was made for us." The question facing the movement's organizers was how to channel popular emotions into a course that could be used not only to extract concessions from the foreigners but also to educate the participants on the realities of modern Chinese life, as the Guomindang and Communists saw them: The blood spilled in Nanking Road was no accident but the inevitable outcome of a foreign domination that restricted China's sovereignty and kept her weak and divided, the better to exploit her.

To meet that goal, the radicals had to make sure they would stay in control of the movement. The new General Labor Union, which opened on 31 May under Li Lisan, Liu Shaoqi, and Liu Hua, acted as an umbrella organization to win over the city's growing labor movement for the Communists. May Thirtieth was more than a workers' protest, however, and from the very beginning the Communists emphasized the need to bring other groups into the united front. On 4 June came the organization of a new group called the Federation of Workers, Merchants, and Students [*Gongshangxue lianhehui*], run by an executive committee representing the General Labor Union, the Federation of Street Unions, the All China Students Union, and the Shanghai Students Union. The General Chamber of Commerce, while giving a guarded blessing to the new body, refused to join, preferring to play an independent role as mediator. In fact, on 7 June (perhaps because Yu Xiaqing's house was bombed), it issued a statement urging an end to disruption while negotiations went on for a settlement of the crisis.[39]

The new Federation now became the central force behind the radical side of the movement, and Qu Qiubai, the literary critic turned Communist organizer, did not exaggerate when he said later that for the next two months it acted "almost as a local government."[40] The Federation was not, strictly speaking, a Communist body, and its diverse membership occasionally took a less radical stand than did the Communists. Yet it was an organ through which the Communists could shape the main outlines of the movement. Not only was the labor organizer Li Lisan one of its guiding spirits, but the General Labor Union, which was Communist controlled and which excluded non-Communist labor organizations from its membership, was its most important constituent body. Communists ran the All-China Students Union, the Shanghai Students Union was at the very least amenable to Communist direction, and the Federation's newspaper, the *Rexue ribao* or "Bloodshed Daily," was edited by Qu Qiubai himself.[41]

Thus, in less than a week after the shooting on Nanking Road, the Settlement found itself almost crippled by a widening general strike, and an organization with a strong Communist influence had been formed to fashion a movement whose interests and demands went far beyond those that had marked the Japanese mill strikes earlier that year. The Settlement was under a state of emergency, foreign sailors and marines had come ashore, and the Municipal Council, after virtually ignoring the first official Chinese protests, was now anxiously hoping to negotiate an end to the affair with leaders of the Chinese community. Stirling Fessenden agreed to accept the mediation of the Chinese General Chamber of Commerce, but nothing came of the move; Fessenden later blamed the Chinese community leaders for their timidity in dealing with foreigners. Meanwhile, the Municipal Council quietly spread the word that it would be better if the special ratepayers' meeting scheduled for 2 June to consider the controversial bylaws was not held. A distraught Mary Dingman, one of the American leaders in the fight for child labor reform, was herself now threatening to vote against that particular measure because of Chinese opposition. To everyone's relief, the meeting failed to turn out a quorum, thus again postponing any action.[42]

On 9 June, the Mixed Court began the trial of the students who had been arrested during the Nanking Road demonstrations. Despite warnings from Consul-General Barton and the police that too much leniency would be dangerous, the American legation urged J. E. Jacobs, the American consular assessor, to be as conciliatory as possible. None of the defendants were imprisoned or fined, and only some eighteen had to sign a personal bond to keep the peace, a judgment that was commonly taken by the Chinese to be tantamount to an acquittal.[43] The hearings also confirmed the Chinese view that the police had behaved with a brutal disregard for life. Everson himself admitted that only ten seconds had elapsed between his warning and the order to fire, and he and other policemen confirmed that they were under orders to "shoot to kill" if life or property were in danger. Though Western witnesses were by no means unanimous in their testimony, several insisted that the crowd had been harmless, and the demonstrators themselves denied having any antiforeign leanings or Bolshevik proclivities. Mere curiosity had drawn him to Nanking Road that day, Qu Qiubai's younger brother (a student at Shanghai University) told the Court (in fact, he had been among the leaders of the demonstrations).[44]

In the meantime, the Municipal Council met in emergency session every day, anxious both to keep its authority intact and to end the affair before the movement got completely out of hand. The senior consul promised the Chinese that there would be an investigation "by the authorities concerned," but no one knew how it would be carried out. Should the Council set up its own board of investigation? or would that seem a sign of weakness? The Council must cooperate with the consular body, Fessenden told his colleagues, but must also maintain its independence and not allow the consuls to dictate a particular course of action.[45] The affair, however, was already passing out of the Council's hands, indeed out of Shanghai's hands, as the movement of protest, with its strikes and demonstrations, spread rapidly beyond the city to other parts of the country.

Hence came the intervention of Peking. Duan Qirui's provisional government thought that the Russians were behind the whole affair but decided to send two officials, Admiral Cai Tinggan and Vice-Minister of Foreign Affairs Zeng Zongjian, to Shanghai to investigate (on 12 June they were joined by Zheng Qian, the civil governor of Jiangsu). The move was a conciliatory one; Zeng was a Cambridge man, very popular in Peking diplomatic circles, and Cai himself was one of the first Chinese educated in America. The Diplomatic Body took a similar step. Shanghai was incapable of considering the situation calmly, argued the comte de Martel—the French minister—and the legations must take matters into their own hands. On 6 June, therefore, the senior minister of the Diplomatic Body told the Waijiaobu—the Chinese foreign ministry—that it would send its own commission south to investigate. At its head would go Jean Tripier, acting counselor of the French legation, accompanied by representatives from the American, British, Japanese, and Italian legations.[46] No one quite knew what their function would be or what powers they would exercise; but the coming of the diplomats questioned the polity of foreign Shanghai, threatening the very independence the Council sought to maintain.

SEVEN

A Danger to the Peace of the World
Shanghai against the Diplomats,
Summer 1925

As both the Chinese government and the foreign diplomats prepared to look into the outbreak of 30 May, neither the movement's radical leaders nor Shanghai's foreigners welcomed the prospect of a solution imposed from the outside. The provisional government set up in the autumn of 1924 had little authority beyond the walls of Peking, and the outside world had never officially recognized it. Premier Duan Qirui was another of Yuan Shikai's old protégés, a man with a reputation tarnished by the loans he had negotiated with Japan in 1918 and who had been driven from public life by the defeat of his faction in 1920. Yet he was back in power again—thanks to the unnatural alliance between the Old Marshal Zhang Zuolin and the Christian warlord Feng Yuxiang—a puppet beholden to these two masters who were growing increasingly resentful of one another. For him, the crisis in Shanghai brought both danger and opportunity: Though the mounting public outrage could further weaken his legitimacy, it also gave him a chance to seize the initiative from the radicals by demanding justice from the imperialists.

Foreign Shanghai and the Municipal Council had several reasons for suspecting the intervention of the Peking legations. To the Westerners who lived there, Shanghai, with its burgeoning trade, its modern industry and banking, was the real center of new China. Only by a historical accident did the capital remain in old Peking, where camel trains still passed under the gray city walls and one wraithlike figure succeeded another as head of state, obedient to whatever warlord dominated the north. "Peking, the Mongolian city of dust, far from China and things Chinese, living in an age closer to Ch'ien-lung than to Republican China, is as out of direct realistic contact with the immediate trend of events in China as a

European or American capital," wrote the *North China*.[1] Dreaming of its
vanished greatness under the northern skies, Peking was a city for archae-
ologists and historians; how could the diplomats, asked the *Écho*, living
in the Nirvana of the Legation Quarter and blessedly indifferent to the
concerns of ordinary mortals, possibly understand the forces making the
new China, the real China?[2]

> Peking is, as one may perceive
> A pleasant land of Make-believe
> Wherein the Governmental Great
> Live, eat, and sleep, and circulate.
> Far, Far from them the Maddening Crowd,
> The Outside World is not allowed
> To injure by its Wild Displays
> The even tenour of its ways. . . .
>
> Although Peking can justly claim
> To play the Diplomatic Game,
> According to established rules,
> To reckon all outsiders fools,
> The ordinary man tends more
> To curse the Diplomatic Corps;
> "T'would function better far," says he
> "If to the Corps, they'd add an 'e.' "[3]

Move the capital to the Yangtze, urged an American journalist in Shanghai, warning the ministers that "they had better wake up or they will be
completely buried in Gobi dust."[4]

There was only one full ambassador in Peking—Leo Karakhan of the
Soviet Union, who had arrived when Russia recognized China in May
1924. The Diplomatic Body recognized him as dean, but only for "cere-
monial purposes," and excluded him from its working meetings when it
gathered periodically under the senior minister. Those meetings were supposed to be secret, but some conjectured that regular leaks to the Chinese
took place (the Spanish minister was suspected).[5] Its minutes, when approved by all, were printed in French at the end of each year, forming a
useful record of what the ministers thought it proper to say to one another,
as distinguished from what they told their governments.

Although Sidney Barton might be the most powerful man in Shanghai,
there was no such commanding British presence in Peking and had not
been since the departure of Sir John Jordan a few years earlier. In February
1925, the British minister, Sir Ronald Macleay, had gone home because
of illness, and until he returned that autumn, Charles Michael Palairet
was appointed acting minister. As counselor of the embassy in Tokyo, he

had distinguished himself in the relief efforts after the great earthquake of 1923. A Roman Catholic, he had become a friend of Paul Claudel, the poet then serving as French minister in Tokyo. Though he knew little of China, he had a firm sense of the justice of the Chinese cause and would show considerable courage in standing up for his own views. But he kept rather to himself, and both his compatriots and his colleagues complained of his aloofness.

Like the British, America's Peking legation also lacked a regular minister at the time of the Nanking Road shooting. Jacob Gould Schurman had gone to the Berlin embassy in late 1924, leaving as chargé d'affaires Ferdinand Mayer, a man of "quick and lucid mind" (Palairet's words) and much liked by his colleagues. In July, the new minister, John Van Antwerp MacMurray, arrived. His knowledge of China was undoubtedly the best of any of the Peking diplomats. A Princeton graduate (like Mayer), he had served in Peking from 1913 to 1917, where he married Lois Goodnow, daughter of the president of Johns Hopkins and sometime adviser to Yuan Shikai. After a brief hitch in Tokyo, he had returned to Washington in 1918 to serve first as chief of the Division of Far Eastern Affairs and then as assistant secretary of state under Charles Evans Hughes. He was an obvious choice for the Peking legation and proved himself an astute observer in China during the revolutionary years. Yet, as time went on, his ideas on what should be America's response to China's new nationalism diverged more and more from those of Frank B. Kellogg, the new secretary of state, and the crisis of 1927 would bring a considerable strain between the legation and the State Department. MacMurray had also published a magisterial summary of China's foreign treaties, and some of his colleagues thought his knowledge too bookish and were put off by his scholastic air. Palairet characterized him as a man at home with books and documents, honest, professorial, and somewhat obstinate. "C'est un homme qui a beaucoup etudié mais qui n'est pas intelligent," was the malicious comment of the French minister,[6] the comte de Martel, who had also served in Peking from 1913 to 1916 but had only taken up his post as head of legation the previous November. Unfortunately, Martel's old-fashioned Gallic disdain for Anglo-Saxon diplomacy was not matched by any fruitful prescriptions for dealing with a country in revolution.

Nor were the Chinese leaders of the May Thirtieth movement any more ready than the guardians of foreign Shanghai to allow Peking to take the initiative in reaching a settlement. The extraordinarily effective kindling of public opinion by the Federation of Workers, Merchants, and Students ensured that no group like the General Chamber of Commerce or Admiral Cai's commission could reach a quiet settlement with the Council or the consuls. May Thirtieth gave Chinese nationalists of all sorts a superb opportunity to enlarge and educate their constituencies. The passions aroused by Nanking Road must not be allowed to die down, and the movement's organizers needed time and had to block any threat of early resolution.

On 7 June, the leaders of the Federation, including the Communists Li Lisan and Lin Jun, drew up a list of seventeen demands. Four preliminary demands called for an end to the state of emergency, the withdrawal of landing parties and demobilization of the Volunteer Corps, the release of those arrested, and the return of the schools (like Shanghai University) that had been occupied. The rest called for apologies and indemnities, the trial of Inspector Everson by a Chinese court, a Chinese commissioner of police in the Settlement, withdrawal of British and Japanese warships, Chinese representation on the Municipal Council, restoration of the Mixed Court to Chinese control, cancellation of the proposed bylaws, the immediate abolition of extraterritoriality, and improved treatment for workers, with the freedom to form unions and to strike.[7] The Federation gave them to Admiral Cai and to Xu Yuan, the special commissioner for foreign affairs, and cabled them to Peking, asking that they become the basis of future negotiations.

There are three points worth making about the demands. First, they spoke to several grievances that had no direct connection with the Nanking Road affair. Second, they addressed not only the interests of the workers, but also those of the Chinese bourgeoisie who had long wanted Chinese representation on the Council and the return of the Mixed Court. Finally, except for the call for the abolition of extraterritoriality, they were local rather than national in scope. In this sense, the demands were less radical than the insistence by both Guomindang and Communists upon the complete abolition of the unequal treaties and the return of all foreign settlements and concessions to China.

Admiral Cai and his colleagues arrived at the Shanghai North Station on the morning of 7 June, while Jean Tripier and the group from the foreign legations came on the tenth. Cai's group visited, or was visited by, representatives of various Chinese groups, including both the General Chamber of Commerce and the Federation of Workers, Merchants, and Students. It called on foreign consuls and on foreign chambers of commerce, finding the French and Japanese ingratiatingly anxious to dissociate themselves from the shooting, while the British and Americans both insisted the strike must end before there could be any talks. It also did its best to obtain evidence, though Cai complained privately that, although his witnesses would talk freely, they were reluctant to sign statements, and thus their testimony was little better than common gossip.[8]

Tripier's group interviewed several Chinese witnesses, including Yu

Xiaqing of the General Chamber of Commerce. They took statements in secret, but not under oath, from Fessenden and McEuen, among others. Both men blamed the unwillingness of Chinese authorities to crack down on the Communists. It was during these secret sessions that it first became clear that McEuen had been absent from the Settlement the day of the shooting, watching the ponies run at Kiangwan.

Finally, Tripier's group held several meetings, formal and informal, with the Cai commission and agreed to try to negotiate an immediate settlement on the spot.[9] But there were substantial obstacles in the way. Most important was local public opinion, both foreign and Chinese. Though the Peking legations had forbidden the Shanghai consuls to take part in the talks, there was a limit how far Tripier and his colleagues could ignore the view of the consuls and the Municipal Council. Thanks to the extraordinarily effective mobilization of public opinion by the Federation, Cai and his colleagues, for their part, were never allowed to forget the rising strength of the movement, which had grown well beyond the possibility of any official control. On 11 June, the Federation sponsored a mass meeting at the Public Recreation Ground near the West Gate of the old Chinese city. Led by Li Lisan of the General Labor Union and Lin Jun of the Students' Union, a crowd of over twenty thousand roared its approval of the seventeen demands, insisting that Peking take them up as its own or face the threat of a nationwide general strike.[10]

Meanwhile, the General Chamber of Commerce, which had had no voice in the formulation of the seventeen demands and which feared the costs of a long strike, set up its own May Thirtieth Committee under Yu Xiaqing to cooperate with the Peking government in reaching a settlement.[11] It thus sought to regain the leadership it had lost on that rainy evening through its reluctance to approve the strike. On 12 June, the chamber announced that it had reduced the Federation's seventeen demands to thirteen, and the changes were significant. Gone was the demand that workers be free to organize and strike, its place taken by a meaningless statement that laborers should enjoy better conditions and be free to decide for themselves whether to work or not. Gone were the demands that Britain and Japan withdraw their gunboats, that the Chinese control the Municipal Police, and for the immediate abolition of extraterritoriality.[12] Perhaps the changes reflected the chamber's political realism. Some, however, suggested that the chamber was looking out for its own interests, less anxious to diminish foreign authority in the Settlement than to prevent the growth of a militant labor movement that could be turned against Chinese as well as foreign capitalism. Though there is some evidence that the Federation's leaders agreed to at least some of the changes,[13] at another mass meeting in Zhabei on the seventeenth, they denounced the Chamber of

Commerce for thwarting the will of the people by compromising with the imperialists. Not that the changes made much difference to foreigners.[14] "Impossible Resolutions of Joint Meeting: Propaganda the Evident Intention," blared the *North China* of the original demands, and the revisions that Chinese radicals saw as a disgraceful sellout brought a similar headline: "Extremists Still in the Saddle: Impossible Proposals: No Discussion Imaginable on Such a Basis."[15]

Though the delegations headed by Cai and Tripier met three times from 16 to 18 June, neither side was willing to give much, and the talks broke off late in the afternoon of the eighteenth, with both sides making statements to the press.[16] The talks failed because of the limitations imposed on the two commissions both by the Peking government and the Diplomatic Body. They failed because of Western insistence, particularly by Tripier and G. B. Vereker, his British colleague, that if McEuen and Everson were to be punished, Chinese official heads must also fall. Above all, they failed because neither Chinese nor foreign public opinion in Shanghai wanted them to succeed. Foreign Shanghai could admit no responsibility by the Municipal Council for the shooting, for it believed that Chinese respected only force, and any signs of doubt or weakness would only lead to more trouble. Cai and Zeng, for their part, worked under the enormous weight of a Shanghai opinion that demanded the humbling of foreign pretensions and sought to push them into a position more radical than they wanted to take. Nonetheless, the evidence they collected for their report, the evidence that came out in the Mixed Court hearings, all seemed to support the contention that Chinese grievances must be met by real concessions, that a mere apology, an indemnity, the perfunctory disciplining of one or two policemen—even if the foreigners had been willing to do this—would not suffice to prevent similar incidents from occurring.

The failure to reach a local settlement left it up to Peking to try to find a solution. On 24 June, the Waijiaobu sent two notes to the Diplomatic Body. One made a sweeping demand for a general revision of the unequal treaties between China and the foreign powers and was not directly concerned with Shanghai. The second formally adopted the Chinese Chamber's thirteen demands as the basis for settlement of the Shanghai case. Three days later, Foreign Minister Shen Ruilin appointed a team of three (including Admiral Cai) to handle negotiations for the Chinese side, while the Diplomatic Body would be represented by the acting Senior Minister Vittorio Cerruti of Italy, the comte de Martel of France, and Ferdinand Mayer, the American chargé.[17] But the two groups never met. Not because of Chinese unwillingness, but because of foreign disagreement on two central questions. How far was the Shanghai Municipal Council an autonomous body, legally capable of handling its own affairs independently of the authority of the Diplomatic Body? And if the Peking legations did exert some disciplinary authority over the Municipal Council, how far—given the temper of China in the summer of 1925—was it wise to press the point?

Although the Communist leader Chen Duxiu was delighted by the breakdown of the talks between Cai and Tripier,[18] Chinese radicals were unhappy at the prospect of a compromise settlement negotiated far away in Qianlong's dusty city. Peking would listen to men like Yu Xiaqing of the Chinese Chamber of Commerce, but popular groups like the General Labor Union and the Federation would have no voice. Their leaders trusted the Chinese government as little as the Municipal Council trusted the legations. They had little to fear, for there were two obstacles to any quick settlement. The first was the explosion of protest from Shanghai to the rest of China; the second was the stubbornness of foreign Shanghai and the powerful voice with which the Shanghai lobby spoke, particularly in London.

Before the end of June, demonstrations against the foreign presence, particularly British and Japanese, erupted in other cities, and again the sound of gunfire was heard in the streets. British rifles killed several Chinese in Hankou on 11 June, and two days later there was a disturbance in the little British concession at Jiujiang on the Yangtze. Downstream at Zhenjiang, bloodshed was narrowly averted on 5 June, and Amoy was in a state of high tension.[19] In Chongqing, in Tianjin, in Peking itself, protests flared up. The most appalling outbreak came in Canton on 23 June. That day the Nationalist rulers of the city staged a huge procession, including cadets from the Whampoa Military Academy, that paraded in front of the British and French concessions on the island of Shameen [Shamian]. Somehow, firing broke out, and when it was all over, fully fifty-three Chinese and one foreigner lay dead. To this day it is not clear who was responsible, but at the time virtually all foreigners blamed the Whampoa cadets for opening fire, and virtually all Chinese held the British and French sailors on Shameen guilty.[20]

After the horrifying slaughter in Canton, it was impossible to calm the country. The Guomindang authorities in Canton called a great general strike against the British in Canton and Hongkong; it lasted sixteen months, badly hurting British trade. Some Nationalist leaders, like the rising young general Chiang Kai-shek, warned that China must prepare for war with Britain.[21] No matter how weak and unrepresentative might be the provisional government in Peking, it could not ignore the passionate fury flaring through the land, especially given the challenge thrown down by Sun Yat-sen's heirs in Canton: On 1 July, they proclaimed the formation of a national government of China, claiming a legitimacy based on a revolution that would sweep away the empty claims of the impotent politicians of the north and assert the independence and sovereignty of a new China, a China of the people.

No local settlement in Shanghai was imaginable at such a time. Back in Peking, Tripier and his colleagues drew up an anodyne report for the Diplomatic Body, whose only specific recommendations had to do with the policing of the Chinese city. It said little of the ways in which the Council might put its own house in order. The ministers were unsatisfied. By 30 June they had drafted their own recommendations: Inspector Everson must be transferred, and Police Commissioner McEuen, who because of his "negligence, lack of judgment, and lack of professional ability" they held chiefly responsible, must be dismissed. Stirling Fessenden had failed to take proper precautions and was thus "not devoid of blame" (the British Vereker later admitted that he had insisted on the criticism of the American Fessenden to counterbalance the censure of the British McEuen). The "shoot to kill" police regulations ("abominable," Palairet called them) must be modified, and finally, Peking was enjoined to punish the officials who had allowed the demonstrations to form on Chinese territory. The senior minister wired these recommendations to the senior consul in Shanghai on 1 July. Show them to the Municipal Council, he was told, and then publish them; if Fessenden and his colleagues proved recalcitrant, threaten to dissolve the Council and put the Settlement under a consular administrative commission.[22]

Even had Chinese Shanghai been willing to agree to so easy a settlement, the more immediate problem came from the foreigners. They had distrusted the Tripier commission even before it arrived (only "missionaries, social workers, and educationists" would welcome it, scoffed the *North China*), and the secrecy with which the diplomats went about their work confirmed all Shanghai's worst suspicions.[23] Tripier's inquiry hardly seemed the impartial investigation promised by the senior consul, and many, such as the British Chamber of Commerce, called for a proper examination.[24] The legations rejected all such appeals. They thought they had enough evidence to go on, and they believed their measures to be (in Palairet's words) "not only just and equitable in themselves but politically essential."[25] No doubt they also mistrusted the impartiality of any investigation based in Shanghai.[26]

Sidney Barton, sitting in his office near the Public Gardens, was furious when he heard what the legations wanted to do. He immediately fired off a protest to Palairet and to the Foreign Office, pleading for reconsideration and warning of the terrible harm that public humiliation of the Council would bring. "In my opinion," he wrote, "issue of an ultimatum to the greatest centre of British interests in China at this critical stage in its life and death struggle with the strike and boycott, when only persistence is needed to secure victory, is more likely to encourage Chinese unreason than to promote a return to normal conditions."[27] He wanted a judicial investigation by a panel of British, American, and Chinese judges; otherwise, he warned, the Council and McEuen would be condemned unheard. "I shall, of course, do all in my power," he went on, "if the Legations insist on their plan being carried out, but I have a sense of injustice to combat."[28]

Back in London, as the Foreign Office learned more about the picture in Shanghai, Barton's reasoning began to seem persuasive. Foreign Secretary Sir Austen Chamberlain worried about publicly humiliating the Council and began to doubt the wisdom of the Diplomatic Body's course. Barton's arguments accordingly carried the day with him, if not with Peking, and at the eleventh hour he ordered Palairet to hold up any publication of the Diplomatic Body's decisions.[29] It was a flat and unilateral veto. It seriously embarrassed Palairet and enraged some of his colleagues on the Diplomatic Body.[30] Chamberlain's action also shifted the balance of power back to foreign Shanghai. Knowing now that London's heavy guns were on its side, the Municipal Council, when it met on 4 July, indignantly refused to play the role of scapegoat. It rejected Peking's findings, maintaining that its own evidence had never been properly taken, and pledged its support to its chairman. Two days later, Fessenden told the senior consul flatly that the Municipal Council would not carry out the recommendations of the Diplomatic Body, reminding him that, although he had promised an "independent and impartial investigation," none had been held. Fessenden closed his letter with what amounted to the Settlement's declaration of independence: "While the Council is quite prepared to give the most weighty consideration to the view of the Diplomatic Representatives, it has to observe that it is primarily responsible only to the electorate of Shanghai."[31]

Never had the constitutional issue been raised quite so starkly. The Municipal Council's action put squarely on the table the question of the Settlement's relationship both to China and to the home countries most concerned with it—America, Japan, and above all, Great Britain. Fessenden the lawyer might have preferred not to force the issue and had earlier urged his Council to work closely with the consuls. But with Barton on his side and the American and Japanese consuls-general sympathetic to his position, Fessenden the municipal councillor fell back on a particular interpretation of the Land Regulations that underscored the self-sufficiency of the Settlement's polity and held the Council virtually immune from decisions made outside it. Only the ratepayers could instruct the Council, for only they had elected it. As long as the Council acted within the scope of the Land Regulations, the consuls and the diplomats—plenipotentiary representatives of their nations though they might be in dealing with the Chinese government—were nothing more than advisory bodies to the management of the Settlement.

The Shanghai municipality [wrote S. P. Waterlow of the Foreign Office] presents the extraordinary anomaly of an international governing body which is legally autonomous, insofar as there is no single government and no superior international body to which, as a body, it is responsible. In practice, this has hitherto worked fairly well, under the guidance of the consular body; but now the strain comes, with a direct conflict of opinion between the diplomatic body (to whom the consuls are responsible) and the municipal Council. The events of May 30 show how necessary it is that the position should be regularized and a definite chain of responsibility established between the council that administers Shanghai and some superior authority. How this can be done will have to be explored. . . . In any case it is now clear that a completely autonomous foreign international municipality in China is a danger to the peace of the world.[32]

Chamberlain's veto badly subverted the authority of the legations and severely tested the cooperation of the powers. At a stormy meeting of the Diplomatic Body on 8 July (joined now by the newly arrived MacMurray), the infuriated Martel, a strong champion of diplomatic supremacy over the Municipal Council, urged his colleagues to leave Britain to climb out of a pit of her own digging.[33] When, a few days later, Barton and his colleagues told the legations that the Council was now ready to accept the "voluntary" resignation of Police Commissioner McEuen as part of a formula to conciliate "native opinion,"[34] Martel scorned it. "The Council knows it has to go to Canossa," he remarked, conjuring up an unlikely vision of Fessenden as the Emperor Henry IV shivering in the Alpine snows, "but it has not quite reconciled itself to the inevitable." Palairet, unwilling at first to allow the Council to save face, gave in at the urging of his staff to avoid "the undermining of an authority in Shanghai which has been for more than fifty years preponderatingly British."[35] Yet, in the confusion of the times, nothing came of the Council's proposal for reconciliation.

London, too, with the passive acquiescence of Washington, also managed to block a further proposal by Martel to redefine the Settlement's position so that its subordination to the diplomats was clear.[36] Meanwhile, despite the secrecy surrounding the negotiations, it was not long before the foreign press learned something of the divisions between the Municipal Council, the consuls, and the ministers.[37] Martel's resignation from the committee established to deal with the Shanghai question and his public statement of 10 July confirmed the fact, if not the details of the dispute. Chinese papers picked up the story, the influential weekly *Guowen zhoubao* reporting it with fair accuracy, though ironically it blamed Palairet—

a proponent of firm action against the Council—for his government's veto of the disciplinary measures against the Settlement's administration.[38]

If the British were the villains in this version of the story, the French emerged as the heroes who had sought to cut Shanghai's pretensions down to size. Such a version of events and the continuing immunity of the French Concession from the summer's troubles helped convince many British, at least, that the French were doing their best to profit from the whole May Thirtieth affair. They were wrong. Martel was appalled at the vision of Barton and Cunningham (as he saw them) coaching the Municipal Council in its obduracy and thought Chamberlain's veto a breach of faith.[39] He went off halfcocked, refused to play any further role in the deliberations, and told Consul-General Jacques Meyrier in Shanghai to remain neutral rather than allow Anglo-Saxon incompetence to threaten France's position.[40]

Martel, however, put his finger on the real issue. "We must know," he wrote home, "if the Council of the International Settlement, an organ elected by a *minority* of ratepayers, can exercise the police and administrative powers contained in the Land Regulations, without limits or any controls by either the diplomatic or consular corps."[41] His outspoken stand upset Paris. Nineteen twenty-five was the year that saw the negotiation of the Locarno Pact, which would guarantee that Europe would never again know another Great War. Like Sir Austen Chamberlain, Foreign Minister Aristide Briand had more important fish to fry than those swimming dimly through the murky waters of the Huangpu and was desperately anxious to stay on the right side of the English. He thus tried to soothe Martel, telling him that France could simply not afford to be blamed for breaking up the solidarity of the legations "to win Chinese public opinion over to our side"[42] (which, of course, was precisely what the British were saying). On 18 July, the Quai d'Orsay blandly published a statement emphasizing Martel's loyalty to his colleagues and asserting that harmony reigned once more within the bosom of the Diplomatic Body.[43]

France's motives were thus not quite as sinister and opportunistic as the British thought. Nor, for that matter, was she any more liberal than the other countries in her approach to Chinese nationalism in the summer of 1925. Martel was a strong champion of the Manchurian warlord Zhang Zuolin and had little interest in treaty revision. He saw the hand of Russia behind the May Thirtieth Movement and would have been quite ready to use force to quash Chinese nationalist pretensions.[44] Yet he also understood the political need to make voluntary concessions to Chinese nationalism rather than acting later under coercion. The foreign position in China, and particularly the French position in Shanghai, must be maintained against the two forces that threatened it: Chinese Bolshevism and its Soviet masters on the one hand, Anglo-Saxon racism and ineptitude on the other.

Meanwhile, in Shanghai, factories and mills stood idle, Britain's trade was coming to a standstill, and her ships, deserted by their Chinese crews, swung idly at their moorings, ensigns limp in the sweltering air of summer. British goods destined for Shanghai were being diverted to Singapore, Kobe, or Manila, while Canton's strike against Hongkong spread rapidly through south China.[45] But how to end the crisis? Chamberlain still pushed for an investigation by a panel of foreign judges, despite the objections of his own chargé and a very cold response from the Peking legations.[46] "I think it right to inform you," wired Palairet, after a meeting with the ministers on 20 July, "that most of my colleagues look on proposal of H.M.G. as a disavowal of authority of foreign representatives here as a result of pressure from Shanghai."[47] By the end of July, however, Paris, Washington, and Tokyo had agreed to London's proposal for a judicial inquiry. More bargaining brought a compromise: McEuen would be suspended, and after an inquiry in October, he would hand the Municipal Council his "voluntary" resignation.[48]

Typically enough, the Chinese government was never consulted, and they learned about the plans from the newspapers. Little wonder Foreign Minister Shen Ruilin refused to have anything to do with it![49] The Chinese press in Shanghai denounced the British initiative. So did the Federation, the Chinese Chamber of Commerce, and most other bodies of opinion in the city.[50] O. M. Green and the North China, on the other hand, were delighted, professing amazement at the suspicion that the inquiry would turn into a whitewash! "To suggest that an impartial court of reputable judges, of which a British judge would be a member, could be guilty of such conduct is almost beneath contempt." Had Shanghai been left to its own devices, the paper continued, the matter would be settled. "One is almost inclined to ask," wrote Arthur Sowerby, editor of the China Journal of Arts and Sciences, "whether the whole thing was not a deliberate attempt, on the part of the diplomats, to get rid of the Council and take over, under the state of emergency, the government of the Settlement."[51]

Through the long summer, Britain's position had won her no friends. Chamberlain's veto had shattered whatever unity the legations had enjoyed. Though Japan and America rode to the rescue, neither was enthusiastic about extricating the British from the mess they had made for themselves. The Peking government was infuriated, the Shanghai Chinese were infuriated, and enough had come out in the papers, both foreign and Chinese, about the whole affair to put Britain's action in the worst possible light.

Why did Chamberlain push so hard to get his own way? Why was he so willing to endanger foreign cooperation in China, which in the best of times was fragile enough? No doubt his government was ready to give the benefit of the doubt to the man on the spot, and Sidney Barton, the commanding figure of the China consular service, spoke with a louder voice than Michael Palairet, the summer stand-in at the Peking legation.[52] Chamberlain himself had promised the House of Commons that there would be a proper investigation,[53] and he did not think the Tripier commission, made up mostly of very junior diplomats with no power to take testimony under oath, an appropriate substitute.[54] No doubt he also worried about the protests that would follow from British Shanghai and its London lobby, even though that lobby was importuning him to reach a quick settlement.[55]

For the time being, foreign Shanghai had won. It won because it had Barton in its corner, and Barton gained it Whitehall's backing. But it also had public opinion—or at least public opinion that counted—on its side. Over in the French Concession, the *Écho de Chine* blamed the troubles on the Soviet consulate ("the Red lair [*officine rouge*] on Whangpoo Road") and called for foreign solidarity—"*Un peu de discipline, s.v.p.*"—while condemning the "ridiculous demands of the strikers." The French naval commander remarked that the Tripier commission had seemingly done its job perfunctorily, condemning Fessenden and McEuen not because the facts warranted it but out of a desire to make a sacrifice to the "*minotaure Chinois.*" Hence, the Council's refusal to act was backed not only by Barton and Cunningham but had "the approval, *in petto*" of much of the consular body.[56] All this opinion undercut the authority of the legations, and Shanghai's interests were left inviolate. The thorny constitutional issue of the Settlement's exact relationship to the Peking government and to the Diplomatic Body remained unsettled. That itself was a victory, for any renegotiation of the Land Regulations, any attempt at a precise definition of the Settlement's legal status, would necessarily confirm the Council's subordination both to the Chinese government and to the legations, and would end foreign Shanghai's long history of independence.

And what of Duan Qirui's government during all this? From the endless telegrams and other dispatches that flew between Shanghai and the legations and Washington and Paris and London, one would hardly know the Chinese government existed. Yet, though it went largely unremarked at the time, Peking did win one victory that would have a bearing on the future of foreign Shanghai. In June, the legations had wanted to talk only about the Nanking Road incident, while the Chinese sought to embrace not only the thirteen demands but also the whole question of treaty revision. By early August, however, the British Foreign Office was beginning to bend, agreeing to the prospect of talks on the "extraneous matters" in the thirteen demands.[57] Finally, in late September and early October, after a good deal of negotiation, an exchange of notes took place between Foreign Minister Shen Ruilin and Senior Minister W. R. Oudendijk of the Netherlands. The Chinese agreed to discuss all questions arising from the Shanghai incident, and Oudendijk, speaking for the legations, listed the steps already taken to meet Chinese wishes—the state of emergency was now canceled, the landing parties withdrawn, the objectionable bylaws never passed. Moreover, he added, the legations stood ready to discuss the questions of the Mixed Court and of Chinese representation on the Council. The question of responsibility for the Nanking Road shooting would need "profound study"—as he delicately referred to the objectionable judicial inquiry.[58]

The Chinese press saw Shen's action as a disgraceful sellout. They would have been much angrier had they known that the letters to which the foreign minister had put his signature had been drafted not by him but by the legations themselves. "A total defeat in the Shanghai case," one journal called it.[59] But in fact, the foreigners had gone some way toward accepting the thirteen demands of June and had agreed to discuss several issues not directly related to the Nanking Road tragedy. Moreover, Peking had its own reasons to want a settlement. Radical demands from groups like the General Labor Union and the Federation of Workers, Merchants, and Students were finding a sympathetic audience and could only benefit Peking's Guomindang and Communist rivals in the newly founded National Government in Canton. In October, the Special Conference on the Chinese Tariff, stipulated by the Washington treaties of 1922, would meet in Peking, and Duan's government, still unrecognized by the powers, badly needed to raise its prestige among the foreign delegates who would soon arrive and to compete with Canton for the support of Chinese public opinion.

The foreign willingness to bend on Shanghai was a victory for China, but a small victory. The calling of the judicial inquiry seemed to suggest that foreign Shanghai still refused responsibility for the atrocity of Nanking Road. The questions of Chinese representation on the Council and the status of the Mixed Court were old ones, and nothing was said about such difficult issues as the external roads. Meanwhile, in Chinese Shanghai, the enthusiasm and unity of the early summer was wearing off. In mid-August, the strikes against Japanese mills and shipping lines came to an end, and a month later workers returned to the British mills. Had foreign Shanghai defeated not only its own legations but also Chinese nationalism? And would it be ready to make any accommodations to prevent another crisis?

EIGHT

Whom the Gods Wish to Destroy
Shanghai on Strike

I confess to an almost quixotic impulse to work with and sustain the position of the British," wrote the American minister on 20 August, "who for reasons of expediency on the part of Chinese radicals are being made to bear the brunt of the attack on the general rights and interests of foreigners in China, including our own." Britain was not an easy ally that summer, however. MacMurray was a strong proponent of cooperation between the Washington powers, yet like the comte de Martel (with whom he had little else in common), he thoroughly distrusted British Shanghai and Barton's influence. Britain, too, believed in the policy of cooperation, particularly since one of its aims was the preservation of general foreign interests in China. But she also wished to maintain her preponderant position in Shanghai. And now that British Shanghai apparently had London's backing, it seemed ready to push for its own interests with an obstinacy that would undercut the policy of cooperation and thus jeopardize the whole foreign position.[1]

After all, the May Thirtieth Movement had started as a protest against all foreign privilege, French and American as well as British and Japanese, calling for the extirpation of all imperialism no matter from what quarter. Granted, apart from a one-day sympathy strike in the concession, the French seemed immune from the movement's fury. Though acting Consul-General Jacques Meyrier landed his marines, he neither declared a state of emergency nor mobilized his volunteers. The Americans played a conspicuous role, however. They had the second largest landing force next to the British; they had the largest contingent of ships in the harbor; and Rear Admiral C. B. McVay, commandant of the Yangtze Patrol Force, was senior naval officer in early June and thus responsible for coordinating the movements of the landing parties with Colonel Gordon of the Shanghai Volunteer Corps.[2] Nonetheless, as the movement went on, it began increasingly to focus on Britain as the chief target. Not unnaturally, the British identified their particular interests with the general interests of foreigners, and not unnaturally, their allies—like MacMurray—came to believe that they were being asked to risk their own stake in China to defend the particular stake of British Shanghai.

One of the first victims of the movement had been the American St. John's University, singled out, said President Hawks Pott, because of its prestige; singled out, said others, because of the obdurate and unsympathetic attitude of Dr. Pott himself. Like other Christian schools, St. John's had faced a problem when the strike call went out on 31 May, and the faculty had agreed to suspend classes for a week. On Tuesday 2 June, Pott reluctantly agreed to a student demand that the Chinese flag be half-masted to honor the victims of Nanking Road (the American flag remained fully raised). Bishop Graves, however, objected that the action would mean taking sides in a political dispute and ordered both flags lowered. Angry students tried to hoist another flag, and Pott decided to shut the university, though he made no threats of expulsion. The result was the resignation of some Chinese faculty members and a mass defection of 552 students from the college and its middle school, many of whom founded a new university that they named Guang Hua [Brilliant China]. Pott blamed the student unions for what had happened, and both he and Graves were convinced that the whole incident had been engineered by student Communists, aided and abetted by the well-meaning but weak-minded leaders of groups like the Y.M.C.A., the Fellowship of Reconciliation, and above all, the National Christian Council (N.C.C.).[3]

The May Thirtieth Movement marked the start of a new and controversial role for the N.C.C. Over the next two years, it would begin to speak with a louder voice in political and social affairs, thus (in the eyes of its friends) bearing Christian witness in troublesome and dangerous times, or (in the eyes of its critics) embroiling itself in politics in a way decidedly improper for a Christian body. On 8 June, David Z. T. Yui [Yu Rizhang], its chairman, and E. C. Lobenstine, its resident secretary, wrote the Municipal Council criticizing the police report on the Nanking Road shooting and calling for a "prompt, thorough, and impartial investigation" by a body "which will command general confidence and on which there shall be adequate Chinese representation." For good measure, they advised adding Chinese members to the Municipal Council to improve Sino-foreign relations and to make it easier to deal directly with questions "which are bound to arise in a growing community such as Shanghai."[4] Meanwhile, the N.C.C. sought to reassure mission boards at home that all was well and to mobilize their support against the forces of reaction. "Movement not blind assault foreigners," wired Yui and Fletcher Brockman to the National Council of the Y.M.C.A. in New York. "Do not confuse this Boxer outbreak requires spirit conciliation and fairness not show force stop wise statesmanship may prevent disaster Shanghai." [5]

Apparently, Fessenden and his colleagues never answered the letter, and it is doubtful whether they would have agreed with the N.C.C. about what would constitute an impartial board. But the N.C.C.'s new political activism and its criticism of the Settlement authorities set off a controversy that would come to divide many missionaries from the rest of foreign Shanghai. [6] Most vocal missionary opinion that summer condemned, by implication if not directly, the actions of the police and the Municipal Council. Moreover, May Thirtieth was a catalyst in the decision of many American and British mission boards to call for an end to the unequal treaties and to dissociate themselves from the policies of their governments. [7] Yet there were dissenters from the beginning. "The police acted with the greatest restraint," wrote Bishop Graves, "even when knocked down they did not fire. In the end they *had to do it* to save their own lives and this Settlement. I don't see how they kept their tempers throughout." [8] He complained to an apologetic Lobenstine that the N.C.C. was being used to inflame the situation, and he looked on David Yui (a St. John's man himself) as little more than a polished opportunist who had built himself an unjustified reputation among Western Christians. Yui, he said, had encouraged the student defection from St. John's, and only with the greatest difficulty was he persuaded to join a group of alumni in signing a statement denying that President Pott's actions had been an insult to the Chinese flag. "He is a most disloyal son of St. John's, and Dr. Pott told him so quite plainly in an interview he had with him last week." [9] Though he spoke out of the passions of the summer and the fear that much of the work of his mission was at risk, Bishop Graves's criticism of the National Christian Council and its leaders was one that a growing number of foreigners—missionaries and others—came to share over the next two years.

The trouble at St. John's (and at Shanghai College, the American Baptist institution that also had to shut down before commencement) [10] was simply one example of the way in which the strike changed the ways in which foreign Shanghai lived. The Municipal Council moved quickly to assure an adequate food supply, and when Chinese workers struck, they drafted volunteer and White Russian labor to help keep the water and power plants going under the protection of foreign bluejackets. Foreign newspapers continued to appear, though reduced sometimes to a few badly printed pages after their typesetters walked out. A plan to join forces in putting out a single daily was scrapped, but J. B. Powell got American naval linotype operators to help publish both the *China Weekly Review* and the *China Press*, and American naval help also kept the *Shanghai Times* and the *North China Daily News* going.[11] Foreign women replaced absent Chinese operators at the telephone company, and it was fear of subversion rather than shortness of staff that led the Municipal Police to order the company to cut off service to members of the Soviet consulate-general and to certain suspect Chinese subscribers (the company reconnected the phones at the end of June since it was losing money).[12]

"Does China need an immigration law to protect Chinese labor from unpaid foreign labor?" asked a sarcastic leaflet published anonymously in English. From an unknown poet, with more than a nodding acquaintance with the American union tradition, came a ballad set to the tune of "John Brown's Body":

> When they have a strike, the Japs just shoot their workers down, it's known,
> Then the S.M.P. get busy with some killings on their own.
> But when they all go out on strike the coppers change their tone,
> And we come marching on.
> Solidarity forever!
> Solidarity forever!
> Solidarity forever!
> And we come marching on.
> When the Japanese assessor sent some students to the can,
> And the others didn't like it, and they said so to a man,
> And the coppers shot the kids down just to see how fast they ran,
> When we come marching on.
> (Chorus)
> When the Chinese got fed up with this, and all threw up their jobs,
> Why, the Council asked us all to scab, both volunteers and gobs,
> And while we did their dirty work, the Council writes of "mobs,"
> And we come marching on.
> Solidarity forever! etc.[13]

In early June, while the Federation and the radical proponents of mass action still held the initiative in the May Thirtieth Movement, the foreign chambers of commerce had approached the Chinese Chamber to help settle the strike and boycott. Yu Xiaqing refused them, unwilling to lose whatever advantage the Cai and Tripier investigations might give the Chinese side. By the time the two commissions returned to Peking, however, many Chinese commercial associations were ready to get back to business and reopen the Settlement's shops. Pressure from the Federation postponed the move until 26 June.[14] The Federation and the Chamber of Commerce then announced that, though the anti-Japanese boycott would continue only until Japanese mill strikes were settled, the movement against Britain would continue until all the demands arising out of May thirtieth had been met.[15] The meaning was clear: The movement's quarrel with Japan was merely over local industrial issues, to be dealt with by management and labor. Britain's case was different. There the issues were political, and not until sweeping changes had come to Shanghai, perhaps to all China, could she expect peace.

Singling out Britain as the primary target represented a victory of Shanghai's moderates over the radicals. The Communists wanted a broader sweep. Writing some three weeks after the Nanking Road tragedy, Qu Qiubai linked the events in Shanghai to a crisis in world capitalism and a heightening of imperialist oppression. Now, he said, a clear line divides true revolutionaries—workers, students, and ordinary merchants—from mere compromisers, who included bureaucrats, capitalist intellectuals, and the kinds of big businessmen represented by the General Chamber of Commerce. Revolutionaries wanted to get rid of all restrictions on China's sovereignty, wanted to abolish the unequal treaties with their economic and legal shackles on the nation's independence, and wanted to reclaim all concessions and settlements. The compromisers, however, had more limited aims: control of the Mixed Court, Chinese representation on the Council, and a settlement on the external roads. Revolutionaries joined with the world's downtrodden in the struggle against all imperialism; compromisers wanted to restrict the scope of the movement to England and Japan alone, or even to England alone. Afraid of taking on all China's oppressors at once, they did not understand that imperialist jealousies would frustrate any attempt to put together a new *baguo lianjun*, an allied army of the sort that had stormed into Peking during the Boxer Rebellion a quarter of a century earlier.[16]

Qu's article was typical of the way radicals tried to keep the General Chamber of Commerce from taking the movement over, while simultaneously appealing to the broader Shanghai bourgeoisie to hold fast to the united front. Yu Xiaqing and his colleagues had given only lukewarm support to the Federation, had watered down the seventeen original demands, and, through their own May Thirtieth Committee, were now trying to settle the affair on their terms rather than those of the masses. Yet, though the radicals might criticize this "narrowing of battle lines" [*suoxiao zhanxian*] that attacked Britain while appeasing the other imperialists, it was a tactic Borodin himself would use two years later to forestall an imperialist alliance against the revolution.

Britain's prominence made her not only an easy target but perhaps also a profitable one. With the British-American Tobacco Company's Shanghai plants idle, its Chinese rivals saw a chance to break the foreign domination of the cigarette market, and the firm of Nanyang Brothers contributed heavily to the strike funds.[17] As a writer in the Chinese Chamber's monthly journal pointed out, his country had been in thrall to England ever since the Opium War, and the boycott would encourage China's economic independence. He thoughtfully appended to his article a list of goods made in Britain or marketed by Britain, together with their brand names. The influential new weekly *Guowen zhoubao* directed most of its attacks against England, and, though a group of prescient Peking University professors warned against "driving out the wolf to let in the tiger" and thus allow Japan to aggrandize herself at England's expense, they agreed that Britain's economic grip must be broken if China were to be saved.[18] The Peking government urged Japan to dissociate herself from Britain and to settle the textile strikes peacefully, and it ordered local officials to direct their fire at Britain alone to avoid any accusations of general antiforeignism.[19]

It is impossible to know just how serious were the effects of the summer's strikes and boycotts against Britain. Nor is it possible to say how far other foreigners profited from her isolation. The seamen's strike hurt badly, as did the boycott of British shipping in south China after the Shameen massacre. Some indication of the harm done to British trade at Shanghai comes from a comparison of the following figures for the shipping that entered and cleared the harbor that summer.

In short, though Britain saw her total tonnage figures drop some 77 percent compared to Japan's 41 percent, her rivals either could or would do little to profit from her discomfiture. The only country to show a substantial growth was little Norway; total entrances and clearances under her flag rose from 30,640 tons in April to 78,049 in July, up 155 percent, and her share of the river and coastal traffic more than tripled.[20]

The Shanghai shipping figures reflect a broad decline in Britain's general China trade in 1925, a year that saw her exports to China (excluding Hongkong) drop by 28 percent, from £20,346,513 in 1924 to £14,633,613.[21] British imports suffered in the Yangtze Valley, where British firms found themselves resorting to all sorts of subterfuges to conceal the origin of their goods, even making contracts in the names of non-British firms. Yet away from Shanghai and Canton, the success of the boycott varied widely, and despite occasional complaints by British businessmen and consuls, it seems that in the hinterland, too, foreigners did not cut far into the British market. There were, after all, reasons other than the boycott to explain the slump in trade. One was the continuation of civil war and the accompanying military exactions that destroyed purchasing power and discouraged investment. Another had nothing to do with Chinese politics: It was the declining competitiveness of British goods. British merchants found themselves undercut not only by Japanese but by Americans and Europeans as well, many of whom also had better marketing strate-

Arrivals by Flag, April 1925

(tons)

	Coast and River	From Home	From India	From Other	Total
Britain	292,861	59,453	26,791	87,084	466,189
Japan	122,674	143,464	11,632	63,743	341,513
U.S.	6,261	94,238		41,870	142,369
China	237,931			907	238,838
France		14,920		15,208	30,128

Clearances by Flag, April 1925

	To Coast and River	To Abroad	Totals
Britain	285,942	233,754	529,696
Japan	149,864	199,934	349,798
U.S.	4,918	141,128	146,136
China	246,311	0	246,311
France	5,309	28,135	33,444

Arrivals by Flag, July 1925

	Coast and River	From Home	From India	From Other	Total
Britain	14,072	18,111	0	72,123	104,306
Japan	26,174	122,934	0	47,102	196,210
U.S.	6,286	93,701	0	34,681	134,848
China	237,266	0	0	4,623	241,889
France	13,904	5,668	0	20,097	39,669

Clearances by Flag, July 1925

	To Coast and River	To Abroad	Total
Britain	30,753	85,504	116,257
Japan	45,618	165,552	211,170
U.S.	2,316	120,000	122,316
China	234,523	916	235,439
France	563	45,623	46,186

gies. In 1925, for the first time, the value of cotton piece goods brought from Japan surpassed those from Britain and her colonies.[22]

However much British shipping and trading houses in Shanghai might suffer, though, some investments—notably those in real estate—could only rise in value as long as Shanghai remained a secure island in a turbulent China. Nor could Britain complain of a lack of diplomatic support.

Both Secretary of State Kellogg in Washington and Foreign Minister Shide-hara Kiijuro in Tokyo resisted all advice to cut their countries loose from London,[23] and in Shanghai itself, neither American Consul-General Cun-ningham nor his Japanese colleague Yada Shichitaro challenged Barton's position.

Yet, like MacMurray, Cunningham grew impatient with those British who continued to insist publicly on the Settlement's international char-acter while privately doing their utmost to preserve British control. That was the nub of the problem for British Shanghai: how to preserve general foreign interests intact against Chinese nationalist attack, while simul-taneously preserving their own predominance among those interests. A cooperative policy was needed to achieve the first aim; but might it destroy the second?

Perhaps the local Chinese authorities and Shanghai's Chinese business-men might be drafted as allies in the defense of the Settlement's integrity. After all, neither could look on the growth of radicalism with much favor. On 12 June, Zhang Xueliang (the "Young Marshal," as foreigners called him to distinguish him from his father, Zhang Zuolin, the "Old Mar-shal") arrived in the city with some two thousand Manchurian cadets of his father's Fengtian army to help keep order. Martel, who was a great champion of the Fengtian clique, took credit for the move,[24] though the Old Marshal hardly needed much urging to reinforce the foothold he had won in Shanghai's winter war. Though the Young Marshal turned down offers from both Cunningham and Barton to provide the names and ad-dresses of the principal agitators, he declared martial law on 22 June. That same day he returned north, leaving behind General Xing Shilian as commander-in-chief of the Shanghai and Wusong district with some six or seven thousand troops. Xing assured the foreigners that when the time was ripe he would move against the propaganda and strike centers. By July, he was issuing a series of increasingly severe proclamations against intimidation and disruption.[25]

To Western Shanghailanders, it was axiomatic that propertied Chinese, responsible Chinese, would identify their own interests with those of the foreign businessmen and bankers who ran the Settlement, must realize that the real enemy was not foreign Shanghai but a Bolshevik-inspired labor movement that threatened them all. Were they to fail to draw the right con-clusions, the Municipal Council had ways of encouraging them to see the wisdom of an alliance against the forces of disorder: On 6 July, it decided to cut off power supplies to bulk electrical users outside the Settlement. Even at the time, few believed the Council's excuse that the strike made the step necessary (particularly since the Council had rejected Chinese guarantees to provide the power plant with both fuel and labor). The most important of the bulk users were the Chinese textile mills and the tobacco factories of Pudong and Zhabei, and it was precisely they, of course, who profited the most while British and Japanese factories lay idle. It was a risky move; the senior consul opposed it, afraid that the tens of thousands who would be thrown out of work would make trouble, and it infuriated the American admiral who had hoped to be able to withdraw some of his sailors.[26] But Barton backed Fessenden and the Municipal Council. The power was cut, though in the end some factories found enough electricity from other sources to continue at least some of their production.[27]

Worried though the Shanghai bourgeoisie may have been about the rise of a radical labor movement, it had its own patriotic agenda, and a share of power in the Settlement's administration was one of its aims. An old story from the *Intrigues of the Warring States* [*Zhanguo ci*] tells of the fisherman who, watching a mussel and a snipe struggle with one another, waits until the bird's beak is held fast in the mussel's shell, then takes both as his prey. Of course, Yu Xiaqing and his colleagues feared the growth of a powerful radical movement; but they also understood how useful the same fear could be in extracting the concessions they wanted from the Settlement's masters. If radical muscle and foreign bird could immobilize one another, perhaps bourgeois nationalism could take the fisherman's profit, winning representation on the Municipal Council and the return of the Mixed Court.

For the Chinese businessmen, this strategy would mean walking a fine line between foreign demands and radical pressure. Radicals pilloried Yu Xiaqing and his colleagues in the Chinese Chamber of Commerce as running dogs of the imperialists and accused the Chinese authorities of collaborating with the British and Japanese to smother the strike and its organizers. Foreign Shanghai, on the other hand, saw Yu as its chief antagonist, more important even than Communists like Li Lisan, Lin Jun, or Liu Hua. "A thorough scoundrel," wrote George Vereker of the British legation; a man "who is suspected of communistic views and [who] certainly subordinates principles for private gain," according to Edwin Cunningham; the man "who has done more than any other single person to encourage the anti-British strike and boycott," complained Barton.[28]

In mid-July, a series of meetings between foreign chambers of commerce and the Chinese Chamber broke down when the British and Japanese refused Yu's demand for strike pay as a condition of settlement.[29] When General Xing Shilian's military authorities closed down the headquarters of the Federation, the Seamen's Union, and the Foreign Employees Union on 23 July, the Chinese Chamber was quick to join the radical organizations in protest. A threat by the Seamen's Union to idle Chinese ships brought pressure on General Xing from the Chinese Chamber to reopen the union headquarters on the twenty-sixth. Two days later when the Federation was reopened, Yu Xiaqing himself was present at the ceremony.[30] It was no coincidence that Yu Xiaqing was a director of the Sanbei Steam Navigation Company and that his colleague Fu Zong-yao [Fu Xiaoan] was a director of the China Merchants Steam Navigation Company. "Two of the most unscrupulous and antiforeign of the local Chinese merchants," an exasperated Barton wrote of them, "whose companies were profiting enormously from the strike."[31] He was incensed by the general's weakness in reopening the unions: "There is no doubt that had Xing not wavered, [the] movement would have collapsed as strike funds are running low and there is bitter discontent with [the] selfish corruption of Union leaders."[32] But the businessmen were not yet ready to cast their radical allies adrift.

Nonetheless, by August the strike was running out of steam. Although almost a hundred thousand workers were still idle at the beginning of the month and there were still over thirteen hundred foreign sailors ashore, most of the Volunteer Corps was now demobilized. On 12 August, the Japanese mill strike came to an end, thanks to the mediation both of the Chamber of Commerce and the Communist organizer Li Lisan. Ten days later, Chinese crews returned to work on Japanese ships, the occasion marked by a waterborne parade of launches accompanied by brass bands and firecrackers. Yu Xiaqing gleefully reported to Peking a manifesto from the Seamen's Union that praised Sino-Japanese brotherhood and that the English—their ships still lying idle—found "very upsetting."[33]

"The Japanese have acted with consummate skill," concluded an American intelligence report, "turning a crisis precipitated by a riot in one of their own mills into a position where they are reaping marked benefits. Their trade has increased materially at the expense of the British, while the steadily conciliatory attitude they have adopted has gone far not only to allay Chinese irritation but to win them Chinese friendship." Or, as the *China Weekly Review* (now appearing without the help of the American navy) wrote, the Japanese "have succeeded in entirely wriggling out of the trouble and left the British holding the bag."[34] Only the Communists and the British objected—the former because they saw all imperialism, not just its British variant, as the enemy, and the latter because they were now more isolated than ever. When the Japanese mill strikes ended, the Municipal Council's sole Japanese member argued that it was time to restore electrical power to users outside the Settlement—where many of the Japanese mills were located.[35] "Treachery," sniffed Barton, and the Council vetoed the move. Fessenden knew, however, that the Council must not seem a British tool, and when the Chinese authorities promised to try to end the strike at the British mills, Barton relented. The consuls ratified the decision to restore power on 27 August, and the following day, as a gesture of conciliation, the Council lifted the three-month-old state of emergency.[36]

As the influence of the Communists weakened on the Chinese side, so did the influence of the diehards on the foreign side. "I have always urged upon my friends in Shanghai," Sir Ronald Macleay told the Manchester Chamber of Commerce in July, "that the day must come when we shall have to give back to the Chinese the control of these big areas. Surely the wisest thing to do will be to educate the Chinese to be prepared for the day when the surrender will be made. . . ."[37] The *North China* attacked the speech; "surrender" was not a term in its vocabulary.[38] The Municipal Council still opposed any indemnity for the victims of Nanking Road and would say nothing in public about the questions of Chinese representation and the Mixed Court. Even at this late date, Barton still hoped to bargain such concessions for Chinese agreement to extend the Settlement's boundaries.[39] Yet, after an exhausting summer, others were ready for a tactical retreat. Some of the leading British China houses, such as the Asiatic Petroleum Company, Jardine Matheson, and the Hongkong and Shanghai Bank, had been pressing the Foreign Office for a conciliatory public gesture. When the China Association (which had been urging Fessenden to make a public statement)[40] and the British Chamber in Shanghai realized that the questions of Court and Council might be negotiated over their heads, they were ready to bend.

Thus it was that on the afternoon of 31 August, some 280 people crowded into a joint meeting of the China Association and the British Chamber of Commerce in their chambers in the Asiatic Petroleum Company building at No. 1 The Bund. London was simply not prepared to take strong action, warned H. W. Lester, the chamber's chairman. There was no hope of armed intervention, and thus "a policy of conciliation, probably entailing concessions, is the only one possible." There was no doubt that the promises made at the Washington Conference dealing with extraterritoriality and the tariff would be carried out, no doubt that the Mixed Court would be given back, no doubt that Chinese would eventually sit on the Council. Better that the British trading community yield gracefully to such changes than see them rammed down its collective throat. He persuaded most of his listeners, and they voted three resolutions: to carry out the Washington Conference's undertakings, to admit Chinese members to the Council, and to return the Mixed Court.[41]

The resolutions took many people by surprise, particularly since just a few days earlier an angry rally of British in Hongkong had demanded military intervention. The *North China Herald* had no comment, but other papers welcomed the step, though many people must have agreed with

MacMurray's private assessment of it as "ludicrously ingratiating in contrast with the previous attitude of the community that they represent."[42] Chinese reaction was less enthusiastic, and while Yu Xiaqing sent the British a tepid note of appreciation, he also told Peking that the British front was cracking and that a "victory without difficulty" was now possible.[43]

But the united front was in trouble. A wave of strikes against several big Chinese firms in August did nothing to encourage unity between businessmen and radicals, and tempers flared when strike funds ran short. As unemployed workers demonstrated against the Chinese Chamber of Commerce, rumors flew through the city that Li Lisan and Liu Hua were taking Japanese bribes. Workers (scabs, or *gongzei* as the Communists called them) attacked the General Labor Union's headquarters in Zhabei. The infighting may have owed something to astute anti-Communist propaganda, but it may also have reflected a struggle between a Communist party growing increasingly strong and the Green Gang, afraid of losing its influence in the labor movement.[44] On 18 September, perhaps at British urging, General Xing Shilian closed and sealed the Union's headquarters and put out a warrant for the arrest of Li Lisan (who managed, however, to flee to Canton). Within a few days, the Federation of Workers, Merchants, and Students, torn by disagreements since August, announced that it was voluntarily winding up its affairs, and General Xing promptly issued a proclamation banning all meetings and demonstrations.[45] This time, the Chinese Chamber of Commerce did not rally to the Federation's defense. By the end of September, the British mill strike was over, and although the boycott and shipping strike officially continued, both of them were petering out and would lose their vitality (at least as far as Shanghai was concerned) by the end of the year.[46]

Although the radical movement began to fall apart under the pressures of unemployment, factionalism, and General Xing Shilian's repression, the Nanking Road affair remained unsolved. Washington and London still disagreed about the plans for the judicial enquiry, and as tempers became frayed in the summer's heat, every day's delay made it less likely that the investigation would solve any problems. MacMurray complained of the "clumsy, dilatory and equivocal way" in which the British behaved, still convinced that British Shanghai was working behind the scenes to prevent any unnecessary concessions or imputation of blame to the Council. It was a view shared by others, including the *China Weekly Review* and—privately—by some of the larger British firms in the city.[47] Chinese opinion saw the enquiry simply as a way to whitewash the Council. Peking tried to block it and ultimately refused to name a Chinese jurist to serve on the panel.[48]

Therefore, when the commission of judges finally did assemble, it included only foreigners. E. Finley Johnson, an associate justice of the Supreme Court of the Philippines, presided. With him served Suga Kitaro, chief justice of the Hiroshima Appeals Court, and Sir Henry Gollan, chief justice of the Supreme Court of Hongkong. Personalities aside, the British choice was unfortunate; though Gollan had no formal connection with Shanghai, he could hardly have been unaffected by opinion in Hongkong where tempers ran even higher than in Shanghai.

The commission met for the first time on 3 October to invite the submission of evidence, then sat in daily session from 13 October through 28 October. Little new evidence came out of the hearings, although under the persistently hard questioning of Justice Johnson, some points emerged more clearly. It was at this time, for example, that McEuen's haphazard behavior on 30 May, including his two-hour, unannounced absence from the Settlement, became a matter of public knowledge. Everson and the other witnesses largely repeated what they had already told the Mixed Court in June. Since only one Chinese witness appeared (a member of the Municipal Police), the picture that emerged almost entirely reflected foreign views.[49] Hence, it was no surprise that Gollan and Suga exonerated the Settlement authorities. "I do not see how," concluded the British judge, "on the facts proved before the Commission, measures in addition to those mentioned by the Commissioner of Police could have been taken to prevent disorder." McEuen had no reason to believe that trouble would break out on 30 May and could not be blamed. Suga defended Everson's decision to open fire, and absolved Fessenden from blame because he had no executive authority.

The troublemaker, in Western eyes, was Justice Johnson. As he admitted privately, he had come to the city suspecting a coverup and was determined to prevent it. "I knew nothing of the facts at the beginning," he wrote Silas Strawn, the American representative at the Peking tariff conference. "I was therefore obliged from time to time to put each of the policemen who went to the witness stand through what they thought a rather severe course of questioning. Except for my course, in my humble opinion, everyone connected with the grettable [sic] incident of May 30 1925, would have been whitewashed."[50] To Secretary of State Kellogg, he complained that the inquiry had been an *ex parte* examination and that only his "fishing" for answers had kept it from becoming a farce that would have put the United States "in much the situation of the Government of our English cousins."[51]

Johnson agreed that Everson had to open fire when he did, since the crowd by then was uncontrollable. That was as far as his concurrence with his colleagues went. At noon, he pointed out, the police stations had

ignored a warning to take special precautions, and as late as 3:25 P.M.—
twelve minutes before the firing—the crowd could still have been controlled with adequate reinforcements. He blamed the police for a lack
of humanity, blamed the authorities for an unclear sense of their duties
and responsibilities, and blamed McEuen for failing to take charge. "I am
fully persuaded," wrote Johnson in his report, "that he does not have a
proper appreciation of his responsibility in the maintenance of peace and
good order within his jurisdiction. I would therefore respectfully recom-
mend that he be substituted by one whose performance of duty shall be
more nearly commensurate with his very high responsibilities." It was a
conclusion not far from that drawn by the Diplomatic Body four months
earlier.

Above all, Johnson blamed foreign Shanghai and its narrow view of
the world around it. Far from restricting himself to the immediate circumstances of the shooting, he listed twenty-five causes, both immediate and
general, that had led to the outbreak. With some of them, any Shanghai-
lander would have agreed: Johnson condemned the agitation of the unions,
condemned the flaccidity of the Chinese police and their authorities, and
condemned the Communists, both local and foreign. But almost all his
other strictures had to do with Chinese grievances, not only in Shanghai
but in the country at large. He pointed to the Mixed Court, to the lack
of Chinese representation on the Council, to the question of the external
roads, to the question of extraterritoriality. He criticized Japanese handling of the mill strikes that spring, and he criticized the proposed bylaws,
as well as the Council's failure to apologize for the incident and to pay an
indemnity. Finally, he blamed "the failure on the part of the foreigners in
China to realize that the Chinese people have made greater achievements
during the past ten years in civics, in the fundamental principles of government and in the better understanding of individual rights under the law,
than they have made in any hundred years during their entire history." [52]

It is hard to imagine a more narrowly didactic American statement,
more certain in its preachiness to drive most of foreign Shanghai wild—
all the more so because it struck home. Johnson's opinions, warned Sir
Ronald Macleay (now back in Peking), would only encourage the Chinese
to make "impossible demands." [53] Austen Chamberlain thought the report
"quite inexcusable" and was shocked by this latest evidence of American
"disloyalty"—to what, it is not quite clear. But John Pratt, now installed
as adviser in the Foreign Office's Far Eastern Department, had no such
doubts. "The chief cause of the dangerous and difficult situation in which
we are placed is not the antics of the American judge, but the failure of
the British judge to do substantial justice. . . ." he argued. "I would certainly come to the conclusion that, had the control of the police been in

competent hands, the tragedy could have been averted." McEuen's failure to come to Louza was "so extraordinary that it is inconceivable how any reasonable person could exonerate him." If Johnson went too far at all, Pratt went on, it was in exonerating Everson for having given the order to shoot. Everson had fired "because that was the simplest and most efficient way of restoring order—not because there was nothing else to be done." Pratt believed that Johnson had done his best to agree with his colleagues, but when he discovered that Gollan was "bent, in the face of all fairness and reason, on a policy of hush up and whitewash, it may be that he decided that it was his duty to speak out. It is no use complaining of American methods—it is the lamentable failure of British justice that is the cause of our trouble." Unless quick action was taken, disaster would strike again, and McEuen should count himself lucky to retire with his pension. "He is a notoriously incompetent loafer. The S.M.C. is a most efficient organization, but 'quod deus vult perdere, prius dementat.' In employing McEuen as Chief of Police and Benbow Rose as Secretary of the Council, Shanghai, in the slang phrase, has been 'asking for trouble.' " [54]

Meanwhile, the Municipal Council's Watch Committee, chaired by the American V. G. Lyman, had held its own private examination into the affair. By 14 December, all but one of them had concluded that neither Everson nor McEuen could be blamed for the shooting. "The Police took all usual and reasonable precautions up to the hour when the shooting took place. . . . Up to the moment when the order to fire was given on that date, such an outbreak could not reasonably have been foreseen or guarded against by the responsible police officials." Only one of the committee members—the lawyer J. H. Teesdale—criticized McEuen for warning his police stations to expect trouble and then leaving the Settlement himself without telling his subordinates.[55]

Obdurate as ever, the Municipal Council now asked whether, with the inquiry over, it might restore McEuen as police commissioner. The gesture of defiance got them nowhere, for Barton had already promised his legation that the Council would oust Everson and McEuen if they could do so in a face-saving way. MacMurray, Macleay, and Japanese minister Yoshizawa told their consuls in Shanghai that the reports of the judges must be published and that the Council must "spontaneously" get rid of the two policemen and pay a "generous compensation" to the Chinese. Tokyo managed to hold up publication for two weeks, giving way only in the face of MacMurray's threat to publish the Johnson report unilaterally. The American minister had also been embarrassed by Johnson's civics lecture, but he knew that suppression would only make things worse.[56] "The fact is," he warned Cunningham, "that Barton is a somewhat stubborn yokemate. I cannot but feel that he has rather bedeviled this business in the past by insistence upon his own views, and by delays and obstacles interposed for the purpose of enabling him to make those views prevail with his Foreign Office behind the back of his Legation. . . . As a result of last July's experience, the members of the Diplomatic Body are prepared to see the devil's horns and tail appearing between the lines of anything that comes from Shanghai."[57]

Fessenden took on the unhappy job of persuading Everson and McEuen to step down, a task complicated by the unreasonably high financial demands the latter appears to have made as the price of a quiet departure (he ultimately was granted a pension of Tls. 12,000 a year—about £1,875).[58] On 23 December, summaries of the judges' findings were given to the press, and simultaneously, the Council announced with regret the resignations of the two policemen. It also said that it would make a grant of $75,000 to the victims of Nanking Road and their families.[59]

"I trust," wrote the American minister in reporting these events to Washington, "this action brings the Shanghai incident to a conclusion as satisfactory as could have been hoped for." Wishful thinking, of course; the Chinese were by no means willing to accept the gesture as a settlement of the case, and Peking, which had demanded a far higher indemnity, ordered the check returned.[60] "It goes without saying," wrote the Communist Qu Qiubai contemptuously, "that the lives of the martyrs of May Thirtieth cannot be bought for a few thousand dollars." He, for one, had no kind words for Justice Johnson. Simply to say, as the Americans had, that the Chinese had made great advances in civics "is no different from saying that a century ago, butcheries could take place freely, but that today aggression must be pursued by other means."[61] Some foreigners shared the view. "These efforts at conciliation came too late to be of any good," stated the *Chinese Recorder*, echoing a view popular among American missionaries. "Furthermore, for a judicial commission investigating so serious an event as this to be composed only of foreigners—virtually the defendants in the case—to sit so long after the event and then to bring in a divided report is almost a fiasco. It does not fit in either with the best ideas of judicial procedure or meet satisfactorily the claims of justice."[62]

Nonetheless, the winding up of the judicial investigation marked, for all practical purposes, the end of the May Thirtieth Movement in Shanghai. The Council had been chastened, if not humbled, by Justice Johnson's strictures, and the departure of Inspector Everson and Commissioner McEuen removed from the city the most visible parties associated with the Nanking Road tragedy. The British business organizations had given a blessing in principle to the return of the Mixed Court and to Chinese representation on the Council. All in all, moderate nationalism of the kind represented by the General Chamber of Commerce had won a considerable victory. It had done so partly because it played on the divisions among the foreigners, particularly between the British and the Japanese. But it had also shown itself able to take advantage of the radical threat growing out of the popular movement, while making no real concessions to the left. At the same time, of course, the divisions between Chinese business circles and the radicals in Shanghai suggested that the united front might well be subjected to increasingly serious strains in the future.[63]

In the meantime, the vicissitudes of China's continuing civil war once again brought political change to Chinese Shanghai. In mid-October, while Johnson and his colleagues were examining the events of Nanking Road, General Sun Chuanfang broke the uneasy truce of the previous January, leading his Zhejiang army north from Hangzhou and expelling the Fengtian forces of Xing Shilian without a fight. The changing of the guard meant little to foreign Shanghai. The General Labor Union, shut down by General Xing on 18 September, remained closed, its Communist leaders once again driven underground. On 29 November, its chief, Liu Hua, was arrested by the Settlement police at a teahouse on Foochow Road and turned over to the Chinese authorities, who executed him at Longhua Arsenal on 17 December.[64] Sun Chuanfang, though a moderate progressive in his way, was no more friendly to the left than Xing had been and maintained a tight control over radical activities and any kind of popular mobilization. In the north, the uncertain powers of Duan Qirui's provisional government were further undercut, weakening any pressure the putative capital might have been able to put on the foreigners. All this gave foreign Shanghai something of a respite from the nationalist movement that had broken out with such force in May 1925, a chance to put its house in order. The calm would not last long, however, for by the summer of 1926, it was apparent that May Thirtieth was only the beginning of a revolution that would eventually embrace all China.

The Embers of a Dying Fire
The Aftermath of May Thirtieth

When Inspector Everson's men opened fire in Nanking Road, three years had passed since the end of the Washington Conference. Since then, the countries that had gathered in the American capital had done little to keep the promises they had made. At Washington, they had agreed on two steps to mitigate, if not eliminate, China's diplomatic subordination under the unequal treaties. First, the Washington customs treaty promised that a special conference would study the question of the Chinese tariff, which had remained at the artificially low level of 5 percent imposed after China's defeat by the French and the British in 1858. It also proposed to allow China to impose small interim surtaxes—the so-called Washington surtaxes—until full tariff autonomy should be restored. Second, the powers agreed that a commission would examine China's progress toward a modern legal system and would consider the future of extraterritoriality. The Washington powers, seeing themselves as China's trustees, considered these concessions to be generous, a recognition that China was moving out of the old imperialism of the nineteenth century into the modern world. China's delegates, however, wanted full sovereignty for their country, and wanted it immediately. Even before the conference met, Sun Yat-sen's regime in Canton (at the time, little more than an uncertain coalition of local politicians and generals) had announced that it would recognize no actions coming out of Washington,[1] and in the passionate nationalism that surged forth from Shanghai after May 1925, the benign promises made three years earlier seemed more inadequate than ever.

The customs question was an enormously complicated one and is beyond the scope of this work, but it was a matter of deep concern both to China and to the outside world. The Chinese Maritime Customs was largely the creation of Sir Robert Hart, who had served as inspector-general from 1865 until 1908, when Sir Francis Aglen succeeded him. By the early twentieth century, many of the duties collected on foreign trade were earmarked for the repayment of foreign loans and obligations, leaving relatively little at Peking's disposal. China's political disunity, grown worse since the Washington conference, further complicated the picture. If the tariff was increased—by the imposition of the Washington surtaxes, for instance—to whom should the new revenues go? To Duan Qirui's weak and unrecognized provisional government in Peking, little more than a facade for the northern warlords like Zhang Zuolin? To the local powers like the Guomindang's National Government in Canton or Sun Chuanfang's government in Shanghai? Or should they simply be held in trust by the foreign powers until China sorted herself out?

To make matters worse, a complicated argument about the way in which China was to repay certain obligations (the gold franc crisis) delayed France's final ratification of the Washington customs treaty until the summer of 1925. As soon as Paris had acted, on 19 August Peking invited the Washington powers to gather that October in the Chinese capital for the tariff conference promised three years earlier. By then, however, Duan Qirui's government had sought to turn to its own advantage the fury that swept the country after the Nanking Road tragedy. On 24 June, when Foreign Minister Shen Ruilin sent the legations a note incorporating Shanghai's thirteen demands, a second communication also called for "the readjustment of China's treaty relations on an equitable basis in satisfaction of the legitimate national aspirations of the Chinese people."[2] Though its call for a mere revision of the treaties was far milder in tone than the Communist and Nationalist demands for their outright abolition, it nonetheless showed Peking's determination to take up the nationalist cause, using the summer's patriotic outpouring to strengthen its own position. The blood shed in Nanking Road gave a new urgency to the unfulfilled promises of Washington, and for the Peking government as for the radicals of Shanghai, May Thirtieth was now no longer a local issue but part of the whole question of foreign privilege in China.

How to reply to Peking's call for reform occupied the legations and their home governments for the better part of the summer and caused almost as much bickering as the Shanghai demands themselves. While the British wanted to postpone any discussion of real change until Peking had restored order,[3] Washington looked on China in a more optimistic light. Secretary of State Kellogg and Nelson Johnson, chief of the State Department's Far Eastern Division, were more willing than either London or Tokyo to appease Chinese nationalism. To do so, they would need to discuss not only the customs surtaxes but also the question of full tariff autonomy, not only to convoke a commission to study China's legal reforms but also be willing to consider the eventual abolition of extraterritoriality. America's liberal outlook left her allies concerned. While Tokyo's foreign minister Shidehara Kiijuro fretted about the effects of too generous a tariff policy on Japanese trade, the British worried that a surrender of extraterritoriality would undermine their position in the treaty ports. Tokyo might concede a few points on extraterritoriality to save the tariff, observed Sir Victor Wellesley of the Foreign Office. For Britain, however, extraterritoriality was a much more important issue, and bend as she might on the tariff, she did not want the sort of change that would threaten the very basis on which her own concessions—and the Shanghai Settlement—were built.[4]

By late August, the powers were ready to reply to the Chinese demand for treaty revision. Britain realized that it was pointless to insist that Peking restore order to a country it could not control, and Washington removed some of the language that London and Tokyo (as well as minister MacMurray) feared might encourage Chinese ambitions. Nonetheless, the response finally made to the Chinese government on 4 September kept open the possibility both of tariff autonomy and the abolition of extraterritoriality. It was a victory for American ideas on treaty reform, but it was also a victory for the furies unleashed by Nanking Road and Shameen. Not that there was any great enthusiasm among radical nationalists for the vague phrases of the foreign response, or even for the calling of the tariff conference; tariff increases and tariff autonomy might be fine in principle, wrote the Shanghai Communist Qu Qiubai, but in China's present state, any increase in customs revenues would only find its way into warlord pockets. Nevertheless, the gesture had its own meaning. "If today warlords, officials, and capitalist exploiters are dreaming of a higher tariff," he continued, ". . . isn't it obvious that without the May Thirtieth Movement, they would not even have got this little sop?"[5]

In fact, they got more than a sop, for on 19 November, less than a month after it first gathered in Peking, the conference not only recognized China's right to tariff autonomy but even set a date—1 January 1929—for her enjoyment of that right. It then turned its attention to the question of the interim surtaxes, wrangling well into 1926 over the question of how China was to collect and use them, without ever reaching agreement. The Commission on Extraterritoriality, which first met in January 1926, took no such action, contenting itself with a pessimistic report the following September setting forth in some detail the kinds of legal reforms the powers would expect China to make before considering any changes.[6] Long before that, however, war was again raging through the north, and the evanescent authority of Duan Qirui's provisional government finally evaporated. On 9 April 1926, Duan himself was deposed and a series of "regency cabinets," more or less under the control of the Zhang Zuolin and his Fengtian armies, now exercised whatever powers of rule remained in the north.[7]

But that is to get ahead of the story in Shanghai. By the autumn of 1925, after the mill strikes ended, after the Federation of Workers, Merchants, and Students had vanished, and after Chinese soldiers had closed the General Labor Union, the city slowly returned to work. When the results of the judicial inquiry appeared, the *China Press* summed up May Thirtieth: Chinese Shanghai had won most of the thirteen demands, and China in general had won the principle of tariff autonomy and the promise of a commission to consider the end of extraterritoriality. "The whole thing comes as a sort of Christmas present to China, although it would be difficult to convince many Chinese that there is much Christmas spirit behind it all. Regardless of that point, China has won a great victory and of tremendous importance has won it without a war."[8]

However hard Justice Johnson might rap the knuckles of the Council, however severe might be his strictures against the police, however quickly Everson and McEuen might pack their trunks and take ship for home, few Chinese, north or south, considered May Thirtieth settled. On 25 November, while the legations were still quarreling about the best way to handle the embarrassing Justice Johnson, the Waijiaobu shocked them with a long and bitter note setting forth Peking's views. Building its case almost entirely on the evidence presented to the Mixed Court in June, it demanded punishment for Everson, McEuen, and the other policemen, both foreign and Chinese, who had participated in the outbreaks of late May and early June. Thirty-two people had been killed and fifty-seven wounded in Shanghai's streets during those bloody days. Surely their lives were worth as much as those of foreigners; Peking would therefore demand precisely the same sums that foreign governments sought when their own citizens were killed or injured in China: $20,000 for each death and $5,000 for each injury, or a total of $925,000 in all. Property claims would come later. To cover the losses from the strikes, for which it held the Council and its police responsible, Peking demanded a lump sum of $1,000,000 to build a local hospital for Chinese. Nor did it stop there: The Mixed Court must be returned, Chinese in the Settlement must have the vote on the same basis as foreigners, and after a six-year period of transition, Shanghai would be governed by a Council consisting of eighteen Chinese and nine foreigners.[9]

"A monstrous document," commented Eric Teichman, of all British diplomats in Peking the most sympathetic to Chinese nationalism. "In all my experience I have never known the Chinese to address so insolent a communication to a legation." To such an embarrassment, the best response was no response. Macleay did not even send it home for two months; MacMurray extracted a promise from the senior minister that the Diplomatic Body would ignore it; and the new Foreign Minister C. T. Wang [Wang Zhengting] never pressed for a reply.[10] By now, however, May Thirtieth had convinced even the taipans of the Shanghai Club that times were changing. So the diplomats went to work on the two questions of Chinese representation on the Shanghai Municipal Council and the return to China at least of the authority over the Mixed Court that the foreigners had assumed in 1912.

The question of Chinese representation on the Council was an old one.[11] Both the legations and the land renters had originally assumed a Chinese voice in the Settlement's governance, but the stipulation had disappeared from the final version of the Land Regulations approved in 1869. After the Mixed Court riots of 1905, various Chinese leaders, including the young Yu Xiaqing, had wanted to form a consultative board to represent the views of the Settlement's Chinese to the Council. The ratepayers turned down the plan, afraid that it would lead to a Chinese demand for active participation. In 1915, the ratepayers approved the principle of a Chinese advisory board in return for an enlargement of the Settlement.[12] That proposal failed too, partly because of Chinese opposition to the Settlement's expansion and partly because Shanghai's foreign lawyers opposed the return of the Mixed Court, which was also part of the bargain.[13] In April 1920, after the threat of strikes and a Chinese refusal to pay an increased municipal rate, the foreign ratepayers, while defeating a motion for Chinese representation on the Municipal Council, did agree to the formation of a Chinese Advisory Committee of five.[14] It was a grudging concession. "From a technical standpoint," wrote Cunningham, echoing a common foreign view, "the Chinese have no right whatsoever to representation on the Municipal Council. The International Settlement is provided as a safe place for the foreigners to live in and transact business in, under their own laws, and those Chinese who are in the Concession are here because they have greater protection than they would in other parts of China."[15] Squabbles over how the Chinese should be chosen vitiated the effectiveness of the arrangement. A new Chinese Ratepayers' Association, made up of roughly 2,500 residents whose property holdings would have entitled them to vote had they been foreign, demanded the right to appoint the advisory committee. The Municipal Council objected and recognized the new committee only when the Chinese gave way. Even then, jealousy and suspicion on both sides stymied any fruitful cooperation over the next several years. Inspector Everson's actions brought the whole experiment to an end, and on 6 June 1925, the entire Chinese Advisory Committee resigned to protest the Municipal Council's handling of the Nanking Road affair.

Though May Thirtieth convinced many leaders of foreign Shanghai to look again at the prospect of Chinese sitting on the Council, the question was not a simple one. Quite apart from whether foreigners should demand anything in return (such as Settlement extension), bringing Chinese on the Council would mean changing the Land Regulations. Article X limited the Municipal Council to nine members; Article XVIII restricted the nominating power to foreigners; and Article XIX restricted the franchise and, by implication, the Municipal Council to foreigners. Second, if Chinese were to be elected on the same basis as foreigners, they would dominate the Council. The number of Chinese seats must therefore be restricted, and Chinese councillors must be appointed rather than elected. But appointed by whom? The Chinese Ratepayers' Association? The Commissioner for Foreign Affairs? Or associations such as guilds and chambers of commerce? Would Chinese members keep the Council's business confidential? How could foreign Shanghai ensure that Chinese members, however chosen, were not the creatures of particular interests or particular factions? How, in other words, might the Council include Chinese members and exclude Chinese politics?

On 18 August, Vittorio Cerruti, the acting senior minister in Peking, asked the Shanghai consuls to consider the question of the Council's "reorganization," a term that (as he explained a few days later) meant primarily adding Chinese members. They acted swiftly, and on 1 September recommended the appointment of two or three Chinese to the Council—not as a matter of right, said the senior consul's letter (which Barton helped draft), nor because anyone imagined that a Chinese presence would improve the Settlement's administration. The move was simply a political gesture to gain Chinese cooperation until the time came for them to assume control of the leading port in Asia "without jeopardizing the material interests involved." [16]

In Peking, Palairet and MacMurray, with Senior Minister Oudendijk, incorporated the consuls' recommendation into a more ambitious proposal that was essentially a restatement of the Greater Shanghai plan of 1923, calling for the creation of a sort of super-Council made up of representatives of all the different parts of the city, Chinese and foreign. Even though the plan was not coupled this time with a proposal to enlarge the Settlement (Chamberlain had opposed such a move), its effect would still have been to turn Shanghai into an international city under a kind of Sino-foreign joint control quite different from anything else under the treaty system.[17] Under a strong and confident Chinese government, such a plan might have worked well; but under a weak government, such a Greater Shanghai would almost certainly have detached itself from anything but the most nominal Chinese control, and the surging Chinese nationalism of the day would never have allowed it to work.[18]

Peking's "insolent" note of 25 November 1925 was a reply to this proposal. The diplomats never answered it, and the rapid erosion of the provisional government's authority in 1926 stalled consideration of the question of representation. The British Foreign Office, conscious that the coming anniversary of May Thirtieth would bring more trouble, pushed Minister Macleay for some action.[19] In Shanghai, the Municipal Council, closely in touch with the leaders of British interests, discussed the matter that winter and finally, on 10 March 1926, decided to put to the April ratepayers' meeting a resolution calling for the seating of three Chinese.[20] Fessenden announced the plan at a dinner for Chinese and foreign dignitaries at the new Majestic Hotel (Shanghai's grandest at that time) on 18 March, adding that the Council would also seek a return of the Mixed Court. His speech was a conciliatory one, but in his stress on industrial questions and his appeal to the business leaders of Chinese Shanghai to deal with union agitation, he seemed to suggest that the problem was between management and labor, missing (or hoping to avoid) its political aspects. Yu Xiaqing's response (apparently drafted by David Yui of the National Christian Council) firmly insisted that Shanghai's problems were not economic but political; they were part of the nationwide drive for the abrogation of the unequal treaties and could not be met by purely local solutions.[21]

Three weeks later, on 14 April, the ratepayers gathered for their annual meeting in the Town Hall. Fessenden gave a brief and rather defensive account of the May Thirtieth affair as the Council saw it, taking issue particularly with some of the press accounts but refusing to elaborate. "A full and frank discussion of matters," he continued, "incidentally but not inseparably connected with the affair of May 30th, would inevitably give serious offense in more than one quarter, no matter how tactful the attempt to avoid offending the sensibility of those concerned might be. No useful object can therefore be attained by stirring up the embers of a dying fire which, if left alone, will burn itself out in time." Worrying about further disturbances in Shanghai's future, he invoked the specter of "hordes of the hardened and callous criminals . . . and more or less desperate characters of all sorts [who had] infested the Settlement" during the summer of 1925. "Like wolves lurking and skulking in the shadows, the dangers of incendiarism, sabotage and mob violence were always present during those troubled days." Nor could he resist a pitying reference to the inability of Chinese to understand "the majesty of the law and impersonal and impartial judicial methods."[22] Nonetheless, when the time came, he put in the resolution to add three Chinese to the Council, and it passed with only one opposing vote (though not before the defeat of an amendment that would have given Chinese the vote on the same basis as foreigners).

It was a shame, commented the *China Weekly Review*, that this liberal gesture had to come after, and not before, the events of 1925. Nevertheless, it warned, it would be madness to act precipitately, and the paper sternly repeated the old view that Chinese representation on the Council was a privilege and not a right.[23] Madness or not, what might have been good enough before Nanking Road, before Shameen, before the mass mobilization of popular feeling, now seemed grudging and inadequate. The day before the ratepayers' vote, newspaper advertisements proclaimed the Chinese Chamber's opposition to any arbitrary limitation of the number of Chinese seats and called for the direct election of Chinese councillors on the same terms as their foreign counterparts. Nor was that the only difficulty. Properly speaking, before the resolution could take effect, the legations must negotiate a change in the Land Regulations with Peking. But by now, what remained of China's government was vanishing into the thin northern air. The ministers finally threw up their hands and told the Shanghai consuls to solve the question locally. A consular subcommittee took the question in hand, and finally on 29 October 1926, Xu Yuan, the commissioner for foreign affairs, agreed to the appointment of three Chinese (precisely how they would be chosen was not clear).[24] By that time, however, central China was caught up in a new kind of civil war, a war in which the revolutionaries marched in step with the generals. By early 1927, when foreign Shanghai faced its greatest crisis yet, the problem remained unsettled.

Nonetheless, the Settlement's leaders had finally accepted the principle of Chinese representation on the Municipal Council, had finally offered the Chinese an olive branch (or at least a twig), and could claim that it was now up to them to respond. Chinese representation, however, was not the only threat a British-dominated Shanghai Municipal Council faced. Ever since the visit of the Tripier commission in June 1925, the British had suspected the French of trying to ingratiate themselves with the Chinese. "Not all the anti-British feeling now being exhibited in China at the present time comes from the Chinese, I can assure you," wrote Commissioner-General Hilton-Johnson in a private letter that August. "Have incontestable evidence," wired the China Association and the British Chamber, "that local French/Italian representatives doing their utmost to utilize Shanghai incident to undermine British prestige and destroy the predominance of British influence in China."[25]

Thus when, in August 1925, the senior minister had asked the Shanghai consuls to study the Municipal Council's reorganization, Barton was quick to smell a rat. The request implied more than simply adding Chinese members, he warned, and was an invitation to "Latin and other small Power consuls" to weaken Britain's position by adding members of other nationalities to the Council. "It should be remembered that most Consuls here are entirely ignorant of the history of the Settlement and of its Anglo-Saxon parentage." But Palairet, unwilling to block the Diplomatic Body again, insisted that the consul-general bite the bullet and keep the question of the Council's internationalization on the agenda.[26]

No mere Italians, like Senior Minister Cerruti or Senior Consul de' Rossi, could out-Machiavelli Sidney Barton. Claiming that he had foiled de' Rossi's attempts to exclude him, Barton got himself named to a subcommittee to study the issue.[27] Eight times the group met that autumn, and eight times Barton insisted, backed by the loyal Cunningham, that they could not have chosen a worse time to consider changes to the policy of foreign Shanghai. Even Fessenden, more flexible than Barton, recommended enlarging the Council to fifteen to handle its increasing work and to allow other nations to be represented. He also wanted to reduce the number of ratepayers necessary for a quorum so that more business could be done at special meetings.[28] The consuls discussed these and other questions, including an extension of the franchise and a consular veto over the Council's actions, similar to that enjoyed by British consuls in purely British concessions. Barton opposed every change without exception, only in the end ("not wishing to appear intransigent," as he put it) agreeing that an enlarged Council might safely consist of representatives of at least five countries other than China.

In December, the subcommittee drafted its report. "Some members were of the opinion that it [the Council] should also be brought into line with modern democratic ideas," they noted rather gingerly; hence their recommendation for an enlarged Council of eleven members representing five nationalities. They left the other issues, including a widened franchise and a consular veto, alone; because of "the peculiar conditions prevailing in Shanghai, its constantly shifting population and the absence, to any great extent, of local patriotism among foreigners, the basis of the franchise must always be the possession of permanent material interests."[29] Finally, they said nothing of the relationship between the Council and the consuls that had been at the center of the dispute in June. Part of the reason for this silence obviously had to do with the need to maintain British predominance. But another part no doubt came from the fear that greater consular control might further encourage the abuses of extraterritoriality that already darkened Shanghai's reputation—such as the shelter of Portuguese citizenship for the ganglord Du Yuesheng. Even Thomas Millard of the *New York Times*, himself no friend of foreign Shanghai's pretensions, justified the Settlement's independence from the diplomats on these grounds.[30]

Eventually, nothing came even of the consuls' timid recommendation. Not until July 1926 did it make its way to the Peking legations, and there it sank without a trace, preempted by more urgent questions. The whole issue of internationalization simply vanished, and in early 1927, when Shanghai seemed to be facing a danger even greater than that of May Thirtieth, the legations agreed to bury it.[31] Once again, British Shanghai, led by Barton, had won. "As long as the Council remains—as it must—predominantly Anglo-Saxon," he wrote later, "it is impossible to expect men of standing to render arduous voluntary service to the community if they are to be subjected to an arbitrary veto imposed as the result of a majority vote given in a body of eighteen consuls, not a few of whom are notoriously corrupt, while others have neither the knowledge of nor interest in local conditions which would justify the exercise of such a power."[32] The Council's foreign membership went unchanged, and the whole curious episode (not a word about which, incidentally, ever made its way into the press) simply illustrates how it was possible for the consular body's most forceful personality to get his way. Not until 1940 was Britain's predominance seriously challenged, and then it was neither the Chinese nor the Latins who insisted on change, but rather the Japanese army.

The other outstanding question to come out of May Thirtieth was the return—rendition, as it was called—of the Mixed Court. The problem here was that, since the revolution of 1911, the foreigners had enjoyed a control over it that was in no way sanctioned by the treaties, and now they were unwilling to surrender that control. In part, this reluctance was based on a fear (a fear exacerbated by the unflattering findings of the Commission on Extraterritoriality) that any increase in Chinese authority would make it more difficult to keep order in the Settlement and would open the Court to the influences of Chinese politics. Another difficulty was less flattering to Western conceptions of the majesty of the law and impartial judicial methods; put simply, since 1911, foreign lawyers had assumed the right to appear in purely Chinese cases, and a good many attorneys were making a good, comfortable living off the Court. Though the British naturally blamed American, Italian, or Spanish lawyers for the disrepute into which the Mixed Court had fallen since 1911, not all British barristers had clean hands themselves. Like lawyers everywhere, Shanghai lawyers knew, as Dickens had written, that "the one great principle of the law . . . is, to make business for itself." How could anyone (but a lawyer) hope to understand the Byzantine complexities of practice in foreign Shanghai with its different jurisdictions, its different kinds of law? *Bleak House* would have been three times longer—and *Jarndyce* v. *Jarndyce* three times as profitable—if the case had been fought in Shanghai.

Though the question of the Court was properly one for the legations and the Chinese government to settle in Peking, again the only sensible procedure in 1926 was to negotiate it locally. Barton took charge of a consular subcommittee to work with Xu Yuan and Ding Wenjiang [V. K. Ting], who had been appointed director general of the Port of Shanghai and Wusong. By July 1926, a draft agreement had gone to the legations for approval. Despite the impassioned pleas of the local American Bar Association and other groups of foreign lawyers, all of whom objected loudly to the prospect of diminished fees, the legations accepted the new arrangement on 31 August.[33]

The agreement did not hand back the Mixed Court so much as it abolished it, putting in its place a Provisional Court whose procedures considerably restricted the license enjoyed by foreigners, and particularly by foreign lawyers, since 1911. The foreign presence did not entirely disappear; the new agreement, though doing away with the old consular assessors, allowed a consular deputy to sit as observer in criminal cases that affected the peace and order of the Settlement and in civil cases where an extraterritorial foreigner was plaintiff.[34] Foreign lawyers could still plead such cases, but—despite efforts made by the Italian government in their behalf—they would be excluded from others. By the end of the year, the final details had been ironed out. On 1 January 1927, the old Mixed Court ended, and the new Provisional Court took its place.[35] With it China gained another small victory in the battle to win control over her own affairs. She did so, moreover—as in the question of representation on the Council—without having to pay the price (usually demanded in the past), of extending the boundaries of the Settlement yet further and giving foreigners a voice in the governance of the Chinese city.

As the British were fighting off both Chinese and foreign challenges to their own authority in the Settlement, they looked jealously at the seemingly unruffled calm of the French Concession during the stormy summer of 1925. That the Frenchtown authorities were able to maintain order without recourse to martial law was seen as clear evidence that they were temporizing with Chinese xenophobia, trying to deflect the wrath of radical nationalism against the British in general and the International Settlement in particular. The British watched with dour disapproval (Anglo-Saxon *"mauvaise humeur,"* the French admiral called it) as parades celebrating liberty, equality, and fraternity marked the Concession's celebration of the *quatorze juillet* of 1925. Martel's public washing of his hands of the Shanghai affair made matters worse. "The stand taken by the French Minister is heartily endorsed by Chinese residents here," wrote Jabin Hsu [Xu Jiabin] of the *China Press* to the American minister. "As a result, many Chinese merchants, students and laborers are participating in the colorful demonstrations being held in celebration of the Fall of the Bastille. The expression of international goodwill between the two peoples is spontaneous." [36] The memory rankled; a year later, when the Chinese authorities formally thanked the French consul-general for his country's help to China in her time of troubles, George Vereker took it as proof that Tripier and his countrymen had been "busily engaged in offering their services as mediators to the Chinese, rather than in helping the Diplomatic Commission to ascertain the real facts and fix the responsibility." [37]

The Concession's freedom from trouble also stimulated speculation that the French were on closer terms than they should be with some of the less attractive elements within their borders. It was a good guess. Though the British did not know it—or at least did not report it—in the spring of 1925, several French authorities, including Captain Étienne Fiori of the *Garde municipale* (he whom Wilden had considered above suspicion), were negotiating with Du Yuesheng of the Green Gang, who was rapidly becoming the most important figure in Shanghai's flourishing and illegal opium trade. Out of the talks came a deal that summer that in effect gave French approval for the distribution of the drug in the Concession. In return, the French police would receive a direct payment for keeping their eyes closed ("pour fermer les yeux"), and more important, they would now have the covert help of Du and his underworld—including, of course, Huang Jinrong, the Green Gang leader who headed the Chinese detectives in the *Garde municipale*—in maintaining order. [38]

Such arrangements would eventually grow into a major scandal that shook the very basis of the French position in Shanghai. But that was later. Though the British may have been right in smelling a French connection with the underworld, they were wrong in thinking that the French were trying to undercut them. The record suggests that French diplomats in China, far from trying to subvert the Settlement authorities in the summer of 1925, were doing their best to save the British from the consequences of their own folly. Not that the French took a more liberal attitude than the Anglo-Saxons toward Chinese pretensions; Martel had little sympathy with Chinese nationalism and was quite prepared to cooperate with the Manchurian warlord Zhang Zuolin in keeping radicalism at bay. But they were desperately afraid that Anglo-Saxon racism and stiff-neckedness— what acting Consul-General Jacques Meyrier called, "Anglo-Saxon superciliousness and its contempt for the Chinese"[39]—would bring the whole structure of foreign privilege in Shanghai crashing down around them all, French as well as British and American.

They thus understood the value of timely concessions—before the first anniversary of May Thirtieth arrived—to keep the Frenchtown Chinese reasonably satisfied. To do so meant, above all, insuring a real Chinese voice in the Concession's affairs, since the arrangement of 1914 to add to two prominent Chinese to the Council as nonvoting members remained a dead letter.[40] Moreover, the French had another problem every bit as important as keeping the Chinese happy. Just as the British fought off attempts to diminish their authority in the Settlement, the French were desperately anxious to stay in control of their own administration. French citizens were becoming increasingly outnumbered in their own Concession as more and more foreigners—particularly Americans and British—moved in, finding that land was cheaper and life pleasanter in Frenchtown than in the frenetic and crowded atmosphere of downtown Shanghai. J. B. Powell himself, the champion of American interests, lived on the rue de Grouchy, and O. M. Green, the voice of British Shanghai, had a house at 54 avenue du Roi Albert. By early 1925, though only about 300 French residents had the franchise, some 1,200 foreigners were qualified to vote. Since many were British and American, the French saw—or thought they saw—the possibility that the Concession would one day be swallowed up by the larger, richer, and more dynamic Settlement.

To make matters worse, some Frenchmen were not above challenging the authority of their own officials. Much to Meyrier's distress, one of the successful candidates in the elections of January 1925 for the *Conseil municipal* was the lawyer du Pac de Marsoulies, whose contract as *avocat conseil* had recently been terminated and who took his revenge by sweeping to victory on a platform that promised to cut down the consul-general's authority over the *Conseil*. Meyrier (who suggested darkly that du Pac wanted to control the police in order to safeguard his rumored interests in opium) countered by taking over the Presidency of the *Conseil* himself.[41] Nonetheless, the appeal made by a Frenchman to non-French interests threatened to subvert France's shaky position. Of course, the consul-general still had a veto power; but how often could he use it and keep the goodwill of his *Conseil*?

Then came the summer of 1925. Demands for the direct election of Chinese to the Municipal Council of the Settlement raised the prospect of similar demands in the Concession. To meet this threat, Meyrier suggested modifying the *Règlement d'Organisation*—the French version of the Settlement's Land Regulations—to enlarge the *Conseil* by adding four Chinese named by Chinese authorities as full councillors and four more

Frenchmen to be named by himself. His plan had several advantages: it would forestall a Chinese demand for direct elections, it would allow the consul-general to choose the right sort of Frenchmen for the *Conseil*, and it would assure a French majority in a body that would now consist of nine Frenchmen (four elected, four appointed, and the consul-general as president), four foreigners, and four Chinese.[42]

The elections to the *Conseil* in January 1926 made the problem more acute than ever. Only 278 of the 915 foreigners who voted were French; 363 were English and 209 American. The new *Conseil*, Meyrier complained, was less French in spirit than ever, and the obstreperous du Pac was still determined to liberate his colleagues from consular control.[43] When Paul-Emile Naggiar arrived in April 1926 as consul-general, his first step was to designate Meyrier to run the *Conseil*, in order to keep a firm hand on it. Neither Naggiar nor the Quai d'Orsay wanted to raise the question of fundamental recasting of the *Règlement* at such a ticklish time, particularly since the Diplomatic Body would have to approve any changes. But there were some steps he could take on his own before the anniversary of May Thirtieth came around. In the April *Bulletin Municipal* appeared a consular *ordonnance* stating that the two Chinese notables designated under the terms of the 1914 agreement would now meet regularly with the *Conseil*. On 23 April, they took their seats.[44]

Obviously (as jealous Anglo-Saxons pointed out), the autocratic power of the French consul-general gave the French *Conseil municipal* a flexibility that the Settlement authorities, bound by their Land Regulations, did not have (and perhaps did not want). Naggiar's step, as it turned out, was only the first of several changes that would be made to keep the French Concession up with the times, and no doubt it helped his bailiwick ride through the difficult days of May 1926. But the International Settlement rode through them too. Though the Chinese Chamber asked for a one-day shop closing and the half-masting of flags on 30 May, and the General Labor Union from its underground headquarters called for a one-day work stoppage in the textile mills, the troops of Sun Chuanfang, the new master of Shanghai, were out in force. There were disturbances in the Settlement, particularly around Nanking Road, and there was a big commemorative meeting at the West Gate and smaller gatherings elsewhere. Cunningham was indignant in reporting to Washington the day's events, but on the whole, foreign Shanghai could count itself lucky for not having to deal with more trouble.[45]

Anyway, the Americans were by no means blameless themselves. On the anniversary of May Thirtieth itself, the Brewer Company of Worcester, Massachusetts, which for years had been importing Fraser's Momilk (a condensed milk) into Shanghai, took out a large advertisement in the local Chinese press. "*Wu wang wusa!*" "Do Not Forget May Thirtieth!" read the large characters that made up the headline. A clear incitement to violence, to antiforeignism? Not at all. May Thirtieth, the small print told the careful reader, marks the beginning of the hot weather, and it would not do to let the day slip by without taking proper precautions for one's health. What better way than by drinking pure, uncontaminated Momilk? Consul-general Cunningham was not amused.[46]

TEN

A Storm Center Once More
Shanghai in 1926

W e came back into the hottest summer I have ever known in Shanghai," wrote Bishop Graves in August 1926, as he returned from his wife's
funeral in California. Another letter described a city in which the ther-
mometer had climbed over a hundred degrees every day for a month,
while the summer rains held back, drying up the rice and cotton crops of
the Yangtze delta.[1] As usual, those who could left Shanghai during the hot
season for cooler parts. Some went to the hills of Korea or Japan or north
to the beaches of Shandong, staying in the old German hotels like the
Strand or the Prince Heinrich in Qingdao, or to Beidaihe near Qinhuang-
dao, which had both an English beach and an American beach. Some—
particularly missionaries—stayed closer to Shanghai. Guling [Kuling] in
Jiangxi's Lushan Mountains above the river port of Jiujiang was a favorite place. You got there via river steamer, then by road, then via sedan
chair carried by coolies up thousands of worn stone steps, the precipices
falling away on either side, to the welcome cool of the Fairy Glen in the
upper valley, thirty-five hundred feet above the sea (in the troubles of 1925,
foreigners making the trip were given military escorts). Or you took the
train from Shanghai to the Grand Canal near Hangzhou, spent the night
on a houseboat, and after landing the next morning, climbed for three
hours through the steep, bamboo-forested hills of Zhejiang to Moganshan
[Mokanshan]. Outsiders could come too, of course—in 1926, Kang You-
wei, the elder statesman whose abortive reforms in 1898 had been crushed
by the Dowager Empress, was there, as was the White Lama.[2] For the
most part, however, both Guling and Moganshan were missionary havens,
dominated by the Anglo-American Protestant ethos of their inhabitants
(twelve of the fourteen members of the Guling Council were missionar-

ies), given to scriptural study, choir concerts, and decorous games for the children.

Most people, of course, had to stay behind and deal with the heat as best they could. Foreign Shanghai's architecture was solider than the colonial style of the southern ports, whose remnants can still be seen on Shamian Island in Canton, and that which used to grace central Hongkong before the buildings gave way to today's anonymous, air-conditioned concrete and glass skyscrapers. The brief winter of south China was a minor inconvenience, and the people there lived and worked in houses designed to catch any breath of wind that might make the summer more bearable. Shanghai's more massive buildings had to cope not only with summer's heat but also with a winter that could bring frost and snow. By late May, as the temperature and humidity rose, huge, wooden ceiling fans would give some relief, and the lucky could escape after work to the cool halls and colder drinks of the downtown clubs, to the public swimming pool on North Szechuen Road, or, best of all, to the lawns and tennis courts, the pergola-shaded roof garden, the *piscine*, and the bar of the new Cercle Sportif that opened in January 1926 on the route Cardinal Mercier.

With the hot weather came the usual warnings from the Public Health Department against the summer's hazards. "Though Shanghai is spoken of as a Model Settlement from the administrative point of view, it is far from being so from the sanitary point of view. The agricultural methods of the Chinese farmer and gardener, the personal habits of the coolie class, the great congestion and overcrowding in certain areas, the existence of foul and stagnant creeks, these are conditions incompatible with an ideal sanitary environment. . . ." The department went on to warn against the dangers of unlicensed iced drinks, uncooked food, cut fruit, jellies, and ice cream.[3] Particularly dangerous was water that had not been boiled, sterilized, or filtered. Cholera was an ever-present danger in Shanghai, and fourteen of the last twenty-six summers had seen outbreaks of the disease. In 1926, a particularly vicious epidemic hit, its source traced to contamination in the Zhabei waterworks. With the help of Settlement engineers, the plant was shut down in early August and thoroughly cleaned out. The incidence of disease began to decline, but not before some two thousand people, most of them in Zhabei, died.[4]

Foreign Shanghai, having made up its mind in April to allow the Chinese a limited voice in the governance of the Settlement, saw the epidemic as a dreadful warning of what might happen if spineless foreign governments were to concede too much to Nationalist demands. They also noted that in May 1926, Sun Chuanfang, publicly contrasting the good order and cleanliness of the foreign settlements with the backwardness of the Chinese city, had established a new Directorate of the Port of Shanghai and Wusong for the building of a new and modern municipality. Foreigners, of course, did appreciate his tribute to the Model Settlement, and they trusted V. K. Ting [Ding Wenjiang], the Edinburgh-educated geologist whom he appointed to oversee the new administration.[5] Such improvements still lay in the future, however. For the moment, just as Chinese dirt and Chinese crime endangered the physical well-being of respectable people, so Chinese disorder endangered the economic well-being of foreign business.

On 23 and 24 June, the Council's commissioner-general, Major Hilton-Johnson, met with a group of leading British businessmen in Jardine, Matheson's Ewo Building on the Bund to discuss ways to cope with the damage done to British trade by the events of 1925. To such men—from the Hongkong and Shanghai Bank, C. H. Arnhold, Ilbert, Butterfield and Swire, and other such firms—it was axiomatic that the success of British commerce depended ultimately on good relations with the Chinese. But weakness would not buy goodwill, and Britain must risk Chinese hostility now for the sake of wider opportunities later. That strategy might even mean a policy of intervention—the word was a vague one that could mean anything from the use of military force to economic diplomacy. Cooperation with Japan in this policy was essential, and with America, desirable, though few believed that Washington would be willing to go along. Above all, the principal treaty port settlements must remain under foreign control, lest they become pawns in the intrigues of Chinese politics.[6]

Though the meeting was private, a copy of the minutes found its way back to the Foreign Office, brought by Lord Southborough. Southborough headed a new China Committee, formed a few months earlier by British trade interests to help (as they put it) the Foreign Office make China policy, or (as the Foreign Office feared) "to keep us up to the mark in Chinese affairs."[7] Out of the June meeting at Jardine's, too, came the formation of China Committees in Hongkong, Shanghai, and several other treaty ports to coordinate the work of local British trade associations with Southborough's group at home.[8] The Foreign Office's Far Eastern Department, which thus far had enjoyed a good deal of independence and had remained remarkably immune from business criticism, looked on the new developments with dismay. "The advice we get from the business community in China on political matters is usually extremely bad," Basil Newton had written a year earlier, "being ill-considered, violent, and fluctuating from one extreme to another. Whenever any incident occurs, they always start by crying out for strong action, while the moment there is any threat of a boycott, they are in favor of giving way."[9] Although moderates like G. Warren Swire realized that the Shanghai mind and its London spokesmen must not be allowed to dictate Whitehall's moves, some of the new committee's members, like Sir Robert Waley Cohen of Asiatic Petroleum, were demanding the use of force against China. Nor did all such calls come from businessmen. As the Canton strike and boycott entered their second year, even old missionaries like W. E. Soothill wanted armed intervention against the Nationalists. "Can *no one* come back from China without advocating force?" asked a despairing William Strang at the Foreign Office.[10]

A little more than a fortnight after the meeting at Jardine's, a far more important gathering took place in Canton. On 9 July, the National Government formally named General Chiang Kai-shek as commander-in-chief of the National Revolutionary Army and proclaimed the start of the long-awaited Northern Expedition. The term was not new; for years Sun Yat-sen had promised a great military campaign that would see vast armies sweep north from Guangdong in a drive to unite all China under the Guomindang's revolutionary banner. In the past, such undertakings had come to nothing; hence, even though the Nationalist armies were already in the field, fighting their way into Hunan, when the Northern Expedition was announced, foreigners paid little attention to Canton's proclamation. Despite the presence of Russian gold, Russian guns, and Russian generals in the Guomindang camp, Canton's advance looked like just another summer campaign that would halt when it came up against the northern commanders: Wu Peifu in the central Yangtze Valley, Sun Chuanfang, master of Shanghai and five eastern provinces, and the strongest of all, Zhang Zuolin, whose Fengtian armies controlled the north from Manchuria to Shandong.

The predictions were wrong, and the Nationalist armies kept going. Douglas Jenkins, American consul-general at Canton, had warned that Chiang's men would fight more effectively than Chinese armies in the past; they were well led, had some "first class airplanes" from the Soviet Union, and the field campaigns would be directed by very able Russians.[11] Sweeping up through Hunan in July and August, the Cantonese and their allies moved toward the Yangtze, just as the Taiping rebels had done three-quarters of a century earlier. By late August over a hundred thousand refugees, afraid less of the southern advance than the prospect of pillage by defeated northern troops, had swollen the foreign concessions in Hankou. On 6 September, Wu Peifu fled the city after the defection of one of his commanders, and the Nationalist soldiers poured into Hankou. Across the river at Wuchang, however, the northern troops put up the stiffest resistance the Nationalist armies had yet seen. There, several American churchmen, including Bishop Logan Roots, worked for a compromise settlement (much to the distress of the American consul-general who thought that men of the cloth should steer clear of political and military affairs). They had almost reached a truce when, on 10 October, the revolutionary armies stormed into Wuchang, raising the white sun and blue sky of the Nationalist flag fifteen years to the day after the outbreak in the very same city of the revolution that had overthrown the Manchu dynasty.[12]

With Hubei province at their feet, the Nationalist troops now pushed northeast into Jiangxi, entering Sun Chuanfang's territory for the first time. As early as 19 September, southern units took the provincial capital of Nanchang, only to be driven out by a northern counterattack. Another assault, directed by Chiang Kai-shek himself, failed before the city gates on 13 October. Then, after reorganizing his forces, on 2 November Chiang ordered a general offensive against the province (a nasty surprise to Sun, who apparently believed the current rumor that Chiang lay dead of his wounds in the Yale-in-China hospital at Changsha). Jiujiang, 450 miles upriver from Shanghai, fell on 4 to 5 November after a brief fight, and three days later on the eighth, the revolutionary armies entered Nanchang, capturing many northern soldiers and their stores to make up for their own substantial losses.[13] Meanwhile, a two-month offensive under General He Yingqin led to the subjugation of the coastal province of Fujian and the occupation of Fuzhou on 18 December. By the end of November, the Nationalists announced that their government would move from Canton to Hankou. South of the Yangtze, only Zhejiang and Jiangsu remained in Sun Chuanfang's hands.

"Whether one likes it or not," wrote the American journalist Rodney Gilbert shortly before the final triumph in the Wuhan cities, "one must admit that the Russo-Cantonese expeditionary force is so efficient that it makes all the northern organizations look like disorganized rabble. Discipline is perfect, control of all officers under a unified command is excellent, and checks upon them ingenious, and when they go into a fight they mean business and carry out their operations with clockwork precision." [14] From him, it was high praise. Gilbert, an American medicine salesman turned journalist and old China hand, was hardly a friendly critic; he despised New China and its ways, held it responsible for the unending series of civil wars, and saw little but Bolshevism behind the nationalist movement. That summer he had published a book called *What's Wrong with China*, which had been devoured by treaty port circles anxious for a work by a man who really understood the Chinese and that would give them facts to back up their own prejudices. Yet here, suddenly, were the Nationalist armies in Fujian, Jiangxi, and Hubei, reaching along the river above Shanghai; and mere prejudice was not likely to stop them.

It was not easy to follow the sinuous course of Canton politics, and the Western view of Chiang Kai-shek was an ambivalent one. That the tensions between moderates and leftists (Communist and otherwise) had grown worse since Sun Yat-sen's death in March 1925 was no secret. The mysterious assassination of the radical leader Liao Zhongkai in July 1925 almost split the two sides, but the uneasy peace between them continued. In November 1925, a right-wing faction of the Guomindang, meeting in the Western Hills near Peking, had denounced the Communists and their supporters, proclaiming themselves to be the true heirs of Sun Yat-sen's revolutionary legacy. Shortly thereafter, they moved to Shanghai and took over the party offices at 44 route Vallon in the French Concession (while representatives of the Canton Guomindang held onto Sun's old house a few blocks away at 29 rue Molière).[15]

In the spring of 1926, the Western Hills faction held its own party congress in Shanghai, denouncing the united front and expelling the Communists from their Guomindang. Chiang Kai-shek and the Cantonese leaders disowned the action, openly defending the alliance with the Communists and the presence of Borodin with his cadre of Soviet advisers. In January 1926, the Second Congress of the Guomindang in Canton marked a clear triumph for the radicals, Communists, and leftists who now held six of the nine seats in the Standing Committee, which was the real power in the Guomindang's Central Executive Committee. Meanwhile, they consolidated their position on the lower levels. Communists, already the most active in organizing labor, peasant, and youth movements, now came to dominate the army's political training units, which were modeled on the Soviet military's commissar system.[16] But Chiang had no intention of becoming an instrument of Soviet policy in China. In March 1926, claiming the discovery of a Communist plot to seize power, he declared martial law in Canton and disarmed some of the more revolutionary units. A tense series of negotiations with Borodin (who had been out of town at the time of the coup) brought an uneasy agreement to continue the united front, though it considerably circumscribed Communist independence. It was hardly a clear victory for the right, however, for at the end of May the moderate Foreign Minister C. C. Wu [Wu Chaoshu] was replaced by the radical Eugene Chen [Chen Yuren], the Trinidad-born, British-educated lawyer who had been Sun's private secretary. C. C. Wu, together with the anti-Communist veteran Hu Hanmin, left Canton for Shanghai, there to strengthen the rightist tinge of the Guomindang's representation in that city.

Chiang's March coup heartened some foreign observers, but left them still confused. "The situation seems to have taken a sudden turn in the direction in which we have always hoped it would," noted a member of the Foreign Office.[17] "No one seems to know how General Chiang stands in the matter of politics," wrote the British consul-general in Canton. "At one moment he will deliver an address to the students of the Kuangtung University breathing fire and revolution and denouncing mission schools as treacherous institutions, and at another he will give assurances pri-

The Bund, looking north to the dome of the Hongkong and Shanghai Bank. From *Shanghai of Today: A Souvenir Album of Fifty Vandyke Gravure Prints of "The Model Settlement,"* 3d edition, revised (Shanghai, 1930).

The Bund, looking north from the Asiatic Petroleum Company building and the Shanghai Club, past the Hongkong and Shanghai Bank, the Customs Building (completed in 1927), the twin towers of the North China Daily News Building, and the tower of Sassoon House (completed in 1930). Today the physical appearance of these buildings is little changed; the Shanghai Club has become a hotel and fast food restaurant, the Hongkong and Shanghai Bank houses the municipal government and party committee, and Sassoon House is the Peace Hotel. From *Shanghai of Today.*

West along Nanking Road in the late twenties. From *Shanghai of Today*.

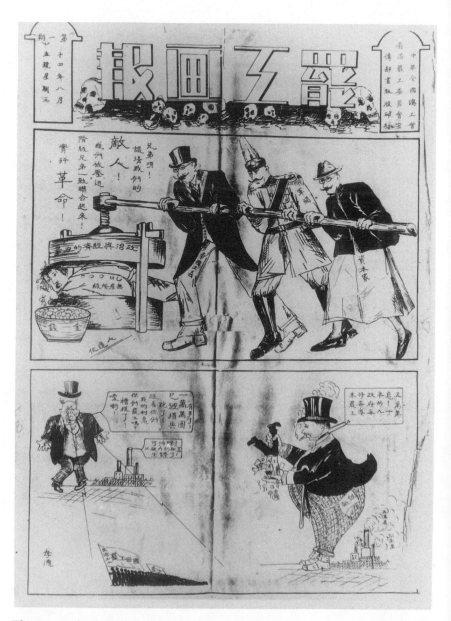

The *Bagong huabao* [Strike Pictorial] of August 1925. The top drawing shows a Chinese capitalist, a warlord, and a foreign imperialist squeezing coins from the mouth of the proletariat in a press labeled "Political and Economic Pressure."
Courtesy of the National Archives.

A worker supports his dying comrade; part of the May Thirtieth Memorial, erected in People's Park (the former International Settlement Recreation Ground) in 1990. The calligraphy is by Chen Yun. Photograph by the author.

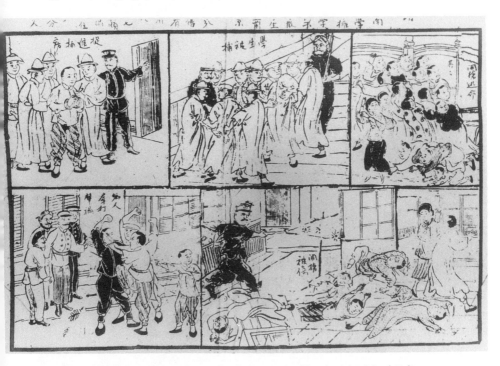

May thirtieth in Nanking Road. A radical paper seized by the Municipal Police shows the events from the arrest of Chinese students to the massacre by foreign police. Courtesy of the National Archives.

Col. Gordon and Stirling Fessenden inspect the American cavalry of the Shanghai Volunteer Force in 1927. The Bettmann Archive.

An armored car company of the Shanghai Volunteer Force, 1927. The Bettmann Archive.

Demonstration in Chinese Shanghai, spring 1927. The banners carry the names of the participating groups. The Bettmann Archive.

Rear-Admiral Reginald Tyrwhitt, British commander-in-chief, and Sir John Duncan, general officer commanding, Shanghai Defence Force, 1927. The Bettmann Archive.

Armed pickets [*jiuchadui*] on parade in Shanghai, spring 1927. The Bettmann Archive.

vately . . . that he is inflexibly opposed to the communist party and their attempts to create disorder."[18] The Communists were still in the minority, warned Douglas Jenkins from Canton, but "they are well organized and know how to fight, whereas the moderates are made up of various cliques and conflicting interests which may or may not unite when the crisis finally comes." Though Chiang had curbed Communist influence, Jenkins reported, he continued to work with Borodin and the Russians who gave him arms, money, and advice, but with a bit of encouragement from Britain and America, he might be weaned away from them. Nonetheless, Jenkins warned that Chiang was antiforeign in general and anti-American in particular.[19]

During the early phases of the Northern Expedition, Chiang struck out hard at the special position of foreigners and its effects on China, alarming the treaty port residents who saw little difference between modern anti-imperialism and old-fashioned, Boxer-style antiforeignism. Americans in south China complained of the increasing hardships suffered by businessmen and missionaries in Guangdong, although their tone suggests that what really upset them was Chiang's failure to fall in with the easy myth that Americans were somehow less imperialist than other foreigners and occupied a particular place in the affections of the Chinese.[20] The British continued to suffer from the long general strike and boycott that had begun after the Shamian shooting a year earlier. Not until October 1926, sixteen months after its start, was it finally settled so that the Nationalists could concentrate on their military campaigns. To an American journalist in Nanchang, Chiang promised that the revolution would not end until all foreign concessions were returned, extraterritoriality abolished, and the unequal treaties ended.[21] If he were to triumph, cautioned the *North China Herald*, Chiang would "set up a Soviet style Government, with Labour as co-partners; after which China will set out hand-in-hand with Moscow her guide and benefactress, to abolish Imperialism throughout the world." The vision was one of Soviet revolution mixed with classic Chinese xenophobia. "We are seeing now a repetition of what happened in 1900. Just as the Manchus then secretly encouraged the Boxers until the latter got out of hand, so the Kuomintang have caressed the mob and it is going too strong for them."[22] Even Powell's *China Weekly Review*, which generally refused to be stampeded by the red menace, ran a series of articles by Charles Dailey of the Chicago *Tribune*, who had no doubts about the Nationalist movement's Communist affiliations and Communist control.[23]

For the moment, Shanghai remained untouched by the war. But on 5 September, above the great Yangtze gorges in Sichuan, British gunboats pounded the city of Wanxian after the local warlord commandeered a

Butterfield and Swire steamer to carry his troops. Though the Wanxian incident had nothing to do with the Northern Expedition, and though old China hands applauded this return of British backbone, the action served only to call up memories of 1925 and to strengthen the image of Britain as an imperialist bully. More ominously, the navy's use of force appeared to have violated the instructions of the British legation—"our naval people on the spot were spoiling for a fight," wrote a Foreign Office observer— and served to remind the diplomats how little control they had over their military representatives.[24]

In Shanghai, however, Sun Chuanfang and the Chinese Chamber between them refused to allow Wanxian to revivify the anti-British movement.[25] In public, Sun declared the neutrality of the five provinces whose overlordship he claimed; in private, he worried both about the Nationalist advance and about the possibility that the Fengtian forces, whom he had ousted from Kiangsu and Shanghai, would use the fighting as an excuse to return south. He also dickered with Chiang Kai-shek, apparently promising to join the Nationalist cause if Chiang would rid himself of the extremists and the Russian advisers. But Chiang's invasion of Jiangxi in early September forced him to choose sides, and on 11 September, after fruitless appeals for British aid, he reluctantly concluded a defensive alliance with Zhang Zuolin's Fengtian group.[26]

The fall of Wuhan and the invasion of Jiangxi brought home to foreign Shanghai the reality of the revolutionary advance as never before. With it came not only the fear of a revolutionary army outside the gates but also of Communist subversion within. Though the anniversary of May Thirtieth had passed with little trouble, June had seen forty strikes break out in the city, the highest ever for a normal period, and although the totals for July and August were somewhat smaller, there was a general current of unrest through the summer and into the fall. In August, the price of rice, which had risen steadily all summer, hit a peak of $19.80 a picul, some 90 percent higher than it had been eighteen months earlier, and the alleged murder of a Chinese docker aboard a Japanese freighter that month ignited a new round of strikes against the Japanese mills. But the real cause of the strikes, as even foreign Shanghai was prepared to admit, was not so much the high price of food or even radical agitation by the underground General Labor Union, but the appalling conditions under which Shanghai's workers continued to labor.[27]

In the summer of 1925, the Shanghai Municipal Council had made a clumsy attempt to combat the May Thirtieth Movement by launching its own anti-Communist campaign. The Council published several numbers of *Chengyan* ("Read the Truth," as it was called in English) that summer, distributed as leaflets and given to the Chinese press. The two dailies, *Shen*

Bao and *Xin Bao*, which were rash enough to publish the first issue—a translation of Austen Chamberlain's speech of 18 June to Parliament—were forced by the Federation to print a public apology, and after that, other means of distribution had to be used. *Chengyan* simply inflamed Chinese anger still further; as a Communist magazine remarked, if the editorials of British Shanghai's press had been translated into Chinese, the anti-imperialist movement would have grown even faster.[28] (In a similar vein, L. A. Lyall, the outgoing commissioner of the Maritime Customs in Shanghai, suggested to a Shanghai audience a year later that Sino-British relations would improve dramatically if the English treaty port papers were printed in Russian; then the Soviets, rather than the English, would get the benefit of Chinese ill will. A hurt editorial in the *North China* showed that they had been stung.)[29]

Though *Chengyan's* origins had been no secret, there were more covert attempts to influence Chinese opinion. Simply putting forward the foreign point of view was not enough, argued a private letter to one of the *North China's* editors. "My own idea is rather more insidious, and, perhaps, Machiavellian. The aim of the propaganda which I have in mind would be directed towards the effecting of a cleavage between the agitators and those who are blindly following them. That can best be secured by enveloping the former in a cloud of distrust and suspicion. . . ." He suggested a series of pamphlets printed in simple Chinese on rough paper, accusing the labor leaders of corruption in the handling of strike pay.[30] Charges of this sort against Li Lisan and the other strike leaders had appeared in the late summer of 1925, though whether or not they came from such a foreign disinformation campaign is impossible to say.

By November 1925, however, a group of British businessmen in Shanghai had begun to form a more or less clandestine group to plan counter-propaganda against radical troublemakers, and shortly thereafter, their movement grew to take in representatives of other nationalities, including Chinese. The move was controversial from the start. "It is obvious from various private letters which we have seen," wrote John Swire and Sons on 4 December 1925 to its Shanghai office, "that quite a number of foreigners in China, who are anxious for a job, consider themselves heaven-born propagandists and, if the matter is taken in hand in the wrong way or by the wrong person, more harm will be done than good." The Shanghai end, however, was convinced that something must be done. "The time has come when the Committee must get on to active work and propaganda by subsiding workers and people in the schools in the same way as the Bolsheviks do, also by using the press and printed matter. To carry this out effectively considerable sums will be required and the firms in China will be asked to contribute."[31]

Out of such plans was born the Constitutional Defence League, which by the spring of 1926 had become a semi-public organization, putting out a monthly magazine called *The Constitutionalist* from its office in the North China Building. Since it appeared only in English, French, and Russian, the journal's effect on Chinese opinion must have been slight. The league claimed, however, that it distributed Chinese translations of anti-Communist books and pamphlets in the outports, using a network of correspondents—particularly missionaries—and that it had won the sympathies of various provincial officials and northern leaders. Under Charles Grosbois, headmaster of the École Municipale, it also set up a "Franco-Chinese Educational Society" as a front organization to sponsor an essay contest for students.[32] It ran its own intelligence service, boasting of its liaison with official secret services, until a shortage of funds forced it to give up that side of its work.

It is not clear how much support the league had from foreign officials. Although Cunningham seems to have given it some encouragement, Macleay warned his consuls to stay clear for fear of violating Britain's 1922 accord with Russia, and Naggiar forced Grosbois to resign as vice-president of the league. The British Secret Service found the league's reports hopelessly superficial and unreliable, as indeed they were if we can take as typical the news that Washington had "voted" $600,000 for propaganda work in China. Above all, the league exemplifies how foreign Shanghai's amateur meddling in diplomacy and intelligence could seriously embarrass the home governments. In mid-1926, it made a clandestine (and unsuccessful) attempt to raise a $2 million loan for Sun Chuanfang through Hongkong; "from being ridiculous," noted a Foreign Office observer of the league's leaders, "they now show signs of becoming a positive danger."[33] Within a year, however, the league had largely faded away, with nothing more to show for their existence than "vague windy reports of enormous length out of which all one could discover was that they themselves thought they were very wonderful people."[34]

South of the avenue Edward VIII, a more professional intelligence service, the French Sûreté, had been furnishing the consul-general with a weekly report on Communist activity in and near the city. It is hard to judge the accuracy of *Actions bolcheviques à Changhaï*, which in any case reported more fully on the activities of Soviet Communists than on Chinese, and probably depended heavily on White Russian informers. As the summer wore on and the southern armies drew nearer, the French police noted an increase in Communist activity throughout the Yangtze Valley, and they kept a close eye on the Soviet ambassador when he visited Shanghai in September. Karakhan arrived on the fourteenth, installing himself in the forbidding, brown building on Whangpoo Road that housed (and still houses) the Soviet consulate-general. There he received a stream of Chinese and foreign visitors, including several officials from the French Concession. Much of his time (said the Sûreté) was spent in meetings to discuss the financing and organization of Communist work in Shanghai, as well as ways to subvert Shanghai through propaganda, strikes, boycotts, and industrial unrest. He called on T. V. Soong, Sun Yat-sen's Harvard-educated brother-in-law, who lived in Seymour Road in the Settlement, and on the Guomindang headquarters at 29 rue Molière. C. T. Wang, who had been foreign minister when China recognized the Soviet Union in 1924, gave him a dinner in the new Palais Oriental on the avenue Joffre. Among the guests was Yu Xiaqing of the General Chamber. Like every tourist, Karakhan went shopping in the big Nanking Road department stores, but he left Shanghai prematurely on the twenty-sixth after the Soviet secret service warned him (said the Sûreté) of a plot against his life.[35]

On Karakhan's return to Peking, Gregor Voitinsky, one of the Comintern's chief Chinese experts, arrived to work with the local Communists. It was his plan—or so the French police thought—to organize local anarchist and criminal groups to create disturbances, including attacks on the concessions, thus provoking massacres and bringing the city a new May Thirtieth.[36] Whether true or not, there was no doubt that tensions within the city were rising as the Nationalist forces drew closer. Shanghai looked like an "armed camp," wrote an American visitor to the city in early autumn, appalled by the sight of the Volunteers on maneuvers, armored cars racing by with machine guns protruding from their turrets, while off the Bund the warships lined up in the Huangpu. "The whole picture struck me as a caricature of what relationships between East and West might be."[37] A few days later came a sudden, sharp scare when Xia Chao, the governor of Zhejiang, declared his independence from his master Sun Chuanfang and led his troops north to attack Shanghai. Sun responded promptly, putting Shanghai under martial law, and though Xia Chao's men fought to within seven miles of the Shanghai arsenal, they were driven back before there was a real military threat to the city.[38]

Though the excitement died down quickly, this brief episode is important. By late 1926, the successes of the Northern Expedition showed that the days of the warlords were numbered and that Shanghai faced an uncertain future. Even as Sun Chuanfang's troops patrolled the Chinese city, behind the scenes a murky battle for control was being fought out by his enemies. The players included Communists, both right-wing and left-wing Guomindang agents, Shanghai businessmen like Yu Xiaqing and his colleagues, and finally, the Shanghai underworld led by men like Du Yuesheng and Huang Jinrong of the Green Gang. Each group was willing to join the others to end warlord control; but each had its own visions of what the city's future should be and who should control that future.[39]

Communist strength was centered in the underground General Labor Union, now under Wang Shouhua who had succeeded the martyred Liu Hua in December 1925. It could field a force of about two thousand *jiuchadui*, or pickets as they were called at the time. A few were armed with guns; the rest had picks, axes, and other makeshift weapons. Simultaneously, Niu Yongjian, a veteran of the 1911 revolution, had arrived in Shanghai to look after Chiang Kai-shek's Guomindang interests and to prepare for the Nationalist arrival. From his house on the route Vallon, Niu built up his own force, helped by the underworld who could furnish recruits from the Green Gang and find arms on the city's black market. Meanwhile, Chinese businessmen, like the members of the Chinese Chamber of Commerce, wanted to keep the fighting away from the city and favored declaring Shanghai independent from both warlords and the revolutionary forces. Under the auspices of Yu Xiaqing, an armed merchant volunteer force [*baoweituan*] had been formed to protect business interests against both the right and the left. In August, Sun Chuanfang ordered them disbanded, thus forcing Yu into a quasi-alliance with the other plotters.

It was this uneasy entente with no clear leadership that sought to liberate the city from Sun's control. Merchant support was ambivalent at best, and Niu Yongjian would have preferred to negotiate the city's surrender rather than fight for it. He had agreed with his Communist allies that an uprising should take place in Shanghai that would be coordinated with Xia Chao's defection to the Nationalist cause (which he himself had helped to arrange). According to Communist versions of the story, however, when Niu learned of Xia's defeat, he did not tell the Communists but simply called off his own guerrillas (though at least some Communists heard the news, and the press reported that Xia's troops were on the run). Hence, the Communist pickets found themselves alone when, on 24 October, according to plan, they attacked police stations in Pudong and Nanshi (a planned rising in Zhabei was canceled in time). Sun's army and police moved in quickly, arrested several of the agitators, and executed them, and the plot came to an inglorious end.

Today, Chinese historians refer to this brief October episode as the first of the Three Armed Uprisings [*sanci wuzhuang qiyi*]. The second would come in February 1927, and the third and successful insurrection a month later. The first rising was a failure, Communist historians tell us today, not only because of weakness and poor planning but because of Chen Duxiu's opportunism, his lack of trust in the workers, and his willingness to concede too much to the bourgeoisie. Nonetheless, it did give the

Communists some experience in street fighting and taught them that they must control their own movements rather than allow their Guomindang and bourgeois allies to take the lead and betray them.[40] Though Chinese accounts are silent, French intelligence at the time also blamed the Soviet consulate for failing to assure coordination between different units and for a last-minute decision not to assign a Soviet military adviser to the operation.[41]

Whatever may be the truth of the matter, the episode represented a marked turn by the radicals from economic action, such as strikes and boycotts, toward an armed political action. Brief as it was, the October insurrection, combined with the advance of the revolutionary armies to the Yangtze, thoroughly scared Shanghai. If Sun were to be defeated, warned Macleay, "we must expect to see student agitations and anti-British demonstrations allowed free rein in Shanghai."[42] Chinese police claimed to have uncovered Cantonese money sent to Shanghai for subversion, and on 25 October, the Municipal Police shut down the *Minguo Ribao* [Republican Daily], accusing it of spreading "false and malicious rumors."[43] "It looks as if Shanghai were shortly to become a storm center once more," wrote Bishop Graves on 27 October. "Apparently no one can do anything to stop the descent to ruin which is before China."[44] Edwin Cunningham, preparing to go home on leave, found the city as nervous as it had been after the Nanking Road shooting. "There is a constant fear that propaganda will be successful in producing strikes and student riots, as the Cantonese are exceedingly active and will seize upon anything which will destroy the confidence of the local people in Sun Chuanfang."[45]

Though Sun held on to Hangzhou, the autumn's fighting left him badly weakened. Of the five provinces that he claimed as his own, two—Fujian and Jiangxi—had already fallen to the Nationalist armies, Zhejiang had almost been carried off by Xia Chao's revolt, and the Red tide would next threaten Jiangsu and Anhui. Sun responded by drawing closer to the northerners. New talks with Zhang Zuolin led to the formation of the *Anguojun*, or National Pacification Army. Zhang Zuolin assumed the position of commander-in-chief on 2 December, and Sun and Zhang Zongchang— the Dog's Meat General from Shandong—were vice-commanders.

As Sidney Barton had foreseen, the fear that Zhang Zongchang might move into the city threatened to drive the whole of the lower Yangtze Valley into the arms of the Nationalists.[46] Moderate leaders, including men like David Yui, C. T. Wang, and Cai Yuanpei, the Guomindang elderly statesman and former chancellor of Peking University, formed a Three Provinces Association (Jiangsu, Zhejiang, and Anhui) to try to keep Zhang's Shandong troops, with their barbaric reputation, out of the city and to win a degree of autonomy for Shanghai. Denouncing Sun's alliance with the northerners, they sought the establishment of a Shanghai Special Administrative District to keep the city neutral. The communists saw in the independence movement a chance to build up their own strength and popularity, to incline the moderate leaders further to the left, and thus to prepare for the next insurrection. Though Sun Chuanfang banned the association, there was little he could do about it since its headquarters, just off the rue Brenier de Montmorand in the French Concession, was safely away from his police—another example, remarked the American consul-general acidly, of the very men who denounced the existence of foreign concessions sensibly using them as a secure base for their political propaganda.[47]

Churchmen too, or at least some of them, were publicly showing a sometimes nervous optimism toward the coming of the new order. On 28 October 1926, the pro-Chinese policies of the Vatican's Celso Constantini had finally borne fruit when the Pope himself consecrated six new Chinese bishops in Rome, the first to be raised to the episcopal dignity since 1685. The ceremony was a sign of Rome's determination that the Church in China no longer depend upon foreign countries, though Vatican officials admitted that they would have to overcome a certain amount of European (read: French) prejudice. Martel, suggesting darkly that Chinese bishops might become heretics "par la pente naturelle de leur esprit," warned that they were apt to use their new positions for their own benefit and that their flocks would desert them when it was evident that they could no longer provide foreign protection.[48] The Quai d'Orsay also suspected that Constantini was behind a refusal by the new bishops to be received by the president of the Republic as they travelled through Paris.[49] Yet, as Constantini told Macleay, the West must realize that it was no longer dealing with a colonial country. It must strengthen China against the Japanese and the Russians, both of whom had their own designs for the country's future.[50]

A few days before the ceremony in St. Peter's, the National Christian Council (N.C.C.) had also wrestled with the questions presented by a Chinese Church at its fourth annual meeting in Shanghai. Though the meeting was, according to E. C. Lobenstine, the most representative in the council's brief history, the N.C.C.'s increasingly active political role put a strain on its membership. Earlier that year, the China Inland Mission, the largest Protestant society in China, had pulled out, and the Presbyterians were cutting back their financial support.[51] Though neither move was publicly linked to the N.C.C.'s politics, the connection seemed obvious to some. A year earlier, a British missionary claimed that he had been forced out of China because he had dared to criticize the council. "The 'N.C.C.' of China is an organization of China that is increasingly attempting to boss the Protestant Missions of China," wrote an irate American Presbyterian. "It has gotten into the hands of a group of Radicals who, as super secretaries, must find something to do to justify their occupancy of their swivel-chair seats; and, as they have no evangelical Gospel to preach, are getting rapidly into the business of meddling in Chinese politics. . . . If the State Department would put its foot down on them (i.e., the ones agitating for political change) about ⅔ of the missionary body would holler 'Amen!' "[52]

According to the N.C.C.'s own polls, however, most of its constituency favored the end of extraterritoriality and of the toleration clauses that had been written into the treaties to guarantee protection for Christianity.[53] David Yui's opening speech to the gathering in October not only called for an early abolition of the clauses but also expressed his gratitude to the "misnamed" anti-Christian movement for having forced Christians to think clearly about their actions.[54] For Yui, at any rate, there was no conflict between the claims of nationalism and the claims of Christianity. "The national spirit is penetrating every institution and movement," he told his audience, warning them that, if they did not become nationalists themselves, their work would fail. "In general it is safe to say that each institution and movement will rise or fall with whether it has the approval or disapproval of the national spirit."[55] (A few months later, in his famous report on the Hunan peasant movement, Mao Zedong would say much the same thing; for him, however, the test was not a middle class nationalism like Yui's but rather violent peasant revolution.)

Nevertheless, the resolutions finally passed by the gathering in October were mild in tone, something of a defeat for those who wanted a strong denunciation of the unequal treaties (the word "unequal" was not used).[56] Still, many were uneasy about the directions in which the N.C.C. was moving. Bishop Graves worried privately that the whole council had been turned over to the Chinese.

The "Chinese Church," which they have been talking about, will no doubt come to pass in time, but if it comes to pass on the lines they lay down it will be Chinese, but with very little Christian spirit and with no connection with the Church throughout the world.

Why the missionary societies at home continue to subsidize the National Christian Council is hard to understand. The expenses of every one of these delegates are paid by the contributions of missionary societies abroad, the amount which the Chinese Christians contribute to the organization being ridiculously small.[57]

In particular, such people were worried by the leadership of David Yui. "Mr. Yui is an able and exceedingly smooth person," Bishop Graves had noted a year earlier. "I have known him from the time when he was a little child and have never trusted him, but he has had quite a remarkable reputation amongst many foreigners."[58] Cunningham found his speech to the N.C.C. "extraordinary, . . . one calculated to create a decided breach between the foreign and Chinese members of this organization. . . . Dr. Yui is regarded by some of his American friends for some time as having passed beyond the bounds of reason" and had "become a dangerous propagandist."[59] "The fact that David's father and himself owe everything they have and are to our mission," wrote Bishop Graves, "witness David's education at Boone and St. John's and Bishop Roots paying for his advanced education at Harvard, ought to have prevented his criticism of missions and missionaries."[60] Such reactions, while perhaps understandable, missed the point. David Yui was one of a number of Chinese, very often mission educated or Western educated, who were useful to liberal Westerners as intermediaries between Chinese nationalism and Western aspirations for China. Just as Western firms trading in China used Chinese compradors to act as mediators between Chinese and Western business practice, so men like Yui—compradors of rhetoric, one might consider them—translated the demands of an often violent and nativist Chinese revolution into terms that enlightened Westerners could understand.[61]

Opinions like those of Bishop Graves, though they did not find their way into the council's publication, were common and worried many of the council's champions. "The National Christian Council has been under fire," wrote one missionary in the *Chinese Recorder*. "It has been wounded in the house of its friends. There are those who say that it cannot speak for the whole church, is not fully representative, and therefore, ought not to speak at all."[62] The next year would bring a more public explosion over the council's political role.

As the Nationalist armies drew closer to the Yangtze, the diplomats tried to convince foreign Shanghai that it need not fear change. Visiting the city on his way to Manila in September, Minister MacMurray reminded a gathering at the American Club that China must work out her problems by herself, without "meddling, interference, or intervention," and he dismissed fears that she would go Communist.[63] A month later, on his way back to Peking, he told the Union Club that Chinese, British, and Americans shared the same ideas of justice and tolerance (unlike other nations, presumably) and had the same high hopes for China's future. Laying it on a bit thick, he praised Shanghai's "historical background of tolerance" and warned that it would be "a tragedy of history" if Shanghai could not adapt itself to the coming age.[64]

In private, MacMurray had little good to say either about the Nationalists or the Shanghai mind. Like other diplomats in Peking, he wanted to make sure that his countrymen in Shanghai would behave themselves in the difficult times that lay ahead and not embarrass their mother country. The same spirit lay behind the public statements of Sir Miles Lampson, who that summer had been named to replace Macleay in Peking. On 14 October, shortly before leaving England, he read the guests at the China Association's annual dinner in London a carefully prepared statement of British policy. It was an olive branch to China but even more of an olive branch to the British communities in that country. Paying high tribute to their "patience and self-sacrifice," promising "resolutely to defend lawful British rights and interests in China," it also sympathized with China in her time of troubles, pointing out that it was up to the Chinese to decide who was to run their country. But the statement could be read two ways: Did it really mean, Rodney Gilbert wondered in the pages of the *North China*, that Britain would insist that the treaties be upheld? or would she simply follow the usual policy of "ruinous conciliation?" [65]

Perhaps it was to reassure his countrymen that Sir Miles stopped in Shanghai before going on to Peking, arriving on 30 November aboard H.M.S. *Despatch*. The *North China* welcomed him, urging him to move around China and get to know parts of the country other than the capital, "for Peking is very remote and its walls are very thick." [66] He immediately plunged into a series of welcoming meetings, tiffins, and dinners, trying to make it clear that any talk of British intervention was "sheer moonshine," though it is by no means certain that he got the point across. His stop in Shanghai was more than a tactful gesture to the city's importance, however. When he left, instead of going straight to Peking to present his credentials, he sailed upriver to visit several of the Yangtze ports. More particularly, he went to Hankou, where the Nationalists had just moved their governmental headquarters. No matter what the diplomats and international lawyers might say, his call on the Nationalists before he had even set foot in Peking implied at least a measure of British recognition of the new regime, suggesting that his country was adjusting itself to a new day in China and lending weight to the warnings of the diplomats that foreign Shanghai must do the same.

Thus, as the Nationalist armies drew closer in the autumn of 1926, various circles in Shanghai, both Chinese and foreign, prepared for the crisis they were certain would come. Foreign businessmen tried to combat Communist propaganda through organizations like the Constitutional Defense League. Christians hurried to declare their allegiance to the new Chinese nation. Sun Chuanfang allied himself with his old enemies in the north and in mid-December quelled another revolt in Hangzhou,[67] while the moderate nationalists of the Three Provinces Association sought to keep Shanghai free both from war and from a radical seizure of power. A strike against the French Tramway Company was settled through the mediation of the every-useful Du Yuesheng.[68] Meanwhile, the French and Settlement police reported the arrival of more and more arms, and more and more Guomindang and Communist agents (one, a certain Zhou—Enlai, perhaps?—had set up headquarters in a Japanese hotel on Seward Road in early November). By late December, there were daily meetings in the Soviet consulate-general between Chinese radicals and their Russian mentors to plan a new uprising.[69]

As the year drew to a close, Americans turned out in larger numbers than ever for the annual Thanksgiving Day service in the normally Anglican preserve of Holy Trinity Cathedral. Foreign Shanghai flocked, as it always did, to the Christmas displays in the Nanking Road department stores (Sincere announced a toy bazaar on the second floor, an assortment of Christmas pies and puddings, sweetmeats of all kinds including California oranges, wine, liquor, brandy, and Chinese embroidered pillows, "really splendid cushions for the ideal home").[70] Meanwhile, six hundred miles up the river, Borodin and the revolutionary government installed themselves in Hankou. To radicals, foreign and Chinese, red Hankou was a sign of hope, pointing the way to China's future. For foreign Shanghai, it was a portent of troubles ahead. Ever since Hankou's fall two months earlier, disturbing reports of economic chaos, radical demands by labor unions, a drying up of trade, interference with banks and business houses, depredations of missionary property, and the like had come downriver.

In Hankou would break the first great storm of the new year. Meanwhile, in Shanghai, the Municipal Council had already taken, in secret, its own first step to prepare for the coming of the revolutionary armies. On 17 November, it decided to delete from the police report for October a reference to an arrest warrant the Municipal Police had issued some years earlier. The warrant was made out in the name of Chiang Kai-shek.[71]

A Last Ditch and an Ebullition of Feeling
Hankou and the Defense of Shanghai

Six hundred miles above the mouth of the Yangtze, the city of Hankou looked to the traveller on the deck of his approaching ship almost like a miniature Shanghai. There were the same tree-lined Bund, the same river steamers lying at their wharves, the same gray destroyers and gunboats moored under foreign flags in the swift, brown current of the river that linked the city to the sea. Everything was a bit smaller, of course, but in the low verandahed buildings of the Bund were the same consulates and banks, the same shipping companies and business houses—Butterfield and Swire, British American Tobacco, Jardine's, the Hongkong and Shanghai Bank. There was also the same division between the broad and orderly roads of the foreign concessions, with their spacious offices and houses, and the maze of little streets, lanes, and alleys into which were crowded the inhabitants of the Chinese city.

Hankou was the greatest of the three Wuhan cities, which, with Wuchang and Hanyang, were clustered together where the waters of the Han River, rising far to the northwest in the mountains of Shaanxi, flow into the Yangtze. Here, in Wuchang on 10 October 1911, had begun the military rising that overthrew the Manchus, and here, fifteen years later, was where the men and women who claimed the inheritance of that revolution established their capital. In December 1926, the National Government arrived from Canton, to oversee the advance of its armies, across the Great River into north China and up to the old capital of Peking, whose fall would establish its claim to rule the country. With it came the Guomindang and their Communist allies, with their organizations of workers, peasants, women, and youth, and with it too came Borodin and his corps of Soviet advisers. Only one element was missing from this picture of unity, and that was the commander-in-chief himself; for Chiang Kai-shek had established his headquarters at Nanchang in Jiangxi province. Although he still protested his loyalty to the National Government, no one was sure how long that allegiance would last.

Wuhan quickly became a symbol of the aspirations of the revolution in a way that had never been true of Canton. In early 1927, it seemed to radiate a kind of rigorous, high-minded purity, free from the factionalism that had divided the heirs of Sun Yat-sen since his death. Unlike Canton, Wuhan was a city of heavy industry with its Hanyang ironworks, its arsenal, and its textile mills, a city with a real industrial proletariat. Here, under a friendly government, the Communists could begin to organize these workers, the masses they still thought would bring to birth China's socialist future. When the government moved to Wuhan, the impetus of the Nationalist armies and the national revolution seemed irresistible. In five months they had brought most of southern China under their control, and it looked as if even the strongest warlords of the north must now give way before them. Now, for a brief period from January to July, Hankou seemed the center not just of the Chinese revolution but of the world revolution, and towering above it all was the figure of Michael Borodin. Seemingly the impresario of insurrection, master of every move and every situation, Borodin was never too busy to receive the throng of foreign writers and journalists who made the pilgrimage that winter and spring to the new Jerusalem on the Yangtze, there to meet and to admire the man whom they praised as the greatest revolutionary of his day.

In the Wuhan cities, crowds greeted the Western new year with parades, demonstrations, and rallies to celebrate the victories of the Northern Expedition and the coming unification of China. Not surprisingly, many of the manifestations took on a strongly anti-British color, particularly with the news of the execution of seven Guomindang activists whom the British police in Tianjin had arrested and turned over to the Fengtian authorities. Borodin seized the chance to step up the movement against Britain, denouncing foreign concessions as counter-revolutionary headquarters that must be seized. In Hankou the day after Christmas, Li Lisan, one of the guiding spirits of May Thirtieth, organized a rally of 100,000 people to denounce Britain and to call for a boycott of British commerce.[1]

The British concession was the oldest and largest of several foreign settlements in Hankou. The marches and demonstrations, the street orators whipping up public passions, led Consul-General Herbert Goffe on 3 January to ask Rear Admiral J. S. Cameron for naval landing parties to join a small marine contingent that was already ashore. Their arrival only further inflamed the crowd, and as the marines rapidly threw up a wall of sandbags that afternoon, there grew the threat of another bloody confrontation between British imperialism and a Chinese crowd. Crouching behind the barricades that shielded them from the stones and bricks thrown by the crowd, the marines held their fire, while Goffe repeatedly called on the Chinese authorities to restore order. Not till 5:30 did a Chinese army detachment arrive, and then its commander agreed to take charge only if his men had sole responsibility for policing the concession. Goffe and Cameron, knowing that their force of 240 men would have no chance in a battle, reluctantly agreed and gave orders for the reembarkation of most of the British forces, who now marched back to their ships in the gray winter twilight.

On 4 January the crowds gathered again, demanding the return of all British sailors to their ships and insisting that China take control of the concessions. That afternoon, as demonstrators began to tear down the barricades, Cameron and Goffe again sought Chinese help. Troops and labor pickets led by the Communist labor organizer Liu Shaoqi entered the British preserve, and that evening a provisional committee that included Foreign Minister Eugene Chen, T. V. Soong, Sun Fo, and others took charge of the concession. With Goffe's consent, the Union Jack was lowered from the administration building, giving way to the Nationalist banner, and Liu Shaoqi took over the British consulate in the name of the Hubei General Labor Union. On 5 January, British women and children mustered on the Bund under an icy rain to board the ships that would take them to the safety of Shanghai, the first of thousands of foreign refugees from the Yangtze Valley who would make the trip during the new year.[2]

A hundred miles downriver, a similar spectacle took place in Jiujiang, where a crowd threatened the British concession on the evening of 5 January and a rumor swept through the town that the Russians wanted to set fire to it. There was no violence at first, but on the seventh throngs forced their way into the concession, and sporadic looting broke out as Chinese authorities took command.[3] Thus by the end of the first week in January, Britain had yielded control of two of its Yangtze concessions to the revolutionary forces. Other than the blow to British prestige, the loss of Jiujiang was of no great moment; but Hankou was a major industrial and trading center, the hub of much of the network of British commerce in central and upper Yangtze Valley, and its surrender might well hurt British pocketbooks as well as British pride. The news of the incident shocked and scared Shanghai, for it seemingly contradicted Eugene Chen's earlier assurances that foreign interests would be protected and that the unequal treaties would be done away with only through peaceful negotiation.

The events at Hankou were a severe blow to British policy. Not three weeks earlier, Sir Miles Lampson had visited Hankou for talks with Eugene Chen. Extraordinary as it might be for the new minister to pay his first call on the revolutionary government, the move was actually part of a long-maturing British plan for détente with the Nationalists. Born out of the failure of the tariff conference the previous July, it reflected a growing view among British diplomats in China and London that the Washington policies had outlived their usefulness and that there must be a radically new—in London's eyes, at any rate—approach to the China question. Such an approach would finally abandon the view that Peking was the only legitimate government and would undertake a broad program of negotiated revision of the old treaties. If that approach meant going it alone, against America, France, and Japan, so be it; it was, as Sir Victor Wellesley argued, a duty that Britain owed China and the only way in which British interests might be preserved in the new China that was emerging.[4]

The proposal had been defined and refined that fall by the Foreign Office and the cabinet, and its presentation was to coincide with the arrival of the new minister.[5] On 18 December, before Lampson reached the capital, British chargé Owen O'Malley presented to his diplomatic colleagues London's suggestion for a common declaration of policy to meet the changes taking place in China. It abandoned the notion that China could only develop under foreign tutelage; it recognized that many of China's claims were just and must be met sympathetically; and above all, it promised Britain's cooperation in negotiating with China a revision of the old treaties. Meanwhile, it was pointless to continue to lodge protests over minor violations of the treaties; it would be better to save protests for what was really important, backing them up when necessary by the strong and united action of the powers.[6]

One of London's suggestions was that China be allowed immediately to impose a 2.5 percent customs surcharge on top of the regular tariff. Though the Washington treaties permitted such a step, it had proved a stumbling block with several of the other powers, notably Japan. Lampson, having now reached Peking, published the British statement on 26 December partly to put a stop to speculation in the press and partly to forestall any attempt by another country to get the jump on Britain. Though Shanghai considered the Christmas memorandum, as it was called, an abject British surrender to American pressure,[7] it was actually no such thing. It had been a British initiative from the start, and its publication was intended at least in part to seize the moral and diplomatic high ground that the Americans had tried to occupy since May Thirtieth. "We have started the ball rolling," boasted George Mounsey at the Foreign Office in London, "and they are at best a bad second."[8]

A few days later came the outbreak at Hankou. At the time, many thought that Borodin and the Communists wanted to provoke a clash between armed Britons and unarmed Chinese, a new May Thirtieth that would strengthen the control of the left over the Wuhan government. This was the way the American journalist George Sokolsky saw it, and the Soviet consul-general in Shanghai reportedly considered the incident a failure because the British had withheld their fire. General MacDonagh of the Asiatic Petroleum Company heard that placards, apparently prepared in advance, had appeared in Changsha and Yichang on 4 January, crying that British machine guns had massacred innocent Chinese, apparent proof, he said, that the radicals had wanted bloodshed.[9] But Borodin had not planned the outburst, and when he heard the news on 3 January, his first reaction was one of fear; good Leninist that he was, he distrusted any show of spontaneity by the revolutionary masses. Only when it became clear that the British would not fight back did he take heart, realizing the extraordinary opportunity before him, and begin to call for a strong stand against the concession's authorities.[10] At the same time, he was desperately anxious to keep England isolated, away from any combined action with America and Japan. While fanning a movement against British imperialism, he must stave off any outburst against imperialism in general; thus the French and Japanese concessions at Hankou were untouched by the troubles. Borodin himself could draw this kind of fine distinction; but could the same be said for the masses caught up in the fervor of revolution? How was he to stay in control, especially considering the success of the spontaneous mass action at Hankou and Jiujiang? How could he prevent similar incidents against other countries, which would bring about the counter-revolutionary alliance that he feared?[11]

Britain's response to Hankou was restrained. No destroyers went storming up the river to bombard Nationalist forts or to retake the concession; there was no retaliation against Canton to harass the enemy's rear. Climate and geography helped the Nationalists: in the low water of the winter river, only ships of shallow draft could mount the six hundred miles from Shanghai to Hankou. More important yet was Britain's fear of playing into the hands of Nationalist extremism. Lampson was at first stunned to learn that British forces had offered no resistance and considered the consul-general little better than a traitor: "The Hankou capitulation is the worst blow to British prestige that has occurred in the last thirty-five years." Only later, when he learned more, did he realize that Goffe and Cameron had met an extraordinarily dangerous crisis with remarkable cool-headedness. What looked like surrender in actuality had prevented another May Thirtieth, another Shamian massacre, another spectacle of British guns and British bayonets spilling innocent Chinese blood. British retaliation at Hankou would have roused the whole country and would have imperiled a good deal more than two concessions on the Yangtze.[12] L. A. Lyall, the former customs commissioner in Shanghai (and the man who had suggested printing the *North China's* editorials in Russian to discredit the Bolsheviks), understood this point and praised his country-men, "who stood being stoned and insulted by a Chinese mob for half a day, without hitting back. It is these things that make one proud of being British." [13] Not many in foreign Shanghai would have agreed.

Instead of military retaliation or economic sanctions, the British lega-tion sent Owen O'Malley and Eric Teichman to Hankou to negotiate with Eugene Chen about the concession's future. Before the events at Hankou, O'Malley himself had urged recognition of the Nationalist Government and direct negotiations on treaty revision. Lampson, though less enthu-siastic, knew that his country must have a good case in the event that the worst happened. "Let us never forget that sooner or later we may be driven, whether we like it or not, to the last ditch," he wrote the day after the Christmas memorandum was published, "and that in that event it will be worth a great deal to have an overwhelmingly convincing case to put before the public." [14] After Hankou, his words seemed even more pertinent. Britain's case must be both rational and morally defensible, and she must be ready to give up what was no longer necessary or could no longer be justified. The Hankou affair would not deflect the policy of the Christmas memorandum, and on 27 January, the British presented both Wuhan and Peking with the most detailed and sweeping foreign proposals for treaty revision yet seen. [15]

Meanwhile, John Pratt had prepared for the Foreign Office a long sum-mary of Britain's position in China under the treaties. The summary is valuable not only for its historical perspective, but also because Pratt, un-like many others, distinguished clearly between the kinds of rights and interests foreigners held by virtue of the treaties (such as the right to live and do business in the open ports) and those that had accrued to them simply by custom, occasionally backed by the threat of force or helped by Chinese inertia (such as the right to establish municipal administra-tions and police forces). [16] A further memorandum praised the advances that the Chinese had made in governing such towns as Qingdao, where foreigners lived happily under Chinese control. The lesson was that con-cessions—even the best of them like those in Hankou and Tianjin—were anachronisms, and the Chinese ought to assume the responsibility for their administration and policing.

There was one great exception to this generalization. "The above re-marks do not apply to Shanghai," he wrote. "The International Settlement at that port is a huge city, with a population of 30,000 foreigners and one and a half million Chinese. It has completely dwarfed the adjacent native city of Shanghai, and it is altogether too big a concern to hand over to a Chinese administration. The annual budget of the Shanghai Municipality is greater than that of most provinces." [17] In other words, British concessions in cities like Hankou and Jiujiang were relics of the past and could survive the coming of Chinese control. Even Nationalist bad faith must not be allowed to hamper the development of trade, which was Britain's central interest. But Shanghai, where the foreign settlements dominated China's most modern city, was different and needed a different approach. Shanghai, in other words, might be the "last ditch."

Shanghai must be defended; but against what? Colonel Gordon of the Volunteers, briefing an informal meeting of consuls, naval officers, and Settlement authorities on 8 December 1926, pointed out two dangers. One was external: the prospect of hostile troops breaking into the foreign settlements as they had threatened to do in 1924. The other was internal: the eruption of Communist-inspired strikes and demonstrations, like those of 1925. This time, Shanghai might have to meet both threats simultaneously. That possibility meant once again reimposing a cordon around the settlements and some of the external roads where foreigners lived. In 1924, twelve hundred men had sufficed to keep order; this time, Gordon warned, four thousand would be needed.[18]

Roughly a month earlier, Lord Southborough of the China Committee had raised the question of Shanghai's defense with the Foreign Office in London. Though he agreed to sound out Barton and Macleay, Foreign Secretary Chamberlain was not anxious to send troops; such a move seemed both unnecessarily provocative and unnecessarily expensive.[19] In mid-December, he and his staff were still reluctant, raising difficulties about the prospect of the planned cordon: It would be too small if there were real trouble and would hurt Shanghai's economic life if it stayed too long in place.[20] Nonetheless, London was worried enough by late December to tell Barton that, if the need arose, he could call directly on Hongkong for a battalion of troops, who could be in Shanghai within a few days.[21]

A few days later, the news from Hankou at once confounded foreign Shanghai and confirmed its worst fears. The China Association warned of plans for mob violence and pleaded for adequate defenses. Brunner Mond's Shanghai director implored his home office to persuade the cabinet to recover Hankou; otherwise "British prestige was finished."[22] A crowded meeting of the American Chamber of Commerce pressed Washington to "oppose with all necessary force any usurpation of the rights now enjoyed by our citizens in these Settlements under existing treaties."[23] Given the nervous temper of American Shanghai, as Gauss commented, the resolution was mild enough, but he and Mayer were relieved that the chamber did not publish it.[24] The Banque Franco-Chinoise and the Messageries Maritimes appealed to Paris for the defense of their concession, as did groups at home, like the Lyon Chamber of Commerce with its interests in the silk trade. "Not since 1900," wrote the French Chamber of Commerce in Shanghai, "has the security of persons, property and economic interests been so threatened. . . . We believe that under present conditions, the abandonment of our essential prerogatives would inevitably lead to catastrophe." It then pointed out the French material interests in Shanghai of Tls. 80,860,000, or about 1,213,000,000 francs.[25]

In Great Britain, the news of the Hankou crisis threatened to undo all the Foreign Office's careful work behind the Christmas memorandum. Until now, Britain's China policy had largely been made in the Foreign Office's Far Eastern Department, where men like Sir Victor Wellesley and John Pratt had persuaded Chamberlain to move toward a gradual accommodation with the Nationalists. The Hankou crisis called into question the advice of the experts. Suddenly, China seemed much more dangerous; now the important decisions would be made by the prime minister, his cabinet, and the military, and the Foreign Office found itself reduced to a mere advisory role.[26]

Right after Hankou, London readied an additional battalion in Hongkong and told Barton that, as soon as Sun Chuanfang suffered a serious defeat, he could call on reinforcements from the colony.[27] The chiefs of staff estimated that it would take a full division of about 12,000 men to hold Shanghai. But the closest British reserves of any size were in India, six to eight weeks away from the China coast. Since Japan alone could produce enough men at short notice, perhaps she could be persuaded to take the lead in putting together a large international force. No one liked the idea of a purely British defense of what was not a purely British settlement; it might well hurt British interests and might even lead to a war whose "consequences and magnitude cannot be foreseen."[28] The Washington policy of cooperation still had its attractions, particularly when expensive, difficult, and dangerous steps had to be taken.

How would Britain's allies—above all, the United States—respond? The Shanghai diplomatic picture was complicated because in November Consul-General Cunningham had gone home on leave, his place taken for several months by Clarence Gauss, who had been in charge of the consulate-general in Tianjin. Gauss was an anomaly in the Foreign Service, a man who had started his career as a mere consular clerk and who, by hard work, high intelligence, and a passion for icy efficiency, had made his way up through the ranks (he would become ambassador to China in 1941). The two men disliked one another, and Gauss suspected Cunningham of turning the American community against him.[29] While Cunningham, like Barton, shared much of the outlook of foreign Shanghai, Gauss maintained a skeptical distance from his countrymen, determined that local Americans must not decide Washington's policy. In mid-December, he and the American naval commander agreed that American forces should protect Americans but should not oppose a Nationalist occupation of the Settlement. Despite MacMurray's objections—"if the foreign powers are not willing to hold the International and French Settlements," wrote a member of his staff, "then the whole bottom will drop out of everything and the denunciation of extraterritoriality and the occupation of the other concessions will be only a matter of weeks or days"—Kellogg agreed with Gauss. If American forces must be landed, they would protect American life and property, but they would not defend the Settlement as such.[30]

After Hankou, Gauss had second thoughts. He had expected the Nationalists to save their energies for Shanghai, but now, by "shooting their bolt," they had shown foreigners what to expect at Shanghai and had shown that their promises were worthless—"apparently the strong Red element of the left wing of the Nationalist Party is in control. . . ." Like Barton, he wanted reinforcements ready as soon as Sun seemed to be in trouble, or as soon as there were signs of local disorder. Nonetheless, he smelled a British rat behind the Council's request of 11 January for the landing of a thousand men, and with his Italian colleague managed to block the move.[31] Four days later, the British, French, Japanese, and American consuls-general met and agreed that no cordon was needed until Sun Chuanfang had been defeated in Zhejiang. Then an international landing force of four to five thousand men (not counting French contingents for the Concession) should start for Shanghai, the British coming from Hongkong and the Americans from Manila, all arriving simultaneously to spare any the onus of being the first ashore. That plan would suffice for local uprisings; but it would take at least twenty thousand men under a general officer to hold the Settlement against Chiang Kai-shek's Nationalist armies.[32]

The meeting of the consuls-general, with its assumption that such an international force would come, marked the high point of foreign cooperation at Shanghai. Even before it had taken place, Admiral Sir Reginald Tyrwhitt, the new commander-in-chief of the China Station, after three days of discussions with Barton and the Council, had dashed talk of a four thousand-man cordon, at least as far as the British were concerned. "Utterly inadequate," said Tyrwhitt; there were too few men for too long a line, and half of them were Japanese or Americans who could not be trusted to hold fast when trouble came. Convinced that there would be an attack on Shanghai, the admiral wanted a full division as soon as possible. The only alternative would be foreign evacuation, and Barton had already warned that that was physically impossible—never mind the political consequences. Sending troops would have other virtues: It would encourage

Britain's "wavering allies" to follow suit and would allow Britain to retake the Hankou and Jiujiang concessions and restore her damaged prestige.[33] Perhaps Tyrwhitt's views were what convinced Colonel Gordon that his earlier plans had been inadequate; rather than a single, international force of four thousand men, he now wanted Britain, Japan, and America each to hold that number ready at Shanghai.[34]

Minister Lampson and Consul-General Barton, still shocked by what had happened upriver, agreed. Britain must draw the line somewhere; either that or, in common decency, warn her people in China and give them time to get out. If Hankou could not be retaken during the winter's low water, then take a stand at Shanghai. "Here everything is in our favor, . . ." wrote Barton, clearly delighted at Tyrwhitt's recommendations. "Extremists have made a big mistake and if we act firmly at once there is no reason why Commander in Chief's plan should not only solve our own difficulties but also lead to elimination by then of discredited Russians without a shot being fired." (So it might, agreed Pratt, back in London. It might also lead to war with China. And once the troops were in China, how do you get them out?)[35]

On 17 January, the cabinet concluded that the Settlement must be held at all costs and ordered preparations to begin for a deployment of troops. Though they hoped Japan and America would join in to build up a division for the city, Britain would act alone if she must; a surrender at Shanghai or an evacuation (even if that were possible) would be disastrous for her position throughout Asia. If Chinese nationalists like Chen could humiliate Britain, what sort of a lesson would Indian nationalists like Gandhi learn? The prospect of the Congress Party becoming an Indian Guomindang was unthinkable. Shanghai might not be part of the British Empire, but Shanghai's future was important to the Empire. (All Asians are alike, Sir Alfred Mond reminded Stanley Baldwin two days later, lumping together in a magnificent sweep all the dusky populations beyond Suez. "The East is one and indivisible and any weakness shown in any part of it by the British Government always reflects itself in attacks on British prestige throughout other parts of the eastern hemisphere.")[36]

Britain's allies proved reluctant to join her. Though the Japanese General Staff was willing at least to consider cooperation, Foreign Minister Shidehara Kiijuro and his diplomats remained unconvinced that there was a real danger of an attack on the settlements. Thus, though he promised the British ambassador to hold a thousand men ready at Kure, he still thought the force of four thousand originally planned would suffice to deal with local troubles. As the Japanese ambassador in London also pointed out, with some 200,000 Japanese in China, Tokyo simply could not run the risk of uniting the country against Japan.[37]

Nor did the Americans do better. The events at Hankou led to a furious argument between MacMurray and Kellogg over the restriction of America's military role to the defense of American life and property. Even Gauss—suspicious as he was of the motives of foreign Shanghai and reluctant to see his country drawn into new difficulties—admitted that it would be hard to draw a line between defending American life and property and defending the Settlement's integrity.[38] According to Barton, Gauss considered the State Department's restrictions an embarrassment and kept them secret from the American colony.[39] MacMurray simply found them unrealistic. In a long and passionately argued telegram on 15 January, he contended that America must be ready for the worst. She had a responsibility not only to protect the lives and property of her citizens, but also to prevent the destruction of a great city.

Conditions in Shanghai are so inflammable that in the event Nationalists extend their control to that area there is bound to be an explosion unless the Nationalist leaders are definitely convinced that the foreign powers have reached the limit of tolerance and are prepared to unite wholeheartedly in making a stand for the protection of their nationals and their interest in Shanghai. I firmly believe the situation is one in which an obvious readiness to use force will afford the only possible escape from the necessity of doing so. With that in view I think there can be no distinction between defending Settlement and defending the lives and property of residents. If the need arises, the forces for the purpose must defend what they can without regard to any question of boundary and without differentiation among the [nationalities] concerned. It would prove equally impossible to distinguish between mob violence and concerted attack by organized forces. . . . Scope of any defensive measures taken for the safeguarding of American and other foreign lives and property should therefore be left to the discretion of those in military command. . . .

I can only give you my best surmise as to the probabilities. I may perhaps err on the side of apprehension; but I submit that in a case potentially involving lives of thousands of our nationals, we must deliberately face the more serious contingencies that may eventuate and plan for the possibility of the worst. I am the more disposed to this view because of my confident conviction that our best assurance of avoiding chance of the burning and looting of one of the world's foremost ports and massacre of an indefinite number of our people (with all the consequences that might be involved) lies in the possibility of joining with other interested nations in presenting a whole-hearted and resolute cooperation in making what would indeed be the last ditch [Lampson's phrase!] stand of foreign rights and interests in China. Jointly with the British and other nationalities participating in the International Settlement we have our legal and moral responsibility for Shanghai.[40]

Though the State Department's Nelson Johnson seems to have echoed these arguments, Kellogg was unmoved.[41] British attempts to play on his fear of Bolshevism (his weak spot, Sir Robert Vansittart called it) were no more successful. On 22 January, Washington announced that 250 marines were on their way from Guam to Manila. By the end of the month, Kellogg told the British ambassador that, though there were 800 men at Shanghai who could be landed and 1,200 more marines embarking from San Diego, the United States would not send any army units. Precisely what he said about the use of these forces is unclear. The American record suggests that they were to be used only to protect American life and property, but the British ambassador, Sir Esmé Howard, understood that America would cooperate with the other powers in the Settlement's defense.[42]

The French needed no British urging to take their own precautions. But they were to be French precautions, not part of any cooperative show of force. Paris agreed to Naggiar's request for a company of Annamites from Hanoi, but it wanted the move kept quiet. The troops would stay aboard ship as long as possible; if they must be landed, perhaps they should be smuggled ashore as mere policemen. The Quai d'Orsay, like the Japanese foreign ministry, was less worried by the possibility of a direct attack on the settlements by Cantonese armies than by the danger of "brigands," and as ambassador de Fleuriau—who had served in Peking before coming to London—told Chamberlain, rich Shanghai Chinese would either buy the revolutionaries off or pay somebody else to fight them.[43]

With no hope of help from her allies, on 21 January the cabinet reluctantly concluded that Britain would have to act alone. To Shanghai would go a full division, one brigade coming from India and two from England and the Mediterranean. With them also would go a battalion of a thousand marines and a cruiser squadron from the Mediterranean capable of landing another thousand men.[44] To Shanghai, in short, was going the largest British force ever sent abroad in time of peace. Added to the other foreign forces ashore and afloat in China that year, it would be by all odds the greatest show of military strength ever made in the country, larger even than the eighteen thousand who had driven the Boxers from Peking in 1900.

"I do not say," Chamberlain told a Birmingham audience on 29 January, "—I am far from saying or wishing you to think—that the threat of bloodshed and massacre hangs over Shanghai. I hope and believe that it does not. But it would be a clear dereliction of duty on the party of His Majesty's Government, to whatever party they might belong, after what has passed at Hankou, to leave the British at Shanghai without effective protection."[45] The Shanghai Defence Force was purely a precaution and would be used strictly for defensive purposes. Major-General Sir John Duncan, who was named general office commanding, was ordered to stay strictly neutral in China's civil war. He must keep his troops within the Settlement's boundaries, moving them out only if the tactical situation required it and then, if possible, only with the "friendly agreement" of Chinese authorities. But neutrality had its limits; his men would be used not only to protect British lives and property in Shanghai but also "to prevent, by force if necessary, the entry of any Chinese military forces into the International Settlement." [46]

Within days, the landings had begun. On 22 January, Barton called for his battalion of Indian troops from Hongkong. The General Labor Union was terrorizing independent workers, he said; British intelligence warned of an attempt against the Settlement; and the Chinese new year's holidays at the end of the month would provide a splendid opportunity for troublemakers. Most important, the Nationalists had resumed their march through Zhejiang, defeating Sun Chuanfang's armies at Lanqi, eighty miles southwest of Hangzhou.[47] On 28 January, in bitterly cold weather, four hundred Punjabis arrived from Hongkong on the *Glenogle* and marched down Nanking Road to their billets at the Race Course. Another four hundred disembarked from the *Empress of Canada* the following day.[48]

Even after the cabinet had given in to the importuning of the men on the spot and had decided to send troops, the Foreign Office continued to hope for a more pacific approach. Conceding the danger to Shanghai, they argued that it made their program of liberal treaty reform more necessary than ever. If the Nationalists would promise to prevent mob violence in the city, perhaps the main body of the Shanghai Defence Force could be held in Hongkong. As Pratt argued,

Chinese psychology is such that force is a most valuable weapon as long as it is kept in the background and never brought out and used. What is most effective of all is the vague threat of the use of an unknown quantity of force, and that is what we should achieve by sending our division to Hongkong. . . . But if we sent the Division to Shanghai, there will first be a howl of "aggression" followed by a boycott, and the familiarity will breed contempt and the Division in their midst will lose its terrors both actual and potential. The Chinese will quickly find that there are various forms of economic pressure which they can bring to bear and against which troops are no protection. Thus we shall have lost our one real weapon, the vague threat of force.[49]

He hoped it might still be possible to work with the Nationalists. In Hankou, O'Malley and Teichman were on the verge of concluding an agreement for the future of the British concession. It was ready for signing on 29 January when suddenly Eugene Chen backed out, demanding that Britain not land her soldiers in Shanghai. At the same time, he sent a message (through British diplomatic channels!) to the Labour opposition, calling on British voters to control the "adventurous element" in their country. It is worth quoting as an example of his outrageously effective public style:

If . . . the massing of armed British forces in the direction of Shanghai is an expression of the type of governing mind that feeds on the bodies of slaughtered men, then it is to be feared that the disablement of British trade and commerce may have to continue until British labour is entrusted by England with the task of arresting the British decline in Far Asia by substituting statesmanship, peace and productive work for the Tory statesmanship of imperialism, war and Byzantine glory.[50]

O'Malley suspected (probably rightly) that Borodin himself had vetoed the Hankou agreement at the last minute.[51] He asked Chen to give a written assurance that the Nationalists would not countenance the use of force against foreign concessions and settlements. Chen replied that the Nationalists had already done so, referring to a vaguely worded statement issued from Wuhan on 24 January. While the pacific Teichman was satisfied, no one else was. O'Malley, Lampson, and Barton were horrified at the prospect of the British troops being halted short of Shanghai and held in reserve. Secret service reports of the arrival of Soviet agitators in Shanghai seemed to show the *mala fides* of the Nationalists, and Barton argued that, though Japanese and American journalists might ridicule British preparations as excessive, their jests only betrayed their "jealous surprise at our ability to act independently."[52]

Throughout this period, Barton himself confused the situation by his brief telegrams that reported no more than the bare essentials. In Hankou, Teichman and O'Malley disagreed with one another; Lampson, working under furious pressure, occasionally sent home contradictory advice. Meanwhile, the Colonial Office, the War Office, and the Admiralty were all getting their own reports from China. No wonder the cabinet, knowing little about China and buffeted by conflicting advice, wavered in its decisions. On 2 February, it decided to give Eugene Chen another chance to guarantee Shanghai's safety before landing troops there. Five days later, on 7 February, responding to a furious reaction from virtually every British official in China save Teichman, it told Tyrwhitt that, though it would be "diplomatically convenient" to hold the troops in Hongkong, ultimately he and Barton were responsible for the protection of the British in Shanghai and must take whatever steps they thought necessary.[53] On 10 February it backtracked again, allowing Chamberlain to tell the House of Commons that day that, if Chen gave the appropriate assurances and signed the Hankou agreement, at least some of the British forces would be held up at Hongkong.[54]

Meanwhile, in the face of a new threat to Hangzhou, Tyrwhitt called for a second brigade of troops to go directly to Shanghai. It was now the Foreign Office's turn to be outraged, and Wellesley pulled Prime Minister Baldwin out of a dinner party on the evening of 16 February so he could order the Admiralty to hold up the sailing of the troops.[55] The very next day, however, the cabinet reaffirmed Tyrwhitt's authority over the Defence Force, and the troop ships continued on course for Shanghai.[56]

Finally, after three weeks of argument, the Hankou agreement was signed on 19 February. O'Malley accepted the Nationalist pronouncement of 24 January as covering the International Settlement in Shanghai. Chen accepted Chamberlain's statement in the House on 10 February as evidence of good faith. When O'Malley worried that the landing of a second brigade at Shanghai might torpedo the whole arrangement, Chen solved the problem neatly by asking not to be informed until after the agreement was signed. Then he would wait one or two days before making a *pro forma* protest. Meanwhile, both sides could save face by not publishing the exchange of correspondence.[57]

It was a practical solution to an awkward problem. But Lampson, pessimistic and disillusioned by dealing with Nationalists, was warning of worse things to come. "The crisis now developing around Shanghai is more fraught with danger to the foreign rights and interests centered there than at any period within recent years, with the probable eclipse of Sun Chuan-fang and the advent of Chang Tsung-Chang with his Shantung 'braves' from the North, and the certainty of recrudescence of internal troops [trouble?], I fear that, as in 1925, the lack of a strong hand in control of the extra-Settlement districts may have far-reaching results."[58]

Writing from London on 8 February, Bertrand Russell predicted that the landing of troops would mean war, unless American or Japanese intervention restrained Britain.[59] He was wrong, of course; and in the end, Pratt and his colleagues lost the battle to hold back the Shanghai Defence Force. The whole new China policy—opening communication with the Nationalists, the Christmas memorandum, and the proposals for treaty revision—had been devised by the Foreign Office's Far Eastern Department. What had happened at Hankou, though, had threatened everything. It was not just that the seizure of the concession showed the hollowness of Nationalist promises to protect foreign interests; it was also that Hankou provided ammunition to those who wanted a stronger British policy. By now, these people included not only the Shanghai diehards, not only Sidney Barton and Admiral Tyrwhitt, but also Sir Miles Lampson and most of his staff. Making the best of a bad thing, the Far Eastern Department argued that sending the Shanghai Defence Force must be seen not as the aggressive antithesis to their own program of conciliation, but rather as its defensive complement. They knew that foreign Shanghai's view would be different, and they worried that the men on the spot might try to use their new military strength for their own aims—had not the Royal Navy shown an alarming readiness to start shooting only a few months ago at Wanxian?

Whatever London may have intended, reported Eric Teichman in late February, foreign Shanghai greeted the coming of the troops as proof that Britain had finally stood up to Nationalist provocation and was clearing for action. The Defence Force, in short, was coming not simply to protect British lives and property but also to keep the Nationalists away from Shanghai, and perhaps to retake the Hankou concession as well. The diehards, warned Teichman, by insisting that the Cantonese and not the warlords were the enemy, would only confirm the views of leftists and nationalists everywhere that the main point of British policy was to shore up Sun Chuanfang and his northern allies. Britain could thus keep Shanghai a foreign enclave in a revolutionary China to further the interests of British imperialism and British trade.[60] Pratt and his colleagues were convinced that Shanghai interests were at work behind the scenes to torpedo any agreement on Hankou. Indeed, the British Chamber of Commerce and the China Association saw the agreement as a capitulation that would only increase antiforeign agitation.[61] Arthur Ransome of the *Manchester Guardian*, who arrived in the city that winter, observed that foreign Shanghai had at first resigned itself to accepting the Hankou agreement and making further concessions to Chinese nationalism. Then came the decision to send troops, and immediately Shanghai's position stiffened. Encouraged by Sidney Barton, it was now determined not to allow any more giveaways to the Chinese and was convinced that the Hankou agreement itself was wrong.[62]

Barton was delighted that Japan and America had stayed out of the Shanghai Defence Force, thus leaving Britain free to act in the difficult days that lay ahead.[63] But in early February, when he suggested that the army might be useful to force a general settlement with China, a red flag went up in the Foreign Office. "A more fatal policy I cannot imagine," snapped Wellesley, and Chamberlain agreed that the Shanghai Defence Force must not become a "bargaining counter" either with China or to secure a diplomatic superiority over America and Japan. Off to Lampson flew a telegram, reminding him of Chamberlain's promise that the troops were there for protection only and asking him to combat the "mischievous and misleading idea" that the Defence Force presaged a new decision to resort to arms for the settlement of difficulties. Lampson, in passing the orders on to Shanghai, hardly reassured his superiors at home. "I cannot help feeling that the F.O. are unduly apprehensive," he wrote Barton. "A certain local ebullition of feeling consequent on relief at what is undoubtedly a change of policy at home, namely at long last decision to take measures, in practice to protect British lives and property at least at Shanghai, was inevitable."[64]

A change of policy indeed! Lampson had arrived in China not much more than a month ago to take charge of Britain's new and constructive approach to the China problem. Was he seeing the world through the jaundiced eye of the old China hand so soon? The telegram was an alarming indication of how far Lampson's views had come to differ from those of the Foreign Office. London's fears, of course, persisted, and for months the Far Eastern Department, no longer in control as it had been, would worry about attempts by British Shanghai to sabotage the Hankou agreement and to turn the Shanghai Defence Force into an offensive task force to retake the upriver concessions.[65]

To Wash Away Eighty Years of Shame
The Second Armed Uprising and French and American Responses to the Crisis

By early February 1927, every steamer arriving in Shanghai from up-river was crowded with foreign refugees. From the outports and the hinter-land arrived the wives and children of missionary families and of foreign companies like Standard Oil, Jardine's, or British-American Tobacco, flee-ing the Nationalist advance for the safety of a city garrisoned by foreign troops. The French, wary of offending the Concession's Chinese citizens, preferred to sneak their Annamite *tirailleurs* ashore disguised as police-man. But Shanghai's defense was a British show, and the troop ships that sailed up the river to Shanghai in February and March carrying the Shang-hai Defence Force were met with all the publicity the British community and its press could provide. Two transports of the British India Line tied up on Saturday 12 February to put ashore two battalions of the Durham Light Infantry and the Gloucesters, the first units of the British brigade from India. On Monday, under a cold gray sky threatening rain, the Royal Marine Band led them up Nanking Road to their billets at the Race Course and the Waterworks on Kiaochow Road. Crowds turned out to see them, "foreigners of other nationality than British [as the *North China* point-edly put it] to whom it was brought home that in the defence of their own nationals, these men marching along with a carefree step and a jaunty swing, were here for the protection of the Settlement and all within its bor-ders." Through the week, other ships arrived with other units, British and Indian. On Thursday, six hundred men paraded through the Central and Western districts, past the Race Club where Admiral Tyrwhitt took their salute and down Nanking Road to the Bund.[1] As more soldiers arrived later, the streets echoed to the sound of marching men, the music of their bands drawing crowds to watch the lines of soldiers tramping from the

Hongkew docks to their quarters. British children might be disappointed that the Coldstream Guards came to China in khaki, their red coats and bearskins left at home, but there was still more than enough excitement for everyone that gray morning in early March when they stepped down the gangplank from the *Kinfauns Castle* at the Old Ningpo Wharf and filed through the rainswept and still deserted streets of the Northern District. "The shrill sound of the fifes pierced the emptiness through which the men were marching," recalled one onlooker, and as the men turned onto Broadway toward the Garden Bridge and the Bund and the crowds grew, the girls of the Loretto School, shepherded by nuns, "burst into a shrill piping chorus of 'Rule Britannia.' " Near the Astor House they came to attention, passing in review before General Duncan. By the time they headed down the Bund to turn right onto Nanking Road for the Race Course and Jessfield, the streets had filled with people, "genuine British hurrahs" drowning out the music of the bands.[2]

Suddenly the city was full of soldiers. "We have Sikhs, Punjabis, a Gloucester regiment, the Durhams, British Marines and Bluejackets, American Marines and Bluejackets, French ditto and the Annamites," wrote an American woman, "so it makes the streets quite gay with uniforms."[3] The British troops were in evidence not only on the boundaries of the Settlement, where barbed wire and sandbags guarded the streets, not only at the strategic intersections manned by Tommies with machine guns and armored cars, but everywhere, day and night. The cold, wet weather made life miserable for soldiers used to India's climate, and several hours of picket duty with nothing more than a small fire of scavenged wood for warmth was followed by a return to inadequately heated stables at the Race Course, which had hurriedly been turned into military billets. Shanghailanders sought to help, inviting soldiers into their houses or forming volunteer groups to meet the needs of their visitors. The grounds of Sir Ellis Kadoorie's huge Marble House on Bubbling Well Road became a center for rest and recreation; the British Women's Association, under Lady Barton, was active in providing canteens, game rooms, libraries, and religious services for the troops. British troops and their officers filled the pews at Holy Trinity and the Community Church to listen to sermons urging fidelity to the high ideals of the Empire. British officers jostled taipans and their juniors at the Long Bar in the Shanghai Club; they danced at the Cercle Sportif, the Majestic, and the Astor; and they ate at the American Club (the Americans also quartered two hundred troops at the Columbia Country Club). Less fortunately, the visitors frequented the still legal brothels of the French Concession and the now illegal brothels that sprang up on the edges of the Settlement. The Defence Force headquarters found itself caught between the demands of the Moral Welfare League to shut them down and the need to police the houses to control the spread of venereal disease among men with little to do, crowded together in make-shift quarters under chilling winter rains and cold gales blowing in from the East China Sea.

The flourish that marked the arrival of the British troops emphasized the inactivity of the other nations at Shanghai. Admiral Tyrwhitt was wrong when he predicted that Britain's allies would fall in behind her. Instead, it seemed, those allies breathed a sigh of relief, delighted that someone else would now protect the city. Paris was determined to defend her concessions at Hankou and Shanghai by force of arms if necessary, but it would be an independent defense.[4] On 28 January, the same day that the Punjabis landed in the Settlement with brass bands playing, 275 Anna-mites quietly came ashore in the Concession. Though Naggiar had his troops, he refused to give Barton any assurances, saying only that France would take whatever steps might be necessary.[5]

The French had distrusted the new directions in British policy an-nounced by the Christmas memorandum—"mal conçue et mal conduite," Ambassador de Fleuriau in London called it.[6] So had the Americans; but their response was more complex. While publicly welcoming Britain's readiness to revise the treaties, in private they were less enchanted, partly because Britain seemed to be trying to break the monopoly Americans fondly imagined their country had on Chinese goodwill.[7] At the State De-partment, Nelson Johnson confessed that he could not understand what the British were up to, and in Peking, MacMurray found Britain's ini-tiative "ill-judged and . . . somewhat antagonistic." He realized, though, that America must go along; to Lampson he remarked that Washington would now want to go the British one better and thus start an "auction" for Chinese favor.[8]

But Secretary of State Kellogg's proposal for an American response to Britain so upset MacMurray that he asked to be called home for consulta-tion and actually left Peking in mid-January, only to be summoned back to the capital as the war clouds gathered.[9] Meanwhile, the pressure mounted on Washington to make its own statement. On 4 January, in part at the instigation of the missionary lobby, Representative Stephen Porter of New York introduced into the House a long resolution calling for the negotia-tion of new treaties.[10] He did so without consulting the State Department, and it was partly to forestall congressional action that Kellogg now drew up his own pronouncement on China.[11]

The American declaration was hastily made public on 27 January, be-fore MacMurray had a chance to comment on it.[12] Opening with the usual protestations of American liberality toward China, it broke far enough with the old cooperative policy to pledge America's willingness to renegotiate her treaties alone if need be. Washington also dropped its earlier proviso that discussions wait until China had a stable government. Yet, by requiring that China "agree upon the appointment of delegates representing the authorities or the people of that country"—delegates acceptable, that is, to both north and south—it was, as Akira Iriye points out, asking the impossible and guaranteeing that there would be no change.[13] Finally, by firmly reminding China that America would protect the lives and property of her citizens, Kellogg left the way open for sending American reinforcements to the Far East. No wonder the Chinese minister in Washington was dismayed, and no wonder he missed the point; for Kellogg's pronouncement made no proposals as specific as those of London. It was concerned less with Chinese realities than with American public opinion, and as a statement of American aspirations for China, it served its domestic purpose admirably.[14]

The declaration did little to parry the charge that America was relying on British forces to protect her citizens in Shanghai, however. Here Kellogg had another idea. Picking up a suggestion from the Navy Department, he proposed to MacMurray a scheme to neutralize Shanghai by having the rival commanders promise not only to stay out of the Settlement but also to keep their troops away from the city's "immediate vicinity." For good measure, he added that his country stood ready to join in "a friendly and orderly negotiation" for changes in the Settlement's administration and status.[15] It was an appallingly bad idea. As the shocked Mac-Murray pointed out, the treaties already bound the Chinese to honor the Settlement's neutrality; to ask the Chinese armies to stay away from the vicinity of Shanghai would be tantamount to American intervention in the civil war. Moreover, a unilateral American offer to discuss changes in the International Settlement's status would not only be an act of bad faith but would encourage the Nationalists to force the issue. Finally, argued the minister, Kellogg's proposal would only endanger Shanghai Americans by embarrassing and impeding "such other nationalities as might have to assume the burden of protecting the lives and interests of our people along with their own." Britain, in other words, was doing America's work, and America should at least stay out of her way.[16]

Kellogg, firmly reminding MacMurray that opinion at home would not tolerate the use of American troops to defend the Settlement, modified the proposal, dropping the more obviously objectionable parts.[17] The British view—in private, at any rate—was scathing. "Unpractical and typical [sic] American," sniffed Lampson. William Tyrrell at the Foreign Office was even less flattering: "I do not think we need be in a hurry to answer this exceedingly foolish proposal put forward by an exceedingly foolish old lady who presides over the State Department!" But he also knew that Britain must not fall out with America, and he told Sir Esmé Howard to make soothing noises in Foggy Bottom while keeping his distance.[18]

From Shanghai, Barton—who disliked any proposal that might tie Britain's hands—hinted darkly that the American initiative had originated with the local Guomindang, who had put it to Gauss and who wanted a stalemate to counter the coming of the Shanghai Defence Force.[19] Though the American plan was in some ways similar to the autonomy movement sponsored by the Three Provinces Association, Barton was almost certainly wrong in seeing a local Chinese initiative behind Kellogg's proposal and probably got the idea from a story by George Sokolsky in the *North China Daily News* on 9 February. Gauss, in fact, thought the neutralization scheme foolish (Washington never asked his opinion, but he volunteered it anyway). Shanghai was simply too rich a prize for any Chinese military or political faction to pass up, and if the city were to become a battleground, the only way to keep the victors (or the vanquished, for that matter) out of the Settlements would be to have a sufficiently large landing force.[20]

On 4 February, Kellogg's neutralization proposal—"that the International Settlement of Shanghai be excluded from the area of armed conflict"—was put to the military commanders on both sides. As MacMurray had predicted, they simply saw it as American interference in their affairs. Sun Chuanfang complained publicly that the foreigners were backing the Guomindang against him.[21] The volatile Eugene Chen accused the United States of "crucifying the Nationalist Government on a cross of technicalities" (one wonders which of his American-educated colleagues gave him the phrase) and warned that the approach would bring on "a serious row."[22] What really miffed him, however, was that the American note had gone not to him but to Chiang Kai-shek at a time when tensions between Hankou and its independently minded commander-in-chief were rapidly building.[23]

Even in 1924, the foreign demand that Shanghai be kept neutral amidst warlord squabbles had had little effect; and in 1927, Shanghai faced a very different kind of war. Kellogg's proposal was in effect a throwback to earlier imperialist practices, and its quick death spared the United States even further embarrassment. In retrospect, the démarche seems little more than another gesture to domestic opinion. Shanghai was very much in the headlines, and though any suggestion of American cooperation with British imperialism would have brought an isolationist outcry at home, Washington had to seem to be doing something. At the same time—as the British ambassador noted—Kellogg left the way open for sending American reinforcements to Shanghai.[24]

Meanwhile, in Shanghai, preparations for the Nationalist arrival continued. Barton and Yada were convinced that the size of the city's foreign population made evacuation impossible, and though the Settlement's police drew up a list of buildings that might be used as "concentration camps" if the outside roads had to be evacuated, their preparations do not seem to have gone much further.[25] Gauss—warning that the American population might grow to six thousand as more refugees came from the interior—put his staff to work on plans to house and feed Americans in emergency shelters near the Bund and perhaps to evacuate them.[26] Right after the Hankou affair, Lampson had advised British subjects in the interior to withdraw to safety, and before the month was out, Gauss told American mission stations in the hinterland to send women and children to Shanghai.[27]

Plans like these were designed to deal with a Shanghai besieged by the Nationalist armies, perhaps even under attack by them. But as Colonel Gordon had earlier warned, the settlements faced a danger from internal radical insurrection as well. "Everybody appears to be expecting an outbreak towards the middle of the month," wrote Bishop Graves early in February. "It is apparently the plan of the Russian leaders of the Southern party to produce a clash between the mob and the authorities and then use the same to excite the Chinese and win the sympathy of the unthinking people in the foreign countries. It is a most devilish plan, but I see no reason why it should not succeed if they are really determined upon it."[28]

On 17 February came the news that Hangzhou, the capital of Zhejiang province and some 130 miles by rail from Shanghai, had fallen to the southerners. Sun Chuanfang's defeat set the stage for what Chinese historians call the Second Armed Uprising, an insurrection within Shanghai that was to be coordinated with the advance of the Nationalist armies and was designed to deliver the city into the hands of the revolutionaries.

But which revolutionaries? Here, though the partisan nature of the sources makes it difficult, it is necessary to understand the relationship between Communists and Nationalists within the city and to distinguish between their aims.[29] Worried by the increasing independence of Chiang Kai-shek from Wuhan and by the increasing influence of the local Guomindang right wing, Shanghai's Communists were anxious to seize control before Chiang's armies could reach the city. Learning from their failure in October, they stepped up the training of their underground pickets [*jiuchadui*] and, by early February, had a central force of about two thousand men, of whom only a hundred had arms. Meanwhile, Niu Yongjian, Chiang's own emissary in the city, saw in Sun's defeats a chance to win Shanghai without fighting by using promises of money and position to induce Sun's commanders to desert a sinking ship.

After his reverse at Hangzhou, Sun gave up his attempt to hold Shanghai and the south bank of the Yangtze and began withdrawing to the north, turning over control of the city to his old rival Zhang Zongchang. The change of command, coupled with Shanghai's hatred of Zhang, promised a period of instability and gave the underground its opportunity. This time, the Communists were determined to stay in control and not allow themselves to be led by Niu Yongjian and the Guomindang. The uprising, however, would take place under the banner of the united front; as the Communist deliberations make clear, the point was to avoid a struggle between the two parties, for then the Communists could only be the losers. Rather, they must encourage the struggle within the Guomindang itself, working with the left against the right, but also staying in control rather than allowing their allies to use them.[30] As the armies drew closer, they made their plans, and when the news came of Hangzhou's fall and of the arrival of the Nationalist vanguard at Jiaxing, some sixty-two miles away, all seemed ready. Early on the morning of 19 February, the General Labor Union put out a call for a general strike. Simultaneously, the Communists demanded the withdrawal of all foreign forces, the return of the concessions, and the formation of a popular municipal government under Wuhan "to build a new Shanghai, free and independent, and wash away eighty years of shame and insult."[31] There was to be no attack on the settlements, however, and the union specifically forbade assaults on foreigners or sabotage in the mills and factories.

Contemporary Communist sources claimed that about 365,000 workers went on strike between 19 and 22 February; Western estimates put the number about two-thirds lower. The city fell silent as factory whistles no longer sounded, trams stopped dead in their tracks, stevedores abandoned their docks, and workers everywhere walked off their jobs. The defense commissioner, Li Baozhang, struck back with a ferocity that Sun's relatively benign government had not shown before. Press reports tell of fifteen-man execution squads patrolling the streets of the Chinese city, each headed by two sword-carrying executioners and the rest armed with rifles. They seized agitators, who were often no more than students handing out propaganda leaflets, and beheaded them on the spot or paraded them through the city before executing them and displaying their heads in public. Two students were said to have been decapitated in front of St. John's, their bodies left in the streets. An unfortunate pedlar whose cry "Mai dabing!" ("Cakes for sale!") was misheard as "Dabai bing!" ("Overcome the soldiers!") was cut down on the spot. The Communists later claimed that thirty-one people were killed and over a hundred arrested in the most ferocious display of official violence in years. Such measures, said Gauss, had "a most salutary effect upon agitators in general," but a Chinese weekly (which gave even higher figures for those executed) pointed to the unrest the repression caused in the Chinese city and the flight once again of refugees to the safety of the settlements.[32] At the same time, the General Labor Union stepped up its own campaign against its enemies (according to Barton's estimates, some thirty anti-union workers were killed by the left from mid-January to mid-March). "The butcheries of the white terror have called into being red revolutionary terror," cried Zhao Shiyan, one of the insurrection's leaders. "To use terror to fight terror is revolutionary behavior," and he accused the Guomindang rightists of being behind Li Baozhang's slaughter.[33]

Meanwhile, the Nationalist army came to a halt at Jiaxing, about halfway up the rail line from Hangzhou. Communist sources claim that, as the right wing was cheering on Li Baozhang's execution squads, Niu Yongjian's Guomindang underground waited to see what would happen before committing themselves to action. After a long debate on 20 February, the Communists decided to go ahead on their own, transforming the strike into an armed insurrection to topple Sun and seize the city. Communist cells on two Chinese gunboats in the river planned to seize the ships, opening fire at six o'clock on the evening of the twenty-second to signal the start of the uprising. Then the warships would ferry armed workers across the river from Pudong to attack the Longhua arsenal, while uprisings would break out in other parts of the city.

By the twenty-second, however, some units had already attacked police stations to seize their arms, while aboard the gunboats the plans leaked out (betrayed by Niu Yongjian, according to a recent Communist historian). The shots that were to announce the start of the uprising thus came an hour late, throwing the plans into confusion. Several shells fell in the Chinese city, and others fell in the French Concession—one in the compound of the American School and another, as Bishop Graves wrote his sister, passing "through the French Club where a lady was delivering a lecture on Chinese culture—rather a rude commentary."[34] In the confusion of a cold and dark winter night, some units never went into battle, while others fought off the police well into the next day. Meanwhile, through the night, detectives of the French Sûreté watched the lights burn late in the Soviet consulate-general on Whangpoo Road. At dawn on the twenty-fourth, the General Labor Union acknowledged defeat once more, telling the workers to go back to their jobs and prepare for even greater uprisings.

The Second Armed Rising had ended. Zhao Shiyan, who had helped plan and lead it, tried to see the bright side. "The experience and lessons gained from these five days, and particularly from their struggles, have shown us a solution, and they surpass any experience and lessons that we have gained since May 30th."[35] Yet, it was undeniably a failure. The ruthlessness of Li Baozhang's repression and the consequent slow return to work of the laborers had hurt it. Modern Communist historians blame the defeat on divisions in their own Party, on Niu's refusal to join the uprising, and on Chiang's orders to his armies to halt at Jiaxing, giving Li Baozhang the chance to crush the Shanghai Communists. That was not the way it looked at the time, however; and contemporary Communist analyses (including a long one written by Qu Qiubai) put the blame entirely on the Party's own organizational and tactical shortcomings. There was no mention of any kind of Nationalist betrayal.[36] A historian on Taiwan blames the Communists for refusing to cooperate with their Guomindang allies and for their treachery in going to ground when military units failed to join the revolt.[37] One of Borodin's Soviet advisers wrote years later that the uprising was premature and ill planned, proof of the shortcomings of the Chinese Communist leadership.[38] Three other Comintern agents, in Shanghai at the time, put the blame not only on the Chinese but on the weakness and indecisiveness of Borodin and his colleagues. "We let slip by an exceptionally favorable historical moment, a rare combination of circumstances, where power lay in the streets but the Party did not know how to take it. Worse yet, it didn't want to take it; it was afraid to."[39]

Modern Nationalist and Communist accounts hardly mention the Soviets. At the time, however, Naggiar's intelligence service reported an increasingly close relationship between Chinese Communists and Comintern agents in the city, with a good deal of money and advice coming in through the Soviet consulate-general. Niu Yongjian himself, who was hiding out in the French Concession, paid high tribute to the role of Soviet money, advice, and arms in the Northern Expedition. According to him, the February uprising had originally been planned to cover a defection by Li Baozhang to the Nationalist side. Sun, however, got wind of the plot and immediately sent out his execution squads, thus ensuring that Li would take the blame for the bloodthirsty repression and be compromised in the eyes of the city's inhabitants.[40] Li, however, stayed in touch with the south and within a month had joined the Nationalist cause.

By now, Sun Chuanfang's tired and dispirited soldiers were leaving the city, and on 25 February, Zhang Zongchang's Shandong troops and his White Russian mercenaries, under the command of Bi Shucheng, began to move into southern Jiangsu.[41] Meanwhile, at Fessenden's urging, the British commander agreed to move his troops outside the Settlement into the external roads. At dawn on 25 February, accompanied by a small Italian contingent, they took up positions on the old 1924–1925 cordon line along the railway loop from Siccawei to Soochow Creek.[42] That same day, Fessenden asked for military help from the warships in the harbor. When Gauss, refusing to be stampeded, would not allow the landing of Americans, Fessenden replied hotly that, since the British alone were prepared to defend the Settlement, he did not care what the Americans did.[43] A day later, on 26 February, the transport *Megantic* arrived, bringing two more battalions of troops. They were accompanied by Major-General Sir John Duncan, general officer commanding, and his chief of staff, Viscount Gort, who—thirteen years later—would become the hero of Dunkirk. The two officers moved into the Astor House Hotel near the Garden Bridge and set up their divisional headquarters at Ewo Terrace.[44]

General Duncan's orders were to keep the Shanghai Defence Force strictly within the Settlement's boundaries until an attack came. The British move to the old cordon line took place the day before he arrived, thus when he landed on the twenty-sixth, he found his troops already in positions that exceeded the War Office's instructions. Perhaps reluctantly, he came to agree with Barton about the strategic virtues of the new deployment, though at this point he refused Barton's request to send troops across the river into Pudong, seeing such a move as tantamount to an invasion of China.[45] Whatever may have been his views, the move beyond the Settlement was not so much a response to the February uprising—which in foreign eyes was no more than a brief general strike—as it was a reaction to the coming of the Shandong troops. But it was also a response to overcrowding in the Settlement. January had brought some eight hundred Westerners, mostly women and children, from upriver ports and mission stations, and more came in February.[46] The heavy rains of the winter made it difficult to find suitable billets and added to fears about the health and morale of the troops. Hence, the British commander jumped at Fessenden's request. The move out to the camp at Jessfield Park, though it might cast doubt on London's earlier pledge to keep the troops within the Settlement, eased a problem brought on as much by bad planning as by the tactical situation.

In 1924, the presence of foreign troops beyond the Settlement's boundaries had provoked little reaction. This time it seemed a clear violation of Chinese sovereignty in the interests of British imperialism. "Look at this: imperialist self-protection at Shanghai!" cried Peng Shuzhi, editor of the *Xiangdao zhoubao*. "The British have brought vast numbers of troops to Shanghai, marching through the streets to overawe the Chinese. 'Shanghai, we are here!' they say. What kind of talk is this? Don't they really mean 'We imperialists are here, who dares to come!' At first the imperialists said they were coming only to guard the Settlements, only for self-protection, but now they occupy Chinese territory outside the Settlements. . . . If stationing troops at Jessfield and Jiangwan is self-protection, then next they will plead self-protection when they occupy Suzhou, Wuxi, and Songjiang, even Hangzhou, Ningbo, and Nanking." British armies had come not to protect Britons but rather "to protect the butcher Sun

Chuanfang and to resist the armies of the Northern Expedition," and Peng called on the revolutionary masses of Shanghai to respond with armed force "to seize the Shanghai concessions, and to drive every imperialist, particularly the British imperialists, out of the country."[47]

To the nervous staff of St. John's University, however, the quartering of a British unit in nearby Jessfield Park brought a sense of security. Warned of trouble from the student union, St. John's had shut down on 6 January. After much soul-searching and laying in of provisions, it had reopened in February with only about two-thirds of its students. Earlier that month, the body of a dead baby had been thrown into the compound of the Episcopal mission. "They do these things when they want to excite the people," wrote Bishop Graves, and, like many other Shanghai Americans, he was relieved when the troops landed. "The British troops give us confidence. It is fortunate that the British have a backbone. All our people seem to have thought of is protection enough to enable us to get aboard and clear out for Manila. If the Southerners get much nearer, the defence of Shanghai will be the only course. We are already surrounded by barbed wire entanglements all along the border."[48]

His reaction was a common one among Shanghai Americans. On 22 February, in the midst of the strike and the uprising and while shells from Chinese gunboats were landing in Frenchtown, Americans were commemorating the birthday of George Washington. President Hawks Pott of St. John's spoke to a Union Club tiffin that day about the father of his country, taking issue with modern historians (presumably like Charles Beard) who sought to debunk his accomplishments. (If, like Mao Zedong some years later, he saw a parallel between 1776 and the Chinese revolution, he did not say so.) That evening, eight hundred men and women were gathered in the ballroom of the new Majestic Hotel on Bubbling Well Road, Stirling Fessenden and Consul-General Gauss in the receiving line of the city's prominent Americans. High above the crowd, the American Club's new portrait of the first president looked down on the proceedings and on the sugar Mount Vernon that decorated the head table. Red, white, and blue ribbons streamed from a chandelier across to the coats of arms of the American Troop and the American Company that decorated the wall. Over the bandstand, next to the Great Seal of the United States, a large bald eagle fashioned from colored lights watched over the proceedings "with a wakeful, blinking eye," as the *North China's* reporter put it.[49]

Was there a bit of editorializing here? Was there a suggestion that although General Washington's vigilance had wakened his people to liberty, President Coolidge had allowed them to fall asleep, oblivious to the dangers faced by their fellow citizens halfway across the world? Two days later, the U.S.S. *Chaumont* arrived with fifteen hundred marines from San

Diego under the command of Colonel Charles Hill, their presence the first stage of a reluctant American military response to Shanghai's troubles. But the men stayed aboard (sulking in their ships like Achilles, commented a British diplomat) when British and Italian troops took up their positions on the twenty-fifth, and they remained embarked as the remnants of Sun Chuanfang's defeated armies decamped toward the north and the savage and unpredictable troops of Zhang Zongchang moved into the city.[50] Only on the morning of 5 March—the same day 450 Japanese marines marched into the Eastern District to guard the textile mills—did they come ashore. Americans and others turned out to watch the marine Fourth Regiment "Devil Dogs" parade down Nanking Road to the Bubbling Well Cemetery, accompanied by a seventy-nine-piece band. It was a good show, but a short one; the marines were back aboard ship in time for lunch.[51]

Officially, Washington continued to insist that the marines were there to protect American lives and property, not to perpetuate the kind of privilege represented by the very existence of the International Settlement. In private, however, Secretary of State Kellogg conceded to an increasingly skeptical MacMurray that it would be up to him and Admiral Williams, as American commander-in-chief, to decide what must be done.[52] If there was to be a battle for Shanghai, Washington could not direct it from nine thousand miles away; thus—just as the British had done—Kellogg gave his men on the spot the freedom to act as necessary.

Meanwhile, he blandly told the Chinese minister in Washington that he knew of no pressure to build up American military strength.[53] If that was true, he was not reading his mail. Gauss was far too good a reporter on Shanghai affairs to ignore the sentiments of the American community, and he was far too good a diplomat to believe that those sentiments should decide American policy. "It is clear that there are no sharper critics today than Americans in China," wrote the *North China Herald* of Washington's apparent inaction, and its issues were filled with letters from Americans deploring the irresolute behavior of their government. Fessenden himself complained to the *New York Sun* about his country's willingness to let the British pull American chestnuts out of the fire. "When I saw the first British troops march through Shanghai, I said, 'Thank God, they're here,'" he told the annual banquet of the St. David's Society on 1 March, apologizing for Washington's apparent ignorance of the true nature of the Chinese crisis.[54] The head of an American firm denounced those, like Senator Borah, who encouraged the president and the secretary of state to shirk their responsibilities and whose "policies and radical utterances are a serious menace to the people of the United States." He concluded with an expression of profound gratitude to the British for their foresight. "I assure you that the first contingent of Indian troops arrived here just in time, for there is no question but what this city would have been taken by the radical Reds fostered by Red Russian agents." Would it give O. M. Green credit for too much subtlety to suggest an editorial motive when the *North China* printed a notice of a new edition of Mrs. Trollope's decidedly unflattering treatment of *The Domestic Manners of the Americans*?[55]

Americans, however, disagreed among themselves about what their country should do. Most missionaries in the Yangtze Valley—vocal ones, at any rate—opposed the use of force, afraid not only that it would violate their Christian principles but also endanger their lives. From Nanking, Rebecca Griest praised the British for holding their fire at Hankou, but she did not trust the Shanghailanders and warned that, if fighting broke out there, American lives and property would be in peril.[56] "The *first shot* fired by an American gunboat just now will absolutely change the whole situation," wrote the Methodist Bishop Birney in January. "It is a *great* opportunity for America if we act on our own initiative, and not in conjunction with other powers." Later that month, a group of Nanking missionaries, headed by A. J. Bowen, the president of the University of Nanking, urged the United States to show the "utmost patience and restraint" at Shanghai.[57] While MacMurray thought London's strong stand would help protect foreigners, Gauss sympathized with the missionary fears and told Barton that his decision to call the Punjabis from Hongkong raised the specter of a massacre in the interior.[58]

From Hankou, Episcopal Bishop Logan Roots urged his skeptical mission board at home to trust the Nationalists. "Chiang Kai-shek has made a wonderful speech lately," he wrote in early March, "indicating to my mind that he has an intellectual grasp of the situation, as well as moral courage and insight of a first order. What interests me especially is his clear statement of his readiness to cooperate with the communists, or rather to have them cooperate with the revolutionary movement in setting forward the Revolution."[59] Yet other missionaries found such views chilling (as would Chiang Kai-shek's left-wing antagonists, had they known of them). Shocked at the destruction of schools and mission compounds, the desecration of churches and chapels, they could see nothing but Boxerism and Bolshevism in the behavior of Canton's forces. Bishop Graves spoke for many when he praised Gauss for his measures to protect Americans but confessed himself unable to understand Washington's passivity. "It is apparently a policy of scuttle all around," he wrote in early January. "People in the United States have been fed so long on the utterances of Chinese students and of optimistic persons out here who hope great things from the Revolution that it will probably require a series of shocks before they awaken to the real facts." He thought the anti-Christian movement "really far more dangerous to Christian work than the Boxer outbreak because it is disguised in all sorts of pleasant words like 'sovereign rights', 'democracy', 'freedom', etc., but the inspiring spirit is the same." [60] He welcomed the coming of the British troops and the security they brought to Shanghai.[61] "How humiliating it is," wrote another Episcopal priest, "to depend for your safety on the soldiers of another nationality because your own government refuses to realize the seriousness of a situation." [62]

Unlike the missionaries, American businessmen in Shanghai were virtually united in wanting firmer action from their government. The American Chamber of Commerce urged Americans to enlist in the Volunteer Corps,[63] and on 19 January, it passed a resolution asking Washington to be ready to use force to protect foreign rights in the Settlement. Ten days later, it praised Kellogg's public statement of 27 January for its firm stand in defense of American lives and property, but the group was silent about its willingness to undertake treaty negotiations.[64]

There was one American in Shanghai who spoke out clearly against turning Shanghai into a foreign fortress, applauding his government for taking precisely the right stand. Although J. B. Powell and his *China Weekly Review* had welcomed London's Christmas call for treaty revision, he could never quite shake off his old-fashioned midwestern fears of the intrigues of British policymakers, and he sometimes confused the voice of British Shanghai with that of the British government. Admitting that Britain's proposals for new treaties went further than those of his own government, he praised Kellogg's statement of 27 January for its assertion that America was prepared to go it alone[65] and praised the Porter resolution for using the same arguments that had led America to reject the dangerous Versailles treaty.[66] Desperately anxious that America and Japan not be taken in by London's scheming for a general intervention to reestablish British ascendancy in China, he warned that following London's lead might bring war with China or, worse yet, with Russia.[67] "The duty of the 'Average American,'" he wrote, "is not to try to push us into a pro-British or pro-Japanese or pro-anything else policy, but to support the policy of Washington, which is to deal with the Chinese, and keep our relations with the Chinese on as friendly a basis as possible, because if that goes there is no point staying around." [68]

Though Powell never actually said the British were wrong in sending troops, he simply could not believe that so many were needed for self-defense and realized that their presence encouraged foreign Shanghai's obduracy. Hence, while toward London he was ambivalent, toward the Municipal Council he was simply scornful. In February, when only nine men were nominated as councillors and the Council duly declared them elected, he lashed out at the private arrangements made by the oligarchy that controlled the administration. "Shanghai Held an Election

Last Week!" cried the *China Weekly Review*, but there was no contest and, "as far as anyone can determine from perusing the correspondence columns of the newspapers or from listening to conversations and the club bars and other common meeting places, no one seems to be interested in the questions, despite the fact that . . . the Settlement is now facing the most serious crisis of its history." Yet an important change had taken place; although there were still two Americans, there were now two Japanese, and Britain had lost a seat. "It would be interesting to the average voter, of which the writer claims to be one, to know just what has taken place and also to know just how it was done to the mutual satisfaction of all parties concerned—and all without an election." [69]

If the crisis came, asked Powell in late February, who would speak for foreign Shanghai—or, at least, for the Settlement, since Naggiar clearly spoke for the Concession? Would it be Fessenden, the American chairman? Or would it be his largely British Council? or the British commissioner-general, the British police chief, or the British commandant of the Volunteer Corps? Or would it be General Duncan of the Shanghai Defence Force? "Assuredly, in a time of crisis there must be somebody in a position of authority who can go ahead and take action as Mr. O'Malley . . . has done at Hankow, and as the French Consul-General, Mr. Naggiar, has been authorized to do in the case of the French Concession here at Shanghai." [70]

Powell's point—and, though he was a voting ratepayer in the Settlement, he lived in the French Concession and had his offices on the avenue Edward VII dividing the two settlements—was that there was at least a clear line of responsibility from the Concession's administration, through the French minister in Peking, up to Paris. French actions were thus less likely to embarrass or even to endanger home governments than were those of an irresponsible Municipal Council. That winter, the French had shown that they could take decisive action; for in January, Martel in Peking and Consul-General Naggiar in Shanghai had dissolved the French *Conseil municipal* and set up a new governing body—with full Chinese representation—in its stead.

To see the French move, as Powell did, simply as a measure to meet the emergency is only partly right. Behind the establishment of the *Commission provisoire* lay also the larger problem of keeping the French Concession under French control rather than see it gradually amalgamated into the International Settlement. A few months earlier, the *Écho de Chine* had launched an embarrassing public campaign to uphold French authority. "Sooner or later," it wrote with a fine rhetorical flourish on 26 October, "it will be necessary to set our Concession free from its foreign yoke and to raise high in triumph him to whom we owe our liberation." [71] Naggiar had already proposed to Paris that more Chinese and Frenchmen be appointed to the *Conseil municipal*, thus turning it into a Franco-Chinese partnership that would diminish the threat of non-French influence.[72] That fall, he, Martel, and the Quai d'Orsay discussed ways of restructuring the *Conseil* so that, when the crisis came, the Concession's Chinese would rally to the support of the French authorities against the extremists.[73] Prudently, he took another step as well: On 12 October 1926, he issued an *ordonnance* amending Article VIII of the *Règlement* to allow the consul-general to suspend the *Conseil municipal* in case of civil war and civil disorder.[74]

Armed with this new power, Naggiar and his superiors now decided to bring the *Conseil municipal* to an end. In mid-January 1927, he suspended it indefinitely under the revised Article VIII, putting in its place a Provisional Commission [*Commission provisoire d'administration municipale*].[75] The new body, installed in the Hôtel Municipale on 17 January, was made up of eight Frenchmen, four foreigners, five Chinese, and a French president. Naggiar did not name du Pac de Marsoulies to the new commission (his term as councillor had expired), but two other French councillors stayed on, joined by several leading French businessmen (including Edouard Charlot, president of the French Chamber of Commerce) whom Naggiar appointed to the new body. The two *notables chinoises* who had been named in 1926 were joined by three others, chosen by the consul-general after discussion with Xu Yuan, the commissioner for foreign affairs.

At the first session of the new commission on 24 January, Naggiar also put into effect new rules strengthening the president's control over the agenda. He also promulgated the statute revising the constitution of the *Conseil*.[76] But from then on, the *Conseil* would exist on paper only; the *Commission provisoire* ran the affairs of the French Concession for the rest of its days.

THIRTEEN

Shanghai Has Become Red!
The Revolution Victorious

The coolest and best-informed foreigners still agree that Shanghai is unlikely to be taken by the Southern armies for many weeks, possibly months," wrote Frederick Moore in mid-March.[1] Recently arrived as correspondent for the *New York Times*, he himself warned that the end might come much sooner. The collapse of the February insurrection and the movement of British troops out to the old defense line had reassured foreign Shanghai for the moment, and the arrival of Zhang Zongchang's Shandong braves and White Russians stiffened the resistance. But Hangzhou had fallen, and the Nationalists were preparing to move up the railway linking the cities. Meanwhile, the different groups who made up Shanghai's political underground—Communist, Guomindang, and others—continued secretly to prepare for the coming of the southerners. Shanghai's fall was no longer in doubt; the real question was who would command the city after the northerners fled.

By the winter of 1927, the cracks in the strained alliance between Communists and Guomindang were noticeably widening. Chiang Kai-shek was increasingly independent of Wuhan, where Borodin and his colleagues had never approved of the advance on Shanghai. Not only would it divert the armies away from the drive to Peking and carry the Northern Expedition farther from the Soviet Union, but Shanghai's wealth would give Chiang and his generals an enormous advantage over the increasingly impoverished Wuhan government and encourage their already dangerous proclivities to give in to the imperialists and the bourgeoisie. By mid-February, the Shanghai Communists had begun a propaganda campaign against Chiang, never mentioning him by name but leaving little doubt that he was a man who would compromise with the Japanese and would turn against the workers.[2] Only in one way could Wuhan neutralize Chiang: by making sure that the leftists were in control when he arrived. Chiang might have most of the army on his side, but the Communists had most of the workers on theirs; and in those days, they still believed that China's future lay in the industrial proletariat, with the Communist party as its revolutionary vanguard.

Given the extraordinary politicization of China's recent historical writing, it is not surprising that we have no dispassionate account of the desperate game played out in the shadows of Shanghai's political underground, when, under the banner of the united front, Communists and non-Communists each plotted to take control of the city as the power of the northerners evaporated. Of course Communist and Guomindang historians disagree, and even within the Communist party itself, factional disputes have muddied the historical writing. Because Chen Duxiu—the general secretary of the Party's Central Committee—was later castigated by Moscow for communism's defeats in 1927, he has generally appeared in orthodox Party accounts as a right-wing opportunist, ready to compromise with the bourgeoisie and distrustful of the proletariat. Only recently has he begun to emerge as a central figure. The real heroes, in the eyes of Party historians, are men like Luo Yinong and Zhao Shiyan of the Zhejiang-Jiangsu Regional Party Committee. So is Zhou Enlai, the head of the Party's Military Affairs Department, who had arrived in Shanghai some months earlier and who was living secretly on the route Lafayette in the French Concession. Though his name does not figure prominently in earlier accounts, more recent writing has elevated him to a position of leadership.[3]

Communist strength lay, as it had since 1925, in the Party's control of the General Labor Union. Driven underground after May Thirtieth and now headed by Wang Shouhua, it had come to dominate much, though by no means all, of the city's labor force. The union also controlled a growing number of irregulars or pickets [*jiuchadui, ziweituan*], armed and unarmed. By the end of February, some five thousand of them were being secretly drilled in the use of weapons under Zhou Enlai's direction. Though arms were scarce, some could be smuggled in, some could be bought on the city's black market, and some obtained from disaffected northern troops. Several pickets managed to infiltrate the self-defense groups [*baoweituan*] set up by merchant associations, thus gaining a different kind of access to arms and arms training.[4] Finally, though nowhere does it appear in Communist accounts, the Party had the support and advice (a dubious benefit, perhaps) of the Soviet consulate-general.

Although the landing of foreign troops and the British move out to Jessfield in February gave the Communists a chance to build up the anti-British campaign ordered by the Central Committee,[5] there is little evidence that their presence posed any serious difficulties for Communist planning. Still, the Party, which by March had come to number some 3,080 members, had problems enough in other quarters. Their public statements at the time spoke of a rising tide of revolutionary sentiment and argued that the February uprising was a victory and not a defeat. Though Communist historians have dutifully echoed these views, the reality was quite different, and the final victory of socialism hardly seemed as inevitable then as it does to later writers. As recently published internal documents show, the Communists continued to suffer badly from disorganization and a lack of discipline. After the brutal repression of February, many workers were fearful and disillusioned, too politically backwards to understand Communist strategies. There were spies everywhere, secret documents were compromised, and the Party found itself unable to mount an effective and convincing propaganda campaign. At the same time, they had to make a desperate attempt to stay abreast of the rapid changes in the military and political picture: Which reports from the battlefield could they believe? Where were the Nationalist armies, and what were their plans? What were the politics of its commanders? And what of their own allies in Shanghai? What of the Guomindang and its agents in the city? What of the bourgeoisie and their plans? Men like Zhao Shiyan, Wang Shouhua, and Luo Yinong met secretly with the Guomindang representative Niu Yongjian, with the gangster leader Du Yuesheng, and with merchants like Yu Xiaqing and Wang Xiaolai ("a bunch of heroes in drinking and womanizing," [*beijiu furen de yingxiongpai*] Luo had scornfully called them).[6] Interestingly enough, they also seem to have been in touch with a member of the Municipal Council, for by early March, the Japanese mill owner T. Funazu, elected the previous month, was intriguing behind the backs of his colleagues to try to save the Japanese mills from further strikes.[7]

The picture of the Guomindang is complicated by the existence of at least two and perhaps three competing party factions in the city. On the right was the dissident Western Hills faction. Though denounced by the official Guomindang, they nonetheless remained an important force on the local level, working from the old party offices at 44 route Vallon in the French Concession.[8] Closer to Chiang and forming a centrist group were some of the most distinguished of the old Guomindang revolutionary comrades. Cai Yuanpei was one; a leader of the New Culture movement and former president of Peking University, he had helped form the Three Provinces Association a few months earlier. Wu Zhihui, the former anarchist, and Niu Yongjian had both arrived in 1926 to work underground to prepare Shanghai for the Northern Expedition. Though still part of the united front, men like these were deeply concerned by the growth of

Communist influence in the councils of their party, particularly after the February uprising, and were increasingly worried by Russian attempts to subordinate Chinese nationalism to the ends of the Soviet Union.[9]

The left wing of the Guomindang, thoroughly committed to the Communist alliance, was represented in the city through the Shanghai Municipality Special Party Bureau and the Jiangsu Provincial Party Bureau, which Wuhan recognized as the city's official party organs. In early March, in a foretaste of the grimmer warfare that would come a month later, a scuffle broke out between radicals and conservatives, both of whom had their headquarters in the relative safety of the French Concession. After gathering at 29 rue Molière to commemorate the anniversary of Sun Yat-sen's death, the leftists—against Communist orders (another breach of discipline in party ranks)—had then marched through the streets shouting, "Down with the reactionaries!" and "Down with the Guomindang right wing!" Their target was the house at 44 route Vallon, whose inmates had already barricaded themselves inside. After some rocks were thrown and some insults shouted, French gendarmes arrived to put a stop to the brawl.[10]

For all practical purposes, the Guomindang left can be grouped with the Communists. The Guomindang center had one enormous advantage over its leftist rivals: General Bai Chongxi, who was leading the Nationalist forces that were advancing on the city, took his orders from Chiang Kai-shek rather than from Wuhan. The hope of the centrists lay in a bloodless conquest, a negotiated surrender that would deliver Shanghai peacefully into the hands of Chiang's armies without the sort of social upheaval that would follow a revolutionary insurrection. Hence, Niu Yongjian opened secret talks with Bi Shucheng, the northern commander, apparently using the gangster Du Yuesheng as go-between.[11] To prevent this kind of an arrangement, the Communists had to proceed as the leaders of an armed, popular uprising carried out under the banner of the revolutionary united front, which would liberate the city from the northerners, install a municipal government under leftist control, and face General Bai and his commander-in-chief with a fait accompli on their arrival. The armed pickets of the General Labor Union would be the shock troops, the vanguard, of the insurrection that would make this feat possible.

Neither the consular reports nor the available Municipal Police reports say much about the part played by the Soviet consulate-general in this contest for power. French police intelligence, however, noted a growing activity at the building on Whangpoo Road since late February and reported the arrival of more Soviet agents to join the Comintern's Gregory Voitinsky, who was already there. Russian money flowed in from Wuhan and from the north, though the enmity between Borodin and the Russian General Galen was said to have delayed the dispatch of $750,000 to the city for arms purchases. The Russians set up the wife of a sympathetic American journalist in a boarding house in Yuen Ming Yuen Road to entertain British officers and extract what information she could (the American manicurist at the Palace Hotel was also rumored to be in Soviet pay). And the consulate-general sent its own representative (disguised as a Chinese to evade police surveillance) to a meeting at C. T. Wang's house in the rue Amiral Courbet to discuss organization of a new municipal administration.[12]

By 16 March, the final campaign in the battle for Shanghai had begun. Bai Chongxi, who led the advance, was one of a trio of talented generals from Guangxi province who had allied themselves with Canton in early 1926, serving with distinction in the first campaigns of the Northern Expedition. Early in 1927, he took command of the Eastern Route Army, and it was his troops that had captured Hangzhou in February. On 19 March, one of his advance units crossed the Huangpu, driving toward Shanghai and Suzhou against little opposition. Twenty-eight miles from Shanghai, the warlord troops guarding the old walled town of Songjiang gave way without a struggle, apparently ordered to withdraw by General Bi Shucheng. That left the way to the city open, and by then the northern leaders were looking out for their own safety. The admiral commanding the small northern naval detachment at Wusong was already flying the Nationalist ensign aboard his flagship, while Bi himself (as he admitted to the British consul-general) was still trying to make his own private arrangements with the Nationalist commanders. Meanwhile, according to French intelligence, a stream of Russian gold poured from the Soviet consulate-general to subvert the already dispirited northern soldiers.[13]

Yet, as Frederick Moore had reported, the sudden fall of Shanghai took many by surprise. Alerted by marine intelligence officers to the coming battle, J. B. Powell and Henry Misselwitz of the United Press finished their Sunday lunch on the twentieth and then drove through the foreign defense lines to find a half-hearted skirmish taking place beyond the city, in fields where grave mounds and occasional clumps of trees provided shelter both for the gray-uniformed northern troops and for their southern opponents.[14] That evening, the sound of distant gunfire reached the Chinese city, and shortly before midnight, the vanguard of Bai's armies entered Longhua Junction.[15] When the sun broke through the grimy haze over Pudong across the river the next morning, southern soldiers were already moving into Siccawei and the arsenal, forcing a retreat by Shanghai's supposed defenders up the railway loop to the North Station.

For the moment, foreign Shanghai paid little attention. The North China Daily News that arrived on the breakfast tables on the twenty-first said nothing to suggest that the Cantonese forces were at the gates of the city (only the *China Press* broke the news in a late bulletin). That very morning, Colonel Hill led his fifteen hundred United States Marines, the early spring sun glinting on their helmets and sidearms, on a march through the International Settlement. The Council had declared no state of emergency; the exercise was simply a chance to get the men ashore for a few hours, away from the cramped quarters of their transport. No doubt, it was also a chance to show Old Glory on the Bund, a chance for the shoppers and office workers of Nanking Road to hear "The Stars and Stripes Forever," a chance to help still some of the criticism of American passivity in the Settlement's hour of need. After parading as far west as the British encampment on the Race Course, the marines returned to the customs jetty to board the Dollar Line tenders that would take them back to the *Chaumont*. Even before they had completed their reembarkation, however, an emergency message ordered them back ashore. Within a few hours, they had taken up their positions in the Settlement, and this time they would stay.[16]

There was very little fighting in Shanghai between the regular armies of the two sides, and in Western eyes at least, the city's fall owed more to bribery and subversion than to the military prowess of the Eastern Route Army.[17] Rumors spoke of a northern arrangement to surrender after a token resistance, and the ease with which Bai Chongxi's troops took over the military headquarters at the Longhua Arsenal severely disillusioned those foreigners who had put their trust in the superior fighting strength of Zhang Zongchang's forces.

Far more important than these skirmishes was the battle fought by the revolutionary insurrectionists in the city's streets, the battle for which the underground had been preparing since its failure in February. For two days, Communist and labor leaders had met almost without a break, anxiously watching the changing military picture and debating their next move. With the arrival of the southerners at Longhua, the moment had come. The first step was the call put out by the General Labor Union on the morning of the twenty-first for a citywide general strike at noon. Ostensibly to welcome the arrival of the southern troops, the strike would also paralyze the city in preparation for the next move. Then, at one o'clock, they would begin the third and greatest of Shanghai's armed uprisings. The operation plan divided the Chinese city into seven tactical districts. From each of these, the workers' pickets, a few armed with guns but most wielding only clubs or axes, would surge out of the shadows to assault the police stations and seize their weapons. Then would come the occupation of buildings already identified as easily defensible strong points. The most important were in the industrial district of Zhabei, where radical strength was at its greatest: the Huzhou Guild, the Commercial Press building, and its workers' club. Another strategic location was the North Station, the city's key rail point, defended not only by the Shandong soldiers but also by the "Great Wall"—one of the armored trains manned by Zhang's White Russian mercenaries.[18] The battle plan (said the French police) had been drawn up with the aid of the Soviet consulate, which had installed one of its own agents (a certain Chusov) in a hotel on Thibet Road to help coordinate the operation.[19]

Thus, as the black ball fell that day on the Bund's semaphore tower to mark the passage of noon, the city's workers began leaving their jobs, and traffic in the streets slowed to a halt. Above the cupola of the Chinese post office on Soochow Creek, long a center of radical strength, the Nationalist colors flew for the first time over the Settlement. Within two hours, the textile mills of the northern and eastern districts were empty, and Chinese workers had abandoned the water and power stations in what was largely a peaceful walkout (only on Nanking Road did the police have to break up a riot among employees of several of the big department stores).

The streets of the Chinese city, emptied earlier that morning by fear of the retreating northerners, were coming to life by noon, filled with tens of thousands of people under a warm spring sun—students, propagandists, strikers, and the simply curious—demonstrating, holding impromptu meetings, celebrating the city's liberation from the Shandong army. Meanwhile, as in the past, a steady stream of Chinese, many of them carrying their bedding and their belongings, poured into the Settlement and the French Concession. Trams and buses came to a stop, deserted by their crews, and Shanghai's rickshaw men suddenly discovered that they could charge whatever fare they wished to carry refugees into the foreign districts. Nor were they the only ones to profit; shops selling flags were emptied within minutes as everywhere throughout the city and the Settlement flags of all descriptions appeared. Some were real Guomindang flags—the white sun on its blue background set against a larger red field—others were only red or only blue and white, and some were simply white cloth with the characters *qingtian bairi* [blue sky, white sun] written on them. Tailors stopped sewing clothes and began turning out flags, printers made flags of paper, and several local tobacco companies (presumably, like the revolutionaries, having prepared for this day) were ready with Warship Cigarettes or Victory Cigarettes in packages decorated with the Nationalist colors. Over shop doors blossomed slogans welcoming the Northern Expedition, welcoming the Guomindang, denouncing the warlords, calling for the unity of the revolutionary forces, and calling on the government to protect workers and peasants. And everywhere in the Chinese city emerged the pickets of the General Labor Union; black-gowned gunmen, as Western onlookers called them, plainclothesmen carrying pistols and rifles sent to keep order and to neutralize and disarm the regular police and Northern stragglers.[20]

As soon as the call for a strike went out, the Municipal Council declared a state of emergency, called in White Russians to man emergency services at the water and power plants, mobilized the Volunteer Corps and the police, and asked the foreign navies to land parties to defend the Settlement. This time the Americans agreed, and Colonel Hill's marines from the *Chaumont* and the *Pecos* began coming ashore for the second time that day. Their billets had already been prepared in the Yangtszepoo and Wayside districts (since they were restricted to the protection of American life and property, the marines were sent to the parts of the Settlement where they were least likely to engage Chinese forces). From the Dutch *Sumatra* and the Italian *Libia* came smaller detachments, and a thousand Japanese sailors took up positions in Hongkew and the Eastern District. In the French Concession, a force of eighteen hundred men—police, volunteers, Annamite and French soldiers from Indochina, and three hundred sailors from the *Jules Michelet* and the *Marne*—went on alert under orders to defend the neutrality of the Concession.[21]

Even before noon, the Shandong troops had disappeared from much of the Chinese city, and the guerrillas had begun to disarm the occasional police patrols still in the streets. Shortly after one o'clock, the sound of scattered gunfire signalled the start of the uprising, as insurgents attacked police stations in the Chinese city, overcoming them and plundering their stocks of arms. Hongkew and Nanshi were first to come under the control of the revolutionaries, and by late afternoon, Pudong and west Shanghai had fallen silent (in Pudong, Communist pickets rescued a *baoweituan* detachment that was standing guard over Du Yuesheng's house).[22] Only in the darkening streets of Zhabei did bitter fighting continue. There, the unremitting sound of small arms fire, punctuated by the deeper crunch of the Great Wall's three-inch gun, drove the terrified inhabitants to what shelter they could find among the decayed, wooden houses of the slums or in the gray concrete and dirty brick factories and warehouses.

By dusk the uprising's leaders, triumphant everywhere else in the city, had moved their headquarters to Zhabei, taking over a former police station on Baoshan Road from which to direct the struggle for the last northern strongholds: the Commercial Press, a fortress of a building where the machine guns of the defenders commanded the streets below; several blocks to the northwest, the Tiantongan train station, held by men made desperate by the destruction of the rail line that cut off their retreat; and the North Station, where the warlord remnants and the White Russians of the Great Wall continued to obey their orders to resist (General Bi Shucheng, still dickering with the Nationalists, had by now prudently sought refuge at the Astor House in the Settlement). Parties of guerrillas, crouched down to avoid fire from the station, tried to tear up the tracks beyond to isolate the armored train and its Russian crew. The cover of darkness only served to make the fighting more furious, and near the police station a fire broke out, spreading rapidly through Zhabei and turning the night sky red. The conflagration destroyed whole blocks of houses and drove fresh crowds of refugees from the flames to join those already trying to escape the battle.[23]

During all this time, it was only in Zhabei that foreigners were in any real danger. "The Chinese have been doing some heavy fighting there but only among themselves," wrote an American to her family at home. "They have no big guns so it's all close range fighting. There are white people living over there—poor Russians and the poor classes of other nationalities who can't afford foreign houses. These people are up against it and their situation is pitiful. When the papers refer to foreigners mixed up in this mess, it is usually some one of this type."[24] By late Monday afternoon, the Council had warned all foreigners living in the danger zone to move to safety, and by Tuesday morning, hundreds of Europeans and Americans from the northern extra-Settlement roads had come to the Public School on North Szechuen Road. The Japanese gathered at their school in the district. That morning, against Gauss's express wishes, Captain J. W. Baldwin of the American Company took an armored car and a detachment of his Volunteers to extricate two American families cut off by sniper fire in their houses on Wonglo Road. Fortunately, a brief truce allowed the beleagured families to escape, "hysterically overjoyed" at their rescue, as one participant wrote.[25] Some hours later, a party made up of Barton, Lord Gort, and several French priests tried to reach the Institute of the Holy Family, a convent on North Honan Road extension in Zhabei, where a group of French and British nuns with two hundred children in their charge were trapped by the fires raging near the North Station. Nationalist soldiers, however, stopped and searched Gort, releasing him only after Barton intervened. Meanwhile, the Jesuit Father Jacquinot took advantage of a lull in the fighting to make his way to the convent to help in its evacuation. He was wounded in the affair and later received the Croix de Guerre for his heroism, but clearly some of the nuns deserved the decoration every bit as much.[26] (Ten years later, during the Japanese invasion of Shanghai, the same Father Jacquinot took the lead in establishing a safe zone for refugees.)

As day broke on the twenty-second and the fire continued to burn out of control, the revolutionaries gradually gained the upper hand in the struggle for Zhabei's streets. The white flag of surrender broke over the Tiantongan railway station at noon. Three hundred soldiers gave themselves up to the insurgents, while others, pursued by pickets, tried to escape. Four hours later, the Commercial Press fell, now to become the center from which the revolutionaries would rally for the final assault on the North Station. Though the exhausted Shandong troops in the building were no longer a threat, the Great Wall remained invulnerable to the rifle fire of the guerrillas. A journalist described the extraordinary sight: There, amidst the fires and wreckage of warfare, was the enormous armored train, a thing of terrible beauty, camouflaged with yellow, black, and brown shapes painted on a sky-blue background. Moving massively and slowly back and forth across Honan Road, it fired intermittently at its impotent attackers, yet without any hope of escape.[27]

As the battle for Zhabei continued, Bai Chongxi and his Nationalist forces had remained at Longhua, still hoping to negotiate a surrender. On the twenty-second, Sidney Barton arranged permission for some of Bai's troops to come up the railway loop to Zhabei, passing through Jessfield Station, which was held by the Durhams. It may have been the arrival of these Nationalist regulars that finally destroyed the resistance of the last defenders of the North Station. Late on the afternoon of the twenty-second, they broke and ran for the International Settlement, crossing Boundary Road and rushing for the British manned barricades on Elgin Road. The first were disarmed and allowed into the Settlement. Then, in the confusion and panic of the late afternoon, British and Chinese began to shoot at one another. About twenty Chinese soldiers died, as did five others in a similar incident on Cunningham Road. At North Honan Road, more northerners tried to force their way into the Settlement and were pushed back, only to die when they came under fire from the guerrillas. Some two to four thousand northern troops, Chinese and White Russian, made it to safety that day in the Settlement, where they were disarmed and allowed to disperse; had they not been let in, reported the police, they would have been murdered by their enemies or torn apart by the mob.[28] By six o'clock that evening, twenty-nine hours after the uprising had begun, all Shanghai beyond the foreign settlements was in the hands of the revolutionary forces.

The next day, the city was quieter. The past two days had seen fair weather and a foretaste of spring, but now on the twenty-third, winter came back. A steady, cold rain—"the best policeman in the world," as the *North China* put it—fell over Shanghai.[29] Though the fires had died down, much of Zhabei was a smoking ruin, a grim foretaste of the fate it would suffer during the brutal Japanese onslaughts of 1932 and 1937. Fifteen hundred houses had been destroyed, thousands were reported dead or in hospitals, and for days the Chinese papers would print lists of the casualties. Wreckage and debris lined the boundary roads, piles of dirty, gray northern uniforms lay in the mud, among them, as a journalist grimly noted, "the red ribbons that had once adorned execution swords." "How much the appearance of the streets had changed in two days!" exclaimed one of the nuns who emerged from the siege of Holy Family. "In front of us, near the boundaries, empty houses, nothing but soldiers in the streets. Further off, lots of activity, the red flag with its blue and white sun in the corner raised over all the Chinese houses, even over the little stores. Shanghai has become red." [30]

Shanghai has become red! For the last two years, Shanghai's foreigners had looked forward with trepidation to this day. What did it mean for the city's future? The fall of the North Station on the evening of the twenty-second completed the rout of the northern armies, and in the end, Zhang Zongchang's forces proved to be no more capable or willing to fight for Shanghai than had Sun Chuanfang's armies. But who had defeated them? The Communist-led revolutionaries had gone into action as soon as they heard of the arrival of the Nationalist vanguard at Longhua, and the ease with which the city's strong points and police stations had surrendered everywhere but in Zhabei showed how carefully they had planned their assault. Armed with only a few antique weapons, claimed a Communist writer, they had nonetheless killed three thousand enemy soldiers and two thousand policemen, winning a total victory so that the Nationalist Army did not have to fire a single shot.[31] An exaggeration, perhaps, but not much of one, for it was not until the afternoon of the twenty-second at the earliest that any of Bai's units joined the fighting at the North Station. If it is true, as Communist accounts maintain, that Bai refused the entreaties of the General Labor Union to send troops earlier, hoping that the workers would be weakened by the continued fighting, he was playing a very dangerous game, for he must have known better than anyone how little stomach the northern armies had for a fight. Or did the Guomindang's Niu Yongjian persuade him to wait in the hope that General Bi Shucheng would agree to a peaceful surrender?[32] At least one foreign journalist repeated the rumor that the unexpected battle in Zhabei had broken out only because Bi had agreed to make common cause with the Guomindang moderates against the Communists.[33]

Foreign reports bear out the claim of the insurrectionists that it was they alone who deserved the glory of victory. "It would be a mistake to say that Northern resistance collapsed," wrote the *North China* on 22 March, "for none was ever offered." Gauss faulted the Nationalists for not moving into the city sooner, thus allowing the city to fall "into the control of agitators, laborers, students and guerrillas, who seized the police stations, armed themselves with rifles and pistols of the police and Chinese

Volunteers of the outside areas, and conducted a reign of terror in the region north of the foreign settlements in the native city." [34] Colonel J. R. V. Steward, the British military attaché, in Shanghai at the time, blamed the collapse of the northern troops on their bad tactics and "the inherent rottenness of their leadership in the face of defeatist propaganda."

> As a result of their entry into Shanghai the Kuo Min-tang forces offer a spectacle that is unparalleled in history, namely an ever victorious army that is composed of troops which, by virtue of their training and armament, could never obtain a victory over the poorest forces outside China, and which have never obtained a victory in China except by means of their civilian allies behind and in the enemies' lines. These allies, armed mainly with automatic pistols, work chiefly by propaganda until the time is ripe for a local *coup de main* against some weakly held headquarters or police station, which *coup de main* completes the moral rout of a badly led and faint-hearted enemy. [35]

Shanghai had fallen to the revolution. But whose revolution was it? The overpowering of the North Station and the defeat of the northerners meant the end of the first stage of the battle for the city. The liberation of Shanghai, cried Zhao Shiyan, was China's February revolution, and Chiang Kai-shek was China's Kerensky; now the struggle must continue, until China had her own October revolution and presumably also her own Lenin. [36]

Well before the fall of Shanghai, the revolutionaries had begun to organize a body to undertake the governance of Shanghai, and even before the fighting was over in Zhabei, they sought to establish its authority over the Chinese city. On the morning of the twenty-second, the Communists Lin Jun of the Students' Union and Wang Shouhua of the General Labor Union, joined by Wang Xiaolai of the Merchants' Association (a Guomindang front set up to displace the more conservative Chamber of Commerce), chaired a meeting in the Xinwutai Theater to choose a committee of nineteen to govern the city. That afternoon the list was ratified at a mass meeting held at the Public Recreation Ground. [37] Superficially, at least, it honored the united front, for together with Communists like Lin Jun, Wang Shouhua, and Luo Yinong could be found the names of Yu Xiaqing, Bai Chongxi, and Niu Yongjian. (Qu Qiubai admitted that they had been included in an attempt to coopt the Guomindang into the new order, and Zhao Shiyan had earlier made it clear that the Communists would act as *houtai laoban*, or backstage bosses.) Wuhan immediately recognized the legitimacy of the new organ, and the very day Shanghai fell, Borodin called an emergency meeting of the government to name a seven-man branch political committee in the city to handle Guomindang affairs. Again the principles of the united front were honored, and Wu Zhihui, Niu Yongjian, and Bai Chongxi were included. How much, if at all, the Guomindang had participated in these preparations is hard to say, but Niu and Bai now refused to play the role assigned to them as pawns of the left. And when the Communist intellectual Guo Moro arrived to Shanghai to take charge of political work in the army, Bai could only have seen that as a step to subvert the loyalty of his troops.[38]

General Bai, at least, wanted no trouble with the outside world. As soon as he arrived, he publicly called on Shanghai's citizens to keep the peace, insisting that questions dealing with the concessions and the unequal treaties be handled by negotiations and not by violence and forbidding any conflict with the foreigners. He also told workers that, though they deserved better treatment, they should return to their jobs, for their employers also suffered from the heavy hand of imperialism and might well go bankrupt if the unions made unreasonable demands.[39]

Most of this jockeying for position was invisible to foreigners in Shanghai at the time. Had they seen it more clearly, it might both have diminished their fears of a general monolithic Chinese nationalism and increased their fears that the treaty ports, like Shanghai, would become pawns in the political fighting between particular Chinese factions. In a sense, it mirrored a similar competition among the foreigners themselves—think of the tensions between the preservation of the general interests of foreigners in Shanghai and the particular interests of the British. Of course, anyone who read the papers knew of the strains between Chiang Kai-shek and Wuhan and could only hope that his subordinates would bring the city's Communists under control. As early as the twenty-second, Consul-General Naggiar was in secret touch with Chiang's agents, who assured him that, though their commander was determined to declare war on the Communists, the left was strong and the battle would be difficult.[40] The following morning, Fu Xiaoan, then the chairman of the Chamber of Commerce, arranged a meeting between General Bai and Barton, Naggiar, and Frederick Maze, the commissioner of customs (Gauss, angry that the authorities were not doing more to restore order, sent word that he was too busy to appear). Bai looked nervous, and his talk was frequently interrupted by an anonymous official, presumably one of the army's political officers making sure that Wuhan's interests were being upheld. Bai did, however, promise to keep the peace by bringing the guerrillas under control and urging the General Labor Union to call off the strike.[41] That day, the union put out a call for a return to work, but it exempted its armed pickets, who kept up their patrols in the Chinese city, as a continuing reminder of the union's influence.[42]

For the moment, an apprehensive quiet settled over the city as the pickets guarded the Chinese districts and foreign troops and volunteers stood watch over the settlements and the western roads. Then, on the morning of the twenty-fifth, came the news of the fall of Nanking the day before and of the death of a British doctor as the Nationalist army had fought its way into the old capital. Within twenty-four hours, the reports grew worse: Dr. John Williams, the American missionary vice-president of the University of Nanking, shot to death, Bertram Giles, the British consul-general, wounded, foreign houses and consulates sacked, and casualties among Nanking's foreigners perhaps far higher. The news stunned foreign Shanghai, already living on its nerves behind its cordon of troops. In the confusion of war, however, with communications upriver possible only through naval radio, there was no way of knowing what had really happened or what could be believed. Around the Settlement flew rumors: Nanking pillaged and in flames, foreign women raped, and, most appalling of all, a general massacre of foreigners by the revolutionary troops.

In a few days, it became known that six foreigners had been killed. A Japanese naval officer was a victim of the Nationalist shelling of the city. An accident, perhaps; but five others, by all report, had been murdered. Two British citizens had been shot to death in their consulate, and three missionaries, French, Italian, and the American Williams, had been killed. The Japanese consul-general, ill in bed, had been shot at but was unhurt; Giles was wounded in the leg, and his consulate looted; John K. Davis, the American consul-general, had escaped as most of the foreign community fled the city. British and Americans sought safety by fleeing to Socony Hill above the Yangtze, and to cover their escape to the river, Davis called on the foreign warships in the river to lay down a protective barrage behind them. U.S.S. *Noa* and H.M.S. *Emerald* responded; a Japanese destroyer remained silent. Estimates of Chinese casualties from the naval bombardment ranged from three or four to more than a hundred. Under cover of the barrage, the foreigners made it to the ships and were taken downstream to Shanghai.

The Nanking outrage, as foreigners called it, was the most serious antiforeign incident in the Chinese revolution of the 1920s. To this day, it is not clear who was responsible for the attacks, nor whether they were premeditated or simply the acts of undisciplined soldiers in the heat of battle. Westerners in Nanking that day were virtually unanimous in their belief that the attackers were Nationalist regulars, and their Hunanese accents seemed to identify them as members of units under General Cheng Qian, who had led the army into the city. Many witnesses, including Consul-General Davis, were further convinced that the soldiers had acted under orders. Eugene Chen's assertion a few days later (echoed by Chiang Kai-shek on 27 March) that defeated and demoralized northern troops were responsible has little evidence to support it, despite a credulous report published in the *Nation* of New York (which is discussed later). What was to become the official explanation by the Guomindang—that leftists had instigated the incident to embarrass Chiang and to thwart his plans for a rapprochement with the foreigners—may have some truth in it, though the affair was bound to hurt Wuhan as well.[43]

Without any firm evidence, it probably makes most sense to assume that the Nanking incident was unplanned and that those responsible were undisciplined troops from Hunan, a province noted for the strength of its radicalism and antiforeignism. Perhaps, as Bai Chongxi later told Powell, unorganized Cantonese sympathizers who had armed themselves were at fault.[44] Cold-blooded as it may sound, what is surprising to the historian is that there were not more incidents of this sort during a revolutionary civil war. Despite the seizure, occupation, and occasional looting of foreign property (largely in mission stations), despite the fierce anti-imperialist rhetoric of both Communists and non-Communists during these years, almost no foreigners were physically harmed by the revolutionary upsurge that began in 1925 (common banditry, of course, north and south, was something else again). That fact contrasted with the May thirtieth tragedy, the Shamian incident, and the British naval bombardment of Wanxian only seven months earlier helps explain why, to Chinese at the time, the "Nanking outrage" meant not the apparently accidental deaths of a handful of foreigners but the apparently merciless bombardment of the city by foreign warships.

Nonetheless, given the fears of foreign Shanghai, given its reaction to the seizure of the Hankou and Jiujiang concessions, it is easy to see why the first reports coming in from Nanking should have produced something close to a state of panic. Within a few days, the first refugees from the old capital had arrived with their stories of the city's fall. "All reports concur," wrote the *North China*, "that the Southern troops in Nanking ran amok like wild animals, shooting foreigners, and looting their houses everywhere." Yet—unlike the sensationalist reports of the *New York Times*—it played down the wilder stories of a general massacre or heavy loss of life.[45] The Nanking affair was the signal for a general evacuation of the foreigners who had remained in the Yangtze treaty ports and the upcountry mission stations. For the next fortnight, British and Japanese river steamers, crowded to their gunwales with exiles in flight from the civil war and often under fire as they steamed downriver, moored off the Bund to discharge their passengers in an already congested city. "How Shanghai can expand to accommodate all these people is a mystery to me," wrote one observer, "but with each new batch that arrives we still find place for them."[46] Most of them were Americans, but they found safety in the foreign concessions under British guard, and the events at Nanking seemed to justify, if any justification were still needed, London's decision to send thousands of troops to the city. On 26 March, Admiral Williams, the American commander-in-chief, asked for fifteen hundred more marines as soon as possible. This time, Washington not only granted the request immediately but for the first time suggested the possibility of sending an army detachment from Manila.[47]

Two days after the Nanking incident, Chiang Kai-shek arrived in Shanghai. His main purpose in coming was to consolidate his control of the city and to begin to tap Shanghai's riches to underwrite his political and military ambitions. He also took advantage of his trip to try to quiet Western fears about the Nanking incident. Arriving on a Chinese gunboat from Jiujiang early in the afternoon of the twenty-sixth, he was driven to the Bureau of Foreign Affairs on route Ghisi. On the way, his driver took a wrong turn and entered the French Concession, allowing the general to see the defense works thrown up around the settlements.[48] The following day in a meeting with foreign reporters, he blamed the Nanking affair on gangsters [*liumang*], deplored the defensive measures, which he called provocative and unnecessary, and denied that there was any danger of Chinese troops overrunning the concessions.[49] At another news conference two days later, he too, like Chen, blamed the northerners for the outbreak at Nanking and condemned what he called the unprovoked foreign bombardment of the city.[50]

Chiang may also have been brought to Shanghai by rumors that the radicals were themselves planning an antiforeign outbreak in the city, perhaps even a direct attack on the concessions.[51] In an announcement appearing on the front page of various Chinese papers on the twenty-sixth, the General Labor Union publicly denied any such intentions, but the reports reaching Western ears were nonetheless unsettling. "It need not be a secret," wrote George Sokolsky in an article published on the twenty-fifth, "that two attempts were made for a demonstration to march upon the Settlement from Chapei for the purpose of working a massacre of Chinese by the foreign troops, and that both efforts were stopped by the Nationalist Army."[52] Sokolsky had by all odds the best contacts in the Guomindang of any Western journalist, but it remains unclear on what he based his charge. French police intelligence reported that, on 25 March, Soviet and Chinese Communists reached a decision for such a move. If true, the attempt was apparently abandoned, perhaps because of opposition from the Comintern.[53]

On the morning of the twenty-seventh, the General Labor Union opened its new offices at the Huzhou Guild in Zhabei. There, representatives of various associations gathered under the chairmanship of Wang Shou-hua to pass resolutions demanding, among other things, the return of the Settlements.[54] That afternoon, a huge public meeting was held, called by the leftist Guomindang's Special Municipal Bureau to welcome the arrival of Chiang Kai-shek. Under fair skies, a crowd variously estimated at from fifty to a hundred thousand people gathered at the Public Recreation Ground. Among them were said to be representatives of fully a thousand different organizations: labor unions, student unions, street unions, commercial associations, women's groups, educational associations, youth groups, and the like.

According to the Chinese press, the tone of the meeting was one of moderation and good sense; while pickets from the General Labor Union kept perfect order, slogans exhorted the citizenry of Shanghai to keep the peace. They must not try to force their way into the settlements; they must not attack foreigners or even give them propaganda pamphlets; there must be no excuse, in short, for imperialist reprisals. The chief speaker was Bai Chongxi, and, while paying tribute to the Shanghai masses for their help in the liberation of the city, he repeated his earlier pleas for order. Foreign policy and military policy were the business of the government and the army, he reminded them and individuals and groups were not to take isolated action.

We are not anti-foreign, and even among Shanghai's foreigners, there are many who are oppressed themselves. What we do want to destroy is the policy of foreign aggression. Therefore we must protect foreign schools, factories and stores. If we act recklessly, we betray our humanity [*renge*], we betray our nationhood [*guoti*], because we are not out to attack foreigners. Everyone must realize that we want to protect foreign life and property.[55]

Western reports of the same gathering gave a rather different picture. Chiang Kai-shek himself was said to have been there (no one seemed quite sure), and though he and Bai tried to keep things calm, the crowds, whipped up by the chairman Lin Jun, nonetheless resolved to resume the general strike if the settlements were not immediately returned. They broke up in a decidedly truculent mood amidst threats of demonstrations against the concessions.[56] One might as well be reading the accounts of two different gatherings. Were the Western reports overblown? Or did the Chinese press fear trouble either with General Bai or the Settlement authorities if it printed the whole story?

Clearly the emergency was not over, and clearly the Nationalist conquest of Shanghai had done little to calm the city down. An indication of its nervousness could be seen from the movements of refugees. Always in the past, the threat of war had brought men and women to the city for safety. Now ominous reports told of travel in the other direction: Tens of thousands of men and women were leaving Shanghai, both from the foreign settlements and the Chinese city, going into the countryside or to the comparative safety of Ningbo or Hangzhou for fear of what was about to happen.[57]

FOURTEEN

Have the Missionaries Been Converted?
Foreign Shanghai under the Nationalists

The rumors blowing down the river from Nanking confirmed a jittery Shanghai's worst fears about the dangers of Nationalist occupation. On 23 March, two days after declaring a state of emergency in the Settlement, the Municipal Council imposed a nighttime curfew. It also forbade any Chinese police or soldiers from entering the Settlement or its roads, and outlawed the carrying of flags and banners in the streets, and the wearing of unauthorized uniforms or any device "bearing any inscription in Chinese or in any Foreign Language" (English, presumably, was a native language). Meanwhile, the Council extolled the Settlement as a haven of peace and security in times of trouble, stressed its neutrality, and emphasized the Council's approbation of many aspects of China's new national spirit. Yet, now was no time "to consider any drastic change in the Shanghai administration." If ther was to be change, it must be evolutionary, not revolutionary, and must take place in an atmosphere of calm and good order.[1] There were two warnings here: one to the Nationalists not to make Shanghai into another Hankou, and another to Washington and London not to negotiate away Shanghai's future over the Council's head. "We are not sure of our respective governments in political matters," wrote the *North China* on 24 March. "We frankly are afraid that we may wake up one morning to find that they have made fatal concessions to the Nationalists, just as was done at Hankow, under the twin delusions that the so-called Nationalist Government is a settled and permanent organization and that its good will may be won by friendly gestures and conciliation."[2]

In the settlements, life went on for foreigners among the difficulties brought by war. Every day the city became more crowded, as refugees from the fighting continued to pour in, and the *North China* deplored the "needless panic" of those who were packing up and shipping home their valuables.[3] Foreign offices might be shorthanded as their men were called out for duty with the Volunteers, but with Yangtze trade at a standstill and inbound ships filled with fugitives from the river ports, business was slow anyway. (On 1 April, Butterfield and Swire's China Navigation Company cut the pay of its foreign officers by 10 percent, thus leading to a long and bitter strike that summer.) The March race meetings were canceled, and people were warned not to travel outside the settlements, although the danger of being hit by a stray rifle shot was not enough to dissuade some passionate golfers from continuing their play on the Hungjao course. Changes there were, however. "How quiet evenings are now that all the young men we know are on duty and the dancing places all closed!"[4] complained a correspondent in the woman's page of the paper. The curfew crippled Shanghai's social life, forcing cafés and cabarets to close at uncommonly early hours, and some of the port's *jeunesse dorée* even discovered the pleasures of a good book by a warm fire on a chilly night. Tea dances, on the other hand, became more popular than ever, and the Eddie Café put on a musical tiffin with dancing and vaudeville from 12:30 to 2:00 in the afternoon.

Within a few days, most of the stores were open again ("the British House for British Troops," Whiteaway's now called itself). Though the Carlton Club canceled its evening boxing matches and the movie theaters their evening shows, one could still see Charlie Chaplin and Jackie Coogan in *The Kid* at the Peking, while at the Isis, John Bowers and Marguerite de la Motte played in *Desire* ("A Brilliant Exposé of High Society"). At the Embassy, however, they were showing newsreels of the January storm at Hankou. Though Mario Paci complained about the competition given his Municipal Orchestra by the Defence Force's military band concerts, his group, like orchestras across the world in 1927, commemorated the centenary of Beethoven's death (on 29 May, it would give Shanghai a performance of the Ninth Symphony, complete but for the last movement).[5]

With over twelve thousand men ashore, tanks and armored cars in the streets, sandbags, barbed wire barricades, concrete pill boxes, and machine gun emplacements at strategic points, the foreign settlements seemed safe from the kinds of horrors Zhabei had suffered, safe from the kind of fury foreigners had suffered in Nanking. Worried that the southern armies would try to seize St. John's, Bishop Graves was relieved when General Duncan ordered a detachment of men from the Jessfield encampment to watch over the university and the American Church Mission. "I tell you it sounds good to hear the heavy boots of the British soldiers on the night patrol in the compound," he wrote later to his sister, and he spoke warmly of their chaplain who had won the Victoria Cross in Mesopotamia.[6] Closer to the city, President F. J. White of Shanghai Baptist College (whose appeal for a warship to be moored near his campus had been refused in January) rejoiced at the sight of American destroyers patrolling the river.[7] "Shanghai's house of defence: the naval wall," a journalist called the warships, elated by "the sleek gray forms creeping up the river from day to day," bringing to Shanghai the largest fleet of foreign men of war the city had ever seen. Most imposing were the U.S.S. *Pittsburgh* and France's *Jules Michelet*, "distinctive in her black paint and, with her large square ports, looking like some great sea castle." Other American cruisers joined those from Japan, Britain, Italy, Spain, and the Netherlands, while H.M.S. *Argus*, the first aircraft carrier to come to Shanghai, lay off Wusong. By late March, twenty-eight ships had arrived. "For a distance of a mile and a half lies an almost unbroken line of grim, silent ships of war, representing the power and rights of seven nations, while scooting about among the larger craft are numerous ships' launches, with business-like machine-guns mounted in the bows, suggesting that foreign property and interests are to be protected on the water no less than in the Settlement on shore. . . ."[8]

Few foreigners doubted that Britain's decision to send troops had saved Shanghai from the fate of Hankou or Nanking, and many Americans were outspokenly critical of their country's inaction. "It was very kind of the American authorities offering to evacuate us all," remarked one of them, "but as we have homes and business interests here, that is nothing to thank them for."[9] Even before he heard the news of Nanking, Bishop Graves wrote home that "Shanghai owes the greatest debt to the British defense forces. If it had not been for them we should have been looted and driven out long before this. The American Marines are now on shore where they ought to have been a month ago. We hear that some 3,000 Marines are standing by at Quantico, Virginia, and some Americans here favor sending a telegram to say that they are glad that Quantico is safe."[10] Frederick Moore of the *New York Times* (like his paper, an alarmist about Shanghai) cabled home reports of American distress at Washington's failure to act more decisively, contrasting the confinement of the marine patrols to the safer sections of the city with the courage of American police and American Volunteers, who gladly accepted dangerous orders from their British commanders.[11] "The British troops have done excellent work and have saved the situation here," wrote an American in the French Concession. "The handful of American marines, while good in themselves, are a joke so far as being really able to protect Americans is concerned—It's the British we have to thank for keeping Shanghai out of trouble and I'd just love to tell Washington what I think of their pusillanimous policy."[12]

However much Washington might wish to limit them, the American marines were now seen—and saw themselves—as an integral part of the Shanghai Defence Force. The American military attaché, arriving the day of the city's fall, reported that the marine units were placed so as "to constitute local support for the British troops on the line of barricades. Technicalities as to the status of the U.S. Marines were no longer being regarded, and to all practical purposes, our Marines had become a component part of the international force and considered themselves subject to General Duncan's orders." [13] On 25 March, the day after Nanking, General Smedley Butler, a veteran of the Boxer days, arrived to take command of the marine detachment. Years later, J. B. Powell remembered that the Quaker general had exasperated other commanders by issuing pacific declarations to the press, but his one interview with the *North China Daily News* did not sound much like a dovish note. It would be the threats to women and children, the general warned, not the threats to property and "vested interests" that would awaken Americans to the real dangers they faced. Then "not a man . . . but would be willing to shoulder a gun, probably given him by one of his own women-folk, to protect the lives of American women and children out here." [14] General Duncan had high praise for Butler's cooperative spirit. Under instructions to try to bring the Americans into the defense of the perimeter, the British commander found Butler willing to "over-ride his instructions" and join the British line if fighting came. [15]

From other quarters came more applause for Britain's stand. The Shanghai Stock Exchange wired London its thanks for the force, "which alone prevents inevitable looting, incendiarism and massacre in Settlements by armed Communists and leaderless Chinese troops." Japanese residents passed a resolution thanking the British, and a Norwegian businessman collected three thousand foreign signatures on a letter praising London for its courage in giving "the lead to the whole civilized world." (The delighted Foreign Office immediately asked Barton [in code] to wire [*en clair*] the names of the leading signatories, "especially the Americans"; Barton's response listed Fessenden, F. F. Fairman, president of the American Chamber of Commerce, and most of the other business leaders.) [16]

Among those joining in the praise for the British was the troublesome Me du Pac de Marsoulies in the French Concession. No doubt he had it in for the authorities, but there were many others in the Concession who thought that Naggiar and his colleagues were not taking the crisis seriously enough. "Capitulons-nous à Shanghai?" cried the *Écho*, contrasting the activism of other countries with French passivity. [17] As the Nationalist armies drew closer, French business circles lobbied Paris for a stronger response; if the British lost, French interests would suffer, and if they won, they would remember that perfidious Marianne had let them down. [18] Nanking brought new fears and new criticisms; the French authorities were "unbelievable," complained one firm, in their willingness to negotiate and to give free rein to the "worst elements of the revolution." [19] "It would be criminal not to understand the anti-foreign character of the present movement fomented and directed by communists," wired the French Chamber of Commerce to Paris. "Against an unleashed horde of barbarians, we cannot insist too strongly on the solidarity of all foreign interests in China, and the need for strong measures and a strong policy with other powers." [20] "British saved us in time—Italy acting conjointly—all with the exception of France realized danger Chinese aim Bolshevism, . . ." wired Fiat's man in Shanghai.[21]

Naggiar himself realized that French weakness might give the British a pretext to intervene in the Concession, and Paris sought to reassure London that the French would hold against armed attack.[22] Discussions between General Duncan and Admiral Basire about measures for defense led to a joint communiqué on 2 April that helped settle some fears.[23] In private, an angry and harassed Naggiar blamed the panic on those who wanted to tie French policy to Britain, hoping for a future amalgamation of the Concession with the Settlement.[24] Such an explanation does not account for the actions of groups like the French Chamber of Commerce, nor presumably for the editorials of the *Écho de Chine*, which, much to the discomfiture of the consul-general, joined in the campaign against the French authorities. Naggiar, as we will see, had his own way of dealing with the crisis, but it was not one that could be made public. Shanghai Frenchmen seem to have behaved much like Shanghai Americans, contrasting Britain's strong stand with their own country's apparently weak response.

Even Gauss, who had tried to block any unnecessary show of force, was seriously worried by late March. After Nanking, he used a broadcast code arranged earlier to warn all the missionaries in his district to come into Shanghai. "William is found to be quite ill," was the signal calling for evacuation of the upcountry mission stations; one woman on hearing it immediately set about praying for the recovery of the American commander Admiral Williams, who she thought had been struck down.[25] To Gauss, Nanking proved the strength of Nationalist radicalism, and he doubted whether Chiang could deal with the leftists. General American opinion, he told MacMurray, "including that of a number of Americans who have in the past strongly opposed firm action by the powers, is that the powers, including prominently the United States, must now take strong measures without further delay in order that the situation and the more moderate Chinese may be strengthened in their position against the radical elements which now dominate the Nationalist Party. . . . I must say frankly that I am strongly of this view." [26]

More and more, Gauss was moving toward the activist line that Mac-

Murray had urged for the last several months. At the end of March, J. B. Powell, afraid that his country might be drawn into a joint military intervention after Nanking, printed a report from Washington that denied any such plans. Gauss wanted to disavow the story, finding it "disconcerting" to Americans who, whatever they might have thought before Nanking, now wanted strong action. Powell's report was, of course, absolutely on the mark, and State's confused and confusing response must have given the consul-general little comfort; Kellogg in effect confirmed what the *Review's* story had said and then added that, since it was obviously untrue, it could safely be repudiated![27]

According to Powell, it was the *Review's* story and the State Department's response to it, which somehow leaked out, that now led the American Chamber of Commerce to put out a public statement, implicitly critical of Washington and asserting that the United States must join the other powers in a strong stand.

Militarism, brigandage, and Bolshevism have destroyed all semblance of law and order throughout the greater part of China, and have brought about a condition where life and property of both Chinese and foreigners are in constant danger from mob violence, military terrorism and unrestrained activities of individual criminals. The repeated assurances of militarists and other spokesmen of political factions that they can and will protect life and property are irreconcilable with the recent deplorable events leading to the necessity for the evacuation of the entire Yangtze Valley. . . . The great mass of conservative and law abiding Chinese have been reduced to a state of helpless intimidation and are unable to take any effective measures to protect either themselves or foreign residents. The adoption of a conciliatory policy by the foreign governments has merely strengthened the position of the lawless elements and encouraged outrages like that of Nanking.

Shanghai alone was safe, it continued, not because of any Nationalist restraint, but simply because of the presence of foreign forces.

We believe that immediate concerted action by the Powers to restore a condition of security for foreign lives and property in all Treaty Ports and to recover all foreign properties which have been destroyed or confiscated will have a far-reaching influence throughout China to the ultimate benefit of the Chinese people. This result should not be difficult to attain with the naval forces now in Chinese waters.

This time, the statement was neither cleared with the consulate nor sent to the State Department. It was a direct appeal to domestic public opinion, and was given to American journalists to send home, but it was not meant for publication in Shanghai. The *North China* printed it, however, thus openly ranging the chamber publicly on the side of those calling for blood to avenge the martyrs of Nanking.[28]

Three of those martyrs had been missionaries, and one was an American. The affair helped bring to a head the continuing quarrel over the National Christian Council's benign attitude toward the revolution. It was not just the N.C.C.'s increasing politicization that worried many but also its readiness to speak in the name of the whole Church in China. Though the N.C.C. denied the charge, there is no doubt that many saw it as representative at least of Protestant Christendom in the country. Already under attack for its earlier public statements, the N.C.C. now found itself in hotter water than ever. In early January, a group of Chinese Christians in Wuhan issued a manifesto giving a virtually unqualified backing to the Guomindang, identifying the cause of Christianity with the cause of anti-imperialism and calling on "any foreign missionaries who love their own countries more than they love Christ . . . to go back to their own countries as soon as possible." They closed by saying that they regarded the anti-Christian movement as their "friend" because, like Jesus, it had called them to repent, presumably of their ties with foreign imperialism.

That was bad enough; but at about the same time the N.C.C. in Shanghai published a large poster to help the cause of proselytization. But, proselytization of what? "Propagate Christianity and Reform [*gexin*] China," the heading cried, while underneath it young representatives of the Chinese Church militant, carrying banners reading "Enlightenment," "Truth," "Justice," "Purity," and "Christian Life," pursued a disordered swarm of hard-faced demons labelled "Cruelty," "Avarice," "Lustfulness," and "Gambling." There might be nothing in that to upset the man of God, perhaps; but critics maintained that to the illiterate, the poster would seem a call by the Church of China to expel the foreign devils (one of the demons was, in fact, named *qinlue*, meaning "invasion"—in the sense of foreign aggression). "Christ leading a mob," an Episcopal priest called it, and Graves agreed that, though in normal times the educated would realize that the poster depicted Chinese students "driving out the devils of corruption, opium, etc., . . . to the illiterate it would appear to be an assault of Chinese students upon a lot of black devils, and of course the only devils they are engaged in driving out just now are the foreign devils."[29]

Not surprisingly, as Gauss pointed out, the Wuhan Christians were trying to preserve themselves in a stronghold of the anti-Christian movement under a government dominated by Borodin and such men as the leftist Xu Qian (himself an old Johannean). Not surprisingly too, newspapers like the *North China* seized on such productions to denounce the N.C.C. for this latest outrage to good taste and good sense. "By their Fruits . . ." it began an editorial on 19 January, attacking the poster and the Wuhan manifesto and thus rekindling the controversy about the Council's political role that had been smoldering since the aftermath of May Thirtieth.

The N.C.C.'s supporters—its American secretary, Edwin Lobenstine, the British Henry Hodgkin, and others—responded, and the fight was on. Yes, Lobenstine admitted, the N.C.C. had published the poster, but it had not produced it; in any case, it had been printed "when the atmosphere was not so electric" and, under the circumstances, would be withdrawn.[30] Other missionaries asserted outright that the Wuhan manifesto had no connection with the N.C.C. and had been drawn up by local Christians without missionary backing as a desperate move to save their church in the face of persecution.[31] In early March, the *North China* attacked another N.C.C. manifesto for its supposedly Bolshevist tendencies, implying that it had been drawn up by Westerners to put radical statements in Chinese mouths. Two weeks later, a scathing letter from Rodney Gilbert railed at the Council as a "Bolshevik Aid Society."

The National Christian Council is on the point of sending delegations to the United States and Great Britain, four or five shameless misrepresenters of fact to each country. They will cover an enormous amount of ground, will fill an endless number of business men, parsons, legislators, labour leaders and soulful uplift folk full of the most poisonous nonsense about China, and there will be no counter propaganda of any sort. . . . Our Chamberlains and our Kelloggs are human politicians, therefore amenable to the discipline of constituencies, therefore weak in the face of a noisy assault and indifferent to the appeal of reason. . . . They tune in to the grand noise and evolve a policy that harmonises with it."[32]

"Long Live the Nationalist Government!" cried the title of a pamphlet put out by the National Christian Literature Association on Museum Road shortly after the city fell to the revolutionaries. It contained several articles by Chinese Christians, as well as Frank Rawlinson's "Towards the New Shanghai," which urged negotiations to change the city's status. "Red Propaganda in Shanghai," bellowed the *North China*, arguing that inflammatory statements like these defied the Municipal Council's prohibitions against seditious literature. Walter Scott Elliott, head of the Christian Fundamentals Mission, publicly accused Rawlinson of rebellion against the Settlement authorities, and for good measure sent a copy of his letter to Fessenden and his colleagues (presumably, in case they were too busy to read the paper).[33] He then called an open meeting in April at the Royal Asiatic Society on Museum Road to denounce the N.C.C. It came to grief, however. This failure was partly because the N.C.C.'s supporters turned out to heckle the speakers; and partly because the Reverend Edgar Strother, an American of pronounced right-wing views, got things off to a bad start when he called the meeting to order by reading all 176 verses of Psalm 119 ("hardly the Psalm many of us might choose for opening the proceedings for a pleasant afternoon," wrote an otherwise sympathetic onlooker). He followed this long appeal for the support of the righteous against the wicked with an only slightly shorter prayer setting forth to the Almighty his own views of the N.C.C.[34]

Good Christians, of course, do not (or should not) allow the press and public opinion to determine their views on religious questions, and most missionaries were undoubtedly firm enough in their faith not to be unduly influenced by newspapers like the *North China* or the odd proceedings on Museum Road. Elliott, Strother, and their ilk aside, the events at Nanking brought an open break between the National Christian Council and some of the most distinguished Protestant leaders of the Yangtze Valley. Upset at the N.C.C.'s plan to send delegations to explain the new China to churches and mission boards in Britain and America, they saw men like Lobenstine and his colleagues simply as "stalking horses" behind which the N.C.C., now completely dominated by young Chinese radicals, could carry on its Guomindang propaganda. An informal meeting, which included Bishop Graves, Hawks Pott, and several others, drew up a statement of protest and presented it privately to the N.C.C. When that body failed to respond, the group, which by now included people like the Methodist Bishop Birney, President A. J. Bowen of the University of Nanking, J. G. Endicott of the United Church of Canada, and seven others, sent a confidential cable to their boards through A. L. Warnshuis of the International Missionary Council in New York. "Nanking tragedy revealed Communist influence dominant government," it read. "Persecution Nanking friends following effort save foreigners. . . . Barrage undoubtedly saved Nanking foreigners much more serious disaster. Safety all foreigners throughout China imperiled while Communists control Nationalist Government. . . . Failure promptly to overthrow rapidly increasing power Communists makes inevitable situation gravest danger. Cooperation America England essential in defense of their nationals and in constructive measures."

"Communicate this to our respective boards," the message finished, and the cable went off, apparently paid for by Lobenstine himself. With more time, wrote Bishop Graves, any number of signatures could have been collected, and just in case the Missionary Council should file and forget it (which, in fact, is precisely what happened), he sent a copy to his own Mission House in New York. A few days later, larger group of missionaries, including Graves, Bishop Molony of Ningbo, Hawks Pott, and A. J. Bowen, met to draw up a more formal account of their grievances against the National Christian Council.[35]

This time they published their statement, which appeared in the press on 12 April. It protested the political stands taken by the Council and objected to the N.C.C.'s efforts to dictate the policy of various churches and mission bodies in the country and its habit of making statements without regard to the wishes of its cooperating bodies. The N.C.C., the writers contended, had lost the confidence of a large part of the missionary body and no longer represented their views and opinions; "We regard its recent policy and methods as dangerous to and subversive of the best interests of the churches in China." The thirty-two signatures included sixteen American and sixteen British missionaries. All were in the mainstream of the Protestant enterprise in China, and presumably they did not try to solicit the support of fundamentalists like Strother and Elliott, whose quarrels with the N.C.C. were as much theological as political.[36]

The *North China* applauded the signers, certain that their stand would give the *coup de grace* to the N.C.C. The American Rodney Gilbert was ecstatic, and in a typically venomous letter to the editor (it covered a full page) excoriated the disloyalty of liberal churchmen to the people who supported them through the Sunday collection plate. "There are close corporations of highly intellectual, horn-rimmed spectacled gentry in Peking, Shanghai, and Canton, who do not mind taking these pennies to finance an excursion to America and Europe for Horatius Peng-Pang or Q.Z. Choo, who goes to lecture on 'nationalism' under heavy subsidy from Soviet Russia and who will hypnotize Chinese communities abroad with his Eurasian eloquence and lift handsome contributions out of them towards the substantial house that he is building in a concession or settlement."[37]

The whole episode was a sad one, not least because it provided an excuse for the obnoxious outbursts of people like Gilbert (one of his solutions to countering missionary propaganda was for Shanghai's Harvard graduates—he had once studied there himself—to draw up a statement that would go to Harvard clubs throughout America). It did not bring about any more defections from the N.C.C., much less its end (the next edition of the *China Christian Yearbook* made only a discreet mention of "some criticism of the Council").[38] But it did mean friction and recriminations between the missionaries and their home boards. J. T. Proctor, one of the Baptist signatories, found himself in trouble with his church's Foreign Mission Society, which thought the statement a call for armed intervention.[39] The embarrassed International Missionary Council never responded. The first cable to Warnshuis had been confidential because its authors were afraid of endangering Chinese who had helped the foreigners escape at Nanking. Nonetheless, when the N.C.C.'s T. Z. Koo [Gu Ziren] saw it (he was in New York at the time), he was said to be infuriated, promising that the signatories would now be finished for work in China. A copy reportedly found its way to the Chinese minister in Washington, and again the signatories protested to Warnshuis this apparent breach of faith.[40]

"You will find out more and more that the Nationalist propaganda in the United States is a very extensive and ably managed business," wrote

Bishop Graves three weeks later, "and that the N.C.C. and the Y.M.C.A. are its helpers. . . . Mr. Lobenstine knows perfectly well what has happened and is happening in China, but his N.C.C. official post does not allow him to state this publicly. He and the other officials in the N.C.C. are entirely dominated by a group of radical young Chinese in their organization." [41]

But the men who, like Graves, signed the public statement were neither trying to kill off the National Christian Council nor calling for armed intervention. The open breach in the Protestant missionary movement nonetheless worried Powell. "Have the missionaries been converted?" asked the *China Weekly Review*, as its editor looked anxiously at the floods of people, many of them missionary refugees from the interior, who were taking ship from Shanghai to return to the States. Would they be more belligerent than earlier, more willing to see their country engaged in the kind of joint intervention that America had so far avoided? He knew how influential they could be. "It may not be generally realized, but as a general rule, what American thinks about China is what the missionaries tell them about it. . . . If we read the missionary sentiment aright, we believe that the missionaries have come to the point where they feel that they have turned the other cheek just once too often." [42] Back in New York, missionary leaders shared the fear and undertook their own version of news management: A. L. Warnshuis wanted to inspire articles in the press to counteract the more sensational stories coming from Shanghai and tried to warn returning missionaries that they must give only "constructive" statements to any journalists who might interview them. [43]

Certainly the signs of change were there, and the revolt against the N.C.C. showed it. The National Council of the Episcopal Church complained to Kellogg that Americans should not have to look to England for protection and asked that the United States take "suitable action" to discharge its responsibilities (it had just learned that Duncan's men were guarding St. John's). A "Veteran American Missionary" in Shanghai, claiming that many of his colleagues were afraid to speak their minds, wanted a mass meeting of the American community to demand stronger action from Washington. A hundred and twenty-seven Nanking missionaries published a statement reminding their readers that, in February, they had protested the use of force and urged conciliation and negotiation. "In but a little more than a month after that, we had to depend on the use of foreign force to save our lives. We have favored the return of the concessions to China, but today a foreign settlement is our only place of refuge." [44]

To some extent, one's beliefs about Nanking became a test of one's attitude toward the revolution. Not surprisingly, leftists were the most willing to swallow Eugene Chen's story that the culprits were the northern troops.

Lewis Gannett told the readers of the *Nation* that Dr. Williams had been shot only after he first drew a revolver.[45] His story, as Gauss discovered in a neat bit of detective work, came originally from G. A. Kennedy, a young schoolteacher at the Shanghai American School who had worked briefly for the Guomindang's *China Courier*. In Nanking, Kennedy had talked to a Chinese, who, while not an eyewitness, nonetheless maintained that Williams had drawn a gun. Kennedy included the statement as hearsay evidence in a piece he wrote for William Prohme, an American journalist working for the Hankou government; Prohme, before he passed the account on to the *Nation*, colored it further by saying that Williams had gestured as though he had a gun. By the time Gannett further improved the report in New York, he had the unfortunate Dr. Williams actually brandishing a revolver at the time he was shot. (A week later, in the face of evidence from William's fellow missionaries, the *Nation* grumpily admitted that there might be other versions of the story, although it never climbed down from its version.)[46]

If Christian missionaries were disillusioned by the events at Nanking, there were others who in 1927 briefly discovered in Hankou the revolution's new Jerusalem. Some were journalists—liberal, leftist, and otherwise—men like Arthur Ransome, Vincent Sheean, or Paul Blanshard who became instant China experts on the strength of a few weeks' or a few months' stay and, above all, on the strength of their access to the charismatic Michael Borodin. Others were missionaries of a secular sort—the three wise men of the Third International, Tom Mann, Earl Browder, and Jacques Doriot—who came that spring to offer their gifts and gaze on the new epiphany in the city on the Yangtze (while King Herod, in the form of Chiang Kai-shek, was sharpening his swords downstream). Many such travellers, of course, passed through Shanghai; it was the easiest way to reach Hankou, and a few days in the fleshpots of the foreign concessions ringed with barbed wire provided good copy and a good contrast to the earnest struggle for high principles that was taking place six hundred miles upriver.

William Prohme, the man who doctored poor G. A. Kennedy's story so that Lewis Gannett could doctor it still further, was one of the most interesting of those who combined journalistic skills with missionary fervor. An American leftist, his reputation (and that of his even more radical wife, Rayna) was already well enough established that, when he first planned to come to China, King George V himself fretted over finding a way to stop him (the Foreign Office quickly advised the monarch that it would never do to ask America to block Prohme!).[47] In the spring of 1927, while Rayna stayed in Hankou editing the Guomindang's English-language *People's Tribune* (and submitting her editorials to Borodin's censorship), William moved between that city and Shanghai, combining his work for the *Tribune* with occasional stories for the *Nation*.[48] The consulate-general put a tail on him when he came to Shanghai in late March, as Prohme soon realized; though when he told Gauss to call off his dogs, the latter blandly denied that he knew anything about it.[49]

Among those Prohme brought to Hankou was the radical American journalist Milly Bennett, and it is she who has left us the most irreverent portrait of the foreigners in Hankou when that city was briefly the headquarters of the Chinese revolution. Coming to China from Honolulu fresh from the breakup of her marriage, she had worked for the Nationalist Zhongmei News Agency in Peking. Arrested there by Zhang Zuolin's police on 5 April, she had been released, had made her way to Shanghai to meet William Prohme, and, with the help of the German journalist Erich von Salzman, had reached Hankou. There she found an earnest competition between Rayna Prohme and Anna Louise Strong for the position of foremost woman revolutionary on the scene. "It makes me sick," Borodin told her, "it makes me sick to leave the Chinese Revolution in the hands of a ladies' pink tea party."[50] She watched with wry amusement the unthinking wonder, almost worship, of the foreign journalists who were "bowled over by Mrs. Sun Yat-sen, Chen and Rayna. Vincent (Jimmy) Sheean came away from his interview with Mrs. Sun Yat-sen, pronouncing her 'the most beautiful woman in the world,' and as for Rayna, he is practically tongue-tied and a bashful and callow youth in her presence. . . . William Henry Chamberlain, Paul Blanshard, Henry Mizzelwitz [sic], . . . one and all, the newspapermen come to Hankow to observe the unorthodox doings and they go away in a dither of hero worship."[51]

At the center of their admiration was, of course, Borodin. "A huge, striking figure, with dark, flashing eyes, set in a face of real distinction, a man with a genius for conversation, a man with a lifetime of Revolutionary experience behind him, which he has a talent for interpreting in a highly romantic way. At his worst, and that was when he was demanding that forty-four things be done at once, Borodin made me think of Major Hoople in the comics. At his best, Borodin, could take a commonplace incident and transform it into something memorable."[52] Bennett refused to fall for the image. "A man of charm, wit, imagination, good looks, and enormous personal magnetism. Nothing more. He is scatter brained, his complete lack of horse sense and discretion is borne out by his posturing on the stage of the China Revolution." She worried, moreover, that by stealing the limelight and posing as "the greatest revolutionist in the world," he upset not only Chiang Kai-shek but also the leaders of the Hankou government. "It galled them. They did not want an outsider taking the credit for being the brains of a revolution which they rightly considered their own." She was right; but neither Borodin nor his foreign entourage agreed.[53]

One of the best of the contemporary accounts of the period came from the pen of Arthur Ransome, the future author of that classic of children's literature, *Swallows and Amazons* (years later, he recalled that he had drawn on Song Qingling for his picture of Missee Lee, the Cambridge girl graduate who insists on daily Latin lessons in her South China pirate hideout). He came through the Yangtze Valley that winter, writing a series of articles for the *Manchester Guardian* that would appear later that year as *The China Puzzle*. J. B. Powell was delighted at last to find an Englishman who agreed with him, but the rest of foreign Shanghai gave Ransome the cold shoulder (had he not already written a book mildly favorable to the Russian revolution?). He repaid the city with his famous piece on "The Shanghai Mind," which made certain that foreign Shanghai would forever be known for a particularly unpleasant and inefficient combination of bigotry and narrowness of vision. Appearing in the *Guardian* on 2 May, it blasted British Shanghai, blasted their unthinking loyalty to Shanghai even when it ran counter to the interests of their own country, and blasted them for their treatment of the Chinese.

They look round on their magnificent buildings and are surprised that China is not grateful to them for these gifts, forgetting that the money to build them came out of China. Controlling the bottle-neck through which the bulk of the China trade must pass, they prosper upon it coming and going and forget that it is the trade that is valuable to England and not the magnificent buildings which profits and small taxes allowed them to erect. English prestige is at stake when their interests are threatened, but unless English policy coincides with their own they are prepared at any moment to be the Ulster of the East. . . .

No Chinese, reading the Shanghai newspapers, could have any other impression than that the important part of British policy was the sending of the troops and that England was fundamentally and irrevocably hostile to the only movement in China which had as its object the freeing of the country from the wholly unscrupulous warlords who secure Shanghai's approval by suppressing labour and the resentment of the whole country by the wholesale armed robbery which is making its normal development impossible.

When the Shanghai British discovered that the Shanghai Defence Force had not come to make war on China, when they discovered that Nanking would not change British policy, they were appalled. "Shanghai will not be satisfied until Sir Austen Chamberlain's winter policy is scrapped, and with high water on the Yangtze, a summer policy takes its place with a naval demonstration up the river, the 'occupation of strategic points,' an open attack on the Nationalists, and attempt to plant the warlords once more on the lid of the boiling Chinese cauldron." And, though he did not say so publicly, Ransome was convinced that Sidney Barton was one of the chief protagonists of a "summer policy" in the British community and was himself working to frustrate Whitehall's efforts to devise a moderate China policy.[54]

The *North China Daily News* had so far managed to ignore the tide of liberal reporters coming through the city, but it could not let this particular piece pass. Articles like Ransome's were damaging because they encouraged wishful thinking about the Nationalists and led to dangerous mistakes, like the arrangement for Chinese control of the British concession at Hankou. "Mr. Bertrand Russell [another of the *North China's bêtes rouges*] would not have made a more hopeless agreement with a non-existent regime that [sic] Mr. O'Malley did."[55] Shanghai would not stand by and see its future negotiated away. But in London, the reaction to Ransome's piece was different. "This article does not overstate the case," wrote Pratt when he read it. "I endorse every word of it."[56]

Squeezed Like a Lemon
Communists, Gangsters, and the Purge of 12 April 1927

The suddenness, the speed, and the scope of the Communist-led insurgency in March had caught Chiang Kai-shek and the Nationalists badly off base, frustrating their plans for a peaceful occupation of Shanghai. While Bai Chongxi had held his troops in check at the Longhua arsenal, the insurrectionists had seized control, and they now policed the Chinese city, armed with the weapons commandeered from the enemy. Sapajou, the *North China's* witty Russian cartoonist, caught the theme: While a Nationalist soldier holds the reins of a toy horse labeled "Lunghua," the Communists escape with the real horse named "Shanghai." Thus, as foreigners sought to come to terms with the Nationalist occupation, the Guomindang and the Communists were beginning a deadly contest for mastery over the city. Much of the struggle took place in the shadows, but though both sides proclaimed their allegiance to the principles of the united front, the rivalry grew more open every day.

"What appears to be certain," wrote the correspondent of the London *Times* a day after the city's fall, "is that the capture of Shanghai by the South has resolved itself into a struggle between the Communists and the moderate Kuomintang for control."[1] Only those blinded by ideology ignored the signs and believed in the sincerity of both sides as they protested their loyalty to the united front. Perhaps because it took on faith what William Prohme was reporting, the *Nation*, for instance, assured its American readers that stories of a breach simply reflected the wishful thinking of Shanghai's diehards. Between Chiang Kai-shek's moderates and Borodin's so-called extremists, there was no opposition, it wrote. "Chiang himself is deeply imbued with Sun Yat-sen's democratic principles, and has always been ready to establish civil rule in the wake of his victories."[2] This kind of deception and self-deception, as Harold Isaacs' classic account argues, echoed the views of the Comintern, which thought it could manage the Chinese revolution from Moscow, six thousand miles distant. As Stalin himself told a meeting on 5 April, "Chiang Kai-shek is submitting to discipline." He and his Guomindang were still useful to the revolution—"they have to be utilized to the end, squeezed out like a lemon, and then flung away."[3] At the other political extreme, a letter in the *North China Daily News* warned that the rumors of rifts in the alliance were simply tricks to make Chiang look like a moderate while his "revolutionary rabble" prepared to seize the Shanghai settlements.[4]

Yet, ever since Chiang had disciplined the Canton Communists over a year earlier, it had been no secret that his relations with the left were tense, no secret that, as the Northern Expedition scattered its enemies before it, the political basis of the alliance between the Guomindang and the Communists had become increasingly rocky. Many foreigners were quite astute enough to realize that Chiang's move on Shanghai had something less than the enthusiastic backing of Wuhan. In mid-March, the Communist and leftist Guomindang members of the Wuhan administration met under Borodin's guidance to reorganize the government, reducing Chiang's influence while elevating that of his chief rival, Wang Jingwei, who was then making his way home from Europe. Meanwhile from Nanchang, Chiang himself issued a statement on 17 March protesting his loyalty to the united front but promising nonetheless to check the influence of the Communists should their "oppression" of the revolution grow too powerful.[5]

Though the general blandly assured foreign reporters in Shanghai on 27 March that he was just a simple soldier who took his orders from the civilians, it took no inside knowledge to realize that he was dissembling. Oddly enough, the *China Weekly Review*, usually the most intelligent and independent of the Shanghai journals, was largely silent about the discord within the Guomindang; perhaps in a time of political uncertainty its editor worried about alienating the Chinese readers and Chinese advertisers who now made up an increasingly important part of the magazine's subscribers. The *North China Daily News* showed no such reticence. Anxious to find signs of weakness in the Cantonese camp, as soon as the city fell it printed stories of clashes between Nationalist troops and the General Labor Union's armed pickets. George Sokolsky, in a detailed analysis of the split on 25 March, warned that the test of strength between Nationalists and Communists would come in Shanghai, as leftists tried to provoke incidents with foreign troops and Chiang's armies sought to neutralize the pickets.[6] Three days later, an editorial openly called on the military leaders to take action, since they stood alone against the Communist tide. "But if General Chiang is to save his fellow-men from the Reds, he must act swiftly and relentlessly. Will he prove himself the man of action and decision, the champion of the true principles of Sun Yat-sen, the defender of his country? or will he too go down with China in the Red flood?"[7]

Sokolsky was at least partly right; a recent Chinese account confirms that the Communists, hoping to undercut Chiang's power and reduce the chances of an attack on the left, decided to step up the anti-British movement. If Chiang opposed the move, he would lose much of his popularity.[8] In general, the insights of Western diplomats in China into the divisions within the Guomindang were no more profound than those appearing in the press. Men like Gauss, Barton, and Naggiar knew that Chiang wanted to strike down the Communists but doubted his ability to do so. Even as Guo Taiqi, Chiang's new commissioner of foreign affairs, was assuring Barton that the general was preparing to move, Barton himself feared that Chiang's position was weakening as the left consolidated its control in the Chinese city.[9] Gauss, too, doubted Chiang's resolve and reported that the general seemed unwilling to take a stand.[10]

In any case, there was little to suggest that foreign interests would be better off under a triumphant Chiang than a triumphant Wuhan. True, in recent months the general had insisted that he would allow no attacks on the settlements and that change must come by negotiation rather than through force; but Eugene Chen had said the same thing—and look what had happened at Hankou and Jiujiang! However moderate Chiang might appear in the Chinese political spectrum, wrote Pratt, his tirades against imperialism showed that he was still "bitterly anti-British."[11] It had been Chiang's armies, after all, that had killed six foreigners at Nanking and had driven the rest from the city. In an unconvincing echo of Eugene Chen, Chiang originally had blamed the northern troops, and though on 31 March he promised to take full responsibility for what had happened at Nanking and to punish the guilty, he did nothing. "A more extraordinary farrago of assertion diametrically opposed to fact . . . it would be impossible to conceive," wrote the *North China Daily News* of the general's public stand, and for once Pratt and his colleagues in London agreed with the voice of the Shanghai diehards.[12]

In the days that followed Nanking, British, French, and Americans in China pushed hard for reprisals, and foreign military officers in Shanghai studied proposals to attack the Wusong forts and the Shanghai and Wuchang arsenals or to block Nationalist troop movements on the river.[13] But they came up against strong resistance from both Washington and Tokyo. The State Department wanted no military action and would do nothing more than join a protest to Wuhan while readying fifteen hundred more American marines for service in China. Nor were the Japanese any more anxious to move. When U.S.S. *Noa* and H.M.S. *Emerald* laid down their barrage at Nanking on the afternoon of 24 March, a nearby Japanese man-of-war had remained silent. Tokyo's reluctance to act came in part from Foreign Minister Shidehara Kiijuro's argument that Chiang Kai-shek, for all his failings, was a man who could be trusted to deal with the extremists. If the Nanking incident had indeed been a plot engineered by the left to embroil Chiang with the powers, it would be folly to fall into the trap, weakening the general and allowing the radicals to profit.[14] Such forbearance carried a price, however; in Shanghai, Consul-General Yada Shichitaro reminded Chiang's emissary that the general must keep order in the city and not allow the revolutionary movement to degenerate into dangerous antiforeignism.[15]

All this came at a time when the British minister in Peking was calling not only for the execution of Cheng Qian and his divisional commanders but also for the public shooting of one out of every ten junior officers and men responsible! Even Pratt wanted the guilty shot and for Chiang to make a public apology and salute the British flag on parade. He understood as well as anyone the splits in the Nationalist camp, but after Nanking he was willing to risk driving Chiang into the hands of the extremists, ready for Britain to act alone even if Japan and America backed out.[16] In the end, thanks to American and Japanese opposition, the Nanking incident brought not even a threat of sanctions, and the British were left infuriated but powerless. "They have no backbone of any sort," wrote Lampson scornfully of the Americans, "and are altogether a feckless people."[17] So too, the French consulate-general was angered by the refusal of Msgr. Prosper Paris and his Vatican superiors to demand indemnities for the deaths of the two Catholic missionaries at Nanking.[18]

Just as Nanking colored the views of foreign diplomats toward Chiang Kai-shek, so it made Chiang more determined than ever to secure his hold over Shanghai and his control over the revolutionary armies. Time was against him, for by now the Communists were showing an alarming growth. Playing on their leadership during the March insurrection, the Communists—who had numbered about forty-five hundred at the time— had increased their membership to eighty-four hundred by early April, and hoped to recruit fifty thousand members by June.[19]

Between Chiang and the left there were three immediate issues. The first was that of the *jiuchadui*, the armed pickets, numbering three to four thousand or more. More determined than ever with their newly acquired weapons, they remained entrenched in a variety of strongholds, particularly in Zhabei, at their headquarters in the Commercial Press Workers' Club, and in the Huzhou Guild that housed the General Labor Union.[20] Chen Duxiu wanted to recruit and train more of them, building a force of some twelve thousand men over the next six months.[21] From the start, however, there was friction with the Nationalist forces. Ten or eleven leftists died in a clash at the Fourth District Police Station in Zhabei on 23 March, and there was an outbreak at the Arsenal the same day. On the twenty-fifth, some three hundred guerrillas at the Temple of the God of War near the West Gate skirmished with the army, and by the end of the month, Bai Chongxi told Powell that his forces had disarmed three thousand plainclothes revolutionists, arresting twenty self-styled "generals" who had organized their own armies under the banner of revolution.[22] Wuhan, though, recognized the pickets as legitimate guardians of the revolutionary order. On 28 March, Chiang promised an envoy from the General Labor Union that the workers would be allowed to keep their arms, and two days later he praised their role to a Japanese reporter.[23]

The second question was how to rule revolutionary Shanghai. Even before the city's fall, the leftists had prepared a provisional government to take power when the Nationalists entered. Established openly on 22 March, it found itself unable to assume control, in part because of the refusal of men like Niu Yongjian, Yu Xiaqing, and Bai Chongxi to assume their places. When it did finally hold its inaugural gathering at the Xinwutai Theater in the Chinese city on 29 March, only thirteen of its members showed up—all either Communists or their supporters. By then, Chiang had ordered it not to take power until the outstanding military problems had been solved—in other words, until he was firmly in control.[24] Though Wuhan had recognized the new organ, Shanghai's political picture remained unsettled.

The third question was about the loyalty of the Nationalist troops. Many of the army's political officers were Communists, men who could use their connections with the officers trained at the Whampoa Military Academy to spread their influence. The news that Wuhan was sending the Communist Guo Moro to Shanghai to oversee the army's political work must have seemed a direct threat to Chiang (though the Shanghai Communists had some questions about his loyalty to the Party).[25] General Duncan's intelligence estimated that, at the end of March, three-quarters of the twelve thousand troops in the city were loyal to Chiang. But when General Li Zongren—like Bai, another brilliant Guangxi general who had joined the Nationalists—arrived in Shanghai on 28 March, he was appalled to find the mass movement almost entirely under Communist control and the army's loyalty uncertain. Chiang was very worried—"I shall resign, I shall resign," he repeated over and over to Li in a hoarse voice, adding that General He Yingqin of the First Army had already threatened to step down because he could no longer control his Communist-dominated troops.[26]

Neither Bai Chongxi nor Li Zongren, allies of long standing from their days in Guangxi, entirely trusted Chiang, but they preferred him to the dangers of Wuhan communism. They therefore took the initiative in a purge of the army as the first step in reducing leftist strength in Shanghai. The plan called for a series of troop transfers to break up Communist concentrations of power and to allow loyal units to oversee the removal of the untrustworthy. After an explosive confrontation between Chiang and his political officers on 5 April, the general ordered Bai to crack down. The purge went smoothly. Many of the agitators were simply cowards and opportunists, Li wrote later, and the army at Shanghai gradually came under the firm control of Bai and his commander-in-chief.[27]

Meanwhile, some of the Guomindang's elder statesmen in Shanghai were pressing Chiang to act quickly. Though not themselves members of the Western Hills Group, they had made their peace with the right wing, worried as they were by the increasing strength of Borodin and the Wuhan leftists. Wu Zhihui had been stunned when on 6 March at a meeting in the French Concession, the Communist leader Chen Duxiu had predicted a Leninist China within twenty years (not a bad prophecy, as it turned out). When Cai Yuanpei presided over a meeting of the Guomindang's Central Supervisory Committee on 28 March, it was Wu who proposed the launching of a new movement to "protect the Party and save the country" [*hudang jiuguo*],[28] thus legitimizing the repression that Chiang was preparing. On 2 April, at a full meeting of the committee, Wu presented a petition [*chengwen*] impeaching the Communists and denouncing Borodin, whose increasing power threatened to turn China into a mere Soviet colony.[29] That afternoon, Huang Fu, who had also been present, told the Japanese consul-general that Chiang would be prepared to move in four or five days.[30]

On 1 April, Wang Jingwei arrived in Shanghai on his way home to China from Berlin and Moscow. Though Wang was associated with the left wing of the Guomindang and was very much a rival of Chiang Kai-shek, he seemed a godsend to Li and Bai. An old revolutionary who had joined Sun Yat-sen's cause well before the 1911 revolution, he had at least as much right as any other to claim the mantle of leadership after Sun's death in 1925. He had left China for Europe in May 1926, in the wake of Chiang's purge of the leftists in Canton, but his prestige remained high. To many, he seemed a civilian leader with the stature needed to reconcile the Guomindang's divisions and control the Communists so that they could help but not harm the Guomindang and the Northern Expedition. Wang's arrival shattered their hopes. He refused to take seriously their apprehensions about Communist behavior, and though he promised not to act as a Communist pawn, he would not join the generals. "I am with the peasants and the workers," he said. "Whoever wants to oppress them will be my enemy!" To Chen Duxiu's prediction of a China turned Red within twenty years, his response was even more disconcerting. "Why twenty years?" he asked, convinced that the Soviet Union had its own plans for China. "Two years will be enough."[31]

Desperately anxious to keep Wang on his side, Chiang told his military commanders to obey Wang's orders, but his private talks with the returned leader were disappointing. If Chiang fought Wuhan and lost, said Wang, then the Guomindang's day would be done and the Communists triumphant; but if the Communists were defeated, the Guomindang would be back where it had been in 1923, Chiang would have no allies, and his political career would be over.[32] Meanwhile, the Communists also wanted to profit from Wang's presence, and perhaps the experience of being courted by both sides went to his head. In any case, all hope of a genuine rapprochement between the two rivals disappeared on 5 April. That morning, the Shanghai papers carried a joint statement by Wang and Chen Duxiu, pledging the continued cooperation of their two parties and promising that the Guomindang would never turn its back on the sainted Sun Yat-sen's policy of cooperation with the Soviet Union. Wu Zhihui was appalled; by what right did Wang presume to speak in the name of the Guomindang? Yes, Sun wanted alignment with Moscow; but surely that did not mean inviting the Soviet Union in as a joint ruler of the country. Wang's defensive protests were unconvincing, and that evening he left Shanghai in secret for Wuhan.[33]

Communist histories would later denounce the Wang–Chen statement as a shameful episode that effectively paralyzed the revolutionary will of the people; but that was hardly the way it appeared at the time.[34] The declaration, and Wang's furtive departure upriver, made it look as if the Communists had won the struggle for his loyalties and no doubt brought the purge closer. Already on 2 April, Wuhan had ordered Chiang to go to Nanking and stick to his military work, leaving politics and diplomacy to others. The same day, the Wuhan Guomindang expelled Guo Taiqi from the party because he had become Chiang's foreign affairs commissioner rather than the leftist they had appointed.[35]

Meanwhile, skirmishes between right and left were beginning to break out in other cities under Nationalist control. At the end of March, a bloody fight erupted in Hangzhou between soldiers and non-Communist workers on the one hand and the city's General Labor Union and student association on the other. A similar outbreak saw the leftist organizations crushed in Chongqing. In Nanchang, however, a Communist coup succeeded on 2 April, when armed pickets organized by Zhu De, the future marshal of the People's Liberation Army, seized the government headquarters and arrested and killed several Guomindang officials. The stroke brought the city, which had been Chiang's stronghold, firmly into the camp loyal to Wuhan.[36]

Simultaneously, Borodin's control of the explosive situation in Hankou was seriously threatened when on 3 April Japanese forces guarding their concession opened fire on a crowd of demonstrators, killing nine people and wounding eight others. The Japanese marines thus did precisely what the British had not done in January, precisely what Inspector Everson's police had done on Nanking Road in May 1925. But this time, Wuhan turned the other cheek. Revolutionary spontaneity must not be allowed to threaten revolutionary strategy, and Borodin could not afford a new May Thirtieth Movement against the Japanese. His policy of keeping Japan isolated from the West had apparently been vindicated when Japanese guns remained silent during the Anglo-American bombardment of Nanking. Desperate to stay on the right side of Tokyo, he counseled patience even when Chinese were gunned down by Japanese rifles, even when local Communists like Liu Shaoqi were crying for vengeance. Soviet Consul-General Linde in Shanghai was said to be furious at Borodin for allowing the mob to get out of hand and threaten the Comintern's policy. By a supreme effort, though, Borodin stayed in control, and the incident was smoothed over.[37]

A third strain in the revolutionary camp came from the action of Zhang Zuolin's soldiers in Peking. On 6 April, the Diplomatic Body allowed them permission to enter the Soviet embassy compound in the Legation Quarter on the flimsy grounds that some of the buildings were being used to plan an uprising in the capital. Though they had no warrant, the troops invaded the embassy itself. There they not only arrested fifty-eight Chinese, including Li Dazhao—one of the chief leaders and theorists of Chinese communism—but also seized a huge mass of material that over the next few months would be translated and released to the world. That the raid was illegal because the troops had entered the embassy building seemed beside the point; the point was that there was now a mass of documentation proving (for those who still doubted it) that the Soviet Union was thoroughly embroiled in the Chinese revolutionary movement.[38]

The episode echoed elsewhere. French police in Tianjin raided Soviet commercial concerns in their concession the next day. Simultaneously in Shanghai, the Shanghai Municipal Police mounted a guard (made up largely of White Russians) outside the Soviet consulate-general on Whang-poo Road, searching all who went in and out of the building (one of those stopped was an angry Guo Taiqi, Chiang's commissioner for foreign affairs). While his worried staff burned or hid their papers, Consul-General Linde of the Soviet Union protested, charging the consular body with complicity. Fessenden responded weakly that the building had been put under guard for its own protection in the face of growing evidence of ill feeling (from whom it was not clear) against the consulate. His explanation could have convinced only the most credulous and, in any case, would hardly explain the searches. Whether the move was linked to the Peking raid or not, its purpose was presumably to disrupt Soviet undercover work in the city. Yet Gauss, Naggiar, and Yada were strongly critical of the Council's behavior, and even Barton admitted that the police had no real evidence of any mischief going on inside the consulate's walls (if true, it suggests either that the Sûreté was not sharing its information or that the Settlement police chose not to believe it).[39]

Finally, Chiang Kai-shek and Wuhan were in a race for control of Nanking. After the city fell on 24 March, the leftists set up both a municipal government and a Jiangsu provincial government, again naming a few Guomindang officials as window dressing.[40] An emergency meeting held secretly at Borodin's house on 7 April decided to move the capital downriver to Nanking to consolidate the control of the left. Chiang Kai-shek, however, got there first, arriving on 9 April. An anti-Communist brawl broke out as his men shut down the local Party and labor union offices, arresting several radical leaders. Within a few days, Chiang's faction was firmly in control of Nanking, and within a week the city would become his capital rather than Borodin's.[41]

Meanwhile in Shanghai, even as Bai Chongxi and Li Zongren were purging their armies of leftists, soldiers and policemen were beginning to move against the Communist strongholds and their unions. Attacks on armed guerrillas in early April left several dozen dead, and some leftist leaders were arrested and sent off to Longhua military headquarters. Bai Chongxi proclaimed a state of martial law in the Chinese city on 5 April, and the next day he shut down the branch of the Political Committee established by Wuhan. Simultaneously, the General Labor Union was busily fortifying the Commercial Press building, storing in it a month's supply of food and arms. They also tried, unsuccessfully, to get warnings printed in the press about the possibility of a reactionary move against the pickets.[42] But there was nothing they could do when, on 7 April, Chiang inaugurated an anti-Communist Federated Association of Shanghai Laborers to counter the General Labor Union, or when, on the eighth, just before leaving for Nanking, he formed a new Shanghai Provisional Governmental Committee under the chairmanship of Wu Zhihui, setting aside the impotent leftist body organized a fortnight earlier.[43]

Such events took place in the open and were reported by the press. Less clear is the precise nature of Chiang's relations with Chinese business and banking circles, who had been in touch with the general long before he arrived in the city and who arranged a loan of $30 million in late March, perhaps conditional on his taking a stand against the left.[44] Finally, deep in the gloom that masked the secret assignations between Chiang's men and the leaders of Shanghai's underworld, still other preparations were being made.[45] Much in the story—particularly about the role played by foreigners—remains unclear, and there is no way to avoid the kind of gossip and speculation that was making the rounds of Shanghai in those days and that has formed part of the myth of April 1927 ever since. There is little doubt, however, that Chiang, prior to his apotheosis as revolutionary military leader in Canton, had formed ties with the Shanghai underworld (the existence of the Shanghai Municipal Police's arrest warrants give some evidence of that) and that these ties were useful when he returned to the city in March 1927.

In particular, Chiang was in touch with the Green Gang leader Du Yuesheng at his base on the rue Wagner in the French Concession. His power and influence substantially increased by the protection the French police afforded his operations since 1925, Du had by now become the most important gangster leader in Shanghai, eclipsing his former patron Huang Jinrong.[46] Heavily engaged in labor recruiting and labor racketeering, the Green Gang had been at times the rival, at times the uneasy ally, of the Communists in the nervous months leading up to Shanghai's capture. By early 1927, presumably convinced that they could no longer work with the Communists, Du and his colleagues apparently tried to sabotage the February uprising.[47] Then, in late March, probably at Chiang Kai-shek's behest, Du turned his many talents to the formation of a group blandly called the China Society for Common Progress [*Zhonghua gongjinhui*]— the name recalling an earlier group active among Shanghai's revolutionaries before 1911. With its headquarters on the rue Brodie Clarke in the French Concession, the organization was no more than a front to recruit Green Gang members into a strong-arm band to do Chiang's work for him. It was members of this group who took part in the various skirmishes with the left in early April.[48] Meanwhile, as worries mounted about the security of their Concession, the French also turned to Du for help in keeping order. On 26 February, Consul-General Naggiar wired Paris asking for ammunition and three hundred rifles to be used by "certain local elements."[49] Three days later, the amount was increased to six hundred rifles, more ammunition, and one thousand steel helmets.[50] In the meantime, Captain Étienne Fiori, the Corsican chief of the *Garde municipale*, arranged a meeting between Du Yuesheng and Stirling Fessenden. At that meeting, Du reportedly asked the French for five thousand rifles and ammunition, and asked Fessenden for permission to move his men through the Settlement to the leftist strongholds in Zhabei.[51]

Moves like these, of course, went unreported in the press. Nor were they mentioned in the dispatches sent home by Barton or Gauss. Even Naggiar was very circumspect about what he told Paris, though he later confirmed his approval of the role played by the French police.[52] The Communists, aware of Chiang's actions, sensed power slipping from them almost as soon as their insurrection had triumphed. "Shanghai has now become the center of counter-revolutionary strength," Luo Yinong told a gathering of activists on 26 March, "and it is the place where the Chinese revolution must be saved." Bai Chongxi, originally warm towards the workers, was now leaning more and more to the right, as was Niu Yongjian; and General Xue Yue, whom the Communists considered most favorable to their cause, was about to be transferred from Shanghai.[53] To counter the dangerous drift to the right, the Communists sought a massive recruitment of new members, and simultaneously launched covert movements against both Chiang Kai-shek and Niu Yongjian. Finally, they considered calling another general strike, this one directed against Britain after the Nanking affair. If Chiang and the right sought to suppress the strike, they would lose their credibility among Chinese patriots, and if they let it go on, it might lead to a mass victory and the return of the Settlements.[54]

In short, the leftists had no reason to trust the Guomindang; regardless of what was known about Chiang's covert actions, his overt actions were quite enough to put the leftists on warning. Their leaders in Wuhan (and in Moscow), however, confused the issue by continuing to argue Chiang's usefulness to the revolutionary cause. Anxious to avoid a clash, on 31 March the Comintern told the Shanghai Communists to hide their arms. An infuriated Luo Yinong hurled the offending telegram to the floor, and Zhao Shiyan burst out that the Party must not allow Chiang to repeat his coup of March 1926.[55]

To Harold Isaacs, writing years later, the Comintern's instructions were an invitation to the Communists to put their heads on the executioner's block. Perhaps so; but they also reflected a note of cautious realism. What chance would three thousand armed workers have against Chiang's troops if a clash came? Was there really any alternative to seeking an accommodation with Chiang?[56] Communist indecision was no match for Chiang's single-mindedness, as he was soon to show. At four o'clock in the afternoon of 11 April, Zhou Fengqi, commander of the Nationalist 26th Army, ordered patrols into the streets of the Chinese city on the pretext that an emergency was developing. (Zhou, a very recent convert to the Nationalist cause, had fought for Sun Chuanfang; years later, he would be murdered as a Japanese collaborator, probably by Du Yuesheng's gunmen.)[57] Disquieting reports reached the Communist headquarters in Zhabei warning that the night would bring an attack against the workers' units, mounted by armed gangsters arriving from the Settlement under foreign protection.

Meanwhile, Du Yuesheng had invited Wang Shouhua, head of the General Labor Union, to dinner at his house in the French Concession—presumably to discuss their joint interest in the labor movement. Wang accepted the invitation, though not before taking the precaution of stationing one of his lieutenants outside the house to spread the alarm if he did not reappear within two hours. His comrades never saw him again; he was murdered, and his body was thrown in a grave near the Longhua arsenal, the first of many victims that night.[58]

At four o'clock in the morning of 12 April, the muffled night noises of the city were broken by a bugle blast, echoed by the siren of a Chinese gunboat moored off Longhua. Immediately, mixed forces of soldiers and their underworld allies began to move—a total of about fifteen thousand men, according to the Municipal Police.[59] Their targets were the picket stations in Zhabei, Nanshi, and Pudong. Gangsters wearing white armbands with the character *gong* (labor) appeared in Zhabei's Baoshan Road, spraying the Commercial Press with small arms fire. A squad of soldiers, arriving ostensibly to break up the fighting, gained admission through a promise to protect the building's inmates and, once inside, seized control. A similar ruse appears to have worked across the street at the Commercial Press Club about an hour later. The Huzhou Guild also fell swiftly, but there was more serious fighting at the Tiantongan railway station where some four to five hundred pickets held out against their assailants. In Nanshi, several truckloads of Du's men emerged from the French Concession and overcame the picket stronghold in the Chinese Tramways Company building near the dingy, red brick pile of the South Station. Similar episodes took place in the sprawling slums behind the docks of Pudong, in Wusong, and everywhere Chiang's soldiers and Du Yuesheng's gangsters were victorious.[60]

When morning came, the General Labor Union was in a shambles. It rallied sufficiently to call a mass meeting in Zhabei, which demanded the return of arms to the workers and the punishment of the military leaders of the operation and sounded a rigorous protest against the Settlement authorities who, they claimed, had bribed the gangsters to do their work for them. A similar meeting in Nanshi under a pouring rain was followed by a march on Longhua military headquarters and the presentation of similar demands. There the demonstrators actually had a conciliatory meeting with one of Bai's deputies. Bai himself put out a statement with his commanders claiming that the army had intervened simply to end the fighting that had broken out between different groups of workers.[61]

But the violence had only begun. A hundred thousand workers responded to the union's call for a general strike on the thirteenth. A mass meeting in Qingyun Road in Zhabei that morning denounced Chiang as a new warlord, condemned his alliance with the imperialists, and again demanded the return of the pickets' weapons. When the meeting broke up, many demonstrators formed a procession to march through the rain to Zhou Fengqi's headquarters in Baoshan Road. Soldiers opened fire on them and, according to Communist reports, killed more than 120 people. (The *North China*, under the headline "Horrible Fight in Chapei," reported that the Communists had put women and children in front of the procession, confident that the soldiers would not shoot.) Near the South Station the same day, the army fired on another procession.[62] Troops and gangsters marched into the headquarters of the General Labor Union and took it over, announcing that, since the union was simply the tool of a small Communist minority, it would now be amalgamated with Chiang's anti-Communist Labor Federation. The new organization would be known as the United Labor Union Committee [*Gonghui zuzhi tongyi weiyuanhui*], dedicated to upholding Sun Yat-sen's Three Principles of the People and to the liberation of the workers from Communist oppression.[63]

The seizure of the Communist-dominated provisional government came on 14 April. That afternoon, troops took over its headquarters, carrying about twenty people off to trial at Longhua. The leftist Special Municipal Bureau of the Guomindang was closed (however, so was the right-wing headquarters at 44 route Vallon), as was the Shanghai Students' Union, its place now taken by a Shanghai Student Movement Leadership Committee. Various other labor headquarters and mass organization headquarters were also raided and shut down.[64] Three Communist leaders, Li Lisan, Nie Rongzhen, and Chen Yannian, arrived secretly the same day from Hankou to try to salvage their organization but found themselves powerless. Zhao Shiyan, who had succeeded the murdered Wang Shouhua as head of the General Labor Union, summoned a secret meeting that had no choice but to declare an end to the strike and order its followers back to work.[65]

Ever since September 1925 when Chinese troops and police had closed it down and arrested its leaders, the General Labor Union had been forced to work underground. For a brief period of three weeks after the fall of Shanghai to the Nationalists in March 1927, it had come into the open and had showed its strength. Now it was again driven into the shadows, and not until the city fell to the Communist armies in the spring of 1949 would it emerge again. Three hundred people had been killed, the union claimed, more than five hundred arrested, and five thousand had fled. Shanghai was now under a terror worse than anything the city had experienced at the hands of the northern warlords.

The imperialists have done all they could to help Chiang Kai-shek and his counter-revolutionary policies, have allowed Chiang's troops and his gangsters to carry arms freely throughout the Settlement, and to search and arrest workers and revolutionaries. Foreign factories have engaged in wholesale firings of those who took part in revolutionary activity. The press and other organs of public opinion are completely under Chiang's control, and all revolutionary and mass organizations, such as the Special Party Headquarters, the Students Union and the City Government, have been shut down or reorganized by the Army, following the disarming of the pickets. Every revolutionary is accused of communism, and every communist seen as someone to be killed. . . . Though Chiang Kai-shek talks revolution, his actions are more counterrevolutionary than those of the Fengtian and Shandong warlords.[66]

The events of the 12 April purge have been described many times, though often with more attention paid to making them into a good story than with regard for the facts. Malraux's *Man's Fate* towers above all other accounts and gives so good a picture of Shanghai in those days that the reader must continually remind himself that he is reading not history but fiction, that Malraux's account serves the novelist's design and not the historian's needs.[67] His purpose is clear enough, however. It is less easy to discern from the other narratives of the period where the historian's truth gives way to the partisan's invention. Nowhere is this more the case than in the question of how much foreign Shanghai knew of the coming attack, and how much its authorities cooperated in Chiang's April crushing of the left.

Chinese Communist sources, both then and now, assume foreign participation, assume that Chiang was doing the work of imperialism and that the matter is so self-evident it needs no documentation. This assumption is clear in the report that the General Labor Union made at the time, and it is evident in two more recent accounts of the 12 April incident.[68] Both of the latter examine the knowledge the foreign powers, particularly Japan and America, had of the rifts within the Nationalist movement, and both assume that, because foreigners wanted to play on these divisions, Chiang Kai-shek became their tool.

That many wanted Chiang to move against the left and the unions is beyond question; witness the *North China's* editorial of 28 March calling on the general to destroy the Communists or be swept away in the Red flood. Not only did the French consul-general know of and support the coup, but the French police played a role in helping it. But the American and British consular reports say nothing about their own knowledge or of the role of the Settlement's authorities. They reported the events of 12 April in the most terse and telegraphic terms, sometimes filling in a few details later. The Municipal Police, however, were well aware of what was happening. "Preparations are being made by the Kung Chin Hui (Joint Progressive Society) to make a surprise attack upon the office of the General Labor Union," read a confidential report of 7 April. "The attack will be made by members of the Ch'ing Pang [Green Gang] with the assistance of soldiers in plain clothes."[69] They did not report whether they gave any assistance, nor did they report the links between the French police and the Gang.

Old men forget, and occasional historical inaccuracies call into question the reliability of memoirs that otherwise have the ring of truth to them. Powell's chronology is skewed—he has Du's gangsters taking control of the city before the Nationalist armies arrived—as is that of the Australian journalist John Pal who remembers interviewing Chiang Kai-shek when his armies reached the outskirts of Shanghai, though Chiang was not there at the time. Pal also remembers that Du Yuesheng put down the Communists before, not after, Chiang reached the city.[70] A young Soviet adviser claimed that the foreigners threatened Chiang with armed intervention if he did not break with the Communists—but she gave no evidence.[71]

Stirling Fessenden, unfortunately, left no reminiscences of his career in Shanghai; whatever records he may have had probably were lost after Pearl Harbor, and he himself perished in a Japanese prison camp. Nor is it likely that he or his colleagues in the Settlement would commit to paper all that they did know. Did he take any of the foreign consuls into his confidence about his deal with Du Yuesheng? The Municipal Council was quite capable of acting without informing the consuls, although Fessenden and his fellow councillors knew that they could trust Barton not to send home everything they told him.

The North China reported at the time that the Settlement authorities had been told of the coup, and it claimed that there was a radical plan to embroil Chinese troops with foreigners.[72] Though it did not actually say that the armed gangs came from the Settlement, a quick look at the map shows that by far the most direct way to reach Zhabei from the French Concession or from most parts of the Chinese city was right across the Settlement, or at least across the western roads that the British had garrisoned since 25 February. The alternatives would have been either a long detour by land to the west of the British defense lines, an arrival by rail at the North Station, or an arrival by water from the Huangpu or Soochow creeks. None of those possibilities makes much sense, and lacking any other evidence, we must conclude that Du's plainclothes gangsters and perhaps uniformed Nationalist troops as well made their way that night through the Settlement, and that neither the Municipal Police nor the foreign landing forces interfered.

SIXTEEN

The Aftermath

Chiang Kai-shek's massacre of the left in Shanghai brought an abrupt change in the fortunes of the Guomindang and in the revolutionary movement it led. The violence that early spring morning signaled the bloody suppression of Communists and radicals in China's other cities: in Canton on 15 April, in Swatow, Amoy, Ningbo, and elsewhere. Within a few weeks, Chiang had almost eliminated Communist power in the cities of south China, shattering the Party's organization and its precarious hold on China's urban workers. Three months later, in July, Wang Jingwei's Wuhan government turned on its own Communists and sent Borodin and his cadre of advisers back to the Soviet Union. Communist-led uprisings later that year, at Nanchang, Changsha, and Canton, seeking to win back an urban base were quickly put down. By the end of 1927, Mao Zedong had led his followers, defeated in the Autumn Harvest uprising in Hunan, to safety in the mountains of the Hunan-Jiangxi border, there to begin the organization of the great peasant revolution that, twenty-two years later, would come to power. Though the Communist party's Central Committee continued to work underground in Shanghai for five more years, it found itself increasingly out of touch with the reality of the Chinese revolution, and finally in 1932, it left the city for the relative security of Mao Zedong's Jiangxi Soviet.[1]

In destroying his enemies on the left, Chiang Kai-shek also betrayed the hopes of many of his allies for the Chinese revolution. April twelfth was a crucial date in the history of the Chinese revolution, a clear division in the fortunes of Chiang's own party. The *qingdang*, or party purge, of 1927 cut the Guomindang—Chiang's Guomindang, at any rate—off from the ideas, the energies, and the organizational skills of many of those who had worked for the party in its revolutionary period. It thus weakened it for the job of national reconstruction that lay ahead.

It is easy to see this today. But Chiang's strike against his rivals caused little stir in foreign circles at the time. "The first shot in the struggle between the Kuomintang and the Communists for mastery in Shanghai," the *North China Herald* called it. While praising Chiang's firmness—"with conditions as they were in this district a fortnight ago, the only thing to do was to act ruthlessly and to shoot down the Communists without mercy"—the paper still warned against putting too much faith in the general.[2] Two months later, it blasted his "heartless opportunism" in the slaughter of innocent workers whose only crime was their failure to understand that the Guomindang line had changed. "Those foreigners who see in the revolt against Soviet dictation, or in the ruthless suppression of communist labor groups, evidence of a sincere change of heart . . . are blind to the fundamental motives behind these changes. Neither in the forwarding of the Bolshevist programme nor in the revolt against it have we ever been able to see anything but cold, calculating hypocrisy, utterly reckless of the miseries imposed upon the Chinese people."[3] Meanwhile, the *China Weekly Review* largely ignored Chiang's coup (its editor was having his own problems, which are described later).

Nor did the foreign diplomats better understand the implications of Chiang's action. "This move by Chiang Kai-shek against the extremists is, to put it mildly, extremely interesting," wrote Lampson to Victor Wellesley of the Foreign Office a week after the purge. "We none of it know how much or what it means."[4] Barton as usual reported little, remarking on only the obvious: that the coup would widen the breach between Chiang and the Communists.[5] According to his French colleague, he remained skeptical of Chiang's intentions, suspecting that the Nationalist authorities were behind a renewal of anti-British agitation that summer.[6] Gauss called the coup a "terrible blow to the communists," but saw no immediate change for the city.[7] Nor do the French reports say much more. Only Naggiar, perhaps because he knew more about the coup's preparation, clearly saw the purge as a dividing line.[8]

The events of 12 April thus brought no great sense of relief to foreigners in the city, no sense of a new and fruitful entente between their interests and Chiang's anticommunism. If foreigners felt secure in their persons and their property, it was because of the British infantrymen and American marines in the streets rather than Chiang's crushing of the left. Although Barton reportedly warned the British-owned *Shanghai Times* (and perhaps the *North China* as well) not to criticize the general,[9] Chiang did not seem to foreigners, either then or later, to be a Chinese leader with whom they could work. "I am afraid that you people at home, in common with the other governments interested, are being just a little premature in your welcome to this gentleman," wrote Lampson to the Foreign Office at the end of April. "He may be all right. But until he has proved himself to be so, I am very chary of accepting him as anything but one form of extremist in place of another. . . . My advice is—do not trust Chiang Kai-shek or anyone else out here further than you can see them." [10] Back in London, both Pratt and Wellesley echoed the fear that the Nationalist movement would degenerate into old-fashioned warlordism, with Chiang becoming "a mere Tuchun playing for his own hand like the rest of them." [11] Meanwhile, the left refused to play dead; Cunningham, who had returned to Shanghai that summer, reported that the General Labor Union was still vigorous, and as late as August, there were fears of a new Communist uprising. [12]

In the new mood of caution among missionaries after Nanking, even the National Christian Council's Bishop Logan Roots welcomed the presence of British gunboats against "banditry" on the Yangtze. [13] Bishop Graves, never a partisan of the Nationalists, told Frederick Moore of the *New York Times* that he could see nothing but trouble ahead, noting that St. John's must remain closed for another year. [14] "It ought to be about time for a healthy opposition to start against the Lobenstine, Warnshuis, Koo and Franklin crowd," he wrote home that summer. "How really sensible men can allow themselves to be fooled as Americans are being fooled by this Soviet-Nationalist propaganda is something that I am entirely unable to understand." [15] Presumably he had in mind such people as Fletcher Brockman of the Y.M.C.A., who was assuring an audience in St. Louis that summer that the Nationalist movement was not Red, but profoundly American. "It was no Chinese who overthrew the Manchu dynasty, but three Americans—George Washington, Thomas Jefferson, and Abraham Lincoln!" (A "diabolically clever speech," commented the *North China Herald*, not because of Brockman's appalling cultural arrogance in planting the American flag firmly over China's own revolution, but because Brockman's Y.M.C.A. on Museum Road owed its safety to the foreign troops.) [16]

Chiang's power remained shaky. In August he retired briefly from his leadership of the Nationalist movement, ostensibly to help reconcile the Wuhan and Nanking branches of the Guomindang. The Northern Expedition continued, and many foreigners no doubt cheered loudly with the *North China Herald* every time the Nationalist troops found themselves checked by the northern armies of the Anguojun. [17] Though George Sokolsky pointed out that for the first time in years the dangerous month of May had passed without serious troubles, [18] most would probably have

preferred the return of Sun Chuanfang to a continued Nationalist occupation, and there were still occasional calls for foreign military intervention
to set China straight.[19] The Shanghai Defence Force, which had numbered
about 14,500 at the time of Chiang's coup, rose to include some 20,000
men, and as long as the Nanking affair remained unsettled, no one was
suggesting that they go home or that the warships riding in the Huangpu
weigh anchor and sail away.[20]

Among foreigners, there were few dissenters from the general chorus of
approbation for the Council's handling of the crisis. The most public split
came over an attempt by the American Chamber of Commerce to oust J. B.
Powell from membership. That body's disappointment that Washington
had not ridden faster to Shanghai's rescue was clear, and Powell's editorials in the *China Weekly Review*, with their unrelenting criticism of the
Municipal Council, had enraged a great many people, Americans as well
as British. "A mischievous man from Missouri," one of his British critics
called him, "with his American-small-town elementary conceptions of the
wide world lying beyond the exclusive orbit of his buck board streets."[21]
Powell, of course, held that he was simply upholding the policy of his
country. He was generally right of course, but what made the matter all
the more infuriating were his suggestions that Britain, ensnared by die-
hard opinion in Shanghai, was trying to inveigle the United States into
doing the dirty work of imperialism.[22]

At the American chamber's annual meeting on 26 April, the chairman,
F. F. Fairman, put forth a resolution asking for the resignation of the *China
Weekly Review*, because its editorial policy differed so markedly from the
views of the chamber's members, thus "lending aid to disruptive instead
of constructive elements." Only George Sokolsky spoke up for Powell, not
to defend his views, but to remind the chamber that it owed its very existence largely to Powell's energies.[23] Powell fought back. "The situation has
become so tense that we are faced with capitulation or war," he wrote to
the *North China Daily News*. "No one of intelligence disputes the obvious
fact that the foreign forces here, chiefly the British, have saved Shanghai
from the fury of the mob, but having saved it, what are we going to do
with it?" The troops could not stay forever, and something would have
to be done to meet Chinese aspirations.[24] Through the spring and summer, he continued to exasperate his adversaries by attacking the chamber
and by printing letters from home congratulating him on his courageous
stand. He complained that American and British firms were pulling their
advertisements from his pages; others saw the *Review*'s increased Chinese
advertising as proof of a Guomindang subsidy.[25] They attributed his anti-
British views to his ouster from the *China Press* in 1925, and suspected
that Powell lay behind a Guomindang attack that August on the American
chamber's imperialistic stance.[26]

James Huskey's work on Americans in Shanghai points out that, by 1927, the chamber had come into the hands of the "parochials," those Americans who had no stake in China beyond Shanghai and who were blind to the larger ramifications of American interests in the country. Frightened by the Nationalist advance, they made the chamber their mouthpiece in a drive to associate America more closely with Britain in the city's defense. When that failed, they turned on Powell as the man responsible for Washington's "pusillanimous policy," as one of their number put it. The attack backfired. They simply condemned themselves, both in the eyes of Shanghai Chinese and in the eyes of public opinion in the United States. By the end of the year, as Shanghai became more peaceful, the breach in the American community was beginning to be healed, and Powell had apparently emerged as victor.[27]

Shanghai grabbed the world's headlines in the spring of 1927, and as the response both to the attack on Powell and to Arthur Ransome's piece on the Shanghai mind showed, many at home did not share Shanghai's flattering views of itself. Even the Municipal Council understood the need to do some political fence mending. Earlier that year, a group of Shanghai firms, with the Council's backing, had gotten into the propaganda business, distributing anti-Communist leaflets in Chinese among the workers of Shanghai's mills and factories. The Council found this sort of covert propaganda "distasteful" and self-defeating, but it also realized that it needed help in its home constituencies as well. What had started as a propaganda effort among Chinese thus turned into a new Publicity Bureau in June 1927, and its audience in the mother countries was at least as important as its local audience. Though formed with the Council's blessing, it was to be financed not by public funds but by commercial interests, both foreign and Chinese. By early 1928, however, only British firms were giving it any active public support, while both the Council and the British consulate-general worked with it behind the scenes.[28]

Emerging first in the summer of 1927, the Shanghai Fascisti represented a more bizarre way of making the case for foreign Shanghai. Again it was respectable British businessmen who took the lead in this organization, announcing that its purpose was to uphold law and order in the Settlement (and by implication, to take matters into their own hands if the Council failed to do so).[29] "The name is unfortunate, but in Shanghai, not unexpected," commented an observer in the Foreign Office,[30] and these British Fascisti on the Bund remind one unavoidably of Roderick Spode—P. G. Wodehouse's sendup of a would-be Man of Destiny who turns out to be a purveyor of ladies' lingerie. "Are we to go sit down quietly and watch this wonderful city of Shanghai go from bad to worse and eventually succumb to a like fate?" cried Bernard Firth of Wheelock and Company. He had just been elected leader of the Fascisti, and was reminding his audience in the Masonic Hall of the terrible example of Hankou. "Better that we die fighting . . . than be led like sheep to the slaughter." [31]

Not surprisingly, the *North China Herald* (where the American Rodney Gilbert was filling in for the vacationing O. M. Green) cheered on the Fascisti. But the Municipal Council drew the line. When the leaders of foreign Shanghai met to give Stirling Fessenden a birthday dinner in September, Firth pledged the support of the Fascisti to the chairman, only to be firmly warned to stay out of trouble and to leave affairs "in the hands of the men who have been chosen by the various governments and the ratepayers who elect them." [32] The point was made, and though the Fascisti illustrate an aspect of the Shanghai mind, they were never to be a force in Shanghai politics.

The celebration for Fessenden was, of course, mostly a tribute to his leadership in the crisis through which the Settlement had just passed. Consul-General Cunningham presided, Naggiar gave an appreciative toast, and when Barton called Fessenden the best representative of the Shanghai mind, he meant it as a compliment. The man from Maine was unquestionably a hero in the eyes of many, particularly in the eyes of the British and the Americans. As the *North China Herald* had written somewhat earlier:

> And yet, though we may disagree
> At times, with U.S. policy,
> We know you, "Fessy," as a man,
> A cent per cent American,
> And while extolling you true blue,
> Regret that you're not British too;
> For Stirling's sterling, just the same
> By nature no less than by name.[33]

Not everyone shared the happy view. Before returning to his post at Tianjin, Clarence Gauss, who had clashed more than once with Fessenden during the spring's crisis, sent the State Department a sharply different valedictory judgment of the Council's chairman. He had been particularly incensed by Fessenden's speech at the ratepayers' meeting that April, not only for its assertion of the Settlement's independence but because of the implicit criticisms of American policy.

The truculent attitude of this American citizen, who, through no fault or favor of the American Government, or its authorities in China, has been hoisted by his colleagues of the Shanghai Municipal Council to the position of its Chairman, and maintains himself in that public position—constantly emphasized in Foreign houses of parliament to show the "International" character of the Shanghai municipal administration—by his attitude of faithful obedience to the will of the reactionary majority of the Council and their supporters, is in my opinion distinctly unbecoming and distasteful. . . . [He is] known openly and persistently to have criticized the American position; he has shown a complete lack of desire in any way to cooperate with the American authorities; and his presence on the Council, and particularly in the position of Chairman, is not only distinctly a liability to the American Government in its position in China, but an open offense to that Government.

In my opinion the time must come shortly when the Powers must impose on the Municipal Council of the International Settlement—if it is to continue its "international" character—some check or control which will make the Council responsible to the official representatives of those powers in Shanghai and Peking. At present, as was so forcibly demonstrated after the May 30th, 1925, incident at Shanghai, the Council holds itself responsible to no one other than the small group of foreign ratepayers who, half-heartedly, annually hold a meeting to confirm them or their carefully chosen successors in office.

MacMurray, however, turned down Gauss's suggestion that they try to block Fessenden's reelection as chairman, and his prestige remained undiminished.[34]

Meanwhile, Naggiar, having strengthened consular control over the machinery of the Concession earlier that year, managed to get rid of one of the chief irritants to his position. The *Écho de Chine* had joined fully in the public outcry against the alleged *fainéant* policy of the consul-general and against France's failure to take a strong stand on Nanking.[35] A wounded Naggiar complained bitterly to Paris; Was this to be the way the Missions Étrangères, who owned the paper, rewarded their French patrons? Shortly thereafter, Msgr. de Guébriant, the superior-general in Paris, shut down the *Écho*, and later that year, a new daily, the *Journal de Changhai*, began publication under the auspices of the French Chamber of Commerce.[36] The *Écho*'s hawkish views no doubt embarrassed the Church even more than Naggiar; and the British, trying to deal with their own *North China Daily News*, must have envied the French this easy imposition of ecclesiastical authority!

No matter how foreign Shanghai might congratulate itself on the way it came through its ordeal, the Nationalist arrival left it with some unfinished business. Two years after May Thirtieth, the question of Chinese representation on the Municipal Council remained unresolved. Although in October 1926, the Chinese authorities had accepted the offer to add three Chinese members, the Nationalist advance on the city threw the whole arrangement up in the air. The villain of the piece, according to Barton and Gauss, was C. T. Wang, who convinced the Chinese Ratepayers' Association to claim a total of nine councillors, and by the summer of 1927, no settlement had yet been reached. Meanwhile, the Council, citing the higher costs of government and particularly of policing a city in disorder, had authorized an increase in the general municipal rate from 14 to 16 percent. (Stupid, Gauss called it; he had tried to dissuade the Council from the move.)[37] The Chinese Chamber protested. So did C. T. Wang, claiming that the Chinese paid 70 percent of the Settlement's rates and implying that the higher taxes were to underwrite the expenses of the foreign troops. The Municipal Council denied both these assertions; according to its figures, the Chinese paid only 55 percent of the rates and held only a tiny part of the debenture investment.[38]

Behind the battle lay an impressive mobilization of Chinese merchants under Guomindang auspices, working through such men as C. T. Wang, Yu Xiaqing, Du Yuesheng, and others whose mixture of persuasion and pressure brought about a merchant unity to back its demands.[39] An apparent compromise in August broke down, a victim again (according to Barton) of politicking by C. T. Wang and the "notorious blackmailer" Wang Xiaolai. At the end of the year, the Chinese Ratepayers' Association was still demanding equality of representation.[40] In January 1928, however, Yu Xiaqing took over the negotiations. The former villain of May Thirtieth now showed himself (wrote Cunningham) to be a "public spirited man" by working for a compromise.[41] Finally, on 3 April 1928, came an agreement: three Chinese to join the Council now, perhaps more later, while six others would sit on various Council committees. Six days later, the three men took their seats, and the Municipal Council at last had its Chinese members.[42] The French, too, had raised their municipal rates, but they got away with it. They already had Chinese councillors, and the ever-useful community leader Du Yuesheng was ready to use his good offices to negotiate a compromise. They thus faced none of the troubles that beset the Settlement.[43]

When the ratepayers met again in April 1928, the city was calmer. Through the summer and fall of 1927, the Shanghai Defence Force had been reduced in size, and by January 1928 its numbers had dropped to forty-five hundred.[44] Despite the vicissitudes in Chiang Kai-shek's fortunes, despite the clashes between his troops and the Japanese in Shandong in 1927 and 1928, the Northern Expedition finally triumphed when his Nationalist armies entered Peking in June 1928, a few days after members of Japan's Kwantung Army murdered the defeated Zhang Zuolin. In March, after long negotiations, MacMurray reached a settlement of American claims in the Nanking incident, with the Chinese government accepting responsibility for the affair although placing the blame on the Communists. A similar British agreement followed in August.[45]

With that out of the way, there were no obstacles left to the diplomatic recognition of the new Nationalist government in Nanking. Though few foreigners saw Chiang as the great leader China needed, for a while, at least, the Nationalists seemed to offer the country more hope of a united and constructive government than anything she had seen since the days of the Manchus. Moreover, in December 1927, Chiang Kai-shek's marriage to the Wellesley-educated Soong Meiling in the splendor of Shanghai's Hotel Majestic seemed to promise a greater Western inspiration for the Nationalist movement. (David Yui had earlier performed the Christian ceremony demanded by the bride's Methodist faith; a few years later, Chiang himself became a convert.) In July 1928, America granted China the tariff autonomy promised by the Special Conference of 1925, and other countries followed suit. Meanwhile, the British took the lead in negotiations that, had they been successful, would have ended extraterritoriality. The arrangement (which would have excluded Shanghai itself for a decade) was almost ready to be signed when the Japanese invasion of Manchuria in the autumn of 1931 stalled the whole enterprise. Though most other nations resigned their claims, the extraterritorial privileges of Britain, France, America, and Japan thus remained intact ten years later, on the day of Pearl Harbor.

Shanghai thus survived the shocks of China's first revolution in the 1920s, but it did not survive unchanged. Never again would either Chinese or foreign Shanghai enjoy the same independence they had known during the years between the overthrow of the Manchus in 1911 and the May Thirtieth Movement. With the Nationalist arrival came a consolidation of power over the Chinese city and a new insistence on Chinese authority. Already in April 1927, the Nationalists sought to impose their control over the independent General Chamber of Commerce, forcing its president, Fu Xiaoan, to flee. (In 1940, as puppet mayor of Japanese-occupied Shanghai, he would be assassinated.)[46] In July, a new municipality of Greater Shanghai was established, seeking to unite and bring under Nationalist control the various parts of the Chinese city.[47]

In at least one instance, the coming of the Nationalist government meant increased cooperation with the foreigners. In 1927, at the urging of Senior Consul Cunningham, a liaison committee was set up between Settlement, Chinese, and French police to check the growth of subversion. It was responsible for a crackdown on leftists in 1930 and probably played a role in many of the arrests of Communists in the next few years.[48] More worrying for foreign Shanghai was the way in which the Nationalists simultaneously began a campaign to extend their influence into the settlements, a campaign that would continue, with varying degrees of success, until they were driven from the city in 1937. In Western eyes, at least, there were three ways in which the Nationalists could pursue this policy. First, they could use the new Provisional Court of 1927 to extend their control over the Settlement's Chinese inhabitants. Almost immediately, foreigners complained of the court's increasing politicization. When Nanking ousted its independently minded president in the summer of 1928, installing a new judge apparently more amenable to Guomindang dictation, the court seemed to become (in Cunningham's words) "nothing but an institution to carry out the orders of the Party and Government, irrespective of whether those orders are based on law or not."[49] Such arguments, of course, ignored the abuses of the old Mixed Court when it was under foreign control. In 1930 and 1931, over foreign objections—particularly from lawyers and real estate interests—the Provisional Court itself gave way to new District Courts within both the International and French Settlements. Foreign assessors played no role in these courts, which now formed an integral part of the modern Chinese judicial system.[50] Foreign complaints continued, and in 1932 the Japanese used the Court's unwillingness to deal with anti-Japanese agitation as an excuse to send their own troops into the city.[51]

The second way to infiltrate the settlements was the new Chinese presence on the Shanghai Municipal Council. By 1930, Chinese occupied five seats, and more and more Chinese were moving into the higher levels of the Settlement's administration. This penetration not only gave them a voice on the Council, it also (muttered the foreigners) gave Chinese authorities a direct line to the Council's inner workings. The Council members, wrote Lampson, functioned "not so much as municipal councillors as political instruments of the Chinese Government and the Kuomintang," even divulging the confidential minutes of Council meetings to Chinese authorities.[52] On the other hand, there is some evidence that the non-Chinese members of the Council occasionally met by themselves.[53]

Third was the challenge mounted by the new Chinese municipality of Greater Shanghai to the Council's murky authority over the external roads. For years, Chinese police would dispute the presence of the Council's own police, and it was not until the 1930s that a *modus vivendi* emerged that lasted until the Japanese invasion of 1937.[54] After visiting the city in the spring of 1929, Lampson remarked that the Chinese authorities, under the control of the Guomindang machine, were "apparently carrying on an intensive campaign for the recovery of control over the Settlement and the curtailment of its existing freedom of action, and to this end driving in at every crack and crevice of the foreigners' position."[55] Cunningham echoed this view, warning that "peaceful penetration" would get for the Nationalists what they could not get by negotiations and would lead eventually to their control of the Settlement.[56]

Finally, where the Nationalists could not extend their legitimate power, they sometimes used illegitimate means. Already by the summer of 1927,

Chiang had turned on his erstwhile supporters among the city's merchants to extract more money from them. Ordinary Nationalist agencies could not operate in the settlements, but the Green Gang's underworld knew no boundaries. It was presumably they who, in the summer of 1927, carried out a campaign of kidnapping and extortion to help finance the military and political ambitions of the new rulers.[57] By the fall of 1927, things were so bad that British and Italian troops were cooperating with the Russian unit of the Shanghai Volunteer Corps and the Settlement police to stop and search suspected kidnappers, but some Chinese complained privately that the French police were in on the racket with the gangsters.[58]

Whether or not the charge was true, the bloody events of April 1927 and the collaboration between the French authorities and the underworld substantially increased the power of Du Yuesheng and his gangsters in the French Concession. His mediation in the rates controversy in 1927 and his influence in the world of labor put the French authorities further in his debt. Operating with French police protection, over the next few years Du and his friends would come to dominate the administrative machinery of Frenchtown. He practically controlled the Concession's Chinese Ratepayers' Association, and through that organization determined the Chinese membership of the *Commission provisoire*. In July 1929, he himself became a member of that body.[59]

His relations with the Nationalist authorities were no less fruitful. In August 1927, the Nationalists established an Opium Suppression Bureau in Shanghai, ostensibly to end the drug traffic by bringing the importation of opium under government control while farming out its sale to a private company. The scheme collapsed, in part because Du would tolerate no rivals. When a Jiangsu Provincial Anti-Opium Bureau appeared six months later, the monopoly was given to Du and his colleagues. The Nationalists now sought to enlist the cooperation of the foreign authorities, who were asked to recognize licenses issued by the monopoly for the importation, sale, and smoking of opium in their districts. The request posed an awkward problem; had the foreigners any right not to cooperate with Chinese law?[60] Though the French consul-general pressed his foreign colleagues for approval—he had learned, he said, that the opium merchants spent $1.5 million annually in bribes for the Shanghai Municipal Police and the *Garde municipale*—the British and Americans managed to block any formal action.[61] At least one of the old British opium firms—E. D. Sassoon and Company—tried (unsuccessfully) to take advantage of the new legality by buying Indian opium for sale to the government's drug monopoly.[62] About the same time, Du Yuesheng himself proposed a deal to Stirling Fessenden: In return for a secret payment of $50 to $100,000 a month to the Council, the Municipal Police would look the other way. Of course Fessenden need not agree, Du admitted; but then the same money would have to be used to suborn the police. A few weeks later, he made a similar proposal to the French authorities, and Paris authorized them to go ahead with the formal agreement as long as the Settlement acted first.[63]

In August 1928, the new anti-opium bureau was closed down, its place now taken by a National Opium Suppression Committee, which quickly passed a new law banning the drug outright save for medical use under government oversight.[64] None of these steps seem to have imposed the slightest curb on Shanghai's importance as a center of the drug trade. "The Chinese triumvirate, who control the underworld in the French Concession . . . are still allowed by the authorities of the French Concession a free hand as regards the sale and smoking of opium in that Concession," reported the British consulate-general in 1929.[65] A year later, there was a brief cleanup campaign in the Concession, timed to coincide with the arrival in Shanghai of a commission of enquiry from the League of Nations. After that body returned to Geneva, the French authorities reportedly raised the price of their averted eyes from $20,000 to $30,000 a month.[66]

Conditions in the French Concession had now become an open scandal. In 1932, Jacques Meyrier, back in Shanghai as consul-general with a new police chief under orders to clean things up, would write that Du's opium racket now dominated the *Garde municipale*, paying off all its Chinese members and many of the French as well. Having started as an ally in French efforts to maintain order in 1927, Du had now become a genuine rival to the French authorities for power in the Concession.[67] Not only did he have his own people on the Provisional Commission, but two of its foreign members—the Swiss Schwyzer (who had been decorated for his role in the troubles of 1927) and the French Blum—were in the pay of the opium racket, the latter acting as its treasurer.[68] The French now attempted to reclaim their authority and reform the Concession, and one of their first steps was to force Du Yuesheng to resign from the *Commission Provisoire*. Within a week, three leading members of the French community were dead: du Pac de Marsoulies of double pneumonia, former Consul-General Koechlin of smallpox while on his way back to France, and Colonel Marcaire of the French military forces of pneumonia. An extraordinary coincidence, perhaps; but no evidence links the deaths to Du.[69]

In short, though the coming of the Nationalists changed the relationship between Chinese and foreign authorities in Shanghai (for the worse, some foreigners would say), it did not solve the Shanghai question—the one posed by the continued existence of the foreign settlements in a Chinese city. Three aspects of that question remained, as intractable as ever.

The first had to do with the protection of foreign interests. Here, the revolution had shown the need for foreigners to bend, to surrender some of their prerogatives and privileges in order to maintain those interests. Out of that realization had come the seating of Chinese on the Municipal Council and the *Commission Provisoire* and the agreements on the courts. The second aspect was in allowing the city to grow and prosper as one of the great ports and trading centers of the world. The Nationalists met this need with their own version of Greater Shanghai—but it still included no more than the Chinese city. Finally, there remained the relationship of foreign Shanghai to its home governments: How far could Shanghai and the Shanghai lobby, working through trade associations, missionary associations, or exotic growths like the Constitutional Defence League, the Publicity Bureau, even the Shanghai Fascisti, be allowed to influence the larger China policies of London and Washington?

All three aspects of the problem were connected. In 1928, Barton defined the Shanghai question thus: "How to effect the withdrawal from the administration of Shanghai of the foreign element, which has been associated with its creation as a world port, without damage to the enormous foreign, and particularly British, vested interests which have come into being as a result of that association and creation?" [70] George Mounsey of the Foreign Office saw the solution in bringing the various parts of the city under a unified administration, ending its division between an efficient but parochial International Settlement, the "absurd anomaly" of the French Concession, and the several districts of the Chinese city, badly administered with no foreign voice. Shanghai would grow all the way to Wusong, along the river that was its life, and its growth must not be impeded by quarrels between its various parts. [71] To John Pratt in the Foreign Office, the Shanghai question was primarily a legal and administrative one, and the concessions to the Nationalists, necessary as they were, only made it more difficult; for in the International Settlement, there was now a clear split between the executive, where the Municipal Council and its police drew their authority from the Land Regulations, and the judiciary, where the Court now came under Nanking's jurisdiction. "That is the problem of Shanghai, and when put in these terms it will be readily perceived that there is, in fact, no solution." [72]

Finally, to Lampson, writing in one of his more exasperated moments, the real Shanghai problem appeared to be simply that the Chinese did not want a solution. They wanted to get Shanghai back for China, no matter what harm it might do foreign and Chinese interests. "That is, and always has been, the real crux of the Shanghai problem." [73] But the unyielding attitude of so much of foreign Shanghai was also part of the problem—particularly for London, for Shanghai remained peculiarly a

British problem. "Whenever real danger threatens the city (as it did in 1927)," wrote Lampson in 1929, "British interests, both economic and political, are so great that British troops must be sent to protect the Settlement, just as though it were a British possession."[74] Leaders of British Shanghai knew this—or sensed it—and the sense had been confirmed in 1927. To some degree, they had their home government over a barrel, and Lampson was very much the man caught in the middle. On the one hand, the Foreign Office continually prodded him to find a solution. The presence of the Defence Force (an expensive presence, London reminded him) should give foreign Shanghai a breathing space in which to put its own house in order (there were rumors that Ramsay MacDonald had sent Labourite agents to Shanghai to prepare a campaign against the Conservative government).[75] On the other hand, British Shanghai seemed to Lampson at times to be "merely stagnating in the comfortable shade of the Defence Force."[76] While he defended Shanghai to London, he prodded Barton to move things along. Barton, however, made things no easier, irritating everyone by his terse and sketchy reports. He indignantly denied that Shanghai was stagnating, but by late 1927 could cite few accomplishments other than the formation of the Publicity Bureau. Even the Peking legation found this progress a bit thin.[77]

But if foreign Shanghai did not deal with its own problems, outsiders would come in and do the job for it. Should not Shanghai, asked George Mounsey of the Foreign Office in early 1928, "admit its incompetence and submit its difficulties as a whole to some outside body of experts in order to get some idea of the way in which they ought to be solved?"[78] But who would those experts be? A suggestion in late 1927 that the new Institute for Pacific Relations (which had examined the Shanghai question at its Honolulu meeting that summer) undertake a study of the city upset the diplomats. "There is no problem less susceptible to amateur solution," objected Barton,[79] and Lampson warned against "outside doctrinaire bodies like the Honoluluites, who though meaning well would almost certainly stir up unfathomable trouble." So when Sir Frederick Whyte, who had headed the British delegation to the meeting, put the question to the Foreign Office, they "poured cold water on in buckets."[80] Roger Greene of the Rockefeller Institute, who had close ties to the Institute for Pacific Relations, agreed, and even the Institute's China group, led by David Yui, wanted no study undertaken while Nationalist fortunes were at a low ebb.[81]

In April 1928 came the agreement to seat Chinese on the Council, and finally another agreement to open the Settlement's parks to Chinese. All forward movement then seemed to stop, nor was it likely to start again under C. H. Arnhold, who replaced Fessenden as chairman in 1929. "Violent," Lampson called him; "rough, unscrupulous, and a die-hard of the worst kind," wrote Pratt. "His ability and a certain rough forcefulness will make him a most dangerous chairman."[82] The kind of sane leadership Shanghai needed was not likely to come from him or from Fessenden— who, though leaving the chairmanship, had assumed a salaried position as director general of the Municipal Council. "Reaction is in the saddle at Shanghai and is riding for a fall."[83]

In July 1929, taking advantage of the presence in Oxford of Stanley Hornbeck, the new chief of the State Department's Far Eastern division, Lionel Curtis of the Royal Institute of International Affairs gathered a group that included Pratt, Malcolm MacDonald, Frank Ashton-Gwatkin, and Sir Frederick Whyte for a weekend at All Souls. There they discussed problems of foreign policy in general and the East in particular. One evening the talk turned to Shanghai, and Hornbeck argued that Britain should take the lead in setting up a commission to study it.[84] The initiative, however, eventually came from Washington. That August, Stirling Fessenden (whose new position, remarked Cunningham ruefully, brought him a salary twice that of his own—and he was senior consul to boot!)[85] visited Washington. Both Hornbeck and Nelson Johnson underscored the State Department's unhappiness at the way in which the Council had insisted upon its independence while simultaneously seeking foreign—including American—protection.[86] Both insisted that Shanghai make the first move. They took the same line with R. Huntley Davidson, the director of the Shanghai Publicity Bureau, who was also in town that summer.

Back in Shanghai that September, Fessenden passed on to the Council's foreign members and to the leaders of British Shanghai the State Department's insistence on an outside study of the Shanghai problem. Meanwhile, Lionel Curtis, travelling through Shanghai on his way to the Institute for Pacific Relations's conference in Kyoto, told his fellow citizens that they must now whole-heartedly accept British policy towards Nationalist China and aid in its execution. When they in turn asked that they have a voice at the forthcoming conference, Fessenden was named to the American delegation. In Kyoto a few days later, he announced that Shanghai would call in outside opinion for advice.[87]

According to the published record of the Institute, a commission of "neutral and impartial experts" was to study the whole question of the city's future municipal organization. In practice, nothing quite so sweeping came to be. In the first place, the study was narrowed to the International Settlement alone; in the second place, Fessenden and the Council decided that they would prefer to deal with a single person rather than with an international commission. A commission would need British and American members, and must therefore also include Japanese. If the Japanese were there, the Chinese would want a voice; and if the Chinese were represented, the group's work would turn from investigation into political negotiation. Arnhold wanted Curtis to do the job, but Curtis pushed for Justice Richard Feetham of South Africa, who already had a reputation for studying problems in his own country and in Ireland. Curtis and Fessenden privately sounded him out by wire, pointing out that Chinese threats to abolish extraterritoriality made reform in the Settlement essential. When he agreed to come, a formal invitation was sent on 29 November 1929.[88]

The Foreign Office never liked the scheme, which they thought had been engineered by Lionel Curtis, and were upset that the State Department had given them no warning of it.[89] Eighteen months later, in the early summer of 1931, Justice Feetham finished his report, which subsequently appeared in three heavy volumes. It was a splendid piece of research, but unfortunately most of the information came from foreign sources. So did most of the opinion, which, equally unfortunately, gave foreign Shanghai exactly what it wanted. Page after page of fact—detailed, Gradgrindian fact—examined foreign accomplishments and Chinese failings in municipal administration, culminating in the recommendation that, although Shanghai must eventually come under full Chinese control, that step must wait until some impossibly distant future when Nanking had established a rule of law on an Anglo-Saxon model. American Consul-General Cunningham found it a splendid piece of work; so did the *North China Daily News*.[90] British officials—privately—had a different view. "The Mountain has produced a mouse," sniffed an observer in the Foreign Office. "It is perhaps fortunate that it is not a more impressive animal, for the odds were greatly against a proposal which would have commended itself to all parties."[91] Lampson recognized the political fatuity of the recommendations. In the midst of delicate negotiations to exclude the city temporarily from the end of extraterritoriality, he did not want British Shanghai stirred up about Chinese shortcomings.[92] Pratt simply threw up his hands. "It is difficult to understand how such proposals can be seriously put forward as a solution of the Shanghai problem. They betray a complete ignorance of the political aims of the Nationalist movement in China, and of its history during the last thirty years."[93] The Feetham recommendations were completely unrealistic, agreed Powell in the *China Weekly Review*; although it was true that a "benevolent foreign control based on real representative government" would serve the city's interests, the same could be said of Chicago or New York.[94]

The Feetham Report provided yet another answer to the Shanghai question: If Chinese control of all Shanghai must come eventually, that day must be postponed as long as possible. Feetham's work thus not only posed no threat to foreign Shanghai, but did much to back up its preju dices and to suggest that life could go on as usual. Despite the insinuation of Nationalist authority, the settlements remained privileged havens for economic enterprise, and in an uncertain and still divided China, Shanghai still seemed a good bet and a good investment. The Indian and London-based Sassoon interests had long been strong in Shanghai, with their background in the opium and textile trades. Sir Victor Sassoon, the new chairman of E. D. Sassoon and Company, looking for sanctuary from the British tax collector, moved millions of dollars from Bombay to Shanghai in the late twenties. Taking over the firm of Arnhold and Company and its Cathay Land Company, he invested heavily in real estate, and his Sassoon House, with its Cathay Hotel, became—and remains—one of the riverfront's landmarks.[95] Though the Great Depression badly hurt trade, money continued to pour in, and the Feetham Report's implication that foreign control would continue encouraged the already powerful land companies.[96] In 1931, British investments in the city reached perhaps £130 million, and by 1937, about £180 million.[97] By 1935, according to one estimate, land prices were triple their 1927 level, and Shanghai was said to boast the tallest buildings in the world outside Manhattan.[98]

Shanghai served Chinese enterprise as well, even though in the 1930s it grew more slowly than in the preceding decade. Yet, as recent studies have shown, for Chinese Shanghai the victory of Chiang's Nationalists meant neither the triumph of the Guomindang nor the triumph of the Shanghai bourgeoisie, and it is no longer possible to see Chiang as the puppet—or even the ally—of China's modern capitalists.[99] Chiang's new regime in Nanking sought to tame the once revolutionary proclivities of the Guomindang, and it tolerated and encouraged only those activities of Shanghai merchants and bankers that supported the regime and contributed to its treasury. In this sense, the Nationalists looked on Shanghai as a source of revenue to tide Nanking through its crises and as a port to bring in what it needed from the outside world. But the city was apparently prosperous. "Before Chiang Kai-shek marched in," wrote an American journalist in 1935, "one could have written the story of Shanghai without invoking the Chinese." Eight years after the Nationalist arrival, however, Shanghai had become a city of Chinese trading companies, mills, factories, department stores, modern public utilities, and above all, banks, particularly the Bank of China built by the able, Harvard-educated T. V. Soong.

Was this to be the model of China's future? Would it lead, the same journalist wondered, to a new China, bourgeois-managed and banker-financed? "Or is this another Russia, a land of peasants and proletariat, who, at some psychological point in history, will sweep the middle classes aside in a few bloody days, drive the foreigners from their dedicated land (for that is an allied issue) and dedicate their immense slice of Asia to themselves?"[100] How deeply had "one generation wonders" like T. V. Soong really changed things? "The government and the economics that he and other westernized Chinese have set up may be merely synthetic, and may never be able to reach down into the masses of China—the farmers, the peasants, the Good Earth." If Nanking failed, the Communists would win, sweeping the foreigner and his works from their precarious perch along the Bund; but if Nanking and its bankers succeeded, their intense nationalism would drive him out just the same. "The only difference being that in the one case he would probably be killed; in the other he would doubtless be given the opportunity to buy a ticket home."[101]

Nothing that the West could do, wracked by depression and faced with the dangers of Europe in the 1930s, was likely to change that ultimate uncertainty. Perhaps that is why Western Shanghai took such an ambivalent attitude toward Japan, an attitude that would contribute eventually to its downfall. In September 1931, three months after the Feetham Report appeared, the Japanese army attacked Manchuria, presently to turn the homeland of the Qing dynasty into a dependency of Tokyo. In late January 1932, a violent battle between Chinese units and a Japanese expeditionary force broke out in Shanghai, and once again large parts of Zhabei were wrecked in the fighting before an armistice was reached in May. Still, some of the influential leaders of foreign Shanghai, narrow-minded as ever, could not see how Japanese intervention had changed the rules of the game, could not see that from now on Japanese militarism, not Chinese nationalism, would be the real threat. Many foreigners, including some leading British and American businessmen, applauded Japan's actions and urged their governments to use the crisis to obtain an extension of the Settlement's boundaries, to force a solution, once and for all, to the outstanding grievances between the Settlement and the Chinese authorities. Cunningham dusted off the old plans for a municipality of "Greater Shanghai" virtually detached from Nanking's authority, and his British colleague suggested that British interests might benefit from a Japanese victory.[102] Powell, who got wind of the plan to turn Shanghai into a free city, claimed that it had been hatched in the Japanese Foreign Office and sold to the British and American real estate interests, who thought they would profit from it.[103] Both Lampson and Nelson Johnson, now the American minister, tried to point out the folly of such ideas. But the pressure continued, and in the elections to the Council in March 1932, those favoring an extension of the Settlement—the Japanese and the British—received the most votes.[104]

These events obviously go well beyond the scope of this work; the point is, however, that despite the Japanese attack on the city in 1932, there were still Westerners who thought of Japan as a policeman that would keep a disorderly Chinese nationalism at bay. As late as 1935, after a visit to Shanghai, the British ambassador to Tokyo expressed his surprise at the strength of pro-Japanese sentiment among his fellow countrymen in the city.[105]

In the end, of course, the forces that finally brought foreign Shanghai to an end came neither from Chiang's nationalism nor Mao's communism, but from Tokyo's aggression. After 1932, much of the International Settlement above the Soochow Creek became a Japanese preserve, subject in fact if not in law to the Japanese consul-general and the Japanese military. In August 1937, a month after Japan's invasion of north China, fighting again broke out in the city. At this point, claims for the Settlement's neutrality were meaningless. Not only did a Chinese bomb intended for the Japanese flagship moored in the Huangpu fall near the Palace Hotel on Nanking Road, killing a thousand people, but Japanese forces moved in to occupy almost all Hongkew and Yangtszepoo. Japanese troops and war material came ashore on the wharves of the International Settlement, and Japanese soldiers kept Westerners away from their properties in the Settlement's Eastern District.[106] The Municipal Council thus found its authority in practice limited to the area south and west of the Soochow Creek, while it desperately sought to stave off as long as possible Japanese demands for an increased role in the policing and governance of the Settlement.[107] In 1940, the British met a Japanese electoral challenge to Council by splitting properties to increase the number of voters and, in the largest poll ever recorded, managed to keep control of the Council in Western hands. A year later, however, after the British chairman had been shot and wounded by a Japanese at a special ratepayers' meeting in January 1941, the Shanghai Municipal Council gave way to a commission to look after the Settlement while a new constitution could be drawn up to replace the Land Regulations.[108] After eighty-eight years, the Land Regulations and the Council for which they provided thus came to an end. The new constitution never appeared. On 8 December 1941, just after midnight, Japanese troops moved across the Garden Bridge and occupied the Bund.

Conclusion

Chen Duxiu's prediction of 1927 that China would be Communist within two decades was not far off the mark. In May 1949, twenty-two years after Chiang turned on his Communist allies, the People's Liberation Army stood at the gates of Shanghai. Again the city's defenders promised an all-out resistance, and again, like Bi Shucheng's Shandong troops of 1927, they melted away after no more than light skirmishing. The first units of the Red Army entered the city on 25 May, moving up from Siccawei through the old French Concession. They advanced along the Bund (now called Zhongshan Road), meeting no serious resistance until they came to the Garden Bridge across Soochow Creek. Within two days, the Nationalist army was gone, and Shanghai was under Communist control.

In 1943, as a gesture of support to their wartime ally, Britain and America had formally ended the unequal treaties, thus giving up their claims to the International Settlement. Under Japanese pressure, Vichy's representative in Nanking had already returned the French Concession to Wang Jingwei's puppet regime, and on 28 February 1946, France joined its allies in renouncing extraterritoriality.[1] In the late summer of 1945, Westerners began to return to Shanghai, joining those who had survived the Japanese internment camps. They tried to put back together the life they had known before the war, but Shanghai was now a Chinese city. There were no longer any protected foreign enclaves, and firms like Jardine's and Andersen Meyer, papers like the *North China Daily News* and the *China Weekly Review*, now found themselves working under the eye of the Nationalists.

Though the rules had changed, victory over Japan nonetheless brought new hope. "Mark my words, this city is in for the biggest boom you can possibly imagine," predicted the American insurance executive C. V. Starr in 1946. "China may fail, but Shanghai will not fail."[2] Others were less sanguine. "Shanghai is a sick city," wrote another observer in early 1946. "It is a huge, bewildered patient that does not know whether it is going to get well or not."[3] Within a few years, Nationalist mismanagement and a wild inflation had proven the pessimists right. The collapse of Chiang's armies in the north brought a rapid Communist advance to the Yangtze Valley. In December 1948, as the decisive battle of the Huai-Hai was unfolding several hundred miles north of the city, the *North China Daily News* drew a parallel with 1927. Again there was talk of putting together an international defense force to protect foreign life and property—one of those who suggested such a move was Du Yuesheng, still active in Shanghai affairs.[4] This time there were no takers for such an obviously anachronistic idea. In 1949, some four thousand Britons remained to look after their country's still substantial investments in the city (estimated at about £107 million in 1947).[5] Most Americans, though, had left before the Communists arrived, worried that Washington's continuing support for Chiang would hurt them under the new regime.

Shanghai's liberation—or its fall, depending upon one's point of view— was met with resignation rather than excitement by its Chinese citizens. Even many foreigners were convinced that the city's plight could hardly be worse than it had been under the Nationalists, and no doubt some remained who thought, as an American reporter had said a few years earlier, that the Chinese would need Western help to make Shanghai work.[6] There were exceptions: The *China Weekly Review*, now put out by William Powell, the son of the former editor, welcomed the new rulers with an almost fawning enthusiasm, publishing what may be the first English version of "The East Is Red," the famous anthem likening Mao Zedong to the rising sun. This time, however, the American Chamber of Commerce agreed with the *Review* that the future looked bright.[7] The mood did not last long. After a brief honeymoon, the city government of Mayor Chen Yi began to crack down on the foreigners. Then came the Korean War, and by 1951 almost all the Westerners—save those whom the new rulers refused to allow to leave—had gone home.

To Chinese patriots and Chinese radicals, both Communist and non-Communist, Shanghai in its days of foreign rule had been an imperialist parasite battening off the country's body, draining its wealth for the benefit of foreigners and their Chinese collaborators. Yet it was also a city whose growth and advance seemed to point the way to China's future. Might Shanghai, under other circumstances, have played such a role in modern China? An unlikely expectation, Rhoads Murphey has argued; Shanghai, like the treaty ports in general, was simply an exotic growth on China's periphery that had little to do, for good or ill, with what was happening in the rest of China—the "real" China of market town and peasant village. Yet to Marie-Claire Bergère, this Shanghai was "the other China," real enough and important enough in its time, even if the forces that drove Chinese history after 1949 ultimately came not from Shanghai capitalists or Shanghai labor unions but from the Red Army and the peasant unions of the interior.[8]

These questions properly concern the historian of China, and today they are echoed in similar questions raised about the role Hongkong will play in the nation's future. Here, however, we are concerned primarily with what Shanghai has to tell us about Western history, about the history of Western empires and their decline. Let us, in summary, look at four aspects of Shanghai during this period.

First is its nature as a colonial community. To caricature foreign Shanghai is easy: Put together a few quotations from the *North China Daily News*, from visiting journalists, from other observers, and you have a picture of the Shanghai mind as Arthur Ransome and others did. This kind of Shanghai fits nicely into Albert Memmi's psychological portrait of colonization; Shanghai shared in the advantages of colonialism, meaning that "in a comparable position, a government employee earns more, a merchant pays fewer taxes, an industrialist pays less for raw materials and labor, than do their counterparts back home."[9] In Shanghai, where democracy was a memory of another clime, could still be found the kind of society of deference that was vanishing from Europe after the Great War. On the Bund, on Bubbling Well Road, or on the avenue Joffre, Englishmen and others could build an idealized home society of the past: Servants who waited on one hand and foot without talking back, and a people grateful for the virtues of the "Model Settlement" built by the energies and skills of the foreigners. Never before had communications been faster, newspapers more complete; yet foreign Shanghai remained in many ways as out of touch as ever with the changes taking place back home. There, Europe was faltering through an uncertain recovery after the First World War, and the real England worried about the rise of socialism, a Labour Party, and the great industrial disputes of the twenties.

Like Memmi's colonialists too, the inhabitants of foreign Shanghai often justified their position not by recourse to the language of the treaties (for many of their privileges had no basis in the treaties), but rather from the contrast they drew between their own virtues in governance and the Chinese vices that were so obvious in Chinese cities. They argued that the Chinese would do better if they were less interested in taking over the foreign settlements and more interested in trying to learn from them. "The shockingly administered Chinese municipalities lie round the International

Settlement and the French Concession," wrote a local British trade journal, "and stand as an object lesson of the failure of the Chinese to grasp even dimly what municipal government means."[10] Such a sentiment is less a reflection of racism (at least in its nineteenth-century, scientific sense) than it is a judgment passed on Chinese shortcomings, a way of attributing failures that sprang from China's political disintegration to Chinese society and culture as a whole. In that sense, it reflected consciously or unconsciously the kinds of judgments that Chinese critics, such as Liang Qichao and Lu Xun, had themselves assigned (and indeed still assign) to their country.[11] It was not true, as Chinese radicals charged, that Westerners were in league with warlords to keep China weak and divided, but it was true that Westerners used the phenomenon of warlordism to argue for the maintenance of the status quo.

Second, we must look at this episode as one in the history of imperial decline. Superficially, Shanghai survived the test posed by the Nationalist revolution of the 1920s. But in the end, because China was not a colony, there was no way of denying the legitimacy of Chinese claims to sovereignty. The day when China would assert control of what was hers, however, could be postponed as long as possible. For that reason, it was essential to maintain and to emphasize the gulf between Chinese and foreign Shanghai. The report of the Extraterritoriality Commission in 1926 (and particularly the speeches of its American member, Simon Strawn) underscored Chinese shortcomings, and the Feetham Report of 1931 stressed the distance China still must travel. Meanwhile, foreign deficiencies were ignored in public. It would not do to talk openly about Western arrogance, about consuls who traded upon extraterritoriality, or about the predatory nature of foreign lawyers and the abuses of the Mixed Court. It would not do to talk openly about the increasing grip of the underworld in the French Concession. Such phenomena must be kept private lest the Chinese use them as sticks to beat the foreigners. Just as French Shanghai worried that Anglo-Saxon racism after May Thirtieth would hasten the end of foreign privilege, so foreign Shanghai later worried that the scandal of French corruption after 1927 would bolster the Chinese claim that the very existence of the concessions was an incentive to crime.

Perhaps the need to postpone the day of reckoning explains why so little was done to prepare the Chinese to assume control. The existence of a cadre of Chinese administrators properly trained to run the settlements would have removed the justification for foreign administration and foreign privilege. Hence, few positions of responsibility in either the Concession or Settlement were open to Chinese, and it took May Thirtieth to get foreign Shanghai to allow Chinese membership on the councils.

When institutions as disparate as the National Christian Council and the Vatican sought to build up a Chinese Church under Chinese control, they were met with skepticism by many old China hands. Look at the scorn for the "uplift" element in so much of foreign Shanghai: If the uplifters were successful, what need would there be for foreign tutors?

Such was the Shanghai view. Yet, as the story of these years shows, the view from Shanghai and the views from its home governments were by no means identical. The myth of British imperialism remained very much alive in the public mind after the First World War.[12] British policymakers in London, faced with industrial disputes at home and with increased trade competition abroad, were far more realistic about the limits of British power and influence in the postwar world that were British Shanghai-landers. In June 1925, a general strike sought to paralyze Shanghai; but in May 1926, another general strike sought to paralyze Britain itself. Both failed, yet just as the first showed the rising strength of China's new radical nationalism, so the second revealed Britain's weakness, her slow recovery from the ravages of war, and her modern industrial decline. The landing of the Shanghai Defence Force in the winter of 1927, the band music echoing on the Bund and Nanking Road, perhaps masked that weakness. London, however, well knew that although the imperial trade routes remained important to Britain's economic well-being, they would have to be protected by means less expensive than the dispatch of armies and navies halfway round the world.

Nothing so dramatic happened in America, but Secretary of State Kellogg, worried as he might be about Bolshevism in Nicaragua and Mexico, knew that American interests in China were comparatively small. He knew his countrymen would not join Britain in any show of force and was thus deaf to MacMurray's pleas that America's interests and honor demanded she match Britain in the defense of Shanghai in 1927. A whole range of American publicists, from Protestant missionaries to men like J. B. Powell (who crowed with delight as he saw British trade giving way to American), called on their country to play a greater part in Chinese affairs. Yet neither American economics nor American political morals would allow the United States in those days to pick up the white man's burden and carry it as Britain had done before 1914. Like Alden Pyle—Graham Greene's "quiet American"—these new spokesmen for American interests wanted clean hands; they saw their country's role as a progressive one that would supersede the reactionary imperialism of the old world, and they assumed that the approbation given them by the Chinese educated at Harvard and Columbia spelled the approbation of all Chinese. Though no one mistook Chiang's triumph over the Communists in 1927 for Western democracy, his marriage later that year to

Sun Yat-sen's American-educated sister-in-law and his conversion to the Methodism of his bride were signs of hope that China would continue along the road of Western progressive Protestantism that Sun Yat-sen had set forth on in 1911. The term "neo-colonialism" had not yet emerged to describe the particular mix of economic, political, and moral influence that would supplant the old imperialism, but something like the phenomenon was at work as America tried to assist in the birth of a particular kind of new China.[13]

Third, we must consider the role of Shanghai in the formation of Western foreign policies. Though foreigners often confused Shanghai with China and the Shanghai question with the China question, Shanghai was in fact only part—and an eccentric part—of the greater problem of China. To the West, a rational China policy meant one that would allow the protection and expansion of trade and investment in China and (particularly for France and America) the freedom of missionary activities. If the old imperialist politics of coercion were no longer possible, it was then necessary to forge a new policy of good relations with all China, the hinterland as well as the treaty ports. To do so meant coming to terms with the new nationalism of the 1920s by meeting those aspirations that did not directly injure Western interests and that, in the long run, might even help with them. Hence, as Pratt never tired of pointing out, foreigners must be willing to do away with old privileges that were no longer useful, that sometimes were of questionable legality at best. Nowhere, of course, were those privileges more tenaciously clung to than in Shanghai.

Governments in Washington, Paris, and London knew they could not allow the narrow interests of treaty port foreigners to dictate China policy as a whole. Those whose interests did not extend beyond Shanghai—small merchants, real estate investors, lawyers, holders of Shanghai securities— were particularly jealous guardians of their privileges. But businessmen whose interests spread throughout large parts of the country understood that the China problem transcended the Shanghai problem and that they must deal with the new China. The lines dividing them were not always clear, and collectively they spoke with a loud voice. Foreign Shanghai lobbied for its local interests in London and Washington, through organizations like the Shanghai Publicity Bureau and the Shanghai Property Owners' Association (formed in 1927). National chambers of commerce mixed concern for a greater China trade with concern for Shanghai's special position. Lord Southborough's China Committee spoke for the great China trade houses but also defended the interests of treaty port residents. Missionaries, taking all China as their sphere of influence, often lobbied for a new order based on new treaties, but some in Shanghai, like Bishop Graves and Hawks Pott, were reluctant to jeopardize the safety of the institutions they had so laboriously built up. It was the consuls, like Barton, Naggiar, and Cunningham, and the ministers in Peking, like Macleay, Lampson, Martel, and MacMurray, who had to mediate between foreign Shanghai and its home governments and who might find themselves (as Lampson and MacMurray did) caught between their sympathies with foreigners in China and their loyalties to their governments.

China's disintegration in the twenties made more difficult the problem of devising a new policy. Europe's empires may have been wounded by the First World War, but the Chinese Empire had collapsed in 1911. Perhaps, as a historian has recently argued, the civil wars reflected a movement towards national integration that culminated in the Nationalist triumph.[14] At the time, however, they seemed chaotic and purposeless, the mere campaigning of selfish men for selfish gain. Part of the China problem for the outside world was thus to protect the foreign stake in the country and to keep it as immune as possible from the damage the quarreling generals were bringing to so much of China.

Finally, it is important to look at the role that Shanghai, with its foreign domination, played in the meeting of cultures. As China's new nationalism learned the language of democracy from the West, it lost its old awe of the West. Meanwhile, it took many of its analytical tools from the Marxist canon. Though by 1924 Stalin may have temporarily abandoned the vision of world revolution, deciding that socialism must first be built in the Soviet Union, Russia was as determinedly evangelical as the United States, and her missionaries found in China's new nationalism an audience that they could both exploit and assist. Rural poverty and peasant deprivation might be at the heart of China's plight, but the Leninist critique of imperialism as the last stage of capitalism was easy enough to adapt to China. The call to arms by both Communist and Guomindang propagandists taught China that she could not overcome her problems until she was mistress in her own house. One of the great accomplishments of the May Thirtieth Movement was to link firmly in the Chinese public mind the problem of "feudal" warlordism with the problem of capitalist imperialism. Each was greedy, and each fed off the Chinese people, both plundering them for their own selfish ends. Together they formed an unholy alliance, united by a common interest in keeping the Chinese people weak, poor, and oppressed.

Such a nationalism took as its very object the existence of cities like Shanghai. Imagine the psychological effect of the great structures on the Bund: The banks, the shipping companies, the hotels spoke of foreign domination. The physical presence of such buildings must have been a daily affront to those who lived there, a constant reminder of the arrogance of white Shanghai.[15] Yet the foreign settlements gave both Chinese businessmen and Chinese radicals a security that their own country did not provide. This city built by Chinese and foreign enterprise represented modernity both to the Communists who put their trust in the emergence of an urban proletariat and to the Nationalists who saw in Shanghai the source for the trade, the revenues, and the enterprise that would build a China safe from communism and in which foreign imperialism had been tamed.

Shanghai was a lens through which one got a distorted vision both of China and of the West. It encouraged both sides to sharpen their prejudices, seeing the worst in one another. If foreigners confused Shanghai with China, so, too, many Chinese confused foreign Shanghai with the West. To them, the exclusion of Chinese from the Settlement's parks mirrored white racism; the contemptuous attitude of papers like the *North China Daily News* mirrored the opinions of all Britons. To foreign Shanghai, the crime, disorder, dirt, and disease of the Chinese city was a perpetual reminder of Chinese incompetence in government. Chinese could claim, however, that Shanghai's divided jurisdiction made it impossible to maintain order in the city as a whole. They were both right. The opium traffic, for example, enjoyed Chinese protection in the 1920s and, after 1925, enjoyed French protection as well. Du Yuesheng's rise to power and influence reflected his French patronage, certainly, but Du enjoyed the patronage of the Nationalists as well.

Much was said in public gatherings during these years of cooperation between Chinese and foreigners about building a great city that would lead China into the modern world. The two sides certainly had common interests. How could the city be kept immune from civil war and disorder, for instance? In 1924, Chinese businessmen talked of foreign protection, and foreigners talked of an international landing force. Then came May Thirtieth, however. Had it simply been a labor dispute, perhaps Chinese and foreign businessmen would have joined to protect their common interests against a radicalism that threatened them both. The movement's leaders, however, made sure that it would become a patriotic crusade cutting across class lines. The arrogant refusal of the Municipal Council to examine its own shortcomings guaranteed that Yu Xiaqing's General Chamber of Commerce and the Shanghai bourgeoisie it spoke for would become the adversary, not the ally, of the foreign establishment, using mass nationalism to extract from the foreigners the concessions it wanted for itself.

In late 1926, as the armies of the Northern Expedition drew closer, both sides again wanted security. But after May Thirtieth, there could no longer be any direct Chinese appeal for foreign protection. Hence, on one side, an autonomy movement was launched by the Three Provinces

Association and their allies, seeking vainly to keep Shanghai out of the orbit of warlord politics; and, on the other side, there came the Shanghai Defence Force. Both sides, in effect, wanted one country with two systems, wanted for Shanghai a special sort of autonomy, like the kind that would be proposed for Hongkong sixty years later. After all, whatever role foreign Shanghai played in the great purge of the left, it had no more confidence in Chiang Kai-shek after 12 April 1927 than it had had before. Shanghai's Chinese businessmen may have briefly turned to Chiang in 1927 as a true nationalist, a leader who represented the best hopes of a progressive, modern China, a China that would end the humiliation they had suffered from foreigners; but it was very soon clear that their hopes would be dashed and that the general's vision of China's future was starkly different from their own.[16] No separatist arrangement for Shanghai could commend itself to Chiang. Whether Hongkong's future will be different remains to be seen.

So 1927 brought no new Sino-foreign alliance, and Chinese and foreign Shanghai distrusted one another as much as ever. But events had changed the setting in which they worked. The new Provisional Court, the addition of Chinese councillors to the Municipal Council and the *Commission Provisoire*, the disputes over taxation and over the policing of the extra-Settlement roads—these, and other facets of municipal administration, chipped away at the power the foreigners had earlier enjoyed. And China triumphed, though, paradoxically in immediate terms, it was not she, but Japan who—in her reversion to direct military imperialism in 1932 and 1937—would bring the old machinery of Western privilege crashing down in 1941.

In the end, Shanghai—the modern Shanghai built by foreigners and Chinese—was not to be the key to modern China, at least for the immediate future. To European Marxists, modern cities embodied the hopes of the future; to Chinese Maoists, they represented the dangers of the past. "This is a battlefield of a different type," says the stalwart political commissar Lu Hua, looking at Shanghai in a play about the city's liberation in 1949. The military enemy had been defeated, but the more dangerous spiritual enemy remained—the luxury of Shanghai that could sap the revolutionary will. "Either we fall here on the Nanking Road or we transform it." [17] Only now, more than forty years after the Communist victory, is the famous old skyline of the Bund at last giving way to modern buildings. Its changelessness during China's years of convulsion are proof that in Mao's years, at any rate, China's leaders believed that their country's revolutionary impulse would come from directions other than those set by the old treaty ports.

Today, Shanghai is changing again, spurred on by Deng Xiaoping's opening to the outside world. Again the foreign colony is growing; new office buildings and new hotels are rising in a city that now numbers close to 12 million. The city is building a subway and digging tunnels under the Huangpu to bring Pudong closer. Joint ventures with foreign firms—Volkswagen, McDonnell-Douglas, and others—are springing up, and both in Pudong and out near Honqiao airport new complexes of offices and apartment buildings hope to lure more foreign residents and foreign investors to the city. Is Shanghai finally to be transformed in a way that owes more to the vision of the 1920s than to the vision of 1949? The future remains uncertain, and the cities remain dangerous, centers of what the Party condemns as spiritual pollution and bourgeois liberalism. On 30 May 1989, sixty-four years after Everson's police squad opened fire in Nanking Road, the students of Peking erected a Goddess of Democracy in Tiananmen Square. Five days later, she was crushed by the tanks and armored cars accompanying the soldiers who shot their way into the center of Peking, ending the calls for democratic change in a horrifying massacre.

In Shanghai, protests, strikes, and demonstrations sputtered after the news reached the city that rainy Sunday morning. Placards and wall posters reminiscent of May Thirtieth went up in the streets, roadblocks halted traffic, students marched, and outside the Party headquarters in the old Hongkong and Shanghai Bank building, an angry crowd gathered to condemn the government's great massacre [*da tusha*] in the capital. In less than a week, as many foreigners boarded evacuation flights for Tokyo and Hongkong, the protests died down. Then, in May 1990, Shanghai unveiled in the People's Park a new monument to honor the martyrs of 1925—a huge, abstract representation of the character *sa* [thirty] towers above a stylized worker supporting a dying comrade in his arms. How long will it be before Peking erects a monument to honor the martyrs of 1989? The answer to that question could tell us much about China's future course and the role that Shanghai will play in it. Perhaps today's Hongkong suggests what Shanghai may become, an open city leading into the modern world that Deng has promised for the next century. Or does today's Shanghai presage the future of Hongkong, a city whose dynamism is an intolerable threat to China's rulers and that must be tamed?

Notes

Abbreviations of Sources used in the Notes

ABAC	"Action bolchevique à Changhaï"
AMAE	Archives de la Ministère des Affaires Étrangères
BDRC	*Biographical Dictionary of Republican China*
CinC	Commander in Chief
CinCAS	Commander in Chief, U.S. Asiatic Fleet
CRG	Li Yunhan, *Cong rong gong dao qingdang*
CWR	*China Weekly Review*
DBFP	*Documents on British Foreign Policy*, 1919–1939
DFZZ	*Dongfang zazhi* [The Eastern Miscellany]
F.O.	Foreign Office
FRUS	*Foreign Relations of the United States*
GMWX	*Geming wenxian* [Documents of the Revolution]
GWZB	*Guowen zhoubao* [The Kuo-wen Weekly Illustrated]
MAE	Ministère des Affaires Étrangères
MGSS	*Zhonghua minguo shishi jiyao* [Republican Historical Documents]
N.C.C	National Christian Council
NCDN	*North China Daily News*
NCH	*North China Herald*
PDR	Police Daily Reports (Shanghai Municipal Police)
RG	Record Group (United States National Archives)
SMA	Shanghai Municipal Archives
S.M.C.	Shanghai Municipal Council
S.M.P.	Shanghai Municipal Police
S.V.C.	Shanghai Volunteer Force
USCGS	Correspondence of the United States Consulate-General, Shanghai

USL   Records of the U.S. Legation, Peking
WJB   Waijiaobu [Chinese Foreign Ministry]
XDZB   *Xiangdao zhoubao* [The Guide Weekly]

Preface (pp. xi–xiv)

1. Charles V. Murphy, "Shanghai: Reopened under New Management," *Fortune*, Feb. 1946, 223.

Chapter 1, Introduction (pp. 1–15)

1. Great Britain, Public Record Office, FO 371 (Foreign Office, General Political Correspondence), F3897/19/10 Pratt to F.O., 30 Sept. 1924. All references to Foreign Office correspondence are to this series unless otherwise noted.

2. United States, National Archives, Central Records of the Department of State, RG (Record Group) 59, 893.00/8564 Gauss to Legation, 24 Feb. 1927. All references to the State Department Archives are to this group unless otherwise specified.

3. Good contemporary accounts of the war's origin can be found in F3897/19/10 Pratt to F.O., 30 Sept. 1924, and F3675/19/10 Macleay to F.O., 11 Sept.; see also George Sokolsky in the *North China Daily News (NCDN)*, 2 Sept. 1924, p. 11.

4. F3102/19/10 China Association and British Chamber of Commerce, wire of 9 Sept. 1924; F51/2/10 (1925) China Association letter of 29 Oct. 1924.

5. *NCDN*, 22 April 1927, p. 7, quoting the London *Daily Mail*.

6. United States, National Archives, Records of the Foreign Service Posts of the Department of State, RG 84, Correspondence of the United States Consulate-General, Shanghai (hereafter cited as USCGS) 1924, part 50, Grace High School to E. S. Cunningham, 1 Jan. 1924.

7. Harry Franck, *Roving through Southern China* (New York, 1925), 16, quoted in James Huskey, "Americans in Shanghai: Community Formation and Response to Revolution, 1919–1928" (Ann Arbor: University Microfilms, 1985), 21.

8. *North China Herald (NCH)*, 29 Nov. 1924, p. 351.

9. Zou Yiren, *Jiu Shanghai renkou bianyi de yanjiu* [Research on Population Change in Old Shanghai] (Shanghai, 1980), 14, 90.

10. Dick Wilson, *Chou: The Story of Chou Enlai, 1878–1976* (London, 1984), 84.

11. Zou, *Renkou*, 40–41; Thomas G. Rawski, *Economic Growth in Prewar China* (Berkeley, California, 1989), 80–81. Zou, *Renkou*, Tables 22 and 23 (pp. 114–15), have statistics on native place origin.

12. In addition to Zou's work mentioned above, the foregoing paragraph owes much to Gail Hershatter, "The Hierarchy of Shanghai Prostitution, 1870–1949," *Modern China* 15 (Oct. 1989): 463–98; Frederick Wakeman, "Policing Modern Shanghai," *China Quarterly* 115 (Sept. 1988): 408–40; Emily Honig, "The Politics of Prejudice: Subei People in Republican-Era Shanghai," *Modern China* 15 (July 1989): 243–374; Brian Martin, "Warlords and Gangsters: The Opium Traffic in Shanghai and the Creation of the Three Prosperities Company, 1913–1926" (Paper read at the Sixth National Conference of the Asian Studies Association of

Australia, Sydney, May 1986); and Bryna Goodman, "New Culture, Old Habits: Native-Place Organization and the May Fourth Movement" (Paper read at the Conference on the History of Modern Shanghai, Shanghai, Sept. 1988).

13. Mary Wright, *China in Revolution: The First Decade, 1900–1913* (New Haven, 1968), 3–23.

14. Arthur Ransome, *The Chinese Puzzle* (London, 1927), 29.

15. *NCH*, 30 June 1923, pp. 883–84; Nicholas R. Clifford, "A Revolution Is Not a Tea Party: The 'Shanghai Mind(s)' Reconsidered," *Pacific Historical Review* 59 (Nov. 1990): 501–26.

Chapter 2, Omnia Juncta in Uno (pp. 16–36)

1. Great Britain, Public Record Office, FO 405 (Foreign Office, Confidential Print [China]), vol. 252B, F472/472/10 Memorandum by J. T. Pratt, 6 Jan. 1927, gives a clear description of the distinctions.

2. For the origins of extraterritoriality, see Wesley R. Fishel, *The End of Extraterritoriality in China* (Berkeley, California, 1953), 5–11.

3. Richard Feetham, *Report of the Hon. Richard Feetham, C.M.G. to the Shanghai Municipal Council* (Shanghai, 1931), 1:40–41.

4. John K. Fairbank, "The Early Treaty System in the Chinese World Order," in *The Chinese World Order*, ed. J. K. Fairbank (Cambridge, Mass., 1968), 257–75.

5. John K. Fairbank, *Trade and Diplomacy on the China Coast, 1842–1854* (Cambridge, Mass., 1964), 445.

6. Hsia Ching-lin, *The Status of Shanghai: Its Future Development and Possibilities through Sino-Foreign Cooperation* (Shanghai, 1929), 28; F. C. Jones, *Shanghai and Tientsin, with Special Reference to Foreign Interests* (London, 1940), 5; F4829/25/10 Memorandum by J. Pratt, 20 May 1927.

7. Feetham, *Report*, 1:316–32.

8. Shanghai Municipal Council (S.M.C.), *Annual Report and Budget, 1926*, 2.

9. F3469/3469/10 "Memorandum on the International Municipal Government of Shanghai," 27 July 1925.

10. Feetham, *Report*, 2:169, has a detailed explanation of the process.

11. 893.102S/86 Cunningham to State, 20 March 1922.

12. F2776/194/10 Minute of 2 July 1925 by S. P. Waterlow of conversation with the American Mahlon F. Perkins.

13. 893.102S/151 Cunningham to State, 15 February 1929.

14. Fessenden to de' Rossi, 1 Oct. 1925, USCGS, 1925, part 61 (the Japanese figures do not include Japanese police); Manley O. Hudson, "International Problems at Shanghai," *Foreign Affairs* 6 (Oct. 1927): 81. Feetham, *Report*, 2:170, shows that there were 501 British in the police and 433 in other branches of the administration in 1931.

15. 893.102S/151 Cunningham to Washington, 15 Feb. 1929.

16. *Finance and Commerce* (Shanghai), 18 Feb. 1925, 90; 22 April 1925, 216.

17. 893.102S/151 Cunningham to Washington, 15 Feb. 1929, which encloses the report of the Council's Economy Commission, published in the *Shanghai Municipal Gazette*, 9 Feb. 1929.

18. Pie Nai-chieng, *Étude sur le Problème des Concessions de Changhaï* (Nancy, 1932), 37–45.

19. Figures drawn from S.M.C. *Annual Reports* of 1926, 1927, and from the

Conseil d'Administration Municipale de la Concession Française, *Compte rendu de la gestion 1926.*

20. *Revue du Pacifique* (Paris), Feb. 1926, 115–16.

21. France, Archives de la Ministère des Affaires Étrangères (AMAE) (Paris), Chine: deuxième partie, Wilden to Ministère des Affaires Étrangères (MAE), 30 Jan. 1924, vol. 336. All references to the French diplomatic archives are to this series unless otherwise noted. For the judgment on Fiori, see Wilden to MAE, 11 March 1924, AMAE, Asie: Affaires communes, vol. 55.

22. Wilden to MAE, 30 Jan. 1924; Meyrier to Legation, 20 Sept. 1925, vol. 336; see also Léon Archimbaud, "La Politique française en Chine," *Revue du Pacifique*, Oct. 1925, 1018, 1020–21; F5382/10/10 (1926) Minute by Strang, 1 Jan. 1927.

23. F2152/1516/10 Lampson to F.O., 18 Jan. 1927; see also J. B. Powell, *My Twenty-five Years in China* (New York, 1945), 153–54.

24. Great Britain, Public Record Office, FO 228 (Foreign Office, Consular and Legation records), vol. 3883, Barton to Lampson, 9 Feb. 1927.

25. Meyrier to MAE, 20 Sept. 1925, AMAE, vol. 336.

26. For background, see 892.102S/184 "Development of the Question of Chinese Representation on the Shanghai Municipal Council until the End of 1927," by Henry S. Waterman, 2 May 1928, 2–32.

27. Feetham, *Report*, 1:50.

28. Feetham, *Report*, 3:1–8; Jones, *Shanghai and Tientsin*, 30–31.

29. Feetham, *Report*, 1:90–110.

30. George Digby, *Down Wind* (New York, 1939), 21; Norwood Allman, *Shanghai Lawyer* (New York, 1943), 99; 893.041/78 Cunningham to State, 1 Aug. 1924, "The Administration of Justice in Chinese and Extraterritorial Courts in China" (written by Vice-Consul J. E. Jacobs).

31. A. M. Kotenev, *Shanghai: Its Mixed Court and Council: Material Relating to the History of the Shanghai Municipal Council and the History, Practice and Statistics of the International Mixed Court* (Shanghai, 1925; reprinted, Taibei, 1968), 176–77, 282; 893.041/78 Cunningham to State, 1 Aug. 1924.

32. F3873/220/10 Brenan to Lampson, 31 May 1931.

33. Quoted in *China Weekly Review (CWR)* (Shanghai), 28 March 1925, 93–95.

34. NCH, 24 Jan. 1925, p. 150; 7 Feb., p. 231; 7 March, p. 404; 2 May, p. 204; 16 Jan. 1926, p. 114; *China Press*, 14 Jan. 1926, p. 1; *CWR*, 28 March 1925, 93–95; F1648/106/87 Delevigne to Foreign Office, 7 May 1925.

35. Allman, *Shanghai Lawyer*, 115–16.

36. F472/472/10 Memorandum of 6 Jan. 1927 by John Pratt, and F4829/25/10 "Memorandum Respecting the International Settlement at Shanghai," 20 May 1927 (also by Pratt), give an excellent summary of the Court and its problems.

37. F4829/25/10 "Memorandum Respecting the International Settlement," 20 May 1927.

38. See Zheng [?] Chaolin, "Diguozhuyi de 'da Shanghai' mengxiang" [Imperialism's Dream of a "Greater Shanghai"], *Xiangdao zhoubao* [The Guide Weekly, hereafter cited as *XDZB*] 93 (3 Dec. 1924): 783–84.

39. F4829/25/10 "Memorandum Respecting the International Settlement," 20 May 1927.

40. Eric Teichman, *Affairs of China: A Survey of the Recent History and Present Circumstances of the Republic of China* (London, 1938), 151.

41. F3069/194/10 Minute of G. W. Moss, 16 July 1925.

42. Digby, *Down Wind*, 11.

43. David C. Wilson, "Britain and the Kuomintang, 1924–1928: A Study of the Interaction of Official Policies and Perceptions of Britain and China" (Ph.D. dissertation, University of London, School of Oriental and African Studies, 1973). There is a copy of this document at the Institute for Historical Research (London) and another at Columbia University, which Sir David kindly allowed me to read.

44. Cyril Pearl, *Morrison of Peking* (Sydney, 1967), 336; FO 228, vol. 3144, Minute of 7 July 1925 by G. Vereker.

45. National Archives, RG 84, U.S. Department of State, Records of the U.S. Legation, Peking, 1925 (hereafter cited as USL), vol. xl, MacMurray to Cunningham, 26 Aug. 1925.

46. F910/170/10 Mounsey to Lampson, 29 Feb. 1928.

47. *Shanghai Municipal Gazette*, 1927, 14 April 1927, 137.

48. *NCH*, 8 Oct. 1927, p. 55.

49. F2939/194/10 and F3469/3469/10 Minute by H. W. Malkin, 9 July 1925.

Chapter 3, Businessmen, Missionaries, and Educators (pp. 37–59)

1. The phrase comes from Marie-Claire Bergère, *L'age d'or de la bourgeoisie chinoise* (Paris, 1986), 69.

2. Rhoads Murphey, *The Fading of the Maoist Vision* (New York, 1980), 25–33.

3. For descriptions of the individual buildings, see Jon Huebner, "Architecture on the Shanghai Bund," *Papers on Far Eastern History* (Australian National University) 39 (March 1989): 128–65.

4. Parkes, as British consul in Canton and later minister to Japan, did much to advance Britain's Far Eastern interests in the mid-nineteenth century; Augustus Raymond Margary's murder in 1875, while surveying a route between southwestern China and British Burma, was used by the British to extract more concessions from China (the Chefoo convention, 1876).

5. *NCH*, 28 May 1927, p. 367.

6. *NCH*, 30 June 1923, p. 886; Lee Feigon, "Lurking in the Shadows: The Architectural Background to the Formation of the CCP in Shanghai" (Paper read at the annual meeting of the Association for Asian Studies, April 1987).

7. *NCH*, 5 July 1924, p. 18.

8. *CWR*, 22 May 1926, 320.

9. Zou, *Renkou*, 90.

10. *CWR*, 18 Dec. 1926, 58–59, has estimates of the numbers of Russians.

11. F1170/1170/10 Board of Trade, "Memorandum Respecting British Interests in China," 5 Feb. 1927.

12. C. F. Remer, *Foreign Investments in China* (New York, 1933), 395.

13. Speech to National Foreign Trade Council, 27 May 1927, in *NCH*, 13 Aug. 1927, p. 305; Cunningham to State, 12 June 1928, USCGS 1928, part 39.

14. F4546/1223/10 Barton to Legation, 20 Aug. 1926. Barton's figures are as follows:

Total land value in Settlement:	Tls. 336,712,494	(£56,211,327)
British registered in Settlement:	Tls. 282,394,408	(£44,209,283)
American registered in Settlement:	Tls. 20,424,927	(£3,191,395)
Japanese registered in Settlement:	Tls. 25,417,652	(£3,971,508)

<table>
<tr><td>Total land value in Concession:</td><td>Tls. 51,821,270</td><td>(£9,034,573)</td></tr>
<tr><td>British registered in Concession:</td><td>Tls. 29,170,000</td><td>(£4,557,813)</td></tr>
<tr><td>French registered in Concession:</td><td>Tls. 16,498,367</td><td>(£2,377,870)</td></tr>
</table>

Conversion at rate of 3s 1.5d = 1 Shanghai tael 1, or £1 = Sh. Tls. 6.40. The rate fluctuated but this represents a good average.

15. A. H. Feuerwerker, "The Foreign Presence in China," in *Cambridge History of China*, vol. 12, part 1, 194.

16. Sherman Cochran, *Big Business in China: Sino-Foreign Rivalry in the Cigarette Industry, 1890–1930* (Cambridge, Mass., 1980), 16, 165.

17. Viola Smith, "Incorporation of American Firms in China," in *China: A Commercial and Industrial Handbook*, ed. Julean Arnold (Washington, 1926), 139–40.

18. Smith, "Incorporation," 140–41.

19. Huskey, "Americans in Shanghai," 31–32; American Chamber of Commerce in China, Shanghai, Annual Report of the President, 1924–1926; *CWR*, 30 May 1925, 334–35.

20. *British Chamber of Commerce Journal: The Journal of the Associated Chambers of Commerce in China and Hongkong* (Shanghai) (Dec. 1928): 307–8.

21. Sherman Cochran, "Japan's Capture of China's Market for Imported Cotton Textiles before World War I: The Role of Mitsui Trading Company," in *The Second Conference on Modern Chinese Economic History*, Academia Sinica (Taipei), Jan. 5–7, 1989, 811–17.

22. Feuerwerker, "Foreign Presence," 196–97; for a good description of the way the system worked, at least for some of the British firms, see F5974/1530/10 Lampson to Chamberlain, 2 June 1927, enclosing a statement of the British Chamber of Commerce, Shanghai; a letter of C. H. Arnhold to Lampson, 23 May 1927; and a statement of various British firms to Lampson, dated 25 May 1927; also F5922/2230/10 Undated memorandum of 1929 by George Pelham. Cochran, *Big Business in China*, 21–24, tells how British-American Tobacco did it.

23. The foregoing generalizations apply to Western firms in Shanghai; for a very successful alternative approach by the Japanese, see Sherman Cochran, "Japan's Capture," 809–42.

24. Rhoads Murphey, *Shanghai: Key to Modern China* (Cambridge, Mass., 1953), 39–40; W. J. Moore, *Shanghai Century or "Tungsha Flats to Soochow Creek"* (Ilfracombe, n.d. [1966?]), 17–18. In 1932, work began on a deeper channel through the Fairy Flats, but onset of the war with Japan interrupted progress.

25. Murphey, *Key*, 46–50, 94–95; Lyman P. van Slyke, *Yangtze: Nature, History, and the River* (New York, 1988), 20. For a graphic description of the perils of the Gorges, see FO 405, vol. 252, F4519/1859/10 "Memorandum on Steam Navigation on the Upper Yangtze," by W. Stark Toller, 23 Oct. 1926.

26. *Finance and Commerce*, 30 June 1926, 305.

27. Feuerwerker, "Foreign Presence," 198.

28. H. G. W. Woodhead, ed., *China Yearbook, 1926–1927* (Tianjin, 1926), 610–12.

29. *Cornelius Vander Starr, 1892–1968* (New York, 1970), 9; Woodhead, ed., *China Yearbook, 1926–1927*, 610–12.

30. Mansfield Freeman, interview with author, August 1987.

31. *NCH*, 1 Nov. 1924, p. 189.

32. *China Stock and Share Handbook (1926)*, compiled by C. R. Maguire (Shanghai, 1926), 35.

33. Figures from Hsiao Liang-lin, *China's Foreign Trade Statistics, 1864–1949* (Cambridge, Mass., 1974), 23–24, 176. The Haikwan (Customs) tael was an accounting unit used by the Maritime Customs. In 1913, it was worth US $.73, or 3s ¼d sterling, and in 1923, it was worth US $.80, or 3s 5 ¾d (Hsiao, 191–92).

34. Much of the following material comes from F4749/4749/87 "Memorandum Respecting the Opium Problem in the Far East," of 10 Aug. 1929 by John Pratt; see also A. M. Kotenev, *Shanghai: Its Municipality and the Chinese* (Shanghai, 1927), 257ff., for information on the opium combine; Brian Martin, "Warlords and Gangsters: The Opium Traffic in Shanghai: The Creation of the Three Prosperities Company, 1913–1926" (Paper read at the Asian Studies Association of Australia, May, 1986; 893.144/144 Reinsch to Washington, 14 Oct. 1916; 893.144/155 Reinsch to State, 23 June 1917; 893.144/172 MacMurray to State, 26 Aug. 1918; 893/144/191 Reinsch to State, 2 Dec. 1918.

35. H. G. W. Woodhead, *The Truth about Opium in China* (Shanghai, 1931), 3.

36. Great Britain, Public Record Office, FO 415 (Foreign Office, Confidential Print [Opium]), F4398/330/10 Alston to F.O., 13 Oct. 1921; *NCH*, 21 Feb. 1923, p. 293; *NCH*, 23 May, pp. 315–16; FO 405, F535/144/10 Macleay to F.O., 17 Nov. 1926; E. C. Lobenstine, "The Fight against Opium," in *The China Mission Year Book, 1925*, ed. Harry Hodgkin (Shanghai, 1925), 330–44; Memorandum by Wilden, "Note sur la Contrebande? La vente et la consommation de l'opium dans la circonscription du consulat-générale de Changhai," 11 March 1924, AMAE, Asie: deuxième série, Affaires communes, vol. 55.

37. Wilden to MAE, 9 July 1923, AMAE, vol. 336; Conseil Municipal, *Compte rendu 1924*, 296; Shanghai Municipal Council, *Annual Report 1924*, 258.

38. FO 415, F942/238/87 Clive to F.O., 12 Feb. 1923.

39. Wilden to MAE, 28 Feb. 1924, AMAE, vol. 336.

40. Wilden to MAE, 21 July 1924, AMAE, vol. 336.

41. Wilden, "Note sur la Contrebande?" 11 March 1924, AMAE, Asie: deuxième série, Affaires communes, vol. 55.

42. Meyrier to MAE, 11 Jan. 1926, Asie: deuxième série, Affaires communes, vol. 56.

43. See F1648/1086/87 Delevigne to F.O., 7 May 1925; F3028/3028/10 Macleay to F.O., 2 June 1926.

44. The culprit was L. G. Husar; see *NCH*, 22 Jan. 1927, p. 114; 14 May, p. 302. For bribery in the Shanghai Municipal Police (S.M.P.), see E. W. Peters, *Shanghai Policeman* (London, 1937), 97–114; see also Brian Martin, " 'The Pact with the Devil': The Relationship between the Green Gang and the French Concession Authorities 1925–1935," *Papers on Chinese History* (Australian National University) 40 (March 1989): 128–65.

45. FO 415, F4749/4749/87 Memorandum by Pratt, 10 Aug. 1929; Y. C. Wang, "Tu Yueh-sheng (1888–1951): A Tentative Political Biography," *Journal of Asian Studies* 26 (May 1967): 433–55.

46. F279/2/10 (1925) Pratt to Macleay, 22 Nov. 1924.

47. F4749/4749/87 Pratt memorandum, 10 Aug. 1929; Wilden, "Note sur la Contrebande?"

48. *NCH*, 17 Jan. 1925, p. 34.

49. *NCH*, 21 Feb. 1925, p. 291.

50. Shanghai Municipal Archives (SMA), Shanghai Municipal Police, Police Daily Reports (PDR), 8 May 1925.

51. Dorothy Borg, *American Policy and the Chinese Revolution, 1925–1928*

(New York, 1947), 68; Remer, *Foreign Investments*, 308, 316; *CWR*, 30 Oct. 1926, 230–31, gives US $15 million as the amount spent a year, and about US $100 million in investment. G. B. Rea, complaining about the power of the missionary lobby, gives $150 million for total American investments, of which $80 million were missionary and uplift investments. He argued that for every dollar America took out in trade profits, it gave back two in charity. (Speech to the National Foreign Trade Council in Detroit, 27 May 1927, in *NCH*, 13 Aug. 1927, p. 305.) Cunningham's survey in 1927–1928 reported $14,927,093 in missionary investments in the Shanghai consular district, compared to $37,107,023 in business; Cunningham to State, 12 June 1928, USCGS 1928, part 39.

52. FO 228, vol. 3291, Letter from H. N. Bishop of the Church Missionary Society, Georges Dubarbier, "A French Criticism of U.S. Policy towards China," *CWR*, 1 March 1924, 12.

53. De Fleuriau to MAE, 24 April 1924, AMAE, vol. 257.

54. See Arthur R. Gray and Arthur Sherman, *The Story of the Church in China* (New York, 1913), 327.

55. National Archives, RG 263, Files of the Shanghai Municipal Police (hereafter cited as S.M.P. Files), IO 9121, report of 18 Feb. 1924. For the Missions Building, see the *Chinese Recorder*, 55, no. 7 (July 1924): 419–21. A biography of Rawlinson will soon be published, but unfortunately I have not been able to see it; John L. Rawlinson, *Rawlinson: The Recorder and China's Revolution: A Topical Biography of Frank Joseph Rawlinson, 1871–1937* (Notre Dame, Indiana, 1990), 2 vols.

56. Shirley Garrett, "Why They Stayed: American Church Politics and Chinese Nationalism in the Twenties," in *The Missionary Enterprise in China and America*, ed. J. K. Fairbank (Cambridge, Mass., 1974), 283–310.

57. G. B. O'Toole, "Work of Catholic Christianity in China," in *The China Christian Year Book 1928*, ed. Frank Rawlinson (Shanghai, 1928), 167.

58. Pascal M. d'Elia, *The Catholic Missions in China: A Short History of the Catholic Church in China from the Earliest Records to Our Own Days* (Shanghai, 1934), 58–60; Louis Hermand, *Les Étapes de la Mission du Kiang-nan, 1842–1922 et de la Mission de Nanking, 1922–1932* (Shanghai, 1933), 27–53.

59. Martel to MAE, 20 Jan. 1926, AMAE, vol. 253.

60. De Fleuriau to MAE, 28 April 1924, AMAE, vol. 257.

61. Cardinal Celso Constantini, *Réforme des Missions au XXe siècle*, trans. from Italian by Jean Bruls (Tournai, 1960), 58–67, 81–93; for French reaction, see Martel to MAE, 7 April 1925, and 27 April 1925, AMAE, vol. 253.

62. Jessie G. Lutz, *Chinese Politics and Christian Missions: The Anti-Christian Movements of 1920–28* (South Bend, Indiana, 1988), has the fullest treatment of the subject; see pp. 42, 64, for the effect of the *Christian Occupation*.

63. Mary Lamberton, *St. John's University, Shanghai, 1879–1951* (New York, 1955), 99.

64. John B. Hipps, *A History of the University of Shanghai* (Richmond, 1964), 63.

65. Quoted in W. B. Nance, *Soochow University* (New York, 1956), 75.

66. Nance, *Soochow University*, 76–77.

67. "La Vie tenace d'une université en Chine," *Revue des Missions* (1929): 61–76 (Archives des Jesuites à Paris [Chantilly], Fonds Chine, No. 2, Carton 51); *Aurora University, Shanghai: General Informations and Curriculum* (Shanghai, 1935), 1–4; Jon Huebner, "L'Université l'Aurore, Shanghai, 1903–1952," *Papers*

on *Far Eastern History* (Australian National University) 40 (Sept. 1989): 133–49. Howard L. Boorman, ed., *Biographical Dictionary of Republican China* ([hereafter cited as *BDRC*] New York, 1967), 2:472. Ma was also instrumental in the founding of the Catholic University of Peking [Furen] in 1925.

68. Peter Fleming, S.J., "Chosen for China: The California Province Jesuits in China, 1928–1957, a Case Study in Mission and Culture" (Ph.D. diss., Graduate Theological Union, Berkeley, California, 1987), 220, 535 n. 156.

69. *Shanghai zhinan* [Shanghai Guide] (Shanghai, 1926), part 3, 1–6; S.M.P. Files, IO 6953 and IO 7241.

Chapter 4, A Memory of Another Clime (pp. 60–78)

1. Great Britain, Board of Trade, *Statistical Abstract for the United Kingdom for Each of the Fifteen Years from 1913–1927*, Cmd. 3253 (London, 1929), table 281, p. 384. The figures do not include Hongkong.

2. *Shanghai Stock and Share Handbook, 1929* (Shanghai, 1929).

3. O. M. Green, *The Foreigner in China* (London, 1942), 8.

4. Barbara Walker, *The Donkey Cart: A Journey in Dream and Memories* (London, 1976), 76.

5. H. G. W. Woodhead, "Shanghai and Hongkong: A British View," *Foreign Affairs* 23 (Jan. 1945): 304.

6. "The Building of Greater Shanghai," supplement to *CWR*, 4 Dec. 1926, 29–31.

7. H. F. Wilkins, "Is Shanghai Outgrowing Itself?" *Far Eastern Review* (October 1927): 448.

8. "The North China Trade Review," Special Supplement to *NCH*, 17 March 1926, p. 29; see also, "The Building of Greater Shanghai," supplement to *CWR*, 4 Dec. 1926, 63, which compares land prices in Shanghai with those of some major Western cities; and "Shanghai's New Billion Dollar Skyline," *Far Eastern Review* (June 1927): 254–64. The *CWR* maintained that Shanghai land was not nearly as expensive as land in major Western cities. The most expensive land (on Nanking Road and the Bund) cost as much as Tls. 350,000 per *mou* (one-sixth of an acre), and it gave as comparable figures Tls. 1,200,000 per *mou* in London, 2,000,000 in Los Angeles, and 2,500,000 in New York, and even more in the Chicago Loop. The figures were based on an exchange rate of US $.72, or 2s 11d sterling for the Shanghai tael.

9. Georges Spunt, *A Place in Time* (New York, 1968), 71.

10. By the mid-twenties, his office at 44 rue Vallon had become the headquarters of the right wing of the Guomindang.

11. Spunt, *Place in Time*, 29–30.

12. Jean Fontenoy, *Shanghai secret* (Paris, 1938), 151.

13. *CWR*, 22 May 1926, 318–21.

14. Yu Dafu, *Nights of Spring Fever and Other Writings* (Peking, 1984), 18–19.

15. S.M.P. Files, IO 9121, report of 18 Feb. 1924. Presumably the reference is either to Wu Peifu in central China or Zhang Zuolin in the north.

16. *CWR*, 20 Nov. 1926, 317 (the member of Parliament was Colonel L'Estrange Malone); F5382/10/10 Minute by W. T. Strang, 1 Dec. 1926.

17. F2942/194/10 (1925) Undated letter from a Miss Arnold; F8053/2/10 "Impressions Gained in China" by Lord Gort, sent by War Office to Foreign Office, 12 Oct. 1927.

18. Ding Ling, "Shanghai in the Spring of 1930(2)," in *Miss Sophie's Diary and Other Stories*, trans. W. J. F. Jenner (Peking, 1985), 88.

19. Digby, *Down Wind*, 9.

20. Warren Cohen, *The Chinese Connection: Roger S. Greene, Thomas W. Lamont, George E. Sokolsky, and American-East Asian Relations* (New York, 1978), 73–85.

21. Edna Lee Booker, *News Is My Job: A Correspondent in War-torn China* (New York, 1940), 7, 20. Powell gives his side of the dispute in *My Twenty-Five Years in China* (New York, 1945), 11; see also *CWR*, 1 May 1926, 215–16; for the other side, see the *China Press*, 16 Jan. 1927, p. 1.

22. Powell, *My Twenty-Five Years*, 13; see also the entry on Powell in the *Dictionary of American Biography*.

23. Feetham, *Report*, 1:234. An incomplete list in the 1926 edition of the *Shanghai zhinan* shows 46 dailies and 110 other periodicals published in all Shanghai (sec. 5, pp. 5–8).

24. S.M.P. Files, IO 9121.

25. S.M.C., *Annual Report*, 1924, 57.

26. Enid Candlin Saunders, *The Breach in the Wall: A Memoir of the Old China* (New York, 1987), 36.

27. *NCDN*, 29 Sept. 1924, p. 16.

28. This was the impression of Harry A. Franck, *Roving through Southern China*, 1–2. See *CWR*, 26 Jan. 1926, 177–78, for a mild rebuttal by J. B. Powell.

29. *NCH*, 20 Aug. 1927, p. 350; *CWR*, 24 Nov. 1926, 367.

30. Huskey, "Americans in Shanghai," 11–13.

31. Janet Fitch, *Foreign Devil: Reminiscences of a China Missionary Daughter, 1909–1935* (Taibei, 1981), 194.

32. C. E. Darwent, *Shanghai: A Handbook for Travellers and Residents* (Shanghai, 1920), 120.

33. Quoted in Jonathan Spence, *To Change China: Western Advisers in China, 1620–1960* (Boston, 1969), 97.

34. W. E. Soothill, *China and England* (London, 1928), 80–81.

35. Wilden to MAE, 30 Jan. 1924, AMAE, vol. 336.

36. Christopher Cook, ed., *The Lion and the Dragon: British Voices from the China Coast* (London, 1985), 29.

37. Huskey, "Americans in Shanghai," 64–65, 173.

38. Arnold, ed., *Handbook*, 10.

39. *Écho de Chine* (Shanghai), 31 Jan. 1926, pp. 1–2.

40. It is unclear how far this was a Chinese and how far a foreign organization; it did, however, issue at least a few numbers of a Chinese periodical in 1924 (the *Chinese KKK Weekly*, or *Zhongguo san K zhoukan*). See S.M.P. Files, IO 5628, and a brief flurry of correspondence between Cunningham and the State Department in June 1924 under file 893.43.

41. Digby, *Down Wind*, 39.

42. *China Press*, 9 Jan. 1927, sec. 2, p. 2.

43. Quoted approvingly in *NCH*, 8 Nov. 1925, p. 255.

44. Hoover Institution, Palo Alto, California, Papers of Milly Bennett [Mildred Jacqueline Bremler], box 11, file 2.

45. Gladys McDermott to her family, no date (1922?); from a private collection kindly lent to me by Mrs. Virginia Molesworth, Mrs. McDermott's daughter; hereafter cited as McDermott letters.

46. *NCH*, 29 Nov. 1924, p. 351.
47. *NCH*, 15 Nov. 1924, p. 296.
48. Huskey, "Americans in Shanghai," 1–31, examines the process for the American community.
49. *NCH*, 7 March 1925, p. 394.
50. 393.11/343 Cunningham to State, 7 Oct. 1924.
51. Cunningham to Evelyn Marx, 18 Nov. 1925, USCGS 1925, part 79.

Chapter 5, A Tragedy of the Most Violent and Bloody Sort (pp. 79–96)

1. Anthony B. Chan, *Arming the Chinese: The Western Armaments Trade in Warlord China, 1920–1928* (Vancouver, 1982), is the best study of this question.
2. S.M.C., *Annual Report, 1924,* 36; *Compte rendu, 1924,* 289; Wilden to MAE, 18 Feb. 1924, AMAE, vol. 336.
3. S.M.C., *Annual Report, 1928,* 54.
4. This was Shen Xingshan; Martin, "Pact with the Devil," 96.
5. I. I. Kounin, *Eighty-five Years of the Shanghai Volunteer Force* (Shanghai, 1938), gives the dates and circumstances of the founding of the various companies.
6. Joseph Fewsmith, *Party, State, and Local Elites in Republican China* (Honolulu, 1985), 43.
7. Wilden to MAE, 18 Feb. 1924, AMAE, vol. 336; Naggiar to MAE, 10 Sept. 1927, AMAE, vol. 342.
8. Though the S.M.C. had no legal right to declare a state of emergency, its doing so had never been challenged. See F2953/156/10 Pratt minute of 22 March 1927.
9. McVay to Cunningham, 30 Aug. 1925; Cunningham to State, 6 March 1926; State to Cunningham, 26 May 1926, USCGS 1926, part 66.
10. Shanghai Municipal Archives, Council for the Foreign Community of Shanghai, Minute Book No. 35 (hereafter cited as S.M.C. Minute Book), meeting of 14 Jan. 1925.
11. For a good background, see F3897/2/10 Pratt to F.O., 30 Sept. 1924.
12. 893.00/5563 Cunningham to State, 25 Aug. 1924; F3654/19/10 Macleay to F.O., 7 Oct. 1924.
13. 893.00/5487 Bell to State, 30 Aug. 1924; 893.00/5495 Bell to State, 6 Sept. 1924; 893.00/5485 Bell to State, 30 Aug. 1924; F3654/19/10 Macleay to F.O., 7 Sept. 1924; F3675/19/10 Macleay to F.O., 11 Sept. 1924.
14. 893.00/5495 State to Bell, 7 Sept. 1924; 893.00/5498 State to Bell, 8 Sept. 1924; 893.00/5518 Bell to State, 12 Sept. 1924.
15. 893.00/5504 Cunningham to State, 9 Sept. 1924; 893.00/5588 Cunningham to State 10 Sept. 1924; *Compte Rendu, 1924,* 183; F3777/19/10 Admiralty to F.O., 10 Nov. 1924; F4011/19/10 (1924) Macleay to F.O., 7 Feb. 1925; Wilden to Legation, 22 Sept. 1924, vol. 231; *NCDN,* 10 Sept. 1924.
16. F3897/19/10 Pratt to F.O., 30 Sept. 1924; 893.00/5612 Cunningham to State, 13 Oct. 1924; 893.00/5750 Cunningham to Legation, 16 Oct. 1924.
17. F3897/19/10 Pratt to F.O., 30 Sept. 1924.
18. 893.00/5569 Cunningham to Legation, 28 Aug. 1924; 893.00/5561 Cunningham to Legation, 3 Sept. 1924; 893.00/5587 Cunningham to State, 8 Sept. 1924. On refugee figures, see F3897/19/10 Pratt to F.O., 30 Sept. 1924; F4179/19/10 Director of Naval Intelligence to F.O., 11 Dec. 1924.

19. *CWR*, 18 Oct. 1924, 220. For Xu, one of Duan Qirui's chief deputies and an important leader of the Anhui clique, who had fled to Sthanghai in Nov. 1923, see *BDRC*, 2:145–46.

20. 893.00/5753 Cunningham to State, 18 Oct. 1924; 893.00/5755 Cunningham to State 17 Oct. 1924; F158/2/10 (1925) Pratt to Macleay, 28 Oct. 1924; *BDRC*, 2:145–46.

21. 893.00/5753 Cunningham to State, 18 Oct. 1924; 893.00/5802 Cunningham to State, 22 Oct. 1924; F158/2/10 (1925) Pratt to Legation, 28 Oct. 1924; *NCH*, 18 Oct. 1924, pp. 94–98; *NCH*, 25 Oct. 1924, pp. 133–38, 140. A similar agreement of 11 November covered the troops at Wusong.

22. 893.00/5894 Davis to State, 2 Dec. 1924.

23. 893.00/5950 Cunningham to State, 31 Dec. 1924.

24. *CWR*, 14 Jan. 1925, 216.

25. Gladys McDermott to her family, 12 Jan. 1925 (McDermott letters).

26. *Écho de Chine*, 13 Jan. 1925, p. 1; 893.00/5979 Cunningham to State, 12 Jan. 1925.

27. 893.00/5938 Schurman to State, 12 Jan. 1925.

28. James E. Sheridan, "The Warlord Era: Politics and Militarism under the Peking Government, 1916–1928," in *Cambridge History of China*, vol. 12, part 1, 286; *BDRC*, 1:125.

29. 893.00/6053 Cunningham to State, 4 Feb. 1925.

30. 893.00/6087 Cunningham to State, 10 Feb. 1925.

31. 893.00/5567 Cunningham to Legation, 29 Aug. 1924; 893.00/5585 Cunningham to State, 5 Sept. 1924.

32. 893.00/5751 Cunningham to State, 14 Oct. 1924.

33. 893.00/5657 Cunningham to State, 25 Sept. 1924; F3897/19/10 Pratt to F.O., 30 Sept. 1924.

34. SMA, PDR, 10 Jan. 1925.

35. F51/2/10 (1925) China Association letter of 24 Oct. 1924, in Leefe to Waterlow, 1 Jan. 1925.

36. 893.00/5979 Cunningham to State, 12 Jan. 1925; 893.00/5938 Schurman to State, 12 Jan. 1925; 893.00/5943 Schurman to State, 13 Jan. 1925; 893.00/5950 Schurman to State, 16 Jan. 1925; 893.00/5952 Schurman to State, 18 Jan. 1925; 893.00/6063 Schurman to State, 29 Jan. 1925; 893.00/6096 Schurman to State, 11 Feb. 1925; F1166/2/10 Pratt to Macleay, 24 Jan. 1925; F1150/2/10 Macleay to F.O., 31 Jan. 1925.

37. 893.00/6096 Schurman to State, 11 Feb. 1925. See also 893.00/5099 Schurman to State, 6 Feb. 1925.

38. *Écho de Chine*, 4–5 Jan. 1925, p. 1.

39. 893.00/5750 Cunningham to Legation, 20 Oct. 1924.

40. 893.00/6053 Cunningham to State, 4 Feb. 1925.

41. F279/2/10 (1925) Pratt to Macleay, 22 Nov. 1924; Martin, "Warlords and Gangsters," 7–14, describes the relationships between the contending sides and the opium underworld.

42. F2304/2304/10 Palairet to F.O., 5 May 1925.

43. F4179/19/10 Director Naval Intelligence to F.O., 11 Dec. 1924.

44. *CWR*, 6 Sept. 1924, 6.

45. Wilden to Legation, 6 Oct. 1924, AMAE, vol. 231.

46 *NCH*, 8 Nov. 1924, p. 224.

47. *CWR*, 24 May 1924, 446–47.

48. F4327/19/10 Minute of 23 Dec. 1926.

49. C. Martin Wilbur, *Sun Yat-sen: Frustrated Patriot* (New York, 1976), 262–63; Lydia Holubnychy, *Michael Borodin and the Chinese Revolution, 1923–1925* (Ann Arbor, Mich., 1979), 443–57; *NCH*, 1 Nov. 1924, p. 180; *NCH*, 8 Nov. 1924, p. 224.

50. F3748/19/10 Admiralty to F.O., 8 Nov. 1924; F268/2/10 (1925) Macleay to F.O., 29 Nov. 1924.

51. S.M.P. report of 19 Nov. 1924, translated in "Shanghai gongong zujie gong-buju jingwuribao xuanze—yu guan Sun Zhongshan beishan bufen," [Selections from the Police Daily Reports of the Municipal Council of the International Settlement about Sun Yat-sen's Trip to the North] in *Lishi yu dangan* [History and Archives] (Shanghai), 1985, 45.

52. 893.00/5852 Cunningham to State, 18 Nov. 1925.

53. F167/2/10 (1925) Eliot to F.O., 11 Dec. 1924.

54. *NCH*, 13 Dec. 1924, p. 436.

55. *CWR*, 27 Dec. 1924, 99.

Chapter 6, China's Bastille (pp. 97–112)

1. C. P. Fitzgerald, "Mao's Cultural Revolution," *Nation* (New York), 9 Oct. 1967, 326.

2. 893.00/6007 Schurman to State, 5 Jan. 1925.

3. *Écho de Chine*, 13 Jan. 1925, p. 1.

4. Wang Jiagui and Cai Xiyao, *Shanghai Daxue: yijiu erer—yijiu erqi* [Shanghai University: 1922–1927] (Shanghai, 1986), 34–35.

5. S.M.P. Files, IO 6952, report of 29 Jan. 1926 by C. D. I. Givens; He Bingyi, "Diguozhuyi roulin Shanghai Daxue de zhuiji," [A Record of the Crushing of Shanghai University by Imperialism], *XDZB* 96 (24 Dec. 1924): 805–6. A Chinese translation of excerpts from the police report appears in Huang Meizhen, You Yuanhua, and Zhang Yun, *Shanghai Daxue shi liao* [Sources for the History of Shanghai University] (Shanghai, 1984), 13. See also S.M.P. report of 2 Dec. 1924 in "Shanghai gongong zujie gongbu jiu jingwuribao xuanze—yu guan Song Zhong-shan beishan bufen," *Lishi yu dangan*, 46.

6. FO 228, vol. 3140, Pratt to Macleay, 19 Jan. 1925.

7. S.M.P. Files, IO 7241, report of 5 Aug. 1926; Lutz, *Anti-Christian Movements*, 30.

8. Chaolin, "'Da Shanghai' mengxiang," 783–84; see also Peng Shuzhi, "Sun Zhongshan xiansheng li Ao lai Hu" [Mr. Sun Yat-sen Leaves Canton and Comes to Shanghai], *XDZB* 92 (19 Nov. 1924): 767–79. There are many articles alleging foreign backing of warlord armies.

9. SMA, S.M.C. Minute Book, meeting of 4 March 1925; SMA, PDR, 26 Feb. 1925.

10. Jean Chesneaux, *The Chinese Labor Movement, 1919–1927*, trans. H. M. Wright (Stanford, 1968), 254–55; 893.5045/50 Cunningham to State, 13 Feb. 1925; 893.5045/67 Cunningham to Legation, 2 April 1925; Fu Daohui, *Wusa yundong* [The May Thirtieth Movement] (Shanghai, 1985), 54–55; see also S.M.P. Files, IO XXX "General Strike May and June 1925 . . ." of 12 June 1925.

11. *NCH*, 14 Feb. 1925, p. 265; Fu Daohui, *Wusa yundong*, 46–60.

12. 893.5045/51 Cunningham to State, 20 Feb. 1926.

13. Chesneaux, *Chinese Labor Movement*, 254–55; Cunningham to State, 2 March 1925, USCGS 1925, part 80; SMA, PDR, 26 Feb. 1925; Fu Daohui, *Wusa yundong*, 36–57, covers the organization of the West Shanghai Workers' Club and its coordinating functions during the strike.

14. Chesneaux, *Chinese Labor Movement*, 256–61.

15. S.M.C. Minute Book, meeting of 19 Jan. 1925.

16. The report of the Child Labor Commission is in Great Britain, State Papers, 1924–1925 Session, vol. 15, China No. 1 (1925), Cmd. 2442; see also FO 405, F2142/2141/10 Memorandum by Pratt of 25 Feb. 1927.

17. *China Year Book, 1925*, 906–7; FO 228, vol. 3140 Pratt to F.O., 30 April 1925; S.M.C. Minute Book, meeting of 1 June 1925.

18. "Unanimous Opposition of the General Chamber of Commerce of Shanghai and Commercial Bodies to Resolutions III through VI . . . ," 29 May 1925, in USCGS 1925, part 61.

19. I am indebted to Jeffrey Wasserstrom for allowing me to read the draft of chapter 3 of his Ph.D. dissertation, "Taking It to the Streets: Shanghai Students and Political Protest, 1919–1949," which deals with the May Thirtieth Movement.

20. Fu Daohui, *Wusa yundong*, 68–77.

21. Ma Chaojun, *Zhongguo laogong yundong shi* [A History of the Chinese Labor Movement], vol. 2 (Taibei, 1958), 376–77.

22. Luo Suwen, "Political Influence of the Chinese Communist Party and the Kuomintang in Shanghai between 1920 and 1927" (Paper read to the Conference on Modern Shanghai, 7–14 Sept. 1988), 26.

23. Quoted in Fu Daohui, *Wusa yundong*, 82–83.

24. The account of the events of 30 May and later days are drawn from a number of sources. Most important are Hu Yuzhi, "Wusa shijian jishi" [A Record of the May Thirtieth Incident], in *Dongfang zazhi wusa shijian linshi zengkan* [*DFZZ*] [The Eastern Miscellany: Special Issue on the May Thirtieth Incident], July 1925, 11–24; Fu Daohui, *Wusa yundong*, 81–90; *Shanghai Municipal Gazette* 18, no. 980, 245–47; evidence given in the Mixed Court trial of 9–11 June 1925; evidence given at the International Judicial Inquiry, 12–27 Oct. 1925; Shanghai Municipal Archives, excerpts from the records of the Watch Committee, 1925 (which conducted its own investigation of the incident); and various accounts in the *North China Herald* and *Shen Bao* appearing over the next few days; 893.5045/158 Mayer to State, 3 July 1925, which includes the complete record of the investigation by the Diplomatic Body in Peking (also contained in F3917/194/10 Palairet to F.O., 6 July 1925); China, Ministry of Foreign Affairs [Waijiaobu] Archives (at the Academia Sinica, Nangang, Taiwan; hereafter cited as WJB), "Hu'an diaocha baogao" [Report of the investigation into the Shanghai case], 4 vols.

25. Darwent, *Shanghai: A Handbook*, 11.

26. Testimony of Captain Martin. Shanghai Municipal Archives: S.M.C. Watch Committee excerpts. Guo Moro, *Geming chunqiu* [Annals of the Revolution] (Peking, 1949), 2:214ff., has an eyewitness account of Nanking Road after the shooting, and the writer Ba Jin, who may well have been there at the time, describes the affair in his short novel *Siqu de taiyang* [Dying Sun] (the relevant passage is translated in Olga Lang, *Pa Chin and His Writings: Chinese Youth between the Two Revolutions* (Cambridge, Mass., 1967), 88–90. A Western eyewitness account is in Booker, *News Is My Job*, 196–200.

27. 893.5045/103 Cunningham to State, 1 June 1925.

28. F2230/2/10 Minute of 13 June 1925.

29. F248/13/10 Minute by Frank Ashton-Gwatkin, 26 Jan. 1926.

30. Hu Yuzhi, "Wusa," 11; Ma Chaojun, *Laogong*, 378; Chang Kuo-t'ao, *The Rise of the Chinese Communist Party, 1921–1927: Volume I of the Autobiography of Chang Kuo-t'ao* (Lawrence, Kansas, 1971), 426–27; Li Lisan, "Jinian Cai Hesen tongzhi" [Remembering Comrade Cai Hesen], *Hongqi piaopiao* [The Red Flag Waves] 5 (1957): 46–48; Fu Daohui, *Wusa yundong*, 90–91.

31. Nicholas R. Clifford, *Shanghai, 1925: Radical Nationalism and the Defense of Foreign Privilege* (Ann Arbor, 1979), 20–21; Hu Yuzhi, "Wusa," 11–12; *Shen Bao*, 1 June 1925, p. 13; "Nanjing lu zhi xue," [Bloodshed on Nanking Road] *Guowen zhoubao* (GWZB) [The Kuo-wen Weekly Illustrated], 7 June 1925, 13–14; Ren Jianshu and Zhang Quan, *Wusa yundong jianshi* [A Brief History of the May Thirtieth Movement] (Shanghai, 1985), 83–85; Fewsmith, *Party, State and Local Elites*, 71.

32. SMA, PDR, 1 June 1925.

33. *Di yici guonei zhanzheng shiqi gongren yundong* [The Workers' Movement during the First Revolutionary Civil War] (Peking, 1954), 73–79; Bureau of Social Affairs, City Government of Greater Shanghai, *Strikes and Lockouts in Shanghai since 1918* (Shanghai, 1933), appendix I, 18–26; 893.5045/104 Cunningham to State, 5 June 1925. There is a useful table of enterprises that were struck in Ren Jianshu and Zhang Quan, *Wusa yundong jianshi*, 100–105.

34. 893.5045/104 Cunningham to State, 5 June 1925.

35. S.M.C. Minute Book, meeting of 1 June 1925; 893.5045/60 Cunningham to State, 3 June 1925; 893.5045/121 Cunningham to State, 8 June 1925; 893.00/6847 MacMurray to State, 9 Nov. 1925; McVay to Cunningham, 6 June 1925, USCGS 1925, part 49; F2009/194/10 Palairet to F.O., 2 June 1925.

36. SMA, PDR, 7–8 June 1925; Cunningham to State, 3 June 1925, USCGS 1925, part 48; 893.5045/121 Cunningham to State, 5 June 1925; 893.5045/121 Cunningham to State, 8 June 1925. There were later reports of a Chinese Police Deserters' Union; see SMA, PDR, 18 June 1925.

37. Hu Yuzhi, "Wusa," 9–10; Wang Jiagui and Cai Xiyao, *Shanghai Daxue*, 38–39; *Di yici guonei*, 71; NCH, 6 June 1925, pp. 411–12; SMA, PDR, 1–6 June 1925.

38. Cunningham to State, 12 June 1925, USCGS 1925, part 48, has photographs of the posters; *Geming wenxian* [GMWX] [Documents of the Revolution], 18:3279–80; "Zhongguo gongchandang wei fankang diguozhuyi yeman canbao de da tusha gao quanguo minzhong," [A declaration of the Chinese Communist Party to the masses of the whole country against the barbaric and violent butcheries of imperialism] *XDZB* 117 (6 June 1925): 1075–77.

39. Hu Yuzhi, "Wusa"; 893.5045/121 Cunningham to State, 8 June 1925.

40. Qu Qiubai, "Guomin huiyi yu wusa yundong" [The National Congress and the May Thirtieth Movement], *Xin qingnian* [New Youth] 3 (25 March 1926): 9.

41. Ren Jianshu and Zhang Quan, *Jianshi*, 151–54; Deng Zhongxia, *Zhongguo zhigong yundong* [A Brief History of the Chinese Labor Movement] (Peking, 1949), 246–47; Chang Kuo-t'ao, *Rise*, 437; Wang Nianhun, *Wo guo xuesheng yundong shihua* [A history of our country's student movement] (Hankou, 1954), 25.

42. 893.5045/103 Cunningham to State, 1 June 1925; 893.00/5045 Mayer to State, 23 June 1925; F2685/194/10 Barton to Legation, 4 June 1925; NCH, 20 March 1926, p. 4; S.M.C. Minute Book, meeting of 2 June 1925; F5493/504/10 Barton to F.O., 14 Dec. 1926. For the role of the Chinese Chamber see Huang

Yifeng, "Wu sa yundong zhong de da zichan jieji" [The upper bourgeoisie during the May Thirtieth Movement], *Lishi Yanjiu* [Historical Research] 3 (1965): 18.

43. FO 228, vol. 3141, Barton to Legation, 4 June 1925; 893.5045/124 Cunningham to State, 16 June 1925; 893.5045/86 Cunningham to State, 12 June 1925. Mayer to Cunningham, 7 June, urged leniency; USCGS 1925, part 48.

44. The complete transcript of the trial is in 893.5045/147 Cunningham to State, 29 June 1925; the student was Qu Jingbai (Wang Jiagui and Cai Xiyao, *Shanghai Daxue*, 77).

45. S.M.C. Minute Book, meetings of 1–11 June 1925.

46. Martel to MAE, 25 June 1925, AMAE, vol. 329; F2106/194/10 Palairet to F.O., 6 June 1925; 893.5045/74 Mayer to State, 6 June 1925.

Chapter 7, A Danger to the Peace of the World (pp. 113–26)

1. *NCH*, 18 July 1925, p. 21.

2. *Écho de Chine*, 1 April 1927, p. 1.

3. *NCH*, 30 April 1927, p. 225.

4. *CWR*, 25 Dec. 1926, 86.

5. FO 405, F2596/2347/10 Macleay to F.O., 26 April 1926.

6. F4882/194/10 Palairet to F.O., 11 July 1925.

7. English text of the seventeen demands in *NCH*, 13 June 1925, p. 413; Chinese text in *GMWX*, 3289–92.

8. WJB, Hu'an diaocha baogao, contains the complete report. Vol. 1 summarizes the activities of Cai and Zeng; see also WJB, Hu'an: yu Hu'an diaochayuan Zeng cizhang Cai duban laidian [Shanghai case: telegrams from the Shanghai investigation members Vice-Minister Zeng and Commissioner Cai], vol. 1. Reports of the meetings can also be found in *Shen Bao*, 8–10 June 1925; and Kong Lingjing, *Wusa waijiao shi* [A Diplomatic History of the May Thirtieth Movement] (Shanghai, 1946), 26.

9. "Commission envoyée à Shanghai par décision du 6 juin 1925: négociations avec les délégués chinois avec 13 annexes," dated 25 June 1925, has the complete report of the Tripier commission's investigations. It can be found in F3917/194/10 Palairet to F.O., 6 July 1925, which includes a memorandum by George Vereker, the British member; and in 893.5045/158 Mayer to State, 3 July 1925, which includes a memorandum by Elbridge Gerry Greene, the American member. Appendix III has the statements of McEuen and Fessenden.

10. SMA, PDR, 12 June 1925; *Shen Bao*, 12 June 1925, p. 11.

11. SMA, PDR, 11 June 1925; WJB, Cai to WJB, two wires received 11 June, Hu'an: yu Hu diaochayuan, vol. 1; Xu Yuan to WJB, received 11 June, Hu'an: yu Hu tepaiyuan lai dian [The Shanghai case: telegrams from the Special Commissioner in Shanghai], vol. 1; *GMWX*, 3296.

12. *NCH*, 20 June 1925, p. 464; *GMWX*, 3293.

13. SMA, PDR, 12 June 1925; *Shen Bao*, 12 June 1925, p. 11, and 13 June, p. 9. A Communist writer, however, later denounced such statements as lies. See Zheng[?] Chaolin, "Diguozhuyi tiedixia de Zhongguo" [China under the iron heel of imperialism], *XDZB* 119 (22 June 1925): 1099; also Chesneaux, *Chinese Labor Movement*, 267.

14. *Shen Bao*, 18 June 1925, p. 13. Nevertheless, when Peking adopted the revised demands ten days later, the Federation declared its support (*Shen Bao*, 28 June, p. 13).

15. *NCH*, 13 June 1925, p. 413, and 20 June, p. 464.

16. "Commission envoyée à Shanghai" and Hu'an diaocha baogao, vol. 3, give details from the sides of the two investigating teams. Other contemporary accounts may be found in *Shen Bao*, 17–19 June 1925; the foreign press had little to say.

17. United States, Department of State, *Foreign Relations of the United States, 1925*, vol. 1 (Washington, 1940) (series cited hereafter as *FRUS*); 793.0093 D 34/187 bis Cerruti to Mayer, 26 June 1925, 670–72; 893.5045/164 Mayer to State, 3 July 1925; F2597/194/10 Palairet to F.O., 19 June 1925; *GMWX*, 3301–4.

18. Chen Duxiu, "Women ruhe ying fu cici yundong de xin jumian" [How we ought to deal with the new situation in this movement], *XDZB* 120 (2 July 1925): 1104–5.

19. For Hankou, see F3694/194/10 Palairet to F.O., 23 June 1925; for Jiujiang, F3899/1984/10 Palairet to F.O., 27 June 1925; for Jinjiang, F3683/194/10 Palairet to F.O., 17 June 1925; for Xiamen, F3897/194/10 Palairet to F.O., 29 June 1925; and Sir Meyrick Hewlett, *Forty Years in China* (London, 1943), 153–79. A contemporary Chinese version can be found in "Bolan," *GWZB*, 21 June 1925, 12–13.

20. David Wilson, "Britain and the Kuomintang," 216–23, examines the evidence carefully but reaches no final conclusions.

21. Chiang Kai-shek to Galen, 26 June 1925, Document 7, in C. Martin Wilbur and Julie Lien-ying How, eds., *Missionaries of Revolution: Soviet Advisers and Nationalist China, 1920–1927* (Cambridge, 1989), 502.

22. Clifford, *Shanghai, 1925*, 37–38; F2690/194/10 Palairet to F.O., 30 June 1925; 893.5045/108 Mayer to State, 2 July 1925; *Séances du corps diplomatique, Année 1925*, USL, vol. 19, meetings of 22 and 30 June 1925, 1 July 1925, 581–92; FO 228, vol. 3150, Minute of Vereker, 23 Sept. 1925.

23. *NCH*, 13 June 1925, p. 1.

24. *British Chamber of Commerce Journal*, June–August 1925, 170.

25. F3914/194/10 Palairet to F.O., 5 July 1925.

26. F2855/2/10 Palairet to F.O., 26 June 1925. G. B. Vereker, however, the British representative on the Tripier commission, also wanted another investigation; FO 228, vol. 3143, Minute of 25 June.

27. F2821/194/10 Barton to Legation, 2 July 1925.

28. FO 228, vol. 3143, Barton to Legation, 28 June 1925; F2891/194/10 Barton to Legation, 4 July 1925.

29. FO 228, vol. 3144, F.O. to Palairet, 5 July 1925.

30. Martel to MAE, 4 July, 6 July, 9 July 1925, AMAE, vol. 184.

31. S.M.C. Minute Book, meetings of 4, 5, and 6 July 1925; Fessenden to de'Rossi, 6 July 1925, USCGS 1925, part 49.

32. F2841/194/10 Minute of 3 July 1925. Waterlow was probably the least sympathetic to Shanghai of the Foreign Office's advisers.

33. Martel to MAE, 9 July 1925, AMAE, vol. 184; 893.5045/118 Mayer to State, 9 July 1925; F2982/194/10 Palairet to F.O., 8 July 1925; F4882/193/10 Palairet to F.O., 11 July 1925; FO 228, vol. 3144, Palairet to Barton, 8 July 1925; *Séances du C.D.*, meeting of 8 July 1925, USL 1925, vol. 19, 605–14.

34. FO 228, vol. 3144, Barton to Legation, 11 July 1925.

35. *Séances du C.D.*, meeting of 13 July 1925, USL 1925, vol. 19, 628–32; FO 228, vol. 3144, minutes of 12 July 1925 by Fox and Palairet.

36. For Martel's proposal, see Martel to MAE, 9 July 1925, AMAE, vol. 184; 893.5045/127 Mayer to State, 10 July 1925. For Washington and London, 893.5045/127 State to Mayer, 13 July 1925; 893.5045/133 Houghton to State, 14 July 1925;

F3069/194/10 F.O. to Palairet, 13 July 1925; 893.5045/168 Memorandum by Johnson of 16 July 1925; Fleuriau to MAE, 16 July 1925, AMAE, vol. 329.

37. *Le Temps* (Paris), 5 July 1925, p. 2; *New York Times*, 10 July 1925, p. 11, 11 July, p. 3, 20 July, p. 5, 23 August, sec. 2, p. 5.

38. "Waijiaotuan polie zhi neimu" [The inner curtain of the Diplomatic Body torn aside], *GWZB*, 19 July 1925, 5–12; "Wusa can'an zhi Beijing jiaoshe" [The negotiations in Peking about the May Thirtieth tragedy], *DFZZ*, 25 July 1925, 1–3. *Minguo ribao*, the Guomindang paper, more accurately saw Barton as villain and Palairet and Vereker as backing the Diplomatic Body; 893.5045/236 MacMurray to State, 28 Aug. 1925.

39. Martel to MAE, 6 July, 9 July 1925, AMAE, vol. 184.

40. Martel to MAE, 9 July 1925, AMAE, vol. 184; Palairet agreed that MacMurray had at first seemed to be unwilling to back up his ministerial colleagues against Shanghai but soon corrected the impression. F4882/194/10 Palairet to F.O., 11 July 1925.

41. Martel to MAE, 31 July 1925, AMAE, vol. 329.

42. "Pour flatter à notre profit le sentiment populaire chinois," MAE to Martel, 23 July 1925, AMAE, vol. 329.

43. *NCDN*, 20 July 1925; on 2 August Martel told the press that British newspapers were wrong in accusing the French of playing their own game; *NCDN*, 3 Aug. 1925.

44. Martel to MAE, 25 June, 1 July 1925, AMAE, vol. 197.

45. F4325/194/10 Department of Overseas Trade to Foreign Office, 1 Sept. 1925, enclosing Brett to Chamberlain, 24 July.

46. F3067/194/10 F.O. to Palairet, 11 July 1925; F3109/194/10 Palairet to F.O., 13 July 1925; 893.5045/136 Houghton to State, 17 July 1925; 893.5045/159 Sterling to Kellogg, 20 July 1925.

47. F3310/194/10 Palairet to F.O., 20 July 1925.

48. Clifford, *Shanghai, 1925*, 46–47.

49. Zhu Zhaoxin to WJB, received 17 July, in Hu'an: zhu Ying Zhu daibiao lai dian [The Shanghai case: telegrams received from Minister Zhu in England], vol. 2; WJB to Zhu, 5 Aug., in Hu'an: yu zhuwai geshi dian [The Shanghai case: telegrams exchanged with various representatives abroad], vol. 1.

50. Clifford, *Shanghai, 1925*, 46; the Chamber's denunciation is in 893.00/6712 MacMurray to State, 22 Sept. 1925.

51. *NCH*, 8 Aug. 1925, p. 113, and 15 Aug., p. 188.

52. Though Macleay and other experts home on leave (perhaps including Pratt?) seem to have agreed that the Diplomatic Body's recommendations ought to be followed. Great Britain, Public Record Office, Cabinet Office, Cabinet minutes (CAB23), Cabinet 34 (25) of 6 July 1925, enclosed in F3031/194/10.

53. Great Britain, Parliamentary Debates, House of Commons, 5th series, vol. 185, col. 922 (18 July 1925).

54. Banque Russo-Asiatique, Shanghai, to Paris Office, undated (July 1925), AMAE, vol. 329.

55. F3229/194/10 Alfred Holt and Co. to Chamberlain, 16 July 1925; F3436/194/10 Letter to Chamberlain from various representatives of China houses, 24 July 1925.

56. *Écho de Chine*, 5 June 1925, pp. 1, 7–8, and 26 June, p. 1; Frochot to Naval Minister, 13 July 1925, AMAE, vol. 185.

57. F3974/194/10 Chamberlain to Zhu Zhaoxin, 22 Aug. 1925.
58. *Séances du C.D.*, meeting of 25 Sept. 1925, USL 1925, vol. 19, 689–95; *NCH*, 10 Oct. 1925, p. 41. Chinese text in *GWZB*, 11 Oct. 1925, 39–40.
59. *DFZZ*, 10 Oct. 1925, 2–3; *GWZB*, 11 Oct. 1925, 1–3, 18.

Chapter 8, Whom the Gods Wish to Destroy (pp. 127–43)

1. 893.5045/188 MacMurray to State, 20 Aug. 1925.
2. McVay to Cunningham, 6 June 1925, USCGS 1925, part 49.
3. Archives of the Episcopal Church (Austin, Texas): Papers of the Rev. F. L. Hawks Pott, for Pott's "The Flag Incident," 2 June 1925; "Recent Events in China in Relation to Christian Education," RG 79–11; Papers of the Rt. Rev. F. R. Graves Papers, RG 64–114, Graves to Wood, 4 June 1925, 10 June, 19 June, 24 June, 2 July; also 893.5045/121 Cunningham to State, 8 July 1925.
4. 893.00/6493 Cunningham to Mayer, 18 June 1925.
5. 893.00/6032 John R. Mott to Coolidge, 22 June 1925.
6. See *NCH*, 25 July 1925, p. 45, and 1 Aug., p. 93. The *NCH* accused the N.C.C. of allowing itself to be used by Chinese propagandists.
7. See, for instance, the missionary correspondence in 892.5045/160 Mayer to State, 2 July 1925.
8. Graves to Wood, 4 June 1925, RG 64–114.
9. Graves to Lobenstine, 9 June 1925; Graves to Wood, 19 June, 24 June, 2 July, 7 July, Graves Papers, RG 64–114.
10. Hipps, *University of Shanghai*, 68.
11. Correspondence between Powell, Cunningham, Adm. McVay, 6 June through 20 July 1925, USCGS 1925, part 49.
12. 893.00B/182 Cunningham to Legation, 11 Aug. 1925; S.M.C. Minute Book, meeting of 29 June 1925.
13. SMA, PDR, 15 June 1925.
14. "Shanghai tanpan tingdun hou zhi wusa shijian" [The May 30th affair after the break off of the Shanghai negotiations], *GWZB*, 28 June 1925, 10; Huang Yifeng, "Da zichan jieji," 20.
15. The joint statement is in Liang Xin, *Guochi shiyao* [A history of national shame] (Shanghai, 1931), 247–48.
16. Qu Qiubai, "Diguozhuyi zhi wusa tusha yu Zhongguo de guomin geming" [The imperialist butchery of May Thirtieth, and China's national revolution], *XDZB* 119 (22 June 1925): 1095–98.
17. According to Sherman Cochran, the ¥100,000 contributed by Nanyang represented about 12 percent of the total that the strikers received from all sources during the May Thirtieth Movement. British sources estimated that there were thousands of agitators on Nanyang's payroll. Cochran, *Big Business in China*, 176–77; F4325/194/10 Brett to Chamberlain, 24 July 1925.
18. Tang Youren, "Dui Ying jingji juejiao" [A rupture of economic relations with Britain], *Shanghai zongshanghui yuebao* [Shanghai General Chamber of Commerce Monthly] 5, no. 6 (June 1925): 1–19, the letter from the Peking professors is in no. 9 (Sept. 1925); "Falü shang zhi wusa shijian guan" [A legal view of the May Thirtieth affair], *GWZB*, 21 June 1925, 3.
19. FO 228, vol. 3144, Barton to Palairet, 7 July 1925.

20. Figures drawn from *British Chamber of Commerce Journal*, June–August 1925, 191.

21. Great Britain, *Statistical Abstract for the United Kingdom for each of the fifteen years from 1913–1927* (London, 1929), table 281, p. 384.

22. The Asiatic Petroleum Company's view is in F2455/194/10 Macleay to Waterlow, 22 June 1925; for more general estimates on trade in 1925, see F710/285/10 George to F.O., 17 Jan. 1926; F1588/1426/10 Undated memorandum of 1926, "Present Trade Situation in China"; see also *British Chamber of Commerce Journal*, Feb. 1926, 36.

23. Akira Iriye, *After Imperialism: The Search for a New Order in the Far East, 1921–1931* (Cambridge, Mass., 1965), 67.

24. Martel to MAE, 18 June 1925, AMAE, vol. 189.

25. F4818/194/10 Palairet to F.O., 14 Aug. 1925; FO 228, vol. 3142, Barton to Legation, 20 June 1925; 893.5045/155 Cunningham to State, 10 July 1925; 893.5045/176 Cunningham to State, 16 July 1925; 893.5045/178 Cunningham to State, 17 July 1925.

26. McVay to Cunningham, 6 July 1925, 3 August, USCGS 1925, part 49; S.M.C. Minute Book, meeting of 6 July 1925.

27. 893.5045/155 Cunningham to State, 6 July 1925; Police Report for July, *NCH*, 22 Aug. 1925, p. 213; Xu Yuan to WJB, received 2 July 1925, in Hu'an: yu Hu tepaiyuan, vol. 1; 893.5945/178 Cunningham to State, 22 July 1925, for Xu Yuan's offer.

28. FO 228, vol. 3146, Vereker minute of 14 July 1925; USL 1925, vol. 32, Cunningham to Legation, 30 Sept. 1925; FO 228, vol. 3147, Barton to Legation, 19 Oct. 1925.

29. Yu Xiaqing to Finance Ministry, in WJB, Hu'an: Yu Hede lai dian [The Shanghai case: telegrams received from Yu Hede (Yu Xiaqing)], telegrams received 7, 13, 14, 16, 17, 19 July 1925; F3281/194/10 Palairet to F.O., 18 July 1925; FO 228, vol. 3146, Barton to Legation, 16 July, Palairet to Barton, 14 July 1925; 893.5045/178 Cunningham to State, 22 July 1925; *NCDN*, 21, 22, and 27 July 1925; *Manchester Guardian*, 22 July 1925, p. 12.

30. SMA, PDR, 25–29 July 1925.

31. Clifford, *Shanghai, 1925*, 59–60; F4818/194/10 Palairet to F.O., 14 Aug. 1925.

32. FO 228, vol. 3147, Barton to Legation, 27 July 1925.

33. Yu Xiaqing to Finance Ministry, received 21 Aug. 1925, in Hu'an: Yu Hede lai dian; *CWR*, 29 Aug. 1925, 263.

34. G-2 report 5609, "Present Situation in China," 14 Sept. 1925, USL, Peking 1925, vol. 32; *CWR*, 29 Aug. 1925, 263.

35. S.M.C. Minute Book, meeting of 13 Aug. 1925; 893.5045/217 Cunningham to State, 14 Aug. 1925, made the point that the refusal put the British in a difficult position and raised the prospect of an alliance between Chinese and Japanese mill owners.

36. F5103/194/10 Barton to F.O., 9 Sept. 1925; F5829/194/10 Barton to Legation, 7 Oct. 1925; S.M.C. Minute Book, meeting of 19 Aug. 1925.

37. *NCH*, 19 Sept. 1925, p. 406.

38. *NCDN*, 12 Sept. 1925, p. 6.

39. S.M.C. Minute Book, meetings of 31 July, 4 Aug. 1925.

40. S.M.C. Minute Book, meeting of 4 Aug. 1925.

41. F5390/348/10 Barton to Legation, 7 Sept. 1925; *British Chamber of Commerce Journal*, Sept. 1925, 223–24.

42. See, for instance, *Finance and Commerce*, 9 Sept. 1925, 125, and 14 Oct., 185; 893.00/6590 MacMurray to State, 9 Sept. 1925.

43. Yu's public statement is in F5390/348/10; his wire of 1 Sept. to Peking is in Hu'an: Yu Hede lai dian.

44. PDR, 28 July 1925, 31 July, 13 Aug., 23 Aug., 24 Aug. in USCGS 1925, part 52; Brian Martin, "The Green Gang and 'Party Purification' in Shanghai: Green Gang–Kuomintang Relations, 1926–1927" (Paper read at the Symposium on the Nanking Decade, Australia National University, 1983), 19. Worst of all, Li was said to have invested some of his ill-gotten gains in a Chinese tobacco company, thereby becoming a capitalist.

45. *NCH*, 26 Sept. 1925, pp. 430–31; F5829/194/10 Barton to Legation, 7 Oct. 1925.

46. F5829/194/10 Barton to Legation, 7 Oct. 1925; F1915/1/10 Macleay to F.O., 18 March 1926.

47. 893.5045/188 MacMurray to State, 20 Aug. 1925; *CWR*, 15 Aug. 1925, 207.

48. 893.5045/252 Jacobs to Legation, 21 Oct. 1925, summarizes Chinese objections, and the *Shen Bao* carried almost daily denunciations in late August of the hearing; WJB to Zhu Zhaoxin, 29–30 July 1925, 5–7 Aug., in Hu'an: yu zhuwai geshi dian, vol. 1; F3803/194/10 Zhu to F.O., 10 Aug. 1925; F3979/194/10 Zhu to F.O., 18 Aug. 1925; 701.0093D 34/259 Oudendijk to MacMurray, 15 Sept. 1925; 701.0093D 34/273 Oudendijk to MacMurray, 30 Oct. 1925 (*FRUS 1925*, 1:707–9).

49. In addition to the reports in the *NCH*, the *Shanghai Mercury* published separately *A Report of the Proceedings of the International Commission of Judges*, a copy of which is in 893.5045/356.

50. 893.5045/274 Johnson to Strawn, 10 Nov. 1925.

51. 893.5045/320 Johnson to Kellogg, 10 Feb. 1926.

52. Public summaries of the judges' reports are in the *China Yearbook, 1926–1927*, 946–55. The full reports were never published, but can be found in 893.5045/314 MacMurray to State, 22 Jan. 1926.

53. F5279/194/10 Macleay to F.O., 28 Nov. 1925.

54. F5729/194/10 Minute of 28 Nov. 1925 by Chamberlain; F5834/194/10 Minute of 4 Dec. by Pratt.

55. SMA, excerpts from Watch Committee minutes of meetings of 14 and 15 Dec. 1925; S.M.C. Minute Book, meeting of 15 Dec. 1925.

56. 893.5045/253 MacMurray to State, 21 Nov. 1925; F5735/194/10 Eliot to F.O., 28 Nov. 1925; 893.5045/259 MacMurray to State, 2 Dec. 1925; State to Houghton, 3 Dec. 1925.

57. Princeton University, Seeley G. Mudd Library, Papers of John Van Antwerp MacMurray, Box 44, MacMurray to Cunningham, 7 Dec. 1925.

58. S.M.C. Minute Book, meeting of 18 Dec. 1925; S.M.C. *Report, 1927*, 442.

59. 893.5045/278 MacMurray to Kellogg, 22 Dec. 1925. "A bit skimpy, the grant," commented Waterlow in the Foreign Office, noting that it amounted only to £7,500 (F6091/194/10 Minute of 21 Dec. 1925).

60. WJB to Xu Yuan, 26 Dec. in Hu'an: yu Hu tepaiyuan, vol. 2; F1231/1223/10 Macleay to F.O., 6 Feb. 1926.

61. Qu Qiubai, "Wusa an zhongcha de jieguo yu guomin geming de lianhe

zhanxian" [The result of the re-investigation of the May Thirtieth affair and the national revolutionary front], *XDZB* 142 (14 Jan. 1926): 1290–92.

62. *Chinese Recorder* (Shanghai) 17 (Feb. 1926): 123.

63. John Fitzgerald, "The Misconceived Revolution: State and Society in China's Nationalist Revolution, 1923–1926," *Journal of Asian Studies* 49 (May 1990): 323–43, discusses this aspect.

64. PDR 30 Nov., 18 Dec. 1925, USCGS 1925, part 52.

Chapter 9, *The Embers of a Dying Fire (pp. 144–58)*

1. Iriye, *After Imperialism*, 20–21.

2. 793.00/46 Mayer to State, 24 June 1925; Chinese text in *GMWX*, 18:3303–4.

3. F2560/194/10 F.O. to Palairet, 2 July 1925.

4. Iriye, *After Imperialism*, 67–68; Great Britain, Cabinet Office, Cabinet Memoranda (CAB 24/181) C.P. 308 (26) memorandum by Wellesley of 9 Feb. 1926.

5. Qu Qiubai, "Wusa yundong hou zhi jiuqi tusha" [The butchery of 7 September in the wake of the May Thirtieth Movement], *XDZB* 130 (18 Sept. 1925): 1192.

6. Fishel, *End of Extraterritoriality*, 120–26; Borg, *American Policy*, 157–79.

7. Andrew J. Nathan, "A Constitutional Republic: The Peking Government, 1916–28," in *Cambridge History of China*, vol. 12, part 1, 282–83.

8. *China Press*, 27 Dec. 1926, p. 12.

9. F1231/1223/10 Macleay to F.O., 6 Feb. 1926; 893.5045/294 MacMurray to State, 18 Dec. 1925.

10. FO 228, vol. 3152, "Rough Notes on Chinese Statement (Mr. Teichman)," and Macleay's memorandum of 28 Jan. 1926; *Séances du C.D.*, 289th meeting of 28 Jan. 1926, in USL 1926, vol. 21, 9–12.

11. Good summaries, at least as the question was seen through Western eyes, can be found in 893.102S/184 "Development of the Question of Chinese Representation on the Shanghai Municipal Council until the End of 1927," by consul Henry S. Waterman, dated 9 May 1928, and F4829/25/10 "Memorandum Respecting the International Settlement at Shanghai," by J. T. Pratt, 20 May 1927.

12. 893.102S/34 Sammons to State, 17 May 1915.

13. Kotenev, *Mixed Court and Council*, 35; F4829/25/10 Pratt memorandum of 20 May 1927.

14. 893.102S/72 Cunningham to Legation, 8 April 1920.

15. 893.102S/72 Cunningham to Legation, 8 April 1920.

16. FO 228, vol. 3177, Décanat circular of 8 Sept. 1925; Barton to Legation, 19 Sept. 1925.

17. *Séances du C.D.*, 278th meeting of 28 Sept. 1925, USL 1925, vol. 19, 697–702; 279th meeting of 9 Oct. 1925, Annex I, 716–17; FO 228, vol. 3177, Palairet to Barton, 1 Oct. 1925; F.O. to Palairet, 5 Oct. 1925.

18. There were a number of schemes for the internationalization of Shanghai, along the model of Danzig, under the League of Nations, and so forth. See, for instance, S. J. Powell in the *China Press*, 22 Nov. 1925, p. 14. "This dream of a greater Shanghai like other schemes we have heard of recently has one great disadvantage—it won't work," wrote J. T. Pratt (minute of 18 June 1926 in F2523/1223/10). Compare more recent ideas to put Hongkong under United Nations trusteeship (*Asian Wall Street Journal*, 28 Aug. 1989, p. 4).

19. F1030/38/10 F.O. to Macleay, 17 March 1926.

20. S.M.C. Minute Book, meetings of 24 Feb. 1926, 10 March, 31 March.

21. "Essentially a politician's reply to a businessman's offer," commented Barton, who distrusted Yui (F3192/1223/10 Barton to Legation, 31 March 1926); 893.5045/330 Cunningham to Legation, 30 March 1926; *NCH*, 20 March 1926, pp. 522–23.

22. S.M.C. *Gazette*, 15 April 1926, 122–24.

23. *CWR*, 24 April 1926, 189–91, and 16 May 1926, 280–82.

24. Xu Yuan to Senior Consul, 29 Oct. 1926, USCGS 1926, part 80.

25. F3833/2/10 China Association and British Chamber of Commerce Shanghai, to China Association London, 5 Aug. 1925; F4695/2/10 Hilton Johnson to Sir Archibald Rose, 6 Aug. 1925.

26. FO 228, vol. 3176, Barton to Legation, 21 Aug. 1925; Palairet to F.O., 25 Aug. 1925; Palairet to Barton, 25 Aug. 1925.

27. Full minutes of all the meetings in USCGS 1925, part 53; a summary of the committee's work through Barton's eyes is in F4546/1223/10 Barton to Legation, 20 Aug. 1926.

28. S. M. Edwards to Cunningham, 2 Sept. 1925; Fessenden to de' Rossi, 1 Oct., 13 Nov., USCGS 1925, part 53.

29. The report can be found in USCGS 1925, part 53; and in F4546/1223/10 Barton to Legation, 20 Aug. 1926.

30. *New York Times*, 14 Aug. 1925, p. 5.

31. FO 228, vol. 3177, minute by Lampson, 7 Jan. 1927.

32. F4546/1223/10 Barton to Legation, 20 Aug. 1926.

33. For the lawyers' lobbying, see *China Press*, 13 July 1926, p. 12, 14 July, p. 1, and 17 July, p. 1; F3699/1223/10 Macleay to F.O., 26 July 1926.

34. F3544/1223/10 Barton to Legation, 15 July 1926, and summary minute by J. T. Pratt, 31 Aug. 1926.

35. F3544/1223/10 Barton to Legation, 15 July 1926; F3474/1223/10 Rosso to Mounsey, 23 Aug. 1926; F1519/25/10 Lampson to F.O., 5 Jan. 1927.

36. Hsu to MacMurray, 14 July 1925, MacMurray Papers, box 75; Frochot to Naval Minister, 21 July 1925, AMAE, vol. 329.

37. F5060/38/10 Vereker to Mounsey, 11 Oct. 1926.

38. Martin, "Pact with the Devil," 100–101; 893.114 Narcotics/208 Jenkins to State, 16 March 1931, includes a copy of the contract and minutes of the meeting of 28 April 1925. Whether this particular agreement actually went into effect is unclear, but there is no doubt that Fiori and other Frenchmen were heavily involved in the opium arrangements.

39. "La morgue anglo-saxonne et le bon marché fait des residents chinois": Meyrier to Legation, 20 Sept. 1925, AMAE, vol. 336.

40. Wilden to MAE, 13 Feb. 1924, AMAE, vol. 336.

41. Meyrier to Legation, 10 Feb. 1925, vol. 336. Du Pac represented the shady N. B. Ezra in the Canton Road opium case of 1925, but there is no evidence linking him to the drug trade. He would also die mysteriously in 1932; see chapter 17.

42. Meyrier to Legation, 20 Sept. 1925, vol. 336.

43. Meyrier to Legation, 13 Feb. 1926, vol. 336.

44. Naggiar to MAE, 7 May 1926, vol. 337.

45. 893.5045/359 Cunningham to Legation, 3 June 1926; *Shibao* (Shanghai), 30 and 31 May 1926; *NCDN*, 31 May 1926, pp. 16–17.

46. *Shibao*, 30 May 1926; see also Cunningham to State, 30 Aug. 1926, USCGS

1926, part 65. The same issue of the *Shibao* carried an advertisement from the China Tobacco Company: "Do not be angry, but just remember!" that the future of the nation's greatness lies in encouraging native products like our cigarettes. Nor were the Peking police amused in June 1990, when they interrogated the American head of a foreign jogging club in the capital; the club had ordered T-shirts made to commemorate their 365th run, which coincidentally (?) was scheduled for the fourth, the first anniversary of the Peking massacre (*South China Morning Post* [Hongkong], 7 June 1990).

Chapter 10, A Storm Center Once More (pp. 159–76)

1. F. R. Graves to Elizabeth Graves, 5 Aug. 1926, RG 141–1–25; to Clara Graves, 12 Aug. 1926, RG 141–1–24.

2. Fitch, *Foreign Devil*, 189; *NCH*, 4 July 1925, p. 515; "Then and Now—Peitaiho/Beidaihe," *The China Connection* 3 (July 1987): 1–2; *China Press*, 20 July 1926, p. 4.

3. The quotation comes from the *Municipal Gazette* of 10 June 1927, p. 201, but the warnings were repeated every summer.

4. *China Press*, 21 July 1926, p. 1, 25 July, p. 10, 13 Aug., p. 1, and 15 Aug., p. 1.

5. *NCH*, 8 May 1926, pp. 252–53.

6. F3125/10/10 Lord Southborough to Mounsey, 30 July 1926.

7. For formation of China Committee, see F285/285/10 Southborough to F.O., 22 Jan. 1926; Minute by W. T. Strang of 18 Nov. 1926, in F4891/285/10.

8. Statement of Brig. E. G. MacNaghten of British chamber, Shanghai, *NCH*, 26 March 1927, p. 497.

9. F3798/2/10 Minute of 11 Aug. 1925. For the department's independence, see Wilson, "Britain and the Kuomintang," 434.

10. F3871/10/10 Soothill to Gwatkin, 1 Sept. 1926, and Minute by Strang of 8 Sept. 1926. See also F3033/10/10 Minute by Pratt of 16 July 1926, of a conversation with Lord Willingdon on 15 July.

11. 893.00/7603 Jenkins to Legation, 2 Aug. 1926.

12. C. Martin Wilbur, "The Nationalist Revolution: From Canton to Nanking, 1923–1928," in *Cambridge History of China*, vol. 12, part 1, 585; 893.00/7743 Lockhart to Legation, 10 Sept. 1926; 893.00/7806 Lockhart to Legation, 20 Sept. 1926; 893.00/7738 Mayer to State, 12 Oct. 1926.

13. 893.00/7964 Lockhart to Legation, 12 Oct. 1926. Wilbur states that the Nationalists had lost at least fifteen thousand men in the Jiangxi campaign, but seven thousand of Sun Chuanfang's men had gone over to the southern side and another forty thousand had been disarmed ("Nationalist Revolution," 586).

14. *NCH*, 2 Oct. 1926, p. 6.

15. Wilbur and How, eds., *Missionaries*, 188–91; Li Yunhan, *Cong ronggong dao qingdang* [From the admission of the communists to the purge of the party, hereafter cited as *CRG*] (Taibei, 1966), 434–50.

16. Wilbur cites a report that three-quarters of the political workers in the National Revolutionary Army were Communists or members of the Guomindang left ("Nationalist Revolution," 562).

17. F1244/1/10 Minute by Mark Patrick, 24 March 1926.

18. F2431/1/10 Brenan to Legation, 3 May 1926.

19. 893.00/7469 Jenkins to Legation, 19 May 1926; 893.00/7446 Jenkins to Legation, 6 May 1926; 893.00/7471 Jenkins to Legation, 25 May 1926.

20. American Association of South China memorandum of 3 May, in 893.00/7468 Jenkins to State, 13 May 1926.

21. Interview with Bruno Schwartz of the *Hankow Herald, NCH,* 27 Nov. 1926, p. 387.

22. *NCH,* 20 Nov. 1926, pp. 339, 343.

23. *CWR,* 27 Nov. 1926, 344; *CWR,* 25 Dec. 1926, 88–89, and 1 Jan. 1927, 116.

24. F4704/3623/10 Minute by Stark Toller, 10 Nov. 1926. The fullest contemporary account of the incident is in a memorandum by Stark Toller of 11 Dec. in F5526/3623/10.

25. F5376/3623/10 Barton to Legation, 15 Oct. 1926.

26. F3821/10/10 Macleay to F.O., 16 Sept. 1926; F3937/10/10 Macleay to F.O., 3 Oct. 1926.

27. S.M.C. *Gazette,* 18 June 1926, 195, 16 July, 234, and 10 Sept., 288; 893.5045/387 Cunningham to State, 9 Aug. 1926; 893.5045/389 Cunningham to State, 15 Sept. 1926.

28. On *Chengyan* see Feng Bolo, "Wusa yundong zhong de diguozhuyi zaoyao pohui de zuizheng" [The criminal evidence of imperialism's destructiveness and rumor-mongering in the May Thirtieth movement], *Jindai shi ciliao* [Materials on Modern History] 1 (1958): 84–87; Shanghai Municipal Council *Annual Report, 1925,* 71; Luren, "Diguozhuyi de baozhi waijiaojia jidujiaotu yu Zhongguo zhi minzu jiefang yundong" [Imperialist newspapers, diplomats, and Christians, and the Chinese people's struggle for liberation], *XDZB* 123 (18 Aug. 1925): 1148–50.

29. *CWR,* 27 Nov. 1926, 348; *NCH,* 18 Nov. 1926, pp. 343–44, 352.

30. SMA, S.M.C. records, mimeographed materials in folder 13, C. Champkin to R. N. Peyton-Griffin, 9 July 1925.

31. F1275/207/10 Barton to Macleay, 16 Jan. 1926; University of London, School of Oriental and African Studies, Papers of John Swire and Sons, 41, JSSII 2/5, B&S to JSS, 4 Jan. 1926, 19 March 1926; B&S Shanghai to B&S Tientsin, 12 Jan. 1926.

32. Naggiar to MAE, 30 June 1926, AMAE, vol. 198.

33. F2341/307/10 SIS [Secret Intelligence Service] to F.O., 7 Sept. 1926, and undated C.D.L. circular; F2604/307/10 Macleay to F.O., 6 May 1926; F4440/10/10 Clementi to Colonial Office, 15 Aug. 1926; B&S Hongkong to JSS, 26 Feb. 1926; W. R. Johnson (American Tobacco) to Cunningham, 17 Feb. 1926, USCGS 1926, part 71. A summary of the league's work can also be found in Carl Crow to Gauss, 13 and 14 Jan. 1927, and Gauss to Legation, 14 Jan., in USCGS 1927, part 96.

34. F6917/6917/10 (1927) Minute by Pratt, 19 Aug. 1927.

35. AMAE, vol. 199: "Action bolchevique à Changhaï," [ABAC], a roughly weekly report by the Sûreté, reports for 28 Sept. 1926, and 4 Oct.; Extracts from Police Intelligence Reports, Sept. 1926, USCGS 1926, part 66.

36. ABAC, 25 Oct. 1926, AMAE, vol. 199.

37. Unknown correspondent to President Wilbur of Stanford, 1 Oct. 1926, in F1161/2/10 of 1927.

38. 893.00/7778 Mayer to State, 12 Oct. 1926; 893.00/7784 Mayer to State, 26 Oct. 1926; F.O. 405, vol. 252, F 2026/144/10 Barton to F.O., 18 Jan. 1927.

39. The account that follows is based on Zhou Shangwen and He Shiyu, *Shanghai gongren sanci wuzhuang qiyi shi* [A History of the Three Armed Uprisings of

the Shanghai Workers] (Shanghai, 1987), 32–49; Huang Yifeng, *Shanghai gong-ren sanci wuzhuang qiyi* [The Three Armed Uprisings of the Shanghai Workers] (Shanghai, 1979), 10–14; and Hua Gang, *Zhongguo da geming shi, 1925–1927* [A History of China's Great Revolution, 1925–1927] (Peking, 1982), 208–10. A very useful collection of internal Communist documents published by the Shanghai Municipal Archives can be found in Zhou Qisheng, ed., *Shanghai gongren sanci wuzhuang qiyi* [The Three Armed Uprisings of the Shanghai Workers] (Shanghai, 1983). It is a *neibu* (internal) publication, but a copy exists in the Hoover Institute Library at Stanford University. Western sources include 893.00/7778 Cunningham to Legation, 21 Oct. 1926; 893.00/7784 Mayer to State, 26 Oct. 1926; F4367/10/ 10 Macleay to F.O., 17 Oct. 1926; F4419/10/10 Macleay to F.O., 19 Oct. 1926; F4484/10/10 Macleay to F.O., 21 Oct. 1926.

40. Zhang Hui and Bao Cun, *Shanghai jin bai nian geming shihua* [A revolutionary history of the last hundred years of Shanghai] (Shanghai, 1963), 139–41; Zhou Shangwen and He Shiyu, *Shanghai gongren*, 50–63. Chesneaux, *Chinese Labor Movement*, 341–42, follows the Communist version of the story.

41. ABAC, 1 Nov. 1926, AMAE, vol. 199, which also has a general account of the uprising.

42. F5376/3623/10 Macleay to F.O., 26 Oct. 1926.

43. *CWR*, 30 Oct. 1926, 249; Extracts from Police Intelligence Reports, 27 Sept. 1926, USCGS 1926, part 66.

44. Graves to Wood, 27 Oct. 1926, Graves Papers, RG 64–115.

45. 893.00/7778 Mayer to State, 23 Oct. 1926.

46. 893.00/7923 MacMurray to State, 9 Dec. 1926; *NCH*, 27 Dec. 1926, p. 365, 11 Dec., p. 485, and 20 Nov., pp. 337–38, which prints the text of a pamphlet by Shanghai-Wusong Citizens' Self Government League that attacks Sun and Fengtian; F5163/4934/10 Macleay to F.O., 30 Nov. 1926.

47. *NCH*, 4 Dec. 1926, p. 335; Gauss to Legation, 6 Dec. 1926, 14 Dec., USCGS 1926, part 67; 893.00/8108 Gauss to Legation, 20 Dec. 1926; F5496/4934/10 O'Malley to Chamberlain, 14 Dec. 1926; ABAC, 13 Dec. 1926, AMAE, vol. 199; ABAC, 20 Dec. 1926, AMAE, vol. 200. For the Communist role in the autonomy movement, see Zhou Shangwen and He Shiyu, *Shanghai gongren*, 82–83; and Zhou Qisheng, *Shanghai gongren*, 83–109.

48. Martel to MAE, 5 May 1926, AMAE, vol. 258; Martel to MAE, 14 April 1926, AMAE, vol. 253.

49. Note pour le Sous-directeur d'Asie, 1 Dec. 1926, AMAE, vol. 253.

50. FO 405, vol. 252 F3189/3027/10 Randall to Chamberlain, 5 Aug. 1926; F4176/3027/10 Russell to F.O., 4 Nov. 1926.

51. C.I.M. to N.C.C., 15 March 1926, *Bulletin of the National Christian Council* (Shanghai), no. 19 (June 1926): 2; Union Theological Seminary, Papers of J. L. Warnshuis, box 68, Evaluation Conference of Presbyterian Missions (North), re N.C.C., Shanghai, 18–20 November 1926.

52. *NCH*, 28 Nov. 1925, pp. 376–77, 396; C. E. Scott to Willys Peck, 24 May 1926.

53. N.C.C. *Bulletin* 20 (Sept. 1926): 11–14.

54. For a similar reaction from a foreign Roman Catholic missionary, see Constantini, *Réforme*, 102–3.

55. N.C.C. *Bulletin* 21 (Nov. 1926): 8–10.

56. N.C.C. *Bulletin* 21 (Nov. 1926): 3–4; Cunningham to Legation, 23 Oct., USL 1926, vol. 12.

57. Graves to Wood, 15 Oct. 1926, Graves Papers, RG 64–115.

58. Graves to Wood, 19 June 1925, Graves Papers, RG 64–113. See also letters to Wood of 2 July and 7 July 1925, ibid.

59. Cunningham to Legation, 28 Sept. 1926, USL 1926, vol. 12.

60. Graves to Wood, 15 Oct. 1926, Graves Papers, RG 64–115.

61. See Clifford, "A Revolution Is Not a Tea Party," 519–20.

62. J. D. Mcrae, "The Significance of the National Christian Council," *Chinese Recorder* 11 (Nov. 1926): 818.

63. *CWR*, 25 Sept. 1926, 92.

64. *CWR*, 23 Oct. 1926, 220; *NCH*, 30 Oct. 1926, p. 218.

65. F4425/10/10 contains the statement; *NCH*, 15 Nov. 1926, p. 296.

66. *NCH*, 2 Dec. 1926, p. 442.

67. F5606/4934/10 Barton to Chamberlain, 18 Dec. 1926; *BDRC*, 1:252–53; 893.00/8036 Gauss to Legation, 20 Dec. 1926; 893.00/8108 Gauss to Legation, 28 Dec. 1926.

68. Zhou Shangwen and He Shiyu, *Shanghai gongren*, 86–87; ABAC, 27 Dec. 1926, AMAE, vol. 200.

69. ABAC, 13 Nov.–27 Dec. 1926, AMAE, vol. 200; MAE memo on Chinese communism, 28 Nov. 1926; 893.00/8036 Gauss to Legation, 14 Dec. 1926; 893.00/8108 Gauss to Legation, 20 Dec. 1926; according to Zhou Shangwen and He Shiyu, Zhou Enlai first arrived in Shanghai in late November from Canton (*Shanghai gongren*, 137).

70. *CWR*, 19 Dec. 1925, 83.

71. S.M.C. Minute Book, meeting of 17 Nov. 1926, 307. In fact, there appear to have been three arrest warrants for Chiang: one dated 22 July 1914 for a crime in Xiaoshadu district, one of 13 Oct. 1917 in connection with a murder committed in 1910, and one of 25 July 1918 in connection with an armed robbery on Seward Road in 1917; see 893.00/8005 Gauss to Legation, 29 Nov. 1926.

Chapter 11, A Last Ditch and an Ebullition of Feeling (pp. 177–93)

1. Jiang Yongjing, *Boloting yu Wuhan zhengquan* [Borodin and the Wuhan Government] (Taibei, 1962), 195.

2. This account is based largely on Jiang, *Boloting*, 100–101; Lee En-han, *China's Recovery of the British Hankow and Kiukiang Concessions in 1927* (Perth, 1980), 9–12; F1722/67/10 Goffe to Lampson, 7 Jan. 1927.

3. Jiang, *Boloting*, 103–4.

4. F2818/2485/10 Minute by Wellesley, 24 July 1926.

5. F5298/10/10 has the final version of the British proposal as it went to the cabinet on 29 Nov.

6. F5688/10/10 contains the statement given by O'Malley to the ministers of the Washington Treaty powers on 18 Dec. 1926.

7. *New York Times*, 1 Jan. 1927, p. 4.

8. F39/2/10 Minute of 3 January 1927.

9. Sokolsky in the *Japan Advertiser* of 14 Feb. 1927, enclosed in F2663/2/10 Tilley to F.O., 14 Feb. 1927; ABAC, 18 Jan. 1927, AMAE, vol. 200; F2145/67/10 Private letter of Gen. MacDonagh, 28 March 1927.

10. Jiang, *Boloting*, 100.

11. Jiang, *Boloting*, 112; Dan Jacobs, *Borodin: Stalin's Man in China* (Cambridge, Mass., 1981), 228–29.

12. F124/67/10 Lampson to F.O., 6 Jan. 1927; F176/67/10 Lampson to F.O., 7 Jan. 1927; Wilson, "Britain and the Kuomintang," 498–500, 529–30.

13. F2660/2610/10 Lyall to Lampson, 12 Feb. 1927.

14. F5764/10/10 Lampson to F.O., 27 Dec. 1926.

15. The proposals for treaty revision are in F953/2/10, given by O'Malley to Chen on 27 Jan. 1927 in Hankou, and by Lampson to Wellington Koo on 28 Jan. in Peking.

16. FO 405, vol. 252, F472/472/10 Memorandum by Pratt, 6 Jan. 1927. The piece is an example of the Foreign Office's ability to take a long historical view of the problems facing Britain. Though various American consular officials produced histories of individual provinces since 1911 in 1924 and 1925, they were far less apt to seek historical explanations for the problems of the day.

17. FO 405, vol. 252, F268/7/10 Memorandum by Pratt, 15 Jan. 1927.

18. 893.00/8911 Gauss to Legation, 11 Dec. 1926; F5496/4934/10 O'Malley to F.O., 14 Dec. 1926.

19. F5182/4934/10 Southborough to Chamberlain, 3 Nov. 1926; F4934/4934/10 F.O. to Macleay, 22 Nov. 1926.

20. F5496/4934/10 F.O. to O'Malley, 20 Dec. 1926; F162/156/10 Pratt minute of 9 Jan. 1927.

21. F5711/4923/10 "Note on Defence of Shanghai," 22 Dec. 1926; F.O. to Lampson, 25 Dec. 1926.

22. F318/156/10 Gull to Mounsey, 12 Jan. 1927; F324/156/10 Shanghai Electric Construction Co. (London) to F.O., 12 Jan. 1927; F491/156/10 S.E.C.C. to F.O., 18 Jan. 1927; F676/67/10 Mond to Baldwin, 19 Jan. 1927.

23. F. F. Fairman to Gauss, 19 Jan. 1927, USCGS 1927, part 37.

24. 893.00/8082 Gauss to State, 19 Jan. 1927; 893.00/8087 Mayer to State, 20 Jan. 1927; 893.00/8266 Gauss to State, 20 Jan. 1927.

25. Banque Franco-Chinoise to Paris, 10 Jan. 1927; Messageries Maritimes (Paris) to MAE, 14 Jan. 1927; Knight to Ministre de Commerce, 24 Jan. 1927; Chambre de Commerce Française de la Chine to MAE, 22 Jan. 1927; Union des Chambres de Commerce Françaises à l'Etranger to MAE, 15 Feb. 1927; Chambre de Commerce de Lyon to MAE, 2 Feb. 1927, AMAE, vol. 264.

26. See Wilson, "Great Britain and the Kuomintang," 529–30.

27. F158/156/10 Lampson to F.O., 7 Jan. 1927; F162/156/10 Lampson to F.O., 7 Jan. 1927; F.O. to Lampson, 8 Jan. 1927.

28. F297/2/10 from Offices of the Cabinet, CAB 23, vol. 54, Cabinet 1(27) of 12 Jan. 1927; F192/156/10 F.O. to Lampson, 12 Jan. 1927.

29. Library of Congress, Papers of Nelson T. Johnson, vol. 4, Gauss to Nelson T. Johnson, 28 Nov. 1926.

30. Gauss to Legation, 11 Dec. 1926, USL 1926, vol. 26; 893.00/7960 Mac-Murray to State, 19 Dec. 1926; 893.00/8111 MacMurray to State, 23 Dec. 1926, which has records of the meetings and gives the size of the Shanghai Volunteer Force (S.V.C.) at fourteen hundred and the S.M.P. at six hundred, *not* including Chinese; 893.00/7960 State to MacMurray, 23 Dec. 1926.

31. 893.00/8212 Gauss to MacMurray, 12 Jan. 1927.

32. 893.00/8264 Gauss to Legation, 16 Jan. 1927; Gauss to Legation, 17 Jan., USCGS 1927, part 37; F421/156/10 Barton to Lampson, 17 Jan. 1927; see also

893.00/8221 Commander in Chief, U.S. Asiatic Fleet (CinCAS) to Opnav, 17 Jan. 1927.

33. F351/156/10 Commander-in-Chief China to Admiralty, 12 Jan. 1927; F3353/2/10 Admiralty to F.O., 9 April 1927, enclosing Commander-in-Chief China to Admiralty, 22 Jan. 1927.

34. 893.00/8212 Gauss to Legation, 12 Jan. 1927.

35. F357/156/10 Lampson to F.O., 15 Jan. 1927; F375/156/10 Lampson to F.O., 14 Jan. 1927, and Pratt minute of 15 Jan. 1927.

36. CAB 23, vol. 54, Cabinet 2(27) of 17 Jan. 1927; F676/67/10 Mond to Baldwin, 19 Jan. 1927.

37. CAB 23, vol. 54, Cabinet 1(27) of 12 Jan. 1927; F573/2/10 Minute by Strang, and F2042/156/10 and F2043/67/10 Tilley to Chamberlain, both 18 Jan. 1927; F334/156/10 Chamberlain to Tilley, 13 Jan. 1927; F706/2/10 Chamberlain to Tilley, 24 Jan. 1927; F2045/156/10 Tilley to Chamberlain, 27 Jan. 1927.

38. Gauss to Legation, 12 Jan. 1927, USCGS 1927, part 37; 893.00/8212 Gauss to Legation, 12 Jan. 1927.

39. F421/156/10 Barton to Macleay, 17 Jan. 1927.

40. 893.00/8061 MacMurray to State, 15 Jan. 1927; see also military attaché Magruder's memo of 13 Jan. arguing this point of view; and his "Comment on Current Events," 1–15 Jan., 18 Jan.: "Nothing is more necessary if the lives of our nationals are to be protected than to secure Shanghai against any sort of disorders. . . . Furthermore, it is idle to draw fine distinctions between Cantonese soldiers and Cantonese mobs. Since in most cases the former have not restrained the latter, one is as dangerous as the other." USL 1927, vol. 25.

41. This statement is based on the presence of an unsigned memorandum of 19 Jan. 1927, presumably by Nelson Johnson (Johnson Papers, vol. 56). If Johnson was the author, Buhite's assertion that he kept Kellogg from following a strong line has to be qualified. See Russell D. Buhite, *Nelson T. Johnson and American Policy toward China, 1925–1941* (East Lansing, 1968), 35.

42. F568/2/10 Chamberlain to Howard, 18 Jan. 1927, and Minute by Vansittart, 18 Jan. 1927; F598/2/10 Howard to Chamberlain, 20 Jan. 1927; F808/2/10 Howard to F.O., 26 Jan. 1927; 893.00/8150 Memorandum by Kellogg of talk with Howard, 27 Jan. 1927; 893.00/8168 Memorandum by Kellogg, 31 Jan. 1927.

43. Naggiar to MAE, 9 Jan. 1927, MAE to Martel, 11 Jan., AMAE, vol. 264; F333/156/10 Chamberlain to Crewe, 13 Jan. 1927.

44. CAB 23, vol. 54, Cabinet 3(27) of 21 Jan. 1927. At its largest, the Shanghai Defence Force consisted of seventeen infantry battalions, one marine battalion, and a cruiser squadron (Wilson, "Britain and the Kuomintang," 502; Brian Bond, *British Military Policy between the Two World Wars* (Oxford, 1980), 89–91.

45. *The Times* (London), 31 Jan. 1927, p. 12.

46. F742G/156/10 War Office to F.O., 25 Jan. 1927; Great Britain, War Office, WO 191, vol. 1: Shanghai Defence Force General Staff, Jan.–March 1927, appendix B.

47. F623/156/10 Barton to Hongkong, 22 Jan. 1927; F651/156/10 Lampson to F.O., 23 Jan. 1927; F421/156/10 Barton to Legation, 17 Jan. 1927; F397/156/10 Lampson to F.O., 16 Jan. 1927.

48. *NCH*, 29 Jan. 1927, p. 137.

49. F979/156/10 Pratt minute of 31 Jan. 1927; see also F351/156/10 Pratt minute of 15 Jan. 1927; F600/156/10 Strang minute (for the Department) of 21 Jan.

1927; F656/156/10 Ashton-Gwatkin memo of 21–22 Jan. 1927; and Pratt minute of 22 Jan. 1927.

50. F998/67/10 O'Malley to Legation, 1 Feb. 1927; for Chen's refusal to sign agreement, F939/67/10 O'Malley to Legation, 31 Jan. 1927; F973/67/10 O'Malley to Lampson, 1 Feb. 1927; F1093/2/10 O'Malley to Legation, 1 Feb. 1927. The Nationalist statement of 24 January is in F708/2/10.

51. For Borodin's role, see Jiang, *Boloting*, 107–9, and Percy Chen, *China Called Me* (Boston, 1979), 101.

52. F1047/67/10 O'Malley to Legation, 2 Feb. 1927; F1057/67/10 Lampson to F.O., 3 Feb. 1927; F924/156/10 Barton to Legation, 31 Jan. 1927; F1127/156/10 Barton to F.O., 5 Feb. 1927.

53. CAB 23(54), Cabinet 6(27) of 2 Feb. 1927; Cabinet 7(27) of 4 Feb. 1927; and Cabinet 8(27) of 7 Feb. 1927.

54. F1245/67/10 F.O. to Lampson, 10 Feb. 1927.

55. F1495/67/10 Minutes by Mounsey and Wellesley, 16 Feb. 1927; F.O. to Lampson 17 Feb. 1927.

56. CAB 23, vol. 54, Cab 10(27) of 17 Feb. 1927.

57. F1604/67/10 Minute by Wellesley, 18 Feb. 1927; F1671/67/10 has the text of the Hankou and Kiukiang agreements and associated documents; O'Malley to F.O., 21 Feb. 1927; F1886/67/10 Barton to Legation, 18 Feb. 1927.

58. F2359/2/10 Lampson to F.O., 26 Jan. 1927.

59. Bertrand Russell, "British Folly in China," *Nation*, 2 March 1927, 227.

60. F4718/2/10 "Analysis of the Chinese Nationalist Complex . . . February, 1927," by Eric Teichman (1 March 1927).

61. F2766/67/10 clipping from *Manchester Guardian*, 16 March 1927; for the department fears about Shanghai interests, see F1494/67/20 Pratt minute of 16 Feb. 1927.

62. F4454/2/10 Mounsey to Wellesley, 2 May 1927, after a talk with Arthur Ransome of the *Manchester Guardian*.

63. FO 228, vol. 3398, Barton to Legation, 26 Jan. 1927.

64. F1096/2/10 Barton to Legation, 4 Feb. 1927; Wellesley and Chamberlain minutes, 5 Feb. 1927; F.O. to Lampson, 6 Feb. 1927; F1715/48/10 F.O. to Lampson, 18 Feb. 1927; Lampson to F.O., 19 Feb. 1927.

65. F1495/67/10 Departmental minute of 16 Feb. 1927; see also F4146/67/10 Mounsey minute of 30 April 1927.

Chapter 12, *To Wash Away Eighty Years of Shame (pp. 194–209)*

1. *NCH*, 19 Feb. 1927, p. 263.

2. Spunt, *A Place in Time*, 130–31; *NCH*, 19 March 1927, p. 443.

3. Gladys McDermott to her family, 19 Feb. 1927, McDermott letters.

4. MAE to Martel, 7 Jan. 1927, AMAE, vol. 264.

5. Naggiar to Legation, 23 Jan. 1927, AMAE, vol. 264.

6. Fleuriau to MAE, 29 Dec. 1926, 5 Jan. 1927; see also Claudel to MAE, 29 Dec. 1926; Naggiar to Legation, 3 Jan. 1927, AMAE, vol. 264; Martel to MAE, 1 Feb. 1927, AMAE, vol. 265.

7. Borg, *American Policy*, 231; Lewis Ethan Ellis, *Frank B. Kellogg and American Foreign Relations, 1925–1929* (New Brunswick, 1961), 126.

8. Johnson to R. S. Greene, 4 Jan. 1927, Johnson Papers, vol. 5; MacMurray

to Silas Strawn, 23 Dec. 1926, MacMurray Papers, box 82; F2/2/10 Lampson to F.O., 31 Dec. 1926.

9. Ellis, *Kellogg*, 126; MacMurray to Kellogg, 30 Dec. 1926, MacMurray Papers, box 82.

10. 69th Congress 2nd Session, H.R. 45. A copy can be found in 793.11/111. The resolution's wording is very similar to that found in a letter from A. L. Warnshuis to Johnson, 27 Dec. 1926 (711.93/106); see also 711.93/110 F. P. Turner to Johnson, 22 Jan. 1927.

11. 711.93/115A State to MacMurray, 24 Jan. 1927; unsigned memorandum [by Nelson Johnson?] of 19 Jan. 1927, Johnson Papers, vol. 56.

12. The statement is in 711.93/116a, State to Mayer, 25 Jan. 1927. In Mac-Murray's absence, Mayer proposed a draft, using Eugene Chen's own flamboyant utterances to undercut the pacific liberalism of the Porter resolution and virtually putting all the blame on China herself for her failure to achieve treaty revision (711.93/116 Mayer to State, 26 Jan. 1927). It was the statement of a debater, not a diplomat, and it may be fortunate it arrived too late.

13. Iriye, *After Imperialism*, 107–9.

14. 711.93/124 Memorandum of 27 Jan. 1927 by Willys Peck; 711.93/130 Memorandum by Johnson, 27 Jan. 1927.

15. 893.00/8164 State to MacMurray, 28 Jan. 1927.

16. 893.00/8164 MacMurray to State, 30 Jan. 1927.

17. 893.00/8164 State to MacMurray, 31 Jan. 1927.

18. F1058/2/10 Lampson to F.O., 3 Feb. 1927; F868/2/10 Tyrrell to Chamberlain, 30 Jan. 1927; F1102/2/10 Lampson to F.O., 4 Feb. 1927.

19. F1096/2/10 Barton to Legation, 4 Feb. 1927.

20. 893.00/8564 Gauss to Legation, 24 Feb. 1927; *NCH*, 12 Feb. 1927, p. 224, has the Sokolsky story; *CWR*, 29 Jan. 1927, 224. The *CWR* first praised the proposal, but later did an about face, attacking the plan because it might lead to an increased foreign control in Shanghai (19 Feb. 1927, 299).

21. 893.00/8164 State to MacMurray, 31 Jan. 1927; 893.00/8448 Davis to Legation, 18 Feb. 1927.

22. 893.00/8467 Lockhart to Legation, 25 Feb. 1927.

23. 893.00/8836 MacMurray to State, 18 March 1927; 893.00/8193 MacMurray to State, 5 Feb. 1927; 893.00/8206 MacMurray to State, 7 Feb. 1927; 893.00/8232 MacMurray to State, 11 Feb. 1927; 893.00/8460 Lockhart to Legation, 12 Feb. 1927.

24. F1652/2/10 Howard to F.O., 21 Feb. 1927.

25. Gauss to Legation, 17 Jan. 1927; Memorandum of talk with Barton, 27 Jan. 1927; Barrett to Spiker, 14 Jan. 1927; undated S.M.C. and French *Commission Provisoire* notices, USCGS 1927, part 37.

26. Emergency Plan of 1 Feb. 1927, USCGS 1927, part 37.

27. F1807/1807/10 Lampson to F.O., 30 Jan. 1928; Gauss to mission heads, 24 Jan. 1927; memo, 26 Jan. 1927, USCGS part 35A; 393.11/461 Gauss to Legation, 24 Jan. 1927.

28. Graves to Wood, 5 Feb. 1927, Graves Papers, RG 64–116.

29. The following account of the strike is taken from Chesneaux, *Chinese Labor Movement*, 354–56; Harold Isaacs, *The Tragedy of the Chinese Revolution*, 2d ed. (New York, 1966), 132–36; 893.00/8822 Gauss to Legation, 9 April 1927; 893.00/8721 Gauss to Legation, 8 March 1927; Zhao Shiyan (Shiying), "Shanghai Zong tongmeng bagong de jilü" [A Record of the Shanghai General Strike],

XDZB, 28 Feb. 1927, 2025–30; *Shibao*, 18–27 Feb. 1927; *GWZB*, 25 Feb. 1927, 1–2; Hua Gang, *Zhongguo da geming shi* [History of the Great Chinese Revolution] (Peking, 1982), 210–16; Huang Yifeng, *Shanghai gongren*, 16–29; Zhou Shangwen and He Shiyu, *Shanghai gongren*, 69–125 (the fullest account); and Zhou Qisheng, *Shanghai gongren*, 123–53, which has the documents for the planning and execution of the uprising.

30. Zhou Qisheng, *Shanghai gongren*, 120.

31. The proclamations are printed in Zhou Shangwen and He Shiyu, *Shanghai gongren*, 93–96.

32. *Shibao*, 27 Feb. 1927; 2035/156/10 clippings from *Manchester Guardian* and *Morning Post* of 22 Feb. 1927; 893/00/8721 Gauss to Legation, 8 March 1927; *GWZB*, 25 Feb. 1927, 1–2. Casualty figures from Huang Yifeng, *Shanghai gongren*, 25.

33. Zhao Shiyan, "Shanghai Zong tongmeng bagong," 2028. Internal Communist documents make frequent mention of the need for a campaign of Red terror during February and March 1927; see Zhou Qisheng, *Shanghai gongren*, 136–37, for an example.

34. F. R. Graves to Elizabeth Graves, 22 Feb. 1927, Graves Papers, RG 141–1–35.

35. Zhao Shiyan, "Shanghai Zong tongmeng bagong," 2030.

36. Zhou Shangwen and He Shiyu, *Shanghai gongren*, 107–25; Zhou Qisheng, *Shanghai gongren*, 154–59, see also 174–79.

37. Li Yunhan, *CRG*, 590.

38. A. J. Cerepanov, quoted in Jean-Marie Bouissou, *Seigneurs de Guerre et Officiers Rouges, 1924–1927: la Révolution Chinoise* (Tours, 1974), 330.

39. N. Nassonov, N. Fokine, A. Albrecht, "Letter from Shanghai," originally published in Paris in 1927, reprinted as an appendix to Leon Trotsky, *Problems of the Chinese Revolution* (Ann Arbor, 1967), 406.

40. Archives de la Ministère des Affaires Étrangères, Papers of Paul-Emile Naggiar, Carton I, Naggiar to Legation, 3 March 1927, for Soviet role; Naggiar to MAE, 4 March 1927, and 8 March 1927, MAE, vol. 266.

41. 893.00/8721 Gauss to Legation, 8 March 1927; 893.00/8721 Gauss to Legation, 8 March 1927.

42. 893.102S/184 Memorandum by N. T. Johnson of interview with Fessenden, 23 Aug. 1929. It is not clear with whom Fessenden made this arrangement; presumably it was either with the acting army commander (Duncan had not yet arrived) or with Admiral Tyrwhitt.

43. 893.00/8324 Gauss to State, 28 Feb. 1927; F1908/156/10 20th Indian Brigade to War Office, 25 Feb. 1927.

44. *NCH*, 5 March 1927, p. 355.

45. WO 191, vol. 1, appendix D; appendix G, Duncan to War Office, 10 March 1927.

46. S.M.P. File for Jan. 1927, quoted in *NCH*, 19 Feb. 1927, p. 288.

47. Peng Shuzhi, "Qing kan, diguozhuyi zai Shanghai zhi ziwei" [Just look at imperialist self-protection at Shanghai], *XDZB* 189 (28 Feb. 1927): 2032–34. See also Ransome, *Chinese Puzzle*, chap. 1.

48. Graves to John Wood, 7 Jan. 1927, 7 Feb., and 23 Feb., Graves papers, RG 64–116; F. R. Graves to Clara Graves, 22 Feb. 1927, RG 141–1–25; Pott to Wood, 15 Feb., 24 Feb. 1927, Pott Papers, RG 64–143.

49. *NCH*, 26 Feb. 1927, p. 323.

50. F2108/156/10 Barton to Legation, 6 March 1927.

51. *NCH*, 12 March 1927, p. 395.

52. 893.00/8300 MacMurray to State, 22 Feb. 1927; State to MacMurray, 25 Feb. 1927; 893.00/8361 State to MacMurray, 9 March 1927.

53. 893.00/8438 Memorandum by Johnson, 15 March 1927.

54. *NCH*, 5 March 1927, pp. 364, 372–73.

55. *NCDN*, 23 March 1927, pp. 6–7.

56. 893.00/8276 Rebecca Griest to W. W. Griest, 16 Jan. 1927.

57. Birney to Gauss, 11 Jan. 1927, USCGS 1927, part 83; 893.00/8096 J. R. Edwards to State, 22 Jan. 1927.

58. MacMurray's views are in F1331/156/10 Lampson to F.O., 5 Feb. 1927, and 893.00/8204 MacMurray to State, 7 Feb. 1927; Gauss to Legation, 25 Jan. 1927, USCGS Part 25A; Gauss memo of 14 Jan. 1927, part 37.

59. Archives of the Episcopal Church, Episcopal Seminary of the Southwest (Austin, Texas), Papers of Bishop Logan Roots, RG 64–236, "Notes of an interview with the Hon. Eugene Chen . . . Jan. 4, 1927," in Roots to Mary Wood, 3 March 1927.

60. Graves to Wood, 7 Jan. 1927, Graves Papers, RG 64–116.

61. Graves to Wood, 11 March 1927, Graves Papers, RG 64–116.

62. Archives of the Episcopal Church (Austin, Texas), Papers of Maurice Votaw, RG 64–142, Votaw to Wood, 28 June 1927.

63. *CWR*, 29 Jan. 1927, 242.

64. 793.93/125 Gauss to State, 31 Jan. 1927.

65. *CWR*, 12 Feb. 1927, 273–74.

66. *CWR*, 5 March 1927, 9–10.

67. *CWR*, 26 Feb. 1927, 332.

68. *CWR*, 19 March 1927, 57–58.

69. *CWR*, 5 March 1927, 3–4.

70. *CWR*, 26 Feb. 1927, 329–30.

71. Naggiar to Legation, 2 Nov. 1926; see also 16 Oct. 1926, AMAE, vol. 337.

72. Naggiar to Legation, 17 Aug. 1926, AMAE, vol. 337.

73. Martel to MAE, 8 Nov. 1926; MAE to Martel, 8 Dec. 1926; Martel to MAE, 8 Nov. 1926; MAE to Martel, 8 Dec. 1926; Naggiar to MAE, 8 Dec. 1926; Naggiar to Legation, 13 Dec. 1926, AMAE, vol. 337.

74. Naggiar to Legation, 8 Sept. 1927; Martel to MAE, 15 Sept. 1927; Naggiar to MAE, 1 Nov. 1927, AMAE, vol. 337.

75. *Compte-rendu 1927*, 4.

76. Naggiar to Legation, 29 Jan. 1927; *Bulletin Municipal*, no. 423 (10 Feb. 1927).

Chapter 13, Shanghai Has Become Red! (pp. 210–26)

1. *New York Times*, 17 March 1927, p. 1.

2. Zhou Qisheng, *Shanghai gongren*, 117–18, 122.

3. Compare the accounts of Xia Zhixu, "Pianduan de huiyi—yi Zhao Shiyan" [Fragments of Memory—Remembering Zhao Shiyan], *Hongqi piaopiao* 5 (15 Dec. 1957): 5–13; and Chang Yi, "Ji Shanghai di sanci wuzhuang qiyi quanhou de Zhao Shiyan lieshi" [In memory of the martyr Zhao Shiyan during the Third Armed Uprising in Shanghai], *Hongqi piaopiao* 16 (October 1961): 65–93, which mention

Zhou's leadership only incidentally, with Huang Yifeng's 1979 account in *Shanghai gongren*, where he has become the central figure. The disgrace of Mao since his death in 1976 has led to a consequent elevation of Zhou Enlai as the beloved hero of the revolution.

4. Zhou Shangwen and He Shiyu, *Shanghai gongren*, 152–56.

5. Zhou Qisheng, *Shanghai gongren*, 117.

6. Zhou Qisheng, *Shanghai gongren*, 87; the figure for membership comes from Luo Suwen, "Political Influences," p. 35.

7. Zhou Qisheng, *Shanghai gongren*, 262, 272–73, 305–6.

8. Li Yunhan, *CRG*, 434–50.

9. For cooperation between the two groups, see Chang Kuo-t'ao, *Rise*, 570.

10. *Shibao*, 13 March 1927; Zhou Qisheng, *Shanghai gongren*, 333.

11. Zhou Shangwen and He Shiyu, *Shanghai gongren*, 143–44.

12. ABAC, 7 March 1927, 14 March 1927, 21 March 1927, *passim*, AMAE, vol. 200. Helen Redko was the wife of a journalist named Howard, who reportedly worked for the *China Courier*. ABAC, 4 April 1927, for Mrs. Williams, the manicurist.

13. *Shibao*, 13 March 1927; *Zhonghua minguo shishi jiyao: Zhonghua minguo liushi nian (yi jiu er qi) yi zhi liu yue* [Important Historical Documents for the Republic of China: January to June, 1927] (Taibei, 1977), 346 (hereafter cited as *MGSS*); F2536/156/10 Barton to Legation, 20 March 1927; ABAC, 14 March 1927, AMAE, vol. 200. The admiral was Yang Shuzhuang.

14. Henry Francis Misselwitz, *The Dragon Stirs: An Intimate Sketch-Book of China's Kuomintang Revolution 1927–1929* (New York, 1941), 18–25.

15. *Shibao*, 21 March 1927.

16. *NCDN*, 22 March 1927.

17. The account of Shanghai's fall is based on many sources, including the reports in the *North China Daily News* and the Shanghai *Shibao*; consular correspondence, particularly 893.00/8006 Gauss to State, 21 April 1927; F5505/2/10 Barton to F.O., 15 April 1927 (report by Vice-Consul Blackburn); Naggiar to MAE, 21 May 1927, in Naggiar Papers, Carton I. The most detailed recent Chinese descriptions are in Huang Yifeng, *Shanghai gongren*, 30–58, and particularly, Zhou Shangwen and He Shiyu, *Shanghai gongren*, 163–92. See also the accounts mentioned below.

18. The battle plan is in Zhou Qisheng, *Shanghai gongren*, 350–59; see also, Chang Yi, "Ji Shanghai di san ci wuzhuang qiyi qianhou de Zhao Shiyan lieshi" [In memory of the martyr Zhao Shiyan during the three armed uprisings of Shanghai], *Hongqi piaopiao* 16 (October 1961): 70. A contemporary account is Zhao Shiying (Shiyan), "Shanghai gongren sanyue baodong jishi," [The March Uprising of the Shanghai Workers], *XDZB* 193 (6 April 1927): 2089–90 (the same article also appears in *Di yici guonei* . . . as "Shanghai gongren di sanci qiyi").

19. ABAC, 28 March 1927, AMAE, vol. 200.

20. "Zui jin Shanghai shehui zhi xiezhen" [Recent Reporting about Shanghai Society], *GWZB*, 10 April 1927, 1–4.

21. 893.00/8140 Gauss to State, 21 March 1927; 893.00/8147 CinCAS to Opnav, 21 March 1927; MAE "Note sur les événements de Chine depuis le 10 février," 19 March 1927, AMAE, vol. 266.

22. Zhou Shangwen and He Shiyu, *Shanghai gongren*, 175.

23. Chang Yi, "Zhao Shiyan," 70; Huang Yifeng, *Shanghai gongren*, 50; for Bi, SMA, PDR 22, 25 March 1927.

24. Gladys McDermott to her family, 25 March 1927, McDermott letters.

25. Private account by Ernest M. Hayes, "The 1927 S.V.C. Mobilization." I am indebted to Mrs. Ambler for letting me see this document.

26. Archives des Jesuites à Paris: Fonds Chine (Chantilly), Msgr. Prosper Paris papers, box 1, Carton 32, undated carbon (presumably by the Mother Superior), "Journées du 21 et du 22 mars 1927 à la Ste. Famille"; 893.00/8006 Gauss to State, 21 April 1927; F2728/156/10 Duncan to War Office, 23 March 1927; *NCH*, 26 March 1927; S.M.C. *Report for the Year 1927*, 7.

27. *NCDN*, 23 March 1927. This account, or one like it, must have furnished the basis for André Malraux's famous description of the train: *Man's Fate* (New York, 1934), 135–36.

28. Various sources, including *NCH*, 26 March 1927, Blackburn, Gauss reports; SMA, PDR, 23 March 1927.

29. *NCH*, 26 March 1927, p. 488.

30. "Journées du 21 et du 22 mars 1927 à la Ste. Famille."

31. Chang Yi, "Zhao Shiyan," 74.

32. Zhou Shangwen and He Shiyu, *Shanghai gongren*, 149, 163, 173.

33. Zhang Hui and Bao Cun, *Shanghai geming*, 148, gives the first explanation; Zhao Shiying (Shiyan), "Shanghai gongren," 209, suggests the second. See also Huang Yifeng, *Shanghai gongren*, 54–55; SMA, PDR, 22 March 1927; *The Times* (London), 22 March 1927, p. 14.

34. Gauss to Legation, 24 March 1927, USL 1927, vol. 27, 1927.

35. F4692/87/10 Lampson to F.O., 6 April 1927.

36. Chang Yi, "Zhao Shiyan," 76.

37. Accounts of the new municipal government appear in *China Correspondence* (Hankou), 15 March 1927, 25; Jiang, *Boloting*, 115–16; Chang Yi, "Zhao Shiyan," 72; *Shibao*, 23 March 1927. These accounts do not all agree on the precise order of events. I've followed mostly the *Shibao* account.

38. Zhou Qisheng, *Shanghai gongren*, 297; Li, *CRG*, 591–92.

39. 893.00/8772 Gauss to Legation, 24 March 1927.

40. Naggiar to MAE, 22 March 1927, MAE, vol. 266. The phrase used of the emissaries is "qu'ils veulent mener d'accord avec Chang-Kai-chek lutte contre communistes."

41. F2680/156/10 Barton to Legation, 23 March 1927; 893.00/8772 Gauss to Legation, 24 March 1927.

42. F2773/156/10 Barton to Legation, 25 March 1927; Zhou Shangwen and He Shiyu, *Shanghai gongren*, 263.

43. The Nanking incident, and summaries of British, American, and Japanese reports can be found in Iriye, *After Imperialism*, 126–30; Wilbur, "Nationalist Revolution," 616–19; Wilson, "Great Britain and the Kuomintang," 575–91; and Borg, *American Policy*, 296–317. The British and American diplomatic documentation is enormous and includes the sworn testimony of several eyewitnesses, mostly missionaries; a small portion of the American record appears in *FRUS 1927*, vol. 2, 164–236. The French side can be found in AMAE, vol. 267. For Chiang's statement, made to foreign reporters in Shanghai, see *NCDN*, 28 March 1927.

44. Undated notes by Powell, USCGS 1927, part 84.

45. *NCDN*, 26 March 1927.

46. Gladys McDermott to her family, 25 March 1927, McDermott letters.

47. 893.00/8478 CinCAS to Opnav, 26 March 1927.

48. *CWR*, 2 April 1927, 121.

49. *NCDN*, 28 April 1927.

50. Naggiar to MAE, 29 March 1927, AMAE, vol. 266.
51. *MGSS*, 420.
52. *NCDN*, 25 March 1927. For the G.L.U. advertisement, see the *Shibao*, 26 March 1927.
53. ABAC, 4 April 1927, AMAE, vol. 200. The Chinese involved were said to be Yang Xingfo and Yu Zehong as well as the executive committee of the Party, which would presumably include such men as Chen Duxiu and Lo Yinong. For the Comintern's veto, see Zhou Qisheng, *Shanghai gongren*, 436–39. A document published after the raid on the Soviet embassy in Peking (see chap. 15) spoke of a plot to engineer such a massacre, but Professor C. Martin Wilbur has concluded that it was a forgery (letter to the author, 26 July 1989).
54. Wilbur, "Nationalist Revolution," 621; SMA, PDR, 27 March 1927; 393.11/506 Gauss to State, 27 March 1927.
55. *Shibao*, 28 March 1927.
56. F2834/156/10 Barton to Legation, 27 March 1927; SMA, PDR, 27 March 1927; *NCDN*, 28 March 1927; 393.11/508 Gauss to State, 28 March 1927.
57. SMA, PDR, 5 April 1927.

Chapter 14, Have the Missionaries Been Converted? (pp. 227–41)

1. Texts in S.M.C., *Municipal Gazette*, 25 March 1927, 85, and 1 April 1927, 107–9.
2. *NCH*, 26 March 1927, p. 495.
3. *NCH*, 12 March 1927, p. 417.
4. *NCH*, 9 April 1927, p. 95.
5. S.M.C. *Report for the Year 1927*, 337–39.
6. F. R. Graves to Clara Graves, 25 April 1927, Graves Papers, RG 141–1–25; Graves to Wood, 26 March 1927, RG 64–116. For the proposed taking of St. John's, see Frederick Moore's interview with Graves in *NCH*, 11 June 1927, p. 488.
7. F. J. White to Gauss, 22 Jan. 1927; Gauss memorandum, 24 Jan. 1927; White to Gauss, 30 March, USCGS 1927, part 33.
8. *NCDN*, 28 March 1927.
9. H.B.R. in *NCDN*, 2 March 1927.
10. Graves to Wood, 25 March 1927, Graves Papers, RG 64–116.
11. *New York Times*, 24 March 1927, p. 1.
12. Gladys McDermott to her family, 25 March 1927, McDermott letters.
13. J. Magruder to Assistant Chief of Staff, G-2, 28 March 1927, in National Archives, Records of the War Department General and Special Staff, RG 165, Microcopy 1444, "Correspondence of the Military Intelligence Division Relating to General Political, Economic and Military Conditions in China, 1918–1941," roll 5. An American serving in the S.V.C. remembered that the Volunteers formed an "interior defense force" to keep order in the Settlement, while British and American regulars constituted an "exterior defense force" to guard against any Nationalist attempt to seize the Settlement. See Ernest M. Hayes, "The 1927 S.V.C. Mobilization," a private account kindly lent to me by Mrs. William W. Ambler.
14. Powell, *My Twenty-Five Years*, 146; *NCH*, 9 April 1927, p. 77.
15. WO 191/2, appendix N, Duncan to War Office, 15 April 1927.
16. For the Stock Exchange, *NCH*, 2 April 1927, p. 18; Japanese residents are

in USCGS 1927, part 33; for the foreign signatures, *NCH*, 26 March, p. 513, and 2 April, p. 19; F2762/156/10 F.O. to Barton, 25 March 1927; F3824/156/10 Barton to F.O., 6 April 1927.

17. *Écho de Chine*, 1 April 1927, p. 1.

18. Compagnie Olivier (Shanghai) to its Paris office, 28 Feb. 1927, AMAE, vol. 341.

19. Établissements Kuhlmann (Paris) to Peycelon, 28 March 1927; Messageries Maritimes (Shanghai) to Paris office, 25 March 1927; Compagnie Olivier (Paris) to MAE, 26 March 1927; Compagnie de Tramways (Paris) to MAE, 27 March 1927, AMAE, vol. 341.

20. Chambre de Commerce Franco-asiatique (Paris) to Briand, 31 March 1927, passing on a wire from Charlot of the French Chamber, AMAE, vol. 341.

21. French Consul-General Turin to MAE, 1 April 1927, AMAE, vol. 342.

22. WO 191/1, appendix W, Staff, SDF to USMC, 28 March 1927; Naggiar to Legation, 6 Feb. 1927; MAE to Fleuriau, 22 Feb. 1927, AMAE, vol. 341.

23. F3039/156/10 Duncan to War Office, 30 March 1927; MAE to Naggiar, 2 April 1927, AMAE, vol. 342; Ministre de la Marine to MAE, 4 April 1927, AMAE, vol. 342; *NCH*, 2 April 1927, p. 16.

24. Naggiar to MAE, 29 March 1927, and 31 March 1927, AMAE, vol. 341.

25. Gauss to State, 24 March 1927, USCGS 1927, part 35A; Graves to Gauss, 30 March, USCGS 1927, part 33.

26. 393.11/506 Gauss to State, 27 March 1927; 893.00/8481 MacMurray to State, 30 March 1927.

27. 893.00/8487 State to Gauss, 30 March 1927; *CWR*, 2 April 1927, 119. See also Powell, *My Twenty-Five Years*, 161–66, for his story of what lay behind this episode.

28. *NCH*, 5 April 1927, p. 54; C. J. Spiker memorandum of 27 June 1927, USCGS 1927, part 37.

29. Graves to Wood, 23 Feb. 1927, Graves Papers, RG 64–116; the poster can be found in 893.00/8267 Gauss to Legation, 21 Jan. 1927, and reproduced in the *NCH*, 19 Jan. 1927, p. 100.

30. *NCH*, 22 Jan. 1927, pp. 100, 103, 106; Lobenstine to Gauss, 21 Jan. 1927, USCGS 1927, part 82.

31. *NCH*, 22 Jan. 1927, p. 106, and 29 Jan. 1927, p. 152.

32. *NCH*, 12 March 1927, p. 419, and 26 March 1927, p. 516.

33. *NCH*, 2 April 1927, pp. 47–48, 81.

34. *NCH*, 23 April 1927, p. 171.

35. Graves to Wood, 2 April, 6 April 1927, Graves Papers, RG 64–116; undated request to Gauss, USCGS 1927, part 36. For the file and forget, see 893.00/8531 Warnshuis to N. T. Johnson, 19 April 1927.

36. *NCDN*, 12 April 1927.

37. *NCH*, 16 April 1927, p. 114.

38. Henry T. Hodgkin, "National Christian Council in 1927," in *The China Christian Yearbook, 1928* (Shanghai, 1928), 71–72. There was no 1927 edition of the *Yearbook*.

39. 893.00/9022 American Baptist Foreign Mission Society to State, 19 May 1927; 893.00/9271 Memorandum by N. T. Johnson, 21 July 1927.

40. Wood to Graves, 7 April, and 18 June 1927; Graves to Wood, 18 May 1927, Graves Papers, RG 64–116.

41. Graves to Wood, 9 May 1927, Graves Papers, RG 64–116.

42. *CWR*, 9 April 1927, 142–43, and 2 April 1927, 118.

43. 393.1163.152 Warnshuis to Johnson, 12 April 1927; 393.1163/157 Warnshuis to Johnson, 19 April 1927.

44. Wood to State, 28 March 1927, USCGS 1927, part 33; *NCH*, 7 May 1927, p. 235, and 14 May 1927, p. 280.

45. *Nation*, 13 April 1927, 388.

46. Gauss to State, 7 April, 13 April 1927, USCGS 1927, part 84; *Nation*, 20 April 1927, 410. The Nanking confusion lives on; a recent account has transformed G. A. Kennedy's story into an American governmental investigation! See Sterling Seagrave, *The Soong Dynasty* (New York, 1985), 224.

47. F4315/1/10 Stamfordham to Tyrrell, 10 Oct. 1926; Tyrrell to Stamfordham, 12 Oct. 1926.

48. Milly Bennett, draft for Autobiography, Bennett Papers, box 10, file 14, box 11, file 4.

49. Prohme to Gauss, 31 March 1927; Gauss to Prohme, 2 April 1927, USCGS 1927, part 84.

50. Bennett Papers, box 10, file 15.

51. Bennett Papers, box 10, file 14.

52. Bennett Papers, box 10, file 14.

53. Bennett Papers, box 10, file 15.

54. F4454/2/10 Minute by Mounsey, 2 May 1927; see also F7793/7793/10 Lampson to Mounsey, 22 July 1927, for the minister's response, which comes to Barton's defense. For Missee Lee, see *The Autobiography of Arthur Ransome*, ed. Rupert Hart-Davis (London, 1976), 326.

55. *NCH*, 28 May 1927, p. 366.

56. F4313/4313/10 contains the *Manchester Guardian's* article of 2 May 1927 and Pratt's minute of 5 May.

Chapter 15, *Squeezed Like a Lemon (pp. 242–56)*

1. *The Times* (London), 22 March 1927, p. 14.

2. *Nation*, 23 March 1927, 302.

3. Isaacs, *Tragedy*, 162.

4. *NCDN*, 12 April 1927.

5. This was the Third Plenum of the Central Executive Committee of the Guomindang; see Wilbur, "Nationalist Revolution," 613, and Li, *CRG*, 545.

6. *NCDN*, 25 March 1927.

7. *NCDN*, 28 March 1927.

8. Zhou Shangwen and He Shiyu, *Shanghai gongren*, 260, 268.

9. F3085/156/10 Barton to Legation, 1 April 1927; F3297/156/10 Barton to Legation, 6 April 1927.

10. 893.00/8547 Gauss to State, 4 April 1927; 893.00/8624 Gauss to State, 8 April 1927.

11. F3077/156/10 Minute of 1 April 1927.

12. *NCH*, 2 April 1927, p. 15; F3077/1530/10 Minute of 1 April 1927; F3460/2/10 Minute of 11 April 1927.

13. WO 191/1, appendix N, Duncan to War Office, 15 April 1927; F3154/1530/10 CinC to Admiralty, 2 April 1927; F3259/1530/10 Admiralty to CinC, 5 April 1927.

14. F3428/1530/10 Tilley to F.O., 8 April 1927.

15. The emissary was Huang Fu; Shen Yu, " 'Si yi er' fan geming zhengbian yu diguozhuyi guanxi zai zhentao" [Another Look at the Relationship of the "12 April" Coup to Imperialism] *Lishi yanjiu* [*Historical Research*] no. 4 (1984): 52–53; F3422/2/10 Tilley to F.O., 3 April 1927; F3043/1530/10 Lampson to F.O., 31 March 1927; F3006/1530/10 Crewe to F.O., 31 March 1927; F3169/1530/10 Tilley to F.O., 4 April 1927 (in which he reported Shidehara's statement that Chiang would take strong action against the extremists).

16. F3859/1530/10 Lampson to F.O., 11 April 1927; F3077/1530/10 Pratt minute, 31 March 1927 (date uncertain); F3116/1530/10 Pratt memorandum, 31 March 1927.

17. F4382/4382/10 Lampson to Wellesley, 27 April 1927.

18. Prosper Paris papers, unsigned memo dated 21 Dec. 1928, "Règlement de l'affaire de NANKIN: 24 March 1927," box 1, Carton 31.

19. Zhou Shangwen and He Shiyu, *Shanghai gongren*, 267.

20. The higher figure comes from the Shanghai Defence Force. F3139/156/10 Duncan to War Office, 31 March 1927.

21. Zhou Shangwen and He Shiyu, *Shanghai gongren*, 263.

22. Undated notes of interview by Powell, USCGS 1927, part 84; 893.00/8906 Gauss to State, 21 April 1927; SMA, PDR, 24–25 March 1927; ABAC, 11 April 1927, AMAE, vol. 201, *passim*, has frequent reports of difficulties between the two sides.

23. F2832/156/10 Barton to Legation, 25 March 1927; Li, *CRG*, 627; Zhou Shangwen and He Shiyu, *Shanghai gongren*, 250.

24. NCDN, 2 April 1927; *Shibao*, 30 April 1927; MGSS, 492. Jiang, *Boloting*, 115–16, lists their names; see also Zhou Shangwen and He Shiyu, *Shanghai gongren*, 248–49, and Zhou Qisheng, *Shanghai gongren*, 430–35, for the organization of the government.

25. Zhou Qisheng, *Shanghai gongren*, 437.

26. F3139/156/10 Duncan to War Office, 3 March 1927; Li Tsung-jen and Te-kong Tong, *The Memoirs of Li Tsung-jen* (Boulder, 1979), 207.

27. Li Tsung-jen and Te-kong Tong, *Memoirs*, 208–9; MGSS, 577; Li, *CRG*, 620.

28. Li, *CRG*, 610–11.

29. Li, *CRG*, 612–13.

30. Shen Yu, " 'Si yi er' fan geming," 54.

31. Li, *CRG*, 615.

32. Li, *CRG*, 615–16.

33. Isaacs, *Tragedy*, 165; Li, *CRG*, 618–19; Zhou Shangwen and He Shiyu, *Shanghai gongren*, 255–58; Feng Chunming, "Guanyu 1927 nian 4 yue Jiang Jieshi Wang Jingwei Shanghai huitan" [Concerning the conversations between Chiang Kai-shek and Wang Jingwei in Shanghai, April 1927], *Lishi yu dangan* [History and Archives], (1983): 122–23.

34. Chang Yi, "Zhao Shiyan," 78; Zhou Shangwen and He Shiyu, *Shanghai gongren*, 309–12, gives a somewhat more balanced appraisal, and Zhou Qisheng, *Shanghai gongren*, 449, the view at the time. Chen Duxiu later blamed the Comintern for ordering him to issue the statement (Wilbur, "Nationalist Revolution," 624).

35. Li, *CRG*, 620; Jiang, *Boloting*, 128 (Yang Xisheng was the Wuhan nominee); F3329/2/10 Goffe to Legation, 2 April 1927.

36. Li, *CRG*, 594–98; Jiang, *Boloting*, 129; Wilbur, "Nationalist Revolution," 626–28.

37. Jiang, *Boloting*, 140–47; Jacobs, *Borodin*, 245; ABAC, 25 April 1927, AMAE, vol. 201.

38. The most thorough examination of the documents and their reliability is in Wilbur and How, eds., *Missionaries*, 1–16, 403–4.

39. Linde to Senior Consul, 7 April 1927; Fessenden to Senior Consul, 13 April, 20 April 1927; Gauss to Legation, 23 April, USCGS 1927, part 97; 893.00/8624 Gauss to State, 8 April 1927; ABAC, 11, April 1927, AMAE, vol. 201.

40. Jiang, *Boloting*, 128.

41. Li, *CRG*, 623–26; Jiang, *Boloting*, 131–35; Wilbur, "Nationalist Revolution," 633.

42. Chang Yi, "Zhao Shiyan," 76–79.

43. SMA, PDR, 4 April, 8 April 1927; Li, *CRG*, 627; Zhou Shangwen and He Shiyu, *Shanghai gongren*, 251. The new government was the *Shanghai linshi zhengzhi weiyuanhui*.

44. Wilbur, "Nationalist Revolution," 610; Isaacs, *Tragedy*, 151–52; Bergère, *L'age d'or*, 241–43; Wu Tien-wei, "Chiang Kai-shek's April 12th Coup of 1927," in F. Gilbert Chan and Thomas H. Etzold, eds., *China in the 1920s: Nationalism and Revolution* (New York, 1976), 151–52.

45. The best account of the role of the underworld is to be found in Brian Martin, "Green Gang and 'Party Purification' in Shanghai."

46. Martin, "Pact with the Devil," 100.

47. Martin, "Green Gang," 21.

48. SMA, PDR, 3–4 April 1927; Martin, "Green Gang," 35; Xu Zhucheng, *Du Yuesheng zhengzhuan* (Fuzhou, 1982), 44–45.

49. Naggiar to MAE, 26 Feb. 1927, AMAE, vol. 340.

50. Naggiar to MAE, 1 March 1927, AMAE, vol. 340. Both Martel and the Quai d'Orsay seem to have assumed that the supplies were for the Volunteers and the police. See MAE to Ministry of War, 2 March, and Martel to MAE, 5 March 1927, AMAE, vol. 340.

51. Powell, *My Twenty-Five Years*, 158–59. Although the chronology in Powell's memoirs is faulty, the story (which he had from Fessenden) has the ring of truth to it. Less convincing is a recent Communist version that has Fessenden reluctant to go along at first, afraid he would call down the wrath of the workers on the Settlement, and giving in only after Du's persuasion. See Zhou Shangwen and He Shiyu, *Shanghai gongren*, 273.

52. Naggiar to MAE, 21 May 1927, Naggiar Papers, carton I.

53. Zhou Qisheng, *Shanghai gongren*, 406; 390, 407 for Xue Yue (who later would build a reputation as a persecutor of the Communists).

54. Zhou Qisheng, *Shanghai gongren*, 374–77, 386, 392, 408–9.

55. Jiang, *Boloting*, 116–17.

56. Isaacs, *Tragedy*, 163; Zhou Shangwen argues that the advice was sound (*Shanghai gongren*, 256, 313–18).

57. Jonathan Marshall, "Opium and the Politics of Gangsterism in Nationalist China, 1927–1945," *Bulletin of Concerned Asian Scholars* 8 (July–Sept. 1976): 40.

58. Shanghai General Labor Union, " 'Si er yi' da tusha jishi," [A record of the great massacre of 12 April], reprinted in *Guonei*, 494; Chang Yi, "Zhao Shiyan," 79; Wilbur, "Nationalist Revolution," 635; Zhou Shangwen and He Shiyu, *Shanghai gongren*, 271–72.

59. SMA, PDR, 12 April 1927.

60. "Da tusha jishi," 495–500; Zhou Shangwen and He Shiyu, *Shanghai gong-ren*, 257–58; Jiang, *Boloting*, 161–63; Isaacs, *Tragedy*, 176–77.

61. "Da tusha jishi," 507–15; Zhou Shangwen and He Shiyu, *Shanghai gong-ren*, 279–84.

62. NCDN, 14 April 1927; "Da tusha jishi," 517–18; Zhou Shangwen and He Shiyu, *Shanghai gongren*, 286–90.

63. "Da tusha jishi," 522–24; Zhou Shangwen and He Shiyu, *Shanghai gong-ren*, 288–89.

64. "Da tusha jishi," 626; Zhou Shangwen and He Shiyu, *Shanghai gongren*, 290–91; Li, *CRG*, 629.

65. SMA, PDR, 14 April 1927; *NCH*, 16 April 1927, p. 104; Chang Yi, "Zhao Shiyan," 82–83; Zhou Shangwen and He Shiyu, *Shanghai gongren*, 299.

66. "Da tusha jishi," 531–33.

67. The terrorist Chen Ta-er's attempted assassination of Chiang Kai-shek never took place. Nor is there any evidence that any of the victims of the purge were burned to death in a locomotive firebox, or that any Russians, like Katov, lost their lives in the slaughter (though several fell victims to the purge in Canton several days later). Above all, Malraux's account diminishes the Chinese role: the Franco-Japanese Kyo Gisors and the Russian Katov lead the Communist forces in Shanghai, the French banker Ferral negotiates Chinese loans to the Guomindang, and Chiang's European police chief König takes charge of the repression. In his suggestion that the Chinese were followers, not leaders, apparently by themselves capable of neither revolution nor counter-revolution, Malraux incongruously reflects a common Western view of the day.

68. "Da tusha jishi," 492, 500, 527–28, gives the version at the time; for recent views, see Shen Yü, " 'Si yi er' fan geming," 46–58; Niu Dayong, "Meiguo dui Hua zhengce yu 'si yi er' zhengbian de guanxi" [The relationship of the 12 April coup to America's China policy], *Lishi yanjiu*, no. 4 (1985): 152–65, as well as the more general works of Huang Yifeng and Zhou Shangwen.

69. SMA, PDR, 7 April 1927.

70. Powell, *My Twenty-Five Years*, 154–59; John Pal, *Shanghai Saga* (London, 1963), 50. Sterling Seagrave's retelling of the story does nothing to clear up the inaccuracies; see *Soong Dynasty*, 221–22.

71. Vera Vladimirovna Vishnyakova-Akimova, *Two Years in Revolutionary China*, trans. Steven I. Levine (Cambridge, Mass., 1971), 308.

72. *NCH*, 16 April 1927, p. 102.

Chapter 16, The Aftermath (pp. 257–75)

1. Lawrence R. Sullivan, "Reconstruction and Rectification of the Communist Party in the Shanghai Underground: 1931–1934," *China Quarterly* 101 (March 1985): 78–97.

2. *NCH*, 30 April 1927, p. 191.

3. *NCH*, 18 June 1926, p. 499.

4. F4382/4382/10 Lampson to Wellesley, 20 April 1927.

5. F3599/2/10 Barton to F.O., 13 April 1927.

6. Naggiar to Legation, 16 April 1927, AMAE, vol. 303; F5546/5439/10 Barton to F.O., 14 June 1927; F5398/5439/10 Barton to Legation, 2 July 1927. Naggiar's

impression was that Barton would have liked to use British troops to solve the Shanghai problem once and for all.

7. 893.00/8655 Gauss to State, 12 April 1927; 893.00/8906 Gauss to Legation, 21 April 1927.

8. Martel to MAE, 15 April 1927, AMAE, vol. 267; Naggiar to MAE, 21 May 1927, Naggiar Papers, Carton I.

9. 893.00/9002 Gauss to Legation, 28 April 1927.

10. F4382/4382/10 Lampson to Wellesley, 27 April 1927.

11. F3599/2/10 Pratt minute of 13 April 1927; F4301/2/10 Wellesley minute of 6 May 1927.

12. 893.00/9339 Cunningham to Legation, 30 June 1927; 893.00/9328 Cunningham to Legation, 19 Aug. 1927. See also S.M.P. report for May in *NCH*, 18 June 1927, pp. 520–21. Though Cunningham did not know it, the secretariat of the Communist party, in a desperate attempt to recover the situation, had proposed on 23 June the launching of a new mass anti-imperialist movement in Shanghai, thus forcing the foreigners to occupy Nanking and Shanghai. The resulting outcry would destroy Chiang Kai-shek's position. The Politburo vetoed this suicidal scheme, however. See Wilbur, "Nationalist Revolution," 665–66.

13. 893.00/9731 Roots to Kellogg, 16 Dec. 1927.

14. *NCH*, 11 June 1927, p. 488.

15. Graves to Wood, 22 July 1927, Graves Papers, RG 64–116.

16. *NCH*, 7 May 1927, pp. 243, 233.

17. See for instance, *NCH*, 20 Aug. 1927, p. 318.

18. *NCH*, 16 June 1927, p. 489.

19. See, for instance, the calls for intervention by Arthur de C. Sowerby (*NCH*, 21 May 1927, p. 356) and by the American General William Crozier, who argued that eight to ten American divisions could take care of the Chinese military threat; there would be no fear of guerrilla war because Chinese lacked the patriotism to make the necessary sacrifices (*NCH*, 3 Sept. 1927, pp. 428–29). The article drew a complimentary response from Ferdinand Mayer (to Crozier, 30 Sept. 1927, USL 1927, vol. 26).

20. The top figure of twenty thousand comes from F6720/3/10 F.O. memorandum of 8 Jan. 1930 in Rohan Butler and J. P. T. Bury, eds., *Documents on British Foreign Policy, 1919–1939*, 2d series (hereafter cited as *DBFP*), vol. 8 (London, 1960): 10.

21. R. N. Bruce Lockhart in the *NCDN*, 26 April 1927, p. 12.

22. *CWR*, 5 Feb. 1927, 250–52, and 26 Feb. 1927, 332; see also, 7 May 1927, 241–42, and 12 May 1927, 37–40.

23. *NCH*, 30 April 1927, p. 209; *CWR*, 30 April 1927, 220–21.

24. *NCH*, 30 April 1927, p. 213.

25. A. Bland Calder to Director, Bureau of Foreign and Domestic Commerce, 19 May 1927, Hoover Institute, Julean Arnold Papers, box 11; Powell to Nelson Johnson, 18 June 1927, N. T. Johnson Papers, vol. 6; and H. T. S. Green to Nelson Johnson, 23 July 1927, vol. 5.

26. Calder to Bureau of Foreign and Domestic Commerce, 31 August 1927, in Julean Arnold Papers, box 11; *CWR*, 3 Sept. 1927, 5–6.

27. Huskey, "Americans in Shanghai," 132–44; the term "pusillanimous" was used by Maj. C. F. Holcomb at the chamber's April meeting.

28. *NCH*, 11 June 1927, p. 473, and 18 June 1927, p. 500, for the public side of

the bureau; Memorandum by R. Huntley-Davidson on the history of the Bureau, enclosed in FO 228, vol. 3883, Garstin to Aveling, 5 Oct. 1928.

29. *NCH*, 13 August 1927, p. 278.
30. F6917/6917/10 Minutes by K. R. Johnson, 17 Aug. 1927.
31. *NCH*, 1 Oct. 1927, p. 14.
32. *NCH*, 1 Oct. 1927, p. 15.
33. *NCH*, 7 May 1927, p. 266.
34. 893.102S/117 Gauss to State, 5 May 1927.
35. Naggiar to MAE, 12 April 1927, AMAE, vol. 259.
36. Naggiar to Legation, 12 Aug. 1927, Naggiar Papers, Carton I; Berthelot to de Guébriant, 7 July 1927, and de Guébriant to Berthelot, 16 July, AMAE, vol. 259.
37. 893.102S/118 MacMurray to State, 3 July 1927; State to MacMurray, 5 July 1927.
38. F5938/5439/10 Barton to Legation, 2 July 1927; *NCH*, 18 June 1927, p. 520, 16 July 1927, p. 107, and 9 July 1927, p. 60. According to the Council's figures, on a per capita basis, each Chinese resident of the Settlement paid about Tls. 6 per year in rates and had about Tls. 7 invested in debentures, while each foreigner paid about Tls. 145 and had about Tls. 1,313 invested. *NCH*, 16 July 1927, p. 108. What the Council's figures ignore is the percentage of the foreign-paid rates that actually came from the pockets of Chinese whose properties were beneficially held by foreigners.
39. Fewsmith, *Party, State and Local Elites*, 135–36.
40. *NCH*, 27 Aug. 1927, p. 363; F9531/5439/10 Barton to Legation, 25 Oct. 1927; FO 228, vol. 3883, Barton to Legation, 31 Dec. 1927.
41. 893.102S/131 Cunningham to State, 17 April 1927; F355/170/10 Lampson to F.O., 23 Jan. 1928.
42. F1424/170/10 Lampson to F.O., 24 March 1928; FO 228, vol. 3883, Barton to Legation, 17 April 1928, has the most detail and much of the supporting correspondence; see also Lampson to F.O., 24 March 1928, Barton to Legation, 31 March, 3 April, 20 April. 893.102S/131 Cunningham to State, 17 April 1928, has Cunningham's report, and he is the source for the statement that Hilton-Johnson did the main work of negotiation.
43. *NCH*, 9 July 1927, p. 60; 893.00 PR Shanghai/1 Cunningham to Legation, 11 Feb. 1928; Meyrier to Legation, 18 Feb. 1928, AMAE, Asie: Affaires Communes, 2ème partie, vol. 56.
44. FO 405, vol. 256, F367/7/10 Extract from the Birmingham *Post*, 10 Jan. 1928.
45. Borg, *American Policy*, 378–85.
46. Fewsmith, *Party, State, and Local Elites*, 130.
47. Marie-Claire Bergère, " 'The Other China': Shanghai from 1919 to 1949," in *Shanghai: Revolution and Development in an Asian Metropolis*, ed. Christopher Howe (Cambridge, 1981), 17.
48. 800.00B International Red Day/51 Cunningham to State, 12 May 1930.
49. 893.00 PR Shanghai/8 Cunningham to Legation, 11 Aug. 1928; 893.00 PR Shanghai/11 Cunningham to Legation, 28 Jan. 1929.
50. F. C. Jones, *Shanghai and Tientsin*, 13, 22; *DBFP*, 2d series, vol. 11, F1158/26/10 Lampson to F.O., 24 Aug. 1933, 570–71; Cunningham to State, 13 March 1930, USCGS 1930, part 91.
51. *FRUS 1931*, vol. 3, Cunningham to State, 12 Oct. 1931, 163–64; and 21 Oct. 1931, 281–82.

52. F658/250/10 Lampson to F.O., 6 Feb. 1929; F3797/250/10 Lampson to F.O., 7 June 1929.

53. As they did in 1929, for instance, in discussing the invitation of outside opinion to examine the Shanghai problem.

54. Bergère, " 'Other China,' " 15.

55. F3797/250/10 Lampson to F.O., 7 June 1929.

56. 893.00 PR Shanghai/11 Cunningham to Legation, 28 Jan. 1929; 893.00 PR Shanghai/14 Cunningham to Legation, 10 April 1929.

57. Parks M. Coble, *The Shanghai Capitalists and the Nationalist Government, 1927–1937* (Cambridge, Mass., 1980), 32–41.

58. Though Barton denied any French role (FO 228, vol. 3883, Barton to Legation, 31 Dec. 1927).

59. Meyrier to Legation, 18 Feb. 1928, AMAE, Asie: Affaires Communes, 2ème partie, vol. 56; Koechlin to MAE, 17 Sept. 1929, AMAE, vol. 338.

60. F522/127/87 Barton to Legation, 1 Dec. 1927; F612/127/87 Barton to Legation, 6 Feb. 1928; Cunningham to Legation, 6 Feb. 1928, 17 March, USCGS 1928, part 122.

61. F4290/127/87 Barton to Legation, 5 May 1928; F4749/4749/87 Pratt memorandum of 10 Aug. 1929; Cosme to MAE, 14 May 1928, AMAE, vol. 56.

62. FO 228, vol. 3887, Brett to Fox, 24 July 1928; Tottenham to India Office, 16 Aug. 1928.

63. Martel to MAE, 10 Feb. 1928; Meyrier to Legation, 18 Feb. 1928; Meyrier to Legation, 15 March 1928; Meyrier to Legation, 13 May 1928; Cosme to MAE, 14 May 1928, AMAE, vol. 56.

64. F6071/127/28 Garstin to Legation, 26 Sept. 1928.

65. FO 228, vol. 4051, Garstin to Legation, 15 April 1929.

66. F3570/184/87 Brenan to Legation, 29 May 1930.

67. Meyrier to MAE, 16 May 1932, AMAE: Asie, Affaires Communes, 3ème Partie, vol. 111; see also Garstin's report on opium traffic in FO 415 F6548/69/87 Lampson to F.O., 22 Oct. 1929, and F4749/4749/87 "Memorandum Respecting the Opium Problem in the Far East," by Pratt, 10 Aug. 1929.

68. Meyrier to MAE, 25 June 1932, AMAE, vol. 111. For Schwyzer's role as commander of the French Special Police—a volunteer force—see *NCH*, 5 Nov. 1927, p. 234.

69. Martin, "Pact with the Devil," 113–14.

70. FO 228, vol. 3883, Barton to Legation, 2 April 1928.

71. F9425/25/10 (1927) Mounsey to Lampson, 18 Jan. 1928.

72. F4209/250/10 Memo by Pratt, 14 Aug. 1929.

73. F307/78/10 Lampson to F.O., 6 Dec. 1929.

74. F6720/3/10 F.O. Memorandum of 8 Jan. 1930 on British policy in China, *DBFP*, 2d series, vol. 8, 19.

75. F9426/25/10 (1927) Mounsey to Lampson, 18 Jan. 1928; FO 228, vol. 3677, Mounsey to Lampson, 28 Sept. 1927.

76. FO 228, vol. 3677, Lampson to Barton, 27 July 1927; F7793/7793/10 Lampson to Mounsey, 27 July 1927, deals with the "anti-Barton campaign."

77. FO 228, vol. 3677, Barton to Legation, 21 Oct. 1927.

78. F9426/25/10 (1927) Mounsey to Lampson, 18 Jan. 1928.

79. F910/170/10 Barton to Legation, 22 Feb. 1928.

80. F910/170/10 Mounsey to Lampson, 29 Feb. 1928.

81. FO 228, vol. 3677, Lampson to F.O., 24 Dec. 1927; F699/170/10 Newton

to F.O., 10 Feb. 1928; F1321/170/10 Lampson memo of 20 Jan. 1928, of talk with J. B. Condliffe, the research secretary of the I.P.R.

82. F760/250/10 Lampson to F.O., 11 Feb. 1929; F1999/250/10 Pratt minute of 22 April 1929. Edwin Cunningham agreed; see 893.00 PR Shanghai/15 Cunningham to Legation, 4 May 1929.

83. F2013/250/10 Minute of 24 April 1929.

84. F307/78/10 (1930) Malcolm MacDonald to Lampson, 22 Nov. 1929.

85. 893.00 PR Shanghai/15 Cunningham to Legation, 4 May 1929.

86. 893.102S/184 Memorandum by N. T. Johnson of interview with Fessenden, 23 Aug. 1929.

87. F5766/250/10 Lampson to F.O., 9 Nov. 1929.

88. F353/78/10 (1930) Lionel Curtis to N. S. Brown, 4 Dec. 1929, enclosing memo on genesis of Feetham Report. See also F107/78/10 (1930), R. Huntley Davidson to G. M. Gillette, 6 Dec. 1929, and F249/78/10 Huntley Davidson to Noel Baker, 6 Dec. 1929. The message from Curtis to Feetham of 11 Nov. 1929 is in USCGS 1929, part 103.

89. F5766/250/10 Minutes by Pratt of 11 Nov., and Orde of 12 Nov. 1929.

90. Cunningham to State, 22 July 1931, including *NCDN* editorials of 25 April, 18 June, and 19 June, USCGS 1931, part 111.

91. F3313/220/10 Lampson to F.O., 5 June 1931.

92. F3810/220/10 Lampson to Godfrey Locker Lampson, 5 June 1931; F1158/26/10 Lampson to F.O., 24 Aug. 1933, *DBFP* 2d series, vol. 11, 579. This dispatch, printed as an appendix to the volume in which it appears, is Lampson's long retrospective look at his service as minister to China from 1926 to 1933.

93. F4904/220/10 Memorandum by Pratt of 10 Sept. 1931.

94. *CWR*, 27 June 1931, 129–32.

95. Stanley Jackson, *The Sassoons* (London, 1968), 210–18; "The Shanghai Boom," *Fortune*, Jan. 1935, 32–38, claimed Mex. $85 million (about U.S. $30 million) as the amount brought from India.

96. *CWR*, 26 Sept. 1931, 125–26.

97. Nicholas R. Clifford, *Retreat from China: British Policy in the Sino-Japanese War, 1937–1941* (London and Seattle, 1967), 15–16, citing E. M. Gull, *British Economic Interest in the Far East* (New York, 1943), 119; C. F. Remer, *Foreign Investments*, 397, 403; *The Times*, 19 and 20 Aug. 1937.

98. Figures from "Shanghai Boom," 32–38, 100.

99. On this point, the recent works of Joseph Fewsmith, Parks Coble, and Marie-Claire Bergère agree.

100. "Shanghai Boom," 40, 110–12.

101. "Shanghai Boom," 112.

102. *DBFP*, 2d series, vol. 9, F1109/1/10 Brenan to Legation, 9 Feb. 1932, 421–22; *FRUS 1932*, vol. 3, Cunningham to State, 19 Feb. 1932, 403–4; Cunningham to State, 4 March 1932, 507–8.

103. *CWR*, 23 April 1932, 240–42, and 14 May 1932, 344.

104. *DBFP*, 2d series, vol. 9, no. 395, F1109/1/10 Brenan to Legation, 9 Feb. 1932, 421–22; no. 583, F1822/1/10 Lampson to F.O., 26 Feb. 1932, 627–28; vol. 10, no. 20, F2166/1/10 Lampson to F.O., 5 March 1932, 23–24; no. 31, F2316/65/10 Lampson to F.O., 8 March 1932, 54; no. 48, F2441/1/10 Lampson to F.O., 9 March 1932, 74–75; see also vol. 21, no. 497, F1023/78/10 Memo by Pratt, 24 Jan. 1938, 667; *FRUS 1932*, vol. 3, State to Wilson, 7 March 1932, 526; Johnson to State, 7 March 1932, 526–27; Cunningham to State, 23 March 1932, 622–23; Johnson to State, 9 April 1932, 682.

105. Clive to Vansittart, 5 Dec. 1935, quoted in Ann Trotter, *Britain and East Asia 1933–1937* (Cambridge, 1975), 26.

106. Clifford, *Retreat*, 25–26.

107. Clifford, *Retreat*, 68–73.

108. Clifford, *Retreat*, 148–50.

Chapter 17, Conclusion (pp. 276–85)

1. Royal Institute of International Affairs, *Survey of International Affairs, 1939–1946: The Far East, 1946*, by F. C. Jones, Hugh Borton, and B. R. Pearn (London, 1955), 17–20, 262.

2. Quoted by Charles V. Murphy, "Shanghai: Reopened under New Management," *Fortune*, Feb. 1946, 143.

3. Lt. Col. Pendleton Hogan, "Shanghai after the Japs," *Virginia Quarterly Review* 22 (Winter 1946): 90.

4. *NCDN*, 13 Dec. 1948.

5. Robert Boardman, *Britain and the People's Republic of China 1949–1974* (New York, 1976), 13, 82.

6. Murphy, "Shanghai," 223.

7. *CWR*, 28 May 1949, 13; 4 June 1949 for "Songs of Liberation." For the American chamber, see Noel Barber, *The Fall of Shanghai* (New York, 1979), 164.

8. Rhoads Murphey, *The Outsiders; the Western Experience in India and China* (Ann Arbor, 1977); Marie-Claire Bergère, " 'Other China,' " 1–34. Bergère contrasts Murphey's more recent view with his earlier work, *Shanghai: Key to Modern China*, which appeared in 1953.

9. Albert Memmi, *The Colonizer and the Colonized* (London, 1974), 64.

10. *Finance and Commerce*, 2 March 1927, 92.

11. On this subject, see Andrew Nathan, *Chinese Democracy* (New York, 1985), esp. 22, 67–86.

12. Trotter, *Britain and East Asia*, 3.

13. See Bergère, *L'age d'or*, 263–64.

14. Shelly Yomano, "Reintegration in China under the Warlords, 1916–1927," *Republican China* 12 (April 1987): 22–27.

15. Lee Feigon, "Lurking in the Shadows."

16. Bergère, *L'age d'or*, 240–43.

17. Shen Ximeng, Mo Yan, Lu Xingchen, *On Guard Beneath the Neon Lights* (Peking, 1966), 87.

Bibliography

I. Published Sources

BOOKS

Alec-Tweedie, Mrs. *An Adventurous Journey: Russia-Siberia-China*. London: Thornton, Butterworth, 1926.

All about Shanghai: A Standard Guidebook. Shanghai: The University Press, 1934–35, reprinted by Oxford University Press, 1983.

Allman, Norwood F. *Shanghai Lawyer*. New York: McGraw-Hill, 1943.

Arnold, Julean, et al. *China: A Commercial and Industrial Handbook* Department of Commerce, Bureau of Foreign and Domestic Commerce Trade Promotion, series no. 38. Washington: Government Printing Office, 1926.

Bamba Nobuya. *Japanese Diplomacy in a Dilemma: New Light on Japan's China Policy, 1924–1929*. Vancouver: University of British Columbia Press, 1972.

Barber, Noel. *The Fall of Shanghai*. New York: Coward, McCann and Geoghan, 1979.

Bergère, Marie-Claire. *L'age d'or de la bourgeoisie chinoise, 1911–1937*. Paris: Flammarion, 1986.

Boardman, Robert. *Britain and the People's Republic of China, 1949–1974*. New York: Harper and Row, 1976.

Booker, Edna Lee. *News Is My Job: A Correspondent in War-Torn China*. New York: MacMillan, 1940.

Boorman, Howard L., and Richard C. Howard, eds. *Biographical Dictionary of Republican China*. 5 vols. New York: Columbia University Press, 1967.

Borg, Dorothy. *American Policy and the Chinese Revolution, 1925–1928*. New York: American Institute of Pacific Relations and Macmillan, 1947. Reprint. New York: Octagon Books, 1968.

Bouissou, Jean-Marie. *Seigneurs de guerre et officers rouges, 1924–1927: la révolution chinoise*. Tours: Maison Mame, 1974.

Brandt, Conrad. *Stalin's Failure in China*. New York: Norton, 1966.

Breslin, Thomas A. *China, American Catholicism, and the Missionary*. University Park: Pennsylvania State University Press, 1980.

Buhite Russell D. *Nelson T. Johnson and American Policy toward China, 1925–1941*. East Lansing: Michigan State University Press, 1968.

Burns, Richard Dean, and Edward M. Bennett, eds. *Diplomats in Crisis: United States-Chinese-Japanese Relations, 1919–1941*. Santa Barbara: A.B.C. Clio Press, 1974.

Cambridge History of China. Vol. 12, part 1, *Republican China, 1912–1949*, ed. John K. Fairbank. Cambridge: Cambridge University Press, 1983.

Candlin, Enid Saunders. *The Breach in the Wall: A Memoir of the Old China.* New York: Paragon House, 1987.

Cary-Elwes, Columba. *China and the Cross: Studies in Missionary History.* London: Longmans Green and Co., 1957.

Chan, Anthony B. *Arming the Chinese: The Western Armaments Trade in Warlord China, 1920–1928.* Vancouver: University of British Columbia Press, 1982.

Chan, F. Gilbert, and Thomas H. Etzold, eds. *China in the 1920s: Nationalism and Revolution.* New York: New Viewpoints, 1976.

Chang Kuo-t'ao (Zhang Guotao). *The Rise of the Chinese Communist Party, 1921–1927: Volume One of the Autobiography of Chang Kuo-t'ao.* Lawrence: The University Press of Kansas, 1971.

Chen, Percy. *China Called Me.* Boston: Little Brown, 1979.

Cherepanov, A. I. *As Military Adviser in China.* Translated by Sergei Sosinsky. Moscow: Progress Publishers, 1982.

Chesneaux, Jean. *The Chinese Labor Movement 1919–1927.* Translated by H. M. Wright. Stanford: Stanford University Press, 1968.

Ch'i, Hsi-sheng. *Warlord Politics in China, 1916–1928.* Stanford: Stanford University Press, 1976.

China Christian Year Book, 1926. Edited by Frank Rawlinson. Shanghai: Christian Literature Society, 1926.

China Her Own Interpreter: Chapters by a Group of Nationals Interpreting the Christian Movement. Edited by Milton Stauffer. New York: John A. Murray, 1927.

China Mission Year Book, 1925. Edited by Henry T. Hodgkin. Shanghai: Christian Literature Society, 1925.

China Stock and Share Handbook. Compiled by C. R. Maguire. Shanghai: North China Daily News and Herald, 1926.

China Yearbook (annual). Edited by H. G. W. Woodhead. Tianjin: The Tientsin Press, 1924–1929.

Clark, Peter Gaffney. "Britain and the Chinese Revolution, 1925–1927." Ph.D. dissertation, University of California at Berkeley, 1973. Ann Arbor: University Microfilms, 1973.

Clifford, Nicholas R. *Retreat from China: British Policy in the Far East 1937–1941.* London: Longmans, 1967.

Clifford, Nicholas R. *Shanghai, 1925: Urban Nationalism and the Defense of Foreign Privilege.* Ann Arbor: Center for Chinese Studies, University of Michigan, 1979.

Clubb, O. Edmund. *20th Century China.* 3d ed. New York: Columbia University Press, 1978.

Coble, Parks M., *The Shanghai Capitalists and the Nationalist Government, 1927–1937.* Cambridge: Harvard University Press, 1980.

Cochran, Sherman. *Big Business in China: Sino-Foreign Rivalry in the Cigarette Industry, 1890–1930.* Cambridge: Harvard University Press, 1980.

Cohen, Warren I. *The Chinese Connection: Roger S. Greene, Thomas W. Lamont, George E. Sokolsky, and American-East Asian Relations.* New York: Columbia University Press, 1978.

Conference on American Relations with China. *American Relations with China: A Report of the Conference held at Johns Hopkins University, September 17–20, 1925, with supplementary materials, and arranged to be of use to discussion groups, current events clubs, and university classes.* Baltimore: Johns Hopkins Press, 1925.

Constantini, Cardinal Celso. *Réforme des Missions au XXe siècle*. Translated and adapted by Jean Bruls. Tournai: Casterman, 1960.

Cook, Christopher. *The Lion and the Dragon: British Voices from the China Coast*. London: Elm Tree Books, 1985.

Cornelius Vander Starr, 1892–1968. New York: C. V. Starr and Co., 1970.

Davidson-Huston, J. V. *Yellow Creek: The Story of Shanghai*. London: Putnam, 1962.

Dayer, Roberta Allbert. *Bankers and Diplomats in China 1917–1925: The Anglo-American Relationship*. London: Frank Cass, 1981.

d'Elia, Paschal M. *The Catholic Missions in China: A short History of the Catholic Church in China from the Earliest Records to Our Own Days*. Shanghai: The Commercial Press, 1934.

Deng Zhongxia. *Zhongguo zhigong yundong* [A brief history of the Chinese labor movement]. Peking, 1949.

des Courtils, Louis. *La Concession Française de Changhaï*. Paris: Librarie du Recueil Sirey, 1934.

Digby, George. *Down Wind*. New York: E. P. Dutton, 1939.

Ding Ling. *Miss Sophie's Diary and Other Stories*. Translated by W. J. F. Jenner. Peking: Panda Books, 1985.

Directory of Protestant Missions in China (Annual, 1924–1927). Shanghai: Kwang Hsueh Publishing House, 1924–1927.

Di yici guonei zhanzhang shiqi gongren yundong [The workers' movement during the first revolutionary civil war]. Peking, 1954.

Dubarbier, Georges. *La Chine contemporaine, politique et économique*. Paris: P. Geuthener, 1926.

Ellis, Lewis Ethan. *Frank B. Kellogg and American Foreign Relations, 1925–1929*. New Brunswick: Rutgers University Press, 1961.

Fairbank, John K. *Trade and Diplomacy on the China Coast, 1842–1854*. Cambridge: Harvard University Press, 1964.

Fairbank, John K., ed. *The Chinese World Order: Traditional China's Foreign Relations*. Cambridge: Harvard University Press, 1968.

Fairbank, John K., ed. *The Missionary Enterprise in China and America*. Cambridge: Harvard University Press, 1974.

Fewsmith, Joseph. *Party, State, and Local Elites in Republican China: Merchant Organizations and Politics in Shanghai, 1890–1930*. Honolulu: University of Hawaii Press, 1985.

Finch, Percy. *Shanghai and Beyond*. New York: Scribners, 1953.

Fishel, Wesley R. *The End of Extraterritoriality in China*. Berkeley: The University of California Press, 1952.

Fitch, Janet. *Foreign Devil: Reminiscences of a Chinese Missionary Daughter, 1909–1935*. Taibei: Chinese Materials Center, 1981.

Flachère, A. *En Route vers les idoles*. Paris: Plon, 1938.

Fontenoy, Jean. *Shanghai secret*. Paris: Grasset, 1938.

Franck, Harry A. *Roving through Southern China*. New York: The Century Co., 1925.

Fu Daohui. *Wusa yundong* [The May Thirtieth Movement]. Shanghai: Fudan University, 1985.

Gaan, Margaret. *Little Sister*. New York: Dodd, Mead & Co., 1983.

Gamewell, Mary Ninde. *The Gateway to China: Pictures of Shanghai*. New York: Fleming H. Revell, 1916.

Gilbert, Rodney. *What's Wrong with China*. London: John Murray, 1926.

Gompertz, G. H. *China in Turmoil*. London: J. M. Dent and Sons, 1967.

Gray, Arthur R. and Arthur M. Sherman, *The Story of the Church in China*. New York: Domestic and Foreign Missionary Society, 1913.

Guide to China: With Land and Sea Routes between the American and European Continents. 2d edition, revised. Tokyo: Japanese Government Railways, 1924.

Gull, E. M. *British Economic Interests in the Far East*. New York: Institute of Pacific Relations, 1943.

Guo Moro, *Geming chunqiu* [Annals of the Revolution]. Peking, 1949.

Hauser, Ernest O. *Shanghai: City for Sale*. New York: Harcourt Brace and Co., 1940.

Hermand, Louis. *Les étapes de la mission du Kiang-nan, 1842–1922 et de la mission de Nanking, 1922–1932*. Shanghai: Imprimerie de la Mission Zi-ka-wei, 1933.

Hewlett, Sir Meyrick. *Forty Years in China*. London: Macmillan, 1943.

Hipps, John Burder. *History of the University of Shanghai*. Richmond: Foreign Mission Board, Southern Baptist Convention, 1964.

Holubnychy, Lydia. *Michael Borodin and the Chinese Revolution, 1923–1925*. Ann Arbor: University Microfilms, for the East Asian Institute, Columbia University, 1979.

Honig, Emily. *Sisters and Strangers: Women in the Shanghai Cotton Mills, 1919–1949*. Palo Alto: Stanford University Press, 1986.

Hou, Chi-ming. *Foreign Investment and Economic Development in China, 1840–1937*. Cambridge: Harvard University Press, 1965.

Hsia Ching-lin. *The Status of Shanghai: Its Future Development and Possibilities through Sino-Foreign Cooperation*. Shanghai: Kelly and Walsh, 1929.

Hsiao Liang-lin. *China's Foreign Trade Statistics, 1864–1949*. Cambridge: Harvard University Press, 1974.

Hsu, Kai-yu. *Chou En-lai: China's Gray Eminence*. New York: Doubleday, 1968.

Hua Gang. *Zhonguo da geming shi yi jiu er wu–yi jiu er chi* [The Great Chinese Revolution, 1925–1927]. Peking: Wenshi ciliao chuban she, 1982.

Huang Meizhen, Shi Yuanhua, and Zhang Yun, eds. *Shanghai Daxue shiliao* [Materials on Shanghai University]. Shanghai: Fudan University, 1984.

Huang Yifeng. *Shanghai gongren sanci wuzhuang qiyi* [The Three Armed Uprisings of the Shanghai Workers]. Shanghai: People's Publishing House, 1979.

Huskey, James Layton. *Americans in Shanghai: Community Formation and Response to Revolution, 1919–1928*. Ann Arbor: University Microfilms, 1985.

Iriye, Akira. *After Imperialism*. Cambridge: Harvard University Press, 1965.

Isaacs, Harold. *The Tragedy of the Chinese Revolution*. 2d revised edition. New York: Atheneum, 1966.

Jackson, Stanley. *The Sassoons*. London: Heinemann, 1968.

Jacobs, Dan. *Borodin: Stalin's Man in China*. Cambridge: Harvard University Press, 1981.

Jiang Yongjing. *Boloting yu Wuhan zhengquan* [Borodin and the Wuhan Government]. Taibei: Biographical Publishing House, 1962.

Jones, F. C. *Shanghai and Tientsin, with Special Reference to Foreign Interests*. London: Oxford University Press, 1940.

Jones, F. C., Hugh Borton, and B.R. Pearn. *Survey of International Affairs, 1939–1946: The Far East*. London: Royal Institute of International Affairs, 1955.

Jordan, Donald. *The Northern Expedition*. Honolulu: University of Hawaii Press, 1976.

Kong Linjing. *Wusa waijiao shi* [A Diplomatic History of the May Thirtieth Movement]. Shanghai, 1946.

Kotenev, A. M. *Shanghai: Its Mixed Court and Council: Material Relating to the History of the Shanghai Municipal Council and the History, Practice and Statistics of the International Mixed Court.* Shanghai: North China Daily News and Herald, 1925. Reprint. Taibei: Ch'eng Wen Publishing Co., 1968.

Kotenev, A. M. *Shanghai: Its Municipality and the Chinese; Being the History of the Shanghai Municipal Council and its Relations with the Chinese, the Practice of the International Mixed Court, and the Inauguration and Practice of the Shanghai Provisional Court.* Shanghai: North China Daily News and Herald, 1927.

Kounin, I. I. *Eighty-Five Years of the Shanghai Volunteer Force.* Shanghai: Cosmopolitan Press, 1938.

Lamberton, Mary. *St. John's University, Shanghai, 1879–1951.* New York: United Board for Christian Colleges in China, 1955.

Latourette, Kenneth S. *A History of Christian Missions in China.* London: Society for Promoting Christian Knowledge, 1929.

Lee Enhan. *China's Recovery of the British Hankow and Kiukiang Concessions in 1927.* Perth: University of Western Australia, Centre for Chinese Studies, Occasional Paper No. 6 (August 1980).

Liang Xin. *Guochi shiyao* [A history of national disgrace]. Shanghai, 1931.

Ling, Pan. *In Search of Old Shanghai.* Hongkong: Joint Publishing Co., 1982.

Ling, Pan. *Old Shanghai: Gangsters in Paradise.* Hongkong: Heinemann Asia, 1984.

Li Tsung-jen and Te-kong Tong. *The Memoirs of Li Tsung-jen.* Boulder: Westview Press, 1979.

Li Yunhan. *Cong ronggong dao qingdang* [From the admission of the Communists to the Party purge]. Taibei: Commercial Press, 1966.

Lo Jialun, ed. *Geming wenxian* [Documents of the Revolution], vol. 18. Taibei, n.d.

Lutz, Jessie Gregory. *China and the Christian Colleges, 1850–1950.* Ithaca: Cornell University Press, 1971.

Lutz, Jessie Gregory. *Chinese Politics and Christian Missions: The Anti-Christian Movement of 1920–1928.* Notre Dame, Indiana: Cross Cultural Publications, Inc., 1988.

Lyall, L. A. *China.* New York: Scribner, 1934.

Ma Chaojun. *Zhongguo laogong yundong shi* [A History of the Chinese Labor Movement], vol. 2. Taibei, 1958.

Maugham, W. Somerset. *The Painted Veil.* New York: George H. Doran Company, 1924.

Maugham, W. Somerset. *On a Chinese Screen.* Reprint. London: Oxford University Press, 1985.

Memmi, Albert. *The Colonizer and the Colonized.* London: Souvenir Press, 1974.

Men of Shanghai and North China: A Standard Biographical Reference Work. 2d ed. Shanghai: The University Press, 1935.

Millard, Thomas F. *China: Where It Is Today and Why.* New York: Harcourt Brace and Co., 1928.

Miller, G. E. *Shanghai: The Paradise of Adventurers.* New York: Orsay Press, 1937.

Miln, Louise Jordan. *The Flutes of Shanghai.* New York: Frederick A. Stokes, 1928.

Misselwitz, Henry F. *The Dragon Stirs: An Intimate Sketch-Book of China's Kuomintang Revolution, 1927–1929.* New York: Harbinger House, 1941.

Misselwitz, Henry F. *Shanghai Romance.* New York: Harbinger House, 1943.

Murphey, Rhoads. *Shanghai: Key to Modern China.* Cambridge: Harvard University Press, 1953.

Murphey, Rhoads. *The Treaty Ports and China's Modernization; What Went Wrong?* Ann Arbor: University of Michigan, Center for Chinese Studies, 1970.

Murphey, Rhoads. *The Outsiders; the Western Experience in India and China.* Ann Arbor: University of Michigan Press, 1977.

Murphey, Rhoads. *The Fading of the Maoist Vision.* New York: Methuen, 1980.

Nance, W. B. *Soochow University.* New York: United Board for Christian Colleges in China, 1956.

Nathan, Andrew J. *Chinese Democracy.* New York: Alfred A. Knopf, 1985.

North-China Desk Hong List, 1924, 1927. Shanghai: North China Daily News and Herald, 1924, 1927.

Pal, John. *Shanghai Saga.* London: Jarrold's, 1963.

Pearl, Cyril. *Morrison of Peking.* Sydney: Angus and Robertson, 1967.

Peters, E. W. *Shanghai Policeman.* Edited by Hugh Barnes. London: Rich and Cowan, 1937.

Pie Nai-chieng. *Étude sur le problème des concessions de Changhaï.* Nancy: Imprimerie Grandville, 1932.

Pott, F. L. Hawks. *A Short History of Shanghai: Being an Account of the Growth and Development of the International Settlement.* Shanghai: Kelly and Walsh, 1928.

Powell, John B. *My Twenty-five Years in China.* New York: MacMillan, 1945.

Problems of the Pacific: Proceedings of the Second Conference of the Institute of Pacific Relations, Honolulu, Hawaii, July 15 to 29, 1927. Edited by J. B. Condliffe. Chicago: University of Chicago Press, 1928.

Problems of the Pacific, 1929: Proceedings of the Third Conference of the Institute of Pacific Relations, Nara and Kyoto, Japan, October 23 to November 9, 1929. Edited by J. B. Condliffe. Chicago: University of Chicago Press, 1930.

Problems of the Pacific, 1931: Proceedings of the Fourth Conference of the Institute of Pacific Relations, Hangchow and Shanghai, China, October 21 to November 3, 1931. Edited by Bruno Lasker and W. L. Holland. Chicago: Chicago University Press, 1932.

Ransome, Arthur. *The Chinese Puzzle.* London: Allen and Unwin, 1927.

Ransome, Arthur. *The Autobiography of Arthur Ransome.* Edited by Rupert Hart-Davis. London: Jonathan Cape, 1976.

Rawski, Thomas G. *Economic Growth in Prewar China.* Berkeley: University of California Press, 1989.

Reed, James. *The Missionary Mind and American East Asian Policy, 1911–1915.* Cambridge: Harvard University Press, 1983.

Remer, C. F. *Foreign Investments in China.* New York: MacMillan, 1933.

Ren Jianshu and Zhang Quan. *Wusa yundong jianshi* [A General History of the May Thirtieth Movement]. Shanghai: People's Publishing House, 1985.

Report of the Hon. Richard Feetham, C.M.G. to the Shanghai Municipal Council. 3 vols. Shanghai: North China Daily News and Herald, Ltd., 1931.

Rigby, Richard W. *The May Thirtieth Movement: Events and Themes.* Canberra: Australian National University Press, 1980.

Seagrave, Sterling. *The Soong Dynasty.* New York: Harper and Row, 1985.

Shanghai zhinan [Shanghai Guide]. 22d ed. Shanghai: Commercial Press, 1926.
Shen Ximeng, Mo Yan, and Lu Xingchen. *On Guard beneath the Neon Lights.* Peking: Foreign Languages Press, 1966.
Snow, Lois Wheeler. *Edgar Snow's China: A Personal Account of the Chinese Revolution Compiled from the Writings of Edgar Snow.* New York: Random House, 1981.
Soothill, W. E. *China and England.* London: Oxford University Press, 1928.
Soviet Volunteers in China, 1925–1945: Articles and Reminiscences. Translated by David Fidlon. Moscow: Progress Publishers, 1980.
Spence, Jonathan. *To Change China: Western Advisers in China, 1620–1960.* Boston: Little Brown, 1969.
Spunt, Georges. *A Place in Time.* New York: G. P. Putnam's Sons, 1968.
Stone, Grace Zaring. *The Bitter Tea of General Yen.* New York: Grosset and Dunlap, 1930.
Sun Yat-sen. *The Three Principles of the People.* Chungking, 1943.
Thomson, John Seabury. *The Government of the International Settlement at Shanghai: A Study in the Politics of an International Area.* Ann Arbor: University Microfilms, 1953.
Trotsky, Leon. *Problems of the Chinese Revolution. With Appendices by Zinoviev, Vuyovitch, Nassonov and Others.* Ann Arbor: University of Michigan Press, 1967.
Trotter, Ann. *Britain and East Asia, 1933–1937.* Cambridge: Cambridge University Press, 1975.
Van Slyke, Lyman P. *Yangtze: Nature, History, and the River.* New York: Addison-Wesley Publishing Co., 1988.
Varg, Paul A. *Missionaries, Chinese, and Diplomats: The American Protestant Missionary Movement in China, 1890–1952.* Princeton: Princeton University Press, 1958.
Vishnyakova-Akimova, Vera Vladimirovna. *Two Years in Revolutionary China.* Translated by Steven I. Levine. Cambridge: Harvard University Press, 1971.
Walker, Barbara. *The Donkey Cart: A Journey in Dream and Memories.* London: New English Library, 1976.
Wang Jiagui and Cai Xiyao. *Shanghai daxue: yijiu erer–yijiu erqi* [Shanghai University: 1922–1927]. Shanghai: Shanghai Academy of Social Sciences, 1986.
Wang Nianhun. *Wo guo xuesheng yundong shihua* [A history of our country's student movement]. Hankou, 1954.
Wei, Betty Peh-t'i. *Shanghai: Crucible of Modern China.* Hongkong: Oxford University Press, 1987.
Wilbur, C. Martin. *Sun Yat-sen: Frustrated Patriot.* New York: Columbia University Press, 1976.
Wilbur, C. Martin, and Julie Lien-ying How, eds. *Communism, Nationalism, and Soviet Advisers in China 1918–1927.* New York: Columbia University Press, 1956.
Wilbur, C. Martin, and Julie, Lien-ying How. *Missionaries of Revolution: Soviet Advisers and Nationalist China, 1920–1927.* Cambridge: Harvard University Press, 1989.
Wilson, Dick. *Chou: The Story of Chou En-lai, 1878–1976.* London: Hutchinson, 1984.
Woodhead, H. G. W. *The Truth about Opium in China.* Shanghai: Evening Post and Mercury, 1931.

Wright, Mary, ed. *China in Revolution: the First Decade, 1900–1913.* New Haven: Yale University Press, 1968.

Wright, Stanley F. *China's Customs Revenue since the Revolution of 1911.* Revised edition. Shanghai: Statistical Department of the Inspectorate General of Customs, 1935.

Wu Chouyi, ed. *Shanghai zujie wenti* [Problems of the Shanghai settlements]. Taibei: Zhengzhong Bookstore, 1980.

Wusa yundong liushi nian jinian ji [A collection of memoirs commemorating the sixtieth anniversary of the May Thirtieth Movement]. Shanghai: General Labor Union, 1985.

Wusa yundong shihliao [Historical Materials on the May Thirtieth Movement]. Edited by the Shanghai Academy of Social Sciences. 2 vols. Shanghai: People's Publishing House, 1981, 1986.

Xu Zhucheng. *Du Yuesheng zhengzhuan* [Biography of Du Yuesheng]. Fuzhou: People's Publishing House, 1982.

Yu Dafu. *Nights of Spring Fever and Other Writings.* Peking: Panda Books, 1984.

Zhang Hui, and Bao Cun. *Shanghai jin bai nian geming shihua* [A History of a Hundred Years of Revolution in Shanghai]. Shanghai: People's Publishing House, 1963.

Zhonghua minguo shishi jiyao: Zhonghua minguo liushi nian (yi jiu er qi) yi zhi liu yue [Important Historical Documents of the Republic of China: 1927, Jan.– June]. Edited by the Committee for Historical Documents for the Republic of China [Zhonghua minguo shishi jiyao bianji weiyuanhui]. Taibei: Center for the Sources of Chinese Historical Research [Zhonghua minguo ciliao yanjiu zhongxin], 1977.

Zhou Shangwen and He Shiyu. *Shanghai gongren sanci wuzhuang qiyi shi* [A History of the Three Armed Uprisings of the Shanghai Workers]. Shanghai: People's Publishing House, 1987.

ARTICLES

Bergère, Marie-Claire. "'The Other China': Shanghai from 1919 to 1949." In *Shanghai: Revolution and Development in an Asian Metropolis.* Edited by Christopher Howe. Cambridge: Cambridge University Press, 1981.

Bergère, Marie-Claire. "The Chinese Bourgeoisie." In *Cambridge History of China*, vol. 12, part 1, 721–825. Cambridge: Cambridge University Press, 1983.

Blakeslee, George H. "The Foreign Stake in China." *Foreign Affairs* 10 (Oct. 1931): 81–91.

Chamberlain, Joseph P. "The Feetham Report in Shanghai." *Foreign Affairs* 10 (Oct. 1931): 145–53.

Chang Yi. "Ji Shanghai di san ci wuzhuang qiyi qianhou de Zhao Shiyan lieshi" [In memory of the martyr Zhao Shiyen during the three armed uprisings of Shanghai]. *Hongqi piaopiao* [The Red Flag Waves] 16 (Oct. 1961): 65–93.

Clifford, Nicholas R. "A Tale of Two Cities: Hongkong and Shanghai." *Commonweal* 8 (Sept. 1989): 453–55.

Clifford, Nicholas R. "A Revolution Is Not a Tea Party: The Shanghai Mind(s) Reconsidered." *Pacific Historical Review* 59 (Nov. 1990): 501–26.

Elvin, Mark. "The Revolution of 1911 in Shanghai." *Papers on Far Eastern History* (Australian National University, Dept. of Far Eastern History) 29 (March 1984): 119–62.

Feng Bolo. "'Wusa' yundong zhong de diguozhuyi zaoyao pohuai de zuizheng" [The criminal evidence of imperialism's destructiveness and rumor mongering during the "May Thirtieth" movement]. *Jindaishi ciliao* [Materials on Modern History] 1 (1958): 84–87.

Feng Chongming. "Guanyu 1927 nian 4 yue Jiang Jieshi Wang Jingwei Shanghai huitan" [Concerning the discussions between Chiang Kai-shek and Wang Jingwei in Shanghai, April 1927]. *Lishi yu dangan* [History and Archives] (Shanghai) 3 (1983): 122–23.

Feuerwerker, Albert. "The Foreign Presence in China." In *Cambridge History of China*, vol. 12, part 1, 128–208. Cambridge: Cambridge University Press, 1983.

Fitzgerald, John. "The Misconceived Revolution: State and Society in China's Nationalist Revolution, 1923–1926." *Journal of Asian Studies* 49 (May 1990): 323–43.

Garrett, Shirley. "Why They Stayed: American Church Politics and Chinese Nationalism in the Twenties." In *The Missionary Enterprise in China and America.* Edited by J. K. Fairbank, 283–310. Cambridge: Harvard University Press, 1974.

Henriot, Christian. "Municipal Power and Local Elites." *Republican China* 11 (April 1986): 1–21.

Hershatter, Gail. "The Hierarchy of Prostitution in Shanghai, 1870–1949." *Modern China* 15 (Oct. 1989): 463–98.

Hogan, Pendleton. "Shanghai after the Japs." *Virginia Quarterly Review* 22 (1946): 91–108.

Honig, Emily. "The Politics of Prejudice: Subei People in Republican-Era Shanghai." *Modern China* 15 (July 1989): 243–74.

Huang Yifeng. "Wusa yundong zhong de dazichan jieji" [The upper bourgeoisie during the May Thirtieth movement]. *Lishi yanjiu* [Historical Research] 3 (1965): 11–24.

Hudson, Manley O. "International Problems at Shanghai." *Foreign Affairs* 6 (Oct. 1927): 75–88.

Hudson, Manley O. "The Rendition of the International Mixed Court at Shanghai." *American Journal of International Law* 21 (July 1927): 451–71.

Huebner, Jon. "Architecture on the Shanghai Bund." *Papers on Far Eastern History* (Australian National University) 39 (March 1989): 128–65.

Huebner, Jon. "L'Université l'Aurore, Shanghai, 1903–1952." *Papers on Far Eastern History* (Australian National University) 40 (Sept. 1989): 133–49.

Huskey, James Layton. "The Cosmopolitan Connection: Americans and Chinese in Shanghai during the Interwar Years." *Diplomatic History* 11 (Summer 1987): 227–43.

Hu Yuzhi. "Wusa shijian jilü" [A Record of the Events of May Thirtieth]. *Dongfang zazhi wusa linshi zengkan* [The Eastern Miscellany]. Shanghai, Special Issue of May Thirtieth (July 1925): 10–34.

Kuhn, Irene Corbally. "Shanghai: The Vintage Years." *Gourmet*, Jan. 1986, 54, 115–17.

Li Lisan. "Jinian Cai Hesen tongzhi" [Remembering Comrade Cai Hesen]. *Hongqi piaopiao* [The Red Flag Waves] 5 (1957): 46–48.

Marshall, Jonathan. "Opium and the Politics of Gangsterism in Nationalist China, 1927–45." *Bulletin of Concerned Asian Scholars* 8 (July–Sept. 1976): 19–48.

Martin, Brian. "Tu Yüeh-sheng and Labour Control in Shanghai: The Case of the French Tramways Union, 1928–1932." *Papers on Far Eastern History* (Australian National University) 32 (Sept. 1985): 99–137.

Martin, Brian. "The Pact with the Devil: The Relationship between the Green Gang and the French Concession Authorities, 1925–1935." *Papers on Far Eastern History* (Australian National University) 40 (March 1989): 94–125.

Murphy, Charles V. "Shanghai: Reopened under New Management." *Fortune* 33, no. 2 (February 1946): 141–48, 206–23.

Niu Dayong. "Meiguo dui Hua zhengce yu 'Si yi er' zhengbian de guanxi" [The relationship of the 12 April coup to America's China policy]. *Lishi yanjiu* [Historical Research] (1985): 152–65.

Orchard, John E. "Shanghai." *The Geographical Review* 26 (1936): 1–31.

"The Shanghai Boom." *Fortune* 11 (Jan. 1935): 30–40, 99–120.

"Shanghai gongong zujie gongbuju jingwuribao xuanze—yu guan Sun Zhongshan beishang bufen" [Selections from the Police Daily Reports of the Municipal Council of the International Settlement about Sun Yat-sen's trip to the north]. *Lishi yu dangan* [History and Archives] (1985): 43–47.

Shen Yü. " 'Si yi er'fan geming zhengbian yu diguozhuyi guanxi zai zhentao" [A reconsideration of the relationship between imperialism and the counter-revolutionary coup of 12 April]. *Lishi yanjiu* [Historical Research] (1984): 46–58.

Sheridan, James E. "The Warlord Era: Politics and Militarism under the Peking Government, 1916–1928." In *Cambridge History of China*, vol. 12, part 1, 259–283. Cambridge: Cambridge University Press, 1983.

Sullivan, Lawrence R. "Reconstruction and Rectification of the Communist Party in the Shanghai Underground: 1931–1934," *China Quarterly* 101 (March 1985): 78–97.

Varg, Paul A. "The Missionary Response to the Nationalist Revolution." In *The Missionary Enterprise in China and America*. Edited by J. K. Fairbank. Cambridge: Harvard University Press, 1974.

Wakeman, Frederick. "Policing Modern Shanghai." *China Quarterly* 115 (Sept. 1988): 408–40.

Wang, Y. C. "Tu Yueh-sheng (1888–1951): A Tentative Political Biography." *Journal of Asian Studies* 26 (May 1967): 433–55.

Wilbur, C. Martin. "The Nationalist Revolution: From Canton to Nanking 1923–28." In *Cambridge History of China*, vol. 12, part 1, 527–721. Cambridge: Cambridge University Press, 1983.

Xia Zhixu. "Pianduan de huiyi—yi Zhao Shiyan" [Fragments of memory—remembering Zhao Shiyan]. *Hongqi piaopiao* [The Red Flag Waves] 5 (Dec. 1957): 5–13.

Yomano, Shelly. "Reintegration in China under the Warlords, 1916–1927." *Republican China* 12 (April 1987): 22–27.

PERIODICALS AND NEWSPAPERS

American Chamber of Commerce, Shanghai. *Annual Reports*. Shanghai, 1923–1926.

British Chamber of Commerce Journal: The Journal of the Associated Chambers of Commerce in China and Hongkong. Shanghai, 1923–1928.

Bulletin of the National Christian Council of China, 1924–1927. Shanghai.

China Association, London. *Annual Reports*, 1915–1928.

China Christian Advocate. Official Organ of the China Section of the East Asia Central Conference of the Methodist Episcopal Church and of the China Mission of the Methodist Episcopal Church, South. Shanghai, 1925–1927.

China Correspondence. Hankow, 1927.
China Weekly Review. Shanghai, 1924–1927.
Chinese Recorder. Shanghai, 1924–1927.
Dongfang zazhi [The Eastern Miscellany]. Shanghai, 1925–1927.
Écho de Chine, 1925–1927.
Guowen zhoubao [The Guowen Weekly Illustrated]. Tianjin, 1925–1927.
Manchester Guardian, 1925–1927.
Nation. New York, 1925–27.
New York Times. 1925–1927.
North China Daily News. Shanghai, 1924–1928, 1945–1949.
North China Herald. Shanghai, 1924–1928.
Revue du Pacifique. Paris, 1925–1928.
Shen Bao (Shun Pao). Shanghai, 1925–1926.
Shi Bao (Shih-pao). Shanghai, 1926–1927.
The Times. London, 1925–1927.
Xiangdao zhoubao [The Guide Weekly]. Shanghai, 1924–1927.

II. Official Sources

China. Maritime Customs. *The Foreign Trade of China* (annual). China Maritime Customs, Shanghai, 1924–1928.
China. Ministry of Foreign Affairs. Records dealing with the May Thirtieth Affair [Hu'an]. Academic Sinica, Taiwan.
City Government of Greater Shanghai. Bureau of Social Affairs. *Strikes and Lockouts in Shanghai since 1918.* Shanghai, 1933.
Conseil d'administration municipale de la concession française à Changhaï. *Bulletin Municipal,* 1924–1928.
Conseil d'administration municipale de la concession française à Changhaï. *Comptes-rendus,* 1924–1928.
France. Ministère des Affaires Étrangères: Archives de la Ministère des Affaires Étrangères.
Great Britain. Board of Trade. *Annual State of the Trade of the United Kingdom with Foreign Countries and British Countries.* London: H.M. Stationery Office, 1925–1929.
Great Britain. Board of Trade. *Statistical Abstract for the United Kingdom for each of the Fifteen Years from 1913 to 1927* (Cmd. 3253). London: H.M. Stationery Office, 1929.
Great Britain. Board of Trade. *Statistical Abstract for the United Kingdom for each of the Fifteen Years 1913 and 1924 to 1937* (Cmd. 5903). London: H.M. Stationery Office, 1938.
Great Britain. Cabinet Office. Cabinet Conclusions (CAB 23), 1924–1927.
Great Britain. Cabinet Office. Cabinet Papers (CAB 24), 1925–1927.
Great Britain. Foreign Office. FO 228. Peking Legation Papers, 1924–1928.
Great Britain. Foreign Office. FO 371. Foreign Office, General Political Correspondence, 1923–1931.
Great Britain. Foreign Office. FO 405, Foreign Office, Confidential Print (China).
Great Britain. Foreign Office. FO 415, Foreign Office, Confidential Print (Opium).
Great Britain. Foreign Office. *Documents on British Foreign Policy, 1919–1939.* Edited by Rohan Butler and J. P. T. Bury. 2d series, vols. 8–10, 21. London: H.M. Stationery Office, 1960–1984.

Great Britain. *Parliamentary Debates,* House of Commons, 5th series (1925–1927).
Great Britain. War Office. W.O. 191. War Diary, Shanghai Defence Force, 1927.
Shanghai Municipal Archives. *Shanghai Gongren Sanci Wuzhuang Qiyi* [The Three Armed Uprisings of the Shanghai Workers]. Edited by Zhou Qisheng. Shanghai: Shanghai Municipal Archives, 1983.
Shanghai Municipal Council. *Annual Reports,* 1924–1928. Shanghai: Kelly and Walsh.
Shanghai Municipal Council (Council for the Foreign Community of Shanghai). Minute Book No. 35, 1925–1926. Shanghai Municipal Archives.
Shanghai Municipal Council (Council for the Foreign Community of Shanghai). Minute Book No. 36, 1927 (excerpts). Shanghai Municipal Archives.
Shanghai Municipal Council. *Municipal Gazette,* 1924–1927. Shanghai, *North China Daily News and Herald.*
Shanghai Municipal Police. Daily Intelligence Reports, 1924–1927. Shanghai Municipal Archives.
Shanghai Municipal Police. Records (various). National Archives, Record Group 263.
United States. War Department. Records of the War Department General and Special Staff. Department of the Army. Correspondence of the Military Intelligence Division Relating to General Political, Economic, and Military Conditions in China, 1918–1941. Record Group 165 (Microcopy 1444). National Archives.
United States. Department of Commerce. *Statistical Abstract of the United States* (annual). Washington: Government Printing Office, 1925–1933.
United States. Department of State. *Papers Relating to the Foreign Relations of the United States, 1924–1932.* Washington: Government Printing Office, 1939–1948.
United States. Department of State. Records of the Foreign Service Posts of the Department of State. Correspondence of the American Consulate-General, Shanghai, 1924–1933. Record Group 84. National Archives.
United States. Department of State. Records of the American Legation, Peking, 1924–1933. Record Group 84. National Archives.
United States. Department of State. Central Records of the Department of State, 1910–1932. Record Group 59. National Archives.

III. Unpublished works

Arnold, Julean. Papers. Hoover Institution, Stanford University.
Bennett, Milly. *See* Bremler.
Bremler, Mildred Jacqueline (Milly Bennett). Papers. Hoover Institution, Stanford University.
Creamer, Thomas. "Hsüeh-yün: Shanghai's Students and the May Thirtieth Movement." Master's thesis, University of Virginia, 1975.
Feigon, Lee. "Lurking in the Shadows: The Architectural Backdrop to the Formation of the CCP in Shanghai." Paper delivered to the annual meeting of the Association for Asian Studies, March, 1987.
Fleming, Peter. "Chosen for China: The California Province Jesuits in China, 1928–1957, a Cast Study in Mission and Culture." Ph.D. diss., Graduate Theological Union, Berkeley, California, 1987.
Graves, F.R. Papers. Archives of the Episcopal Church, Episcopal Seminary of the Southwest, Austin, Texas.

John Swire and Sons Papers. University of London, School of Oriental and African Studies.

Johnson, Nelson T. Papers. Library of Congress.

Kellogg, Frank B. Papers (film). Minnesota Historical Society.

Luo Suwen. "Political Influence of the Chinese Communist Party and the Kuomintang in Shanghai between 1920 and 1927." Paper presented to the Conference on Modern Shanghai, 7–14 Sept. 1988.

MacMurray, John Van Antwerp. Papers. Seeley Mudd Library, Princeton University.

Martin, Brian. "The Green Gang and 'Party Purification' in Shanghai: Green Gang–Kuomintang Relations, 1926–1927." Paper delivered at the Symposium on the Nanking Decade, 1928–1935, National Australian University, 15–17 Aug. 1983.

Martin, Brian. "Warlords and Gangsters: The Opium Traffic in Shanghai and the Creation of the Three Prosperities Company, 1913–1926." Paper delivered to the Asian Studies Association of Australia, Sydney, 11–16 May 1986.

Maze, Sir Frederick. Papers. University of London, School of Oriental and African Studies.

McDermott, Gladys. Letters, in the possession of Mrs. Carlton Molesworth, Jr.

Naggiar, Paul-Emile. Papers. Papiers d'Agents, Archives de la Ministère des Affaires Étrangères, Paris.

Pott, F. L. Hawks. Papers. Archives of the Episcopal Church, Episcopal Seminary of the Southwest, Austin, Texas.

Roots, Logan. Papers. Archives of the Episcopal Church, Austin, Texas.

Society of Jesus. Archives des Jesuites à Paris, Fonds Chine, Chantilly.

Votaw, Maurice. Papers. Archives of the Episcopal Church, Episcopal Seminary of the Southwest, Austin, Texas.

Warnshuis, A. L. Papers. Missionary Research Library, Union Theological Seminary, New York.

Wilson, David C. "Britain and the Kuomintang, 1924–1928: A Study of the Interaction of Official Policies and Perceptions of Britain and China." Ph.D. diss., University of London, 1973.

Index

UNIVERSITY PRESS OF NEW ENGLAND publishes books under its own imprint and is the publisher for Brandeis University Press, Brown University Press, Clark University Press, University of Connecticut, Dartmouth College, Middlebury College Press, University of New Hampshire, University of Rhode Island, Tufts University, University of Vermont, and Wesleyan University Press.

Library of Congress Cataloging-in-Publication Data

Clifford, Nicholas Rowland.
  Spoilt children of empire : Westerners in Shanghai and the Chinese revolution of the 1920s / Nicholas R. Clifford.
    p. cm.
Includes bibliographical references and index.
ISBN 0–87451–548–3 — ISBN 0–87451–595–5 (pbk.)
  1. Shanghai (China)—Foreign population. 2. China—History—1912–1928. 3. Exterritoriality. I. Title.
DS796.S29C57 1991
951′.132041—dc20   ⊗   90–50904